The Unforgiving Rope

The Unforgiving Rope

Murder and Hanging on Australia's Western Frontier

Simon Adams

UWA PUBLISHING

First published in 2009 by
UWA Publishing
Crawley, Western Australia 6009
www.uwap.uwa.edu.au

UWAP is an imprint of UWA Publishing
a division of The University of Western Australia

THE UNIVERSITY OF
WESTERN AUSTRALIA
Achieving International Excellence

National Library of Australia
Cataloguing-in-Publication entry:

Adams, Simon, 1968–
    The unforgiving rope : murder and hanging on Australia's
    western frontier / Simon Adams.

    ISBN 978 1921401 22 0 (pbk.)

    Includes index.
    Bibliography.

    Hanging–Western Australia–History.
    Murder–Western Australia–History.
    Western Australia–History–19th century.
    Western Australia–Social conditions–19th century.

364.6609941

Cover image: Brian S. Kusumonegoro

Printed by McPherson's Printing Group

For my grandmother, Clarie Coleman, who always warned me that I was a 'bloodthirsty creature'.

Contents

Contents

Acknowledgements

I started the research for this book in 2001. The project was immediately delayed by the tragic events of 11 September. At the time I was writing for the newspapers and doing a large amount of political commentary on the developing 'War on Terror'. Besides my job at the University of Notre Dame, the book that eventuated from that work – *All The Troubles: Terrorism, War and the World After 9/11* – took up most of my time in 2002 and 2003. There was also the birth of two of my children to contend with. However, the morbid historian in me kept secretly returning to the dark idea of, as my wife described it, 'that hanging book'.

One accumulates favours and debts writing any book. My wife Amanda, as always, suffered most – enduring my obsessions, my grisly tales of murder most foul, and my relentless avoidance of household chores while investigating hangings. This time around I am also thankful to the staff at the Battye Library in Perth as well as those at the Local History Unit at the Fremantle Library. Scott Wilson and Moya Sharp from the Eastern Goldfields Historical Society were helpful in finding out more about Tagh Mahomet. Tom Gannon put up with me, my daughter Aislinn and a 300 kilometre drive in summer heat to go find an abandoned stone cottage in the bush where a double murder and double hanging took place in 1840. My father similarly drove a thousand kilometres with me to visit the site of a double murder and quintuple hanging in 1865. My University of Notre Dame colleague Dr Deborah Gare provided great critical feedback on some of this work. Professors Bruce Scates and Rae Frances provided inspiration and guidance, often without even realising they were doing so. I thank all these people for their time, support and patience. I must, however, absolve them from any responsibility for any errors in the final text.

Simon Adams

Author's Note

I first developed the idea for this book around 2001 after visiting the Abrolhos Islands. It was on these pristine islands almost four centuries earlier in 1629 that the infamous *Batavia* mutiny took place. I was appalled and intrigued by this most bloodthirsty of all Australian mass murders and multiple hangings. Closer to home I was also disturbed to learn about the hanging of John Gavin in Fremantle during April 1844. The fifteen-year-old boy had been executed and secretly buried only a few metres from where I was then working at the University of Notre Dame in Western Australia. Soon afterwards, on yet another tourist trip to the historic convict-built Fremantle Prison with a visiting relative, I was struck by the fact that more than forty people from all over the world ended their lives in that one darkened chamber. The idea for this book emerged from a desire to explore Australian history through the lives, crimes and deaths of these men and women.

This book begins with the hanging of Barrabong and Doodjeep from a sturdy gum tree in 1840 and ends inside Fremantle Prison in 1909, where Martha Rendell's corpse swings slowly in the confinement of the dark pit beneath the gallows. Although nineteen more people will hang after her it is the end of an era, and not just because she was the last woman hanged. It is eighty years since Captain Fremantle first stepped ashore in 1829 and claimed the whole western third of the Australian continent in the name of the British Crown. The Swan River Colony has become the state of Western Australia. Traditional Aboriginal people have been displaced by a new European-derived society born of sweat, blood and noble intent. And more than a hundred miscreants have been hanged to maintain British law and order.

Writing in my office in the 'historic West End' of Fremantle, the remnants of this history were all around me. Just outside were the steps to the Roundhouse and Arthur's Head, where young John Gavin had been broken at the end of a rope on Easter weekend of 1844 – the first European to be hanged under British law in Western Australia. The earthly remains of that young murderer lay beneath the sand hills that run from Arthur's Head towards the few broken pieces of the old Fremantle Jetty that still stick out like rotting teeth from the water at low tide. I would sometimes sit on those sand hills to have my lunch and gaze into the Indian Ocean. I often spared a thought for John Gavin, who had been hanged before his sixteenth birthday.

On Cliff Street, the very same street my office was located, also stands the Old Convict Establishment, now a Maritime Museum. Inside the museum are a skull and partial skeleton of one of the more than one hundred victims of Jeronimus Cornelisz's mutinous reign of terror – the person was hacked to death with a cutlass on the Abrolhos Islands in 1629. The hanging of Cornelisz and his confederates from an improvised gallows on a windswept beach of the Abrolhos was Australia's first recorded hanging, and a multiple hanging at that. The condemned had been tortured, to obtain full confessions, prior to execution. In all, the remains of seven convicted murderers and mutineers were left hanging under a blazing sun as the Indian Ocean lapped against the treacherous Abrolhos reefs.

Also on Cliff Street, towards what was once the ocean and is now the Esplanade Park, there previously stood the store of George French Johnson, who died following a duel with William Nairne Clark during August 1832. Clark was found not guilty of manslaughter, but left the colony a few years later. Johnson's store was closed down, although eight months later an Aboriginal man named Domjum was shot dead trying to break in and steal food. It was Domjum's death that led his brother Yagan towards his own fatal confrontation with white settler society. The now infamous deadly encounter between Yagan and two young Swan River settlers is symbolic of the entire tragic encounter between the original inhabitants of Western Australia and the society that dispossessed them. The consequences still linger today.

Finally, to the east of my old office on the outer fringes of 'Old Fremantle' is the Fremantle Prison, whose modern gallows (built in 1888) took the lives of forty-three men and one woman before it swung open its fatal trapdoor for the last time. In all, between 1840 and 1964, 154 human beings forfeited their lives at the end of a rope in Western Australia, with almost a third of those executions taking place in the tiny port town of Fremantle.

In April 1915, only six years after Martha Rendell died upon the Fremantle gallows, Australian troops stormed another distant shore. After the sacrifice at Gallipoli the Federal Commonwealth of which Western Australia was a reluctant inductee apparently started to feel like a nation. Among those young men whose blood was needlessly mixed with Mediterranean sand and Turkish dirt at the Dardenelles were many West Australians. In all, more than 6,000 'Sons of the West' would be killed, and 11,000 horribly wounded, before the Great War ended. Ironically, back home there was a noticeable downturn in the number of public executions. Indeed, in the eight-year period between 25 April 1915 and March 1923 there was not a single hanging in the state. This was, in fact, the longest break in public executions in Western Australia's history since 1840.[1]

The first convoy of Anzacs had sailed from Albany on 1 November 1914. Sitting below decks on a troopship carrying them to the battlefields of World War One, perhaps some of the West Australian men aboard may have felt a sense of history. The trip to Egypt, where the Anzacs trained, was long and boring. The men apparently swapped stories with one another, and fortified themselves against the challenges they were about to face. Perhaps as the various troopships cut across the Indian Ocean some of these young Anzacs may have wiled away the hours at sea by retelling the terrible story of the *Batavia* mutiny of 1629. I wonder if they waited until night and the lulling of the ship on the dark sea before embarking upon the tale of Jeronimus Cornelisz and murder most foul.

I also wonder if these young West Australians were aware of John Gavin? What did they know of Captain Fremantle's naked 1829 'show and tell' encounter with the Indigenous inhabitants of the area that would eventually bear his name? Could they recall the Afghan cameleers who once carried water to the Eastern Goldfields? Had they heard of Tagh Mahomet or his murder in the Coolgardie Mosque? What did these young men know of their history, of crime and punishment, life and death, and of the struggle to establish the 'Swan River Colony' on Australia's westernmost frontier? This then is a history of the people who made Western Australia, and of the beautiful and brutal country that made them.

WARNING:

This book contains stories about people who were murdered or executed in extremely violent circumstances. This book may not be culturally appropriate for some Aboriginal people.

Introduction: Young John Gavin and the Spectacle of Death

On the morning of his hanging young John Gavin's executioners worried that the skinny teenage boy's neck wouldn't break. They feared that instead he would hang twisting at the end of the noose, wetting his pants in terror as he was slowly throttled to death. The assembled Fremantle townspeople who had trundled up to Arthur's Head to observe the Swan River Colony's first official hanging of a European were expecting to watch in silence as John Gavin died quickly and quietly at the end of a rope. They had come to see the public spectacle of a murderer hanged. No one wanted to witness a frightened, fifteen-year-old boy go to a slow agonising death, his eyes bulging and itching under the hangman's hood as he slowly lost his battle with the suffocating noose. And so Sheriff Stone, whose job it was to supervise the public execution of the young murderer, made the decision to weigh down John Gavin's legs so that his neck would break as soon as the rope snapped tight.

Having solved the technical problem of killing him quickly, Sheriff Stone then discovered that John Gavin was unable to walk to the gallows. The terror of his impending death immobilised him. Instead the teenaged boy had to be gently assisted as he ambled towards the execution platform. By sunset on 6 April 1844, Easter Saturday, John Gavin – or Johnny as he was known – was in a shallow grave in the sand hills that run along the southern foreshore nearby. His hanging was supposed to be a dignified occasion of legal retribution; an eye for an eye, with the blessing of the Crown, the Governor and Almighty God. It turned out to be a particularly ignoble moment in the history of public execution in Western Australia; the most remote, hot and sandy periphery of the British Empire.

John Gavin (sometimes recorded as Gaven) was a 'Parkhurst Boy', one of the troubled young males sent out from the infamous reformatory system in Britain to work in the colonies and help ease the acute labour shortage in Western Australia. Slavery had been abolished throughout the British Empire in 1833, and the founders of the Swan River Colony had not wanted to formally establish it as a convict colony – that other great source of cheap labour in the antipodes. As a result they were forced to depend upon indentured labour in establishing the settlement. But it was not enough.

No less than twelve shipments of Parkhurst Boys were sent to the Swan River Colony between 1842 and 1861. Of these, 334 boys were sent between 1842 and 1853. The boys (some were as young as twelve) were serving sentences of three to five years at Parkhurst before transportation. Officially designated as 'juvenile immigrants' and apprenticed out to local farmers and businessmen, they were the first (largely unacknowledged) convict workforce of Western Australia. One can only imagine how lonely and frightening their entry into the Swan River Colony must have been for them. Of their families, friends and the private worlds they left behind very little is known.[1]

The Parkhurst Boys were used to drive down the cost of labour. While their employers were compelled under the legislation governing the juvenile immigrant system to take care of their moral and religious instruction, as well as their material comfort and wellbeing, fierce corporal punishment was meted out to any boy who was insubordinate, lazy, or troublesome. While some boys were given early freedom in return for their hard labour, others were punished for failing to live up to the expectations of their employers. According to the reports of Mr John Schoales, who was responsible for the boys in Western Australia, Parkhurst Boy 'No.32' was 'incorrigible' and was constantly being punished. Meanwhile boy 'No.34' was returned to the government by his employer because he was 'too small and weak'.[2]

John Gavin was born in 1828 and started work as a 'spoon polisher' when he was still a child. He was no more than thirteen years old when he was sent first to Parkhurst and then to Western Australia. Gavin arrived in Fremantle in 1843, was quickly apprenticed, and sent to work on a farm in the employ of John Pollard of North Dandalup (now Pinjarra). It was for the crime of murdering Pollard's seventeen-year-old son George that Gavin was sentenced to death.[3]

Gavin allegedly confessed to hitting George Pollard with an adze. He also confessed of conspiring to murder Mrs Pollard, although he had apparently decided against it after killing George. Three of the four witnesses who appeared in court to testify against Gavin were relatives of the deceased (including Mrs Pollard, who had discovered her son's bloody body in his bed). According to John Schoales, who as guardian of juvenile immigrants had the 'melancholy duty' to report the matter to the Governor, Gavin was sentenced to death in Fremantle on a Thursday, spent Good Friday with 'his ghostly adviser' and promptly went to his death Saturday morning. The *Perth Gazette* reported that at eight in the morning the preparations for execution were complete:

> The prison bell then began to toll, and the melancholy procession set off from the condemned cell to the scaffold: the Sheriff and his deputies and constables, the Rev. G. King, reading appropriate passages of Scripture, the prisoner, supported by Mr Schoales, and lastly, more constables closed the train. The boy was deeply affected and was assisted up the steps to the platform. From this time the proceedings were rapid, and at ten minutes after eight the cart moved forward, and the criminal was launched into eternity.[4]

John Schoales's version of events, in his letter to the Governor, revealed the horror of the occasion:

> At the boy's earnest, passionate request I carried him to the scaffold and took my leave of him at the foot of the ladder. I am told that he suffered little. I was not able to witness the death pangs. After hanging for an hour they transferred him to me and by my direction placed him in a decent shell and at 4pm I laid him without a rite of church in the sandhills south west of the jail.

The *Perth Gazette* offered additional details, reminding readers that John Gavin's body was so light that, 'with humane attention, heavy weights were attached to the legs of the sufferer, a precaution the propriety of which was evinced in the fact that apparently the pangs of the unhappy boy were very few'. In other words, Sherriff Stone conducted a good hanging – no choking rope. John Gavin's body was cut down and buried in the sand hills by prisoners from the Roundhouse gaol.[5] The *Perth Gazette* commented that on the western precipice of the Australian continent:

> There, without rite or ceremony, the remains of this miserable lad were inhumed, but though the place of his sepulchre be unknown to all, yet may

God grant that awful example made on so young a lad, may ever be before the minds of all of us young or old.[6]

The newspaper's final warning to its readers was that, 'the boy's faults were many – let them sleep in his grave'.[7]

The Roundhouse, the first major public building in Fremantle – in front of which John Gavin died – was built on the edge of the Indian Ocean and overlooked the Swan River, the infant colony's lifeline to the world. The gaol had been designed by Henry Willey Reveley, the colony's civil engineer and a friend of the doomed English poet Percy Bysshe Shelley. In the early days of the Colony the Roundhouse served as a warning, and a comfort, to the inhabitants of the small sandy settlement at Fremantle, reminding them by its dominating presence and the yellow glare of its limestone walls that British justice reigned there. During those foundation years the Roundhouse was the first visible sign of civilisation new settlers could see as their ships cut in against the West Australian coastline. Nearly two centuries later the Roundhouse and the convict-built Fremantle Prison still mark out the historic boundaries of central Fremantle.

Exiled to remote Western Australia and exploited for his cheap labour, John Gavin had been denied a Christian burial after his execution. Such a policy on behalf of the British authorities – along with earlier ones regarding gibbeting felons, anatomising murderers and decapitating traitors – deliberately sought to exploit the anxieties of ordinary people regarding the afterlife.[8] To this day John Gavin's earthly remains are still interred in the sandhills near the Roundhouse. Tourists trudging through the 'historic West End' to soak up the atmosphere of its colonial heritage are given no indication that a fifteen-year-old murderer rests underfoot. His bones, like most of our history of crime and punishment, remain unacknowledged.

::

Hanging has a gruesome pedigree. It began in tenth century Britain as an extremely public and deliberately slow punishment. The first gallows were trees and in those days all that was needed was a strong branch and an unforgiving rope. The first victims were choked to death. The intent was to extend the suffering and humiliation of the condemned for long enough to amuse the crowd and impress upon them the cruel majesty of the law. It was this tradition of hanging that arrived in Australia with the First Fleet in 1788.

With time, however, social changes required more sophistication and delicacy in execution. Refined nineteenth-century ladies and gentlemen insisted upon reform. No more would a doomed criminal be paraded around town in a cart and publicly tormented prior to be being 'launched into eternity'. Condemned cells were purpose-built beside new scientific gallows within model nineteenth-century prisons. Hanging became a quick, private and precise art. Specialist hangmen, rather than fellow prisoners looking for a reprieve, were employed. These discrete men took their morbid means of making a living very seriously. Fine ropes were measured, weights taken, drops calculated, improved gallows arduously designed and constructed. The emphasis was on ritual efficiency and cold protocol.

Yet despite the sterile pretence, hanging remained a barbarous act. No matter how much science was injected into the process, killing another human being remained intrinsically...human. Some prisoners faced their appointment with the rope with grim stoicism. But some still begged for life, forgiveness and mercy. People still shook with fear upon the scaffold. Trembling lips sometimes muttered final prayers as well as farewells to loved ones. Afterwards, some condemned prisoners convulsed and twitched while dangling from the noose. Corpses wet themselves. No wonder that hangmen and prison warders who regularly witnessed hangings had a tendency to drink. They had much to forget.

Which brings me to the purpose of this book. History is more than organised remembering. When we look at these cases of men and women facing death upon the gallows, at these instances of crime and punishment, we look deep into the soul of our society. We see our history at its most unedifying. And yet these horrible yet fascinating cases of murder – legal or otherwise – have much to teach us about ourselves. As Tim Castle has written with regard to nineteenth-century newspaper reports of executions in New South Wales, such stories 'enable the modern reader to understand the 'moral universe' of colonial society, in which capital punishment was supported as a necessary part of maintaining secular social order, as well as conforming to contemporary beliefs about divine justice'.[9]

Western Australia was the final frontier in the expansion and occupation of the continent by Europeans. Despite various Dutch, French and English expeditions since the seventeenth century, prior to 1829 no one had annexed 'New Holland', as it was called, because no European power wanted it. The land was considered too wretchedly barren and inhospitable for habitation by civilised people. One member of a 1818 French expedition to New Holland described the land as 'a picture of desolation' where 'sterility and death' reigned.[10] Therefore, despite the infant colony at Sydney, after 1788 entire swathes of the continent stretching from the dry reaches of western New South Wales to the hills to the east of Perth, were entirely unexplored and unsettled by Europeans. In these places Aborigines continued to live as they always had, unmolested by people from the world of steel and steam.

All that changed when Captain Fremantle raised the British flag and erected a rudimentary fort at the mouth of the Swan River during May of 1829 (on the site of a town that would soon be named after him). By that simple act Fremantle annexed one million square miles of land in the name of the British monarchy. This dubiously acquired possession, Western Australia, was ten times bigger than Britain and was protected by only a few lonely and bored soldiers of the Crown.[11] The settlers who arrived soon afterwards in June of 1829 came carrying the intellectual baggage of imperial Europe in all its splendour. They unpacked upon this continent not only their bedraggled possessions – hammers, clothing, rifles, flour and other items useful for colonisation – but also ideas about science and society. Books on Enlightenment philosophy, Christian morality, literature and life were carried aboard ships plying their way to the Swan River.

European Australia was still in its infancy. Adelaide and Melbourne did not exist in 1829 when Fremantle and Captain James Stirling arrived to establish the Swan River Colony. Sydney and Hobart were convict outposts. Indeed, nearly half the white population of Australia were exiled prisoners of the British Crown.[12] Nevertheless, the Europeans who settled Western Australia in 1829 were, for the most part, fanatically curious about their new home. They explored their surroundings, enjoining the colonial project with a luminous idealism. They collected samples of leaves and pressed flowers to send home to friends and museum curators. They observed the fauna and made noble attempts to describe, for example, the wonder of seeing a jumping kangaroo or a fornicating quokka for the first time. The settlers also explored the local environment and cautiously regarded the Indigenous inhabitants.

Much of nineteenth-century Western Australian history is the story of a fragile outpost of the British Empire struggling to survive. Even the weather and parched environment seemed to conspire against the settlers. Despite numerous attempts to penetrate inland the white newcomers were continually driven back (by lack of water as much as anything else) and continued to cluster near the coast. It really felt as though the Swan River Colony, wedged between the Indian Ocean and a vast desert, was perched upon the edge of the earth.

Given the remoteness of the colony, settlers naturally clung to ideological and political structures that anchored their society – Christianity, the Empire, and an abiding belief in the innate majesty and fairness of British law and order. The law provided certainty and safety in a place of isolation. Cases of murder and hanging were therefore only the most dramatic examples of a people struggling to build a new society on the margins of the known world.

::

The All Saints' Church of the Upper Swan stands on land that was first 'settled' by Frederick Chidley Irwin, who ruled the Swan River Colony during Governor James Stirling's absence from 1832 until 1834. Irwin, a career soldier, had been decorated during the Napoleonic wars and was sent to Western Australia in 1829 as Captain of the 63rd Regiment. He was soon promoted to major and made commander of all military forces in the colony. A deeply religious man, Irwin donated to the Anglican Church an acre of land upon which Stirling and his men had camped during Stirling's original exploration of the Swan River in 1827. Stirling had made it as far up the Swan as the modern suburb of Guildford before returning to his ship and England. He named the narrow waterway near where All Saints now stands Ellen Brook, in honour of his wife. The foundation stone of the All Saints' Church was laid in 1839 – a decade after the official arrival of British settlers.

Visiting the quaint church a few years ago I walked upon its heavy creaking wooden floorboards, where the saw cuts of the settlers who built it are still visible, and was struck by a simple memorial plaque on the wall.

> In memory of James Minchin who came to the Swan on the ship 'Caroline' 12th October 1829. Buried on the riverbank 20th July 1837, beside five other settlers who were killed by natives before this church was built. Aged 38 years. Descendants to the 5th generation have erected this memorial as a token of esteem – 1st November 1936.

Gazing upon the plaque I was much moved by it. I imagined these brave pioneers leaving kith and kin in Britain and embarking upon a journey to the ends of the earth in search of hope, prosperity and land. Instead they found, not the uninhabited paradise they had been promised, but a rugged countryside occupied by Aborigines armed with spears. I sympathised with the local Aborigines – who, after all, were defending their ancestral inheritance – but I also felt sympathy for these dead settlers, cut down in a country they never had a chance of comprehending.

Except that James Minchin was not killed by Aborigines at all. Leaving the Church I came across an information sheet explaining that James Minchin died, not from Aboriginal spears, but 'as a result of swallowing a bone'. The only real dispute, according to the Church's information leaflet, was what kind of bone it was that killed him – 'Some say a chicken bone, others say a fish bone'. I walked back into the Church to check the plaque again and noticed that while it implied, by loose association, that Minchin had been killed by Aborigines, it did not actually state it. Unfortunately the site of the graves of the murdered settlers, and details of the circumstances which led to their deaths at the hands of local Aborigines, have been lost.

The entire episode got me thinking about the way in which we draw false inferences or mythologise our past. When the famous Elizabethan pirate and explorer Sir Walter Raleigh was being held prisoner in the Tower of London he dedicated his hours to writing a history of the world. Legend has it that Raleigh was well on his way to writing the second volume when he witnessed a fight between some workmen from the window of his cell. One of the men was beaten to death and Raleigh became obsessed with finding out the cause of the argument which had precipitated the violence. Despite the fact that he had actually been an eyewitness to the scuffle, its causes and motivations remained a mystery to him. As legend has it, Raleigh was so demoralised by his inability to get an adequate explanation that he set fire to his unfinished manuscript and abandoned his history of the world.

George Orwell, commenting upon this incident, wrote that if the legend of the burnt volume was not actually true then 'it certainly ought to be'. Orwell reflected on the professional dilemma that had ended Raleigh's career as a historian (Raleigh's other career as a courtier, explorer and colonist ended when he was beheaded in 1618). If historians cannot determine the truth and meaning of things that pass before their very eyes, what hope do they have of disentangling truth from myth in the past?

Orwell was, of course, himself a famous journalist and author of two of the most important pieces of political literature produced last century – *Animal*

Farm and *1984*. Writing under the dark shadow of Nazism and at a time when Stalin's Soviet Union was still expanding its 'gulag archipelago', Orwell feared for the future of the past. Comparing his own experience to that of Raleigh, Orwell wrote in 1944 that 'up to a fairly recent date, the major events recorded in the history books probably happened'. He used, as his examples, the fact that it is safe to assume that the battle of Hastings was actually fought in 1066 and that Colombus probably did arrive in America (although Colombus thought it was Asia) in 1492. Orwell contrasted this with the disputed facts of historical events during World War Two:

> In no case do you get one answer which is universally accepted because it is true: in each case you get a number of totally incompatible answers, one of which is finally adopted as the result of a physical struggle. History is written by the winners. In the last analysis our only claim to victory is that if we win the war we shall tell less lies about it than our adversaries.[13]

For Orwell the truly monstrous thing about his times was that totalitarianism was undermining the very concept of objective truth – 'it claims to control the past as well as the future'. It was this reworked phrase that appeared a few years later in his monumental *1984* – 'who controls the past controls the future: who controls the present controls the past'. Orwell remained profoundly worried over how future historians would reveal or conceal the lies, propaganda and truth in history.

Reading Orwell I was struck by how troubled he would have been by contemporary debates in Australia over the meaning and momentum of our own history – not least of all in the area of relations between 'settlers' and 'natives' on the Australian frontier. Australian people agree on only the barest essentials regarding our shared past. We all acknowledge that the First Fleet arrived in 1788. But was Australia peacefully settled, or violently invaded by the British? Was Australia largely uninhabited land which the settlers were free to take and develop, or should prior Aboriginal sovereignty be meaningfully acknowledged in our history books and legal system? Was there an actual war on the Australian frontier, or only sporadic and inconsequential violent skirmishes which have been much exaggerated? Closer to home, did the violent clash between Aborigines and Governor Stirling's men at Pinjarra in 1834 constitute a 'battle' or a 'massacre'? And so on.

When J.S. Battye published his famous history of Western Australia in 1924, he pointed out that conflicts with Aborigines loomed large over the early stages of the colony's development.

> Even the advocates of kindly treatment felt that drastic steps ought to be taken. As a result the history of 1833 and part of 1834 is practically the tale of native aggression and repulsion. Thefts were incessant, murders increasingly frequent, and the settlers lived in continual fear of an outbreak, a fear that was enhanced by their knowledge of the treacherous and cunning nature of the natives.[14]

While the language may trouble us now, this was an acceptable historical truth in 1924. More importantly, while the conquest of Western Australia was still afoot, relations between 'native' and 'settler' were at the forefront of debates about justice, crime and punishment. While the complex frontier cultures of resistance and accommodation that affected Aboriginal–white relations are only one aspect of our disputed history, the problem of a fractured and partisan understanding of Western Australia's past remains.

Crime and punishment are social constructs. Contending societies – Bardi and British for example – have diverging cultural notions of justice. Even within European society laws have been altered over time and what could get you hanged in 1607 might only get you a fine, or result in no legal sanction whatsoever, in 2009. Institutions of the law, and the notion of the equality of all people before the law, are the foundation upon which our civilisation supposedly rests. Yet, the law is not above history. It is contested terrain where issues of wealth, poverty, corruption, morality, religion and ethnicity are in constant creative tension. This book seeks to explore the dark social frontier between the law, the gallows and the history of Western Australia.

Western Australia was the last state in the nation to officially do away with hanging. Although capital punishment was not abolished until 1983, the last man hanged was Eric Edgar Cooke, who went to the gallows on 26 October 1964 in Fremantle Prison – 124 years after the first public hanging (and gibbeting) at the Swan River Colony. Of Cooke much has already been written. His murder spree is largely credited with changing the way that people in Perth felt about their city and about crime. Prior to Cooke's murderous rampage, Perth was considered a peaceful suburban backwater where people left their doors unlocked at night and the grim realities of the modern world were kept at bay. After Cooke's capture, trial and execution, Perth people were presumed to be a little less trusting, a bit more cautious, a touch fearful and 'modern'. Curtains were drawn, doors locked. Darkness descended upon the suburbs.

Cooke, however, was actually the forty-fourth person to be legally executed inside Fremantle Prison's walls. More than three-dozen men and one woman had gone to the gallows before him. In all, 154 people were legally hanged in Western Australia between 1840 and 1964. Many of those executed committed crimes just as heinous and equally notorious in their own era. Some were hanged because they had killed for profit, for vengeance, out of jealousy, because of misunderstanding or madness, or just because they thought they could get away with it. Others were hanged simply because the nature of the times and the prejudicial ideas of the age led them inexorably towards the gallows.

There could be no greater evidence of a society's struggle with its historical demons than to look at who it hanged and why. This is a book about the history of colonial Western Australia. It is a history that has been made not just by noble proclamations, adventurous sea captains, stoic pioneers and imperial ambition, but also by murderers, thieves, rapists, and those who resolved to break their necks at the end of a rope.

I

The Basest Treachery and Blackest Ingratitude: Barrabong and Doodjeep Versus the British Empire, 1840

A double murder committed by Aborigines results in a double execution; this being the first legal hanging ever conducted at the Swan River Colony.

Western Australia existed in the twilight between dreams and reality for the Europeans who first settled the colony. Long before Captain James Stirling established the Swan River Colony in 1829, the western coast had already been rendered infamous by Dutch explorers, English pirates and various other European interlopers. The Dutch had been exploring the coastline since the early 1600s and their dog-legged journey from Africa to their colonial possessions in the East Indies vomited up shipwrecks upon the treacherous coast. Some survived to tell about the dry harsh land the Dutch named 'New Holland'. Others starved to death or suffered unknown fates as castaways. A few did gruesome violence to one another.

In the most notorious case, when the Dutch ship *Batavia* was shipwrecked in June 1629 upon the Abrolhos Islands, off the coast of modern Geraldton, more than a dozen men embarked upon a mutinous orgy of rapine and murder. The head mutineer Jeronimus Cornelisz established a reign of terror over the more than 200 abandoned survivors of the shipwreck. By the time *Commandeur* Pelsaert returned to rescue the castaways, only seventy-four were left alive. More than 115 men, women and children had been murdered by Cornelisz and his confederates. Pelsaert arrested the mutineers, assembled the bedraggled remains of *Batavia*'s hapless passengers and crew, and held a trial. The ringleaders were sentenced to death and hanged, including Cornelisz who was given the maximum punishment available – mutilation, death and confiscation of all his worldly possessions.

I

Such extreme measures were necessary, to use Pelsaert's words, 'in order to turn us from the wrath of God and to cleanse the name of Christianity of such an unheard of villain'.[1]

On the windswept Abrolhos on the morning of 2 October 1629 seven of the mutineers were hanged from a rudimentary gallows. As a gruesome warning to others, both Cornelisz's hands were chopped off with a hammer and chisel before he was hanged. He died unrepentant. Even as the blood from his amputated hands dripped upon the hot sand, he continued to shout 'Revenge!' as he mounted the gallows and the noose was slipped over his head. The rope failed to break his neck and so Cornelisz died a slow choking death. He was followed by six other mutineers, their corpses left dangling from the gallows like rotten meat.[2] Nine lesser conspirators were taken by Pelsaert to the Dutch East Indies where they were imprisoned. Some were tortured in order to obtain confessions. One of the mutineers, Daniel Cornelissen, was keel hauled three times and given 100 lashes during the voyage to the East Indies. After arrival he had his right hand amputated and was then hanged. In all, five of the nine lesser conspirators were eventually hanged. Three more were severely flogged and exiled. One, 'Stone-Cutter Pietersz', was broken on the wheel – dying the most gruesome death of all.[3]

This was Western Australia's first acquaintance with European justice and the hangman's noose. No wonder Henrietta Drake-Brockman, just one of the many writers drawn to the morbid tale of the *Batavia*, described it as 'the greatest dramatic tragedy in Australian history', and as a story which made the Mutiny on the Bounty look like 'an anaemic tale'. Interestingly, two of the *Batavia* mutineers, Wouter Loos and Jan Pelgrom, were spared the rope. Pelsaert had them marooned on the nearby Australian mainland instead. Before he sailed for the East Indies with the remaining survivors of the *Batavia*, Pelsaert gave Loos and Pelgrom provisions as well as beads and some toys so that they could befriend any 'natives' they came across. They were then abandoned near present-day Kalbarri, never to be seen again. They were quite possibly the first European residents of Western Australia.[4]

When the grim tale of the *Batavia* shipwreck first became known in Europe it seemed to confirm people's suspicions regarding this malignant desolate shore. At least two accounts of the *Batavia* mutiny were printed in Dutch and French. As Simon Leys has written:

It can be said without exaggeration that, in its time, the tragedy of the *Batavia* had a greater impact on the public imagination than did the wreck of the *Titanic* in the 20th century.[5]

Later meanderings along the Kimberley coast by the English pirate William Dampier were famously recorded for posterity in his own 'best selling, rollicking' book, *A New Voyage Round the World*.[6] Dampier was an extraordinary man by any measure. He was the first man to sail around the world three times, visiting five continents. He was the first Englishman to describe in print the sensation of tasting soy sauce in Southeast Asia, as well as the effects of smoking marijuana ('Some it keeps sleepy, some merry...others it makes mad.'). Despite being an enthusiastic scientific adventurer, he was lucky not to end his life upon the gallows like his pirate acquaintance Captain Kidd. Instead, Dampier's vivid travel writings inspired both Daniel Defoe and Jonathan Swift, causing his biographers to comment that, 'Without Dampier there might have been no Yahoos, no Robinson Crusoe, no Man Friday.'[7]

Dampier first arrived in Western Australia in January 1688, north of Broome. Dampier and his pirate crew are the first Englishmen known to have explored the Australian mainland. Local stories passed down among Aboriginal Bardi elders tell of how Dampier's ship, the *Cygnet*, first arrived in one of the bays off King Sound, northwest of Ardyaloon (One Arm Point) Aboriginal community. According to Irene Davey and other elders, local people did not call out 'gurry, gurry' as Dampier later recorded, but 'ngarri, ngarri', believing the white sailors to be devils, ghosts, evil spirits. Bardi people ran from the strange visitors. Dampier's descriptions of the area speak of a land without nourishment, although the Bardi could have easily led the buccaneers to sources of water and 'bush tucker' if only the cultural gulf between the two peoples had not been so great.[8]

Notoriously, Dampier later described the Aborigines he encountered as the most miserable looking people he had ever seen in the world. His physical description of the Aborigines, with eyelids 'always half-closed, to keep the flies from their eyes', black like 'a negroe' and differing 'little from brutes', was hardly an edifying portrait of these still proud and wonderful people. Joseph Banks, travelling with Captain Cook almost a century later on the 1770 voyage where Cook discovered the easterly passage to Australia, wrote about how as they approached the coast they spied several humans on the shore. The five Aborigines 'appeared through our glasses to be enormously black; so far did the prejudices which we had built on Dampier's account influence us that we fancied we could see their colour when we could scarce distinguish whether or not they were men'.[9]

As a regular visitor to Bardi-Djawi country, what I find most remarkable is how unimpressed Dampier was with the peninsula that now carries his name. Its blinding white sands, clear turqoise water and magnificent blood red dirt did not enchant him. He found its Indigenous people curious, but repulsive. He viewed the land as infernally hot, and with little potential for trade or settlement. Dampier and the crew of the *Cygnet* retreated to the sea, turning their backs upon Western Australia.

Dampier returned to what is now called Shark Bay, Lagrange Bay and Broome in 1699, but remained unimpressed by New Holland's prospects. Working now for the British Admiralty, at Shark Bay Dampier's men killed an eleven-foot shark inside which they discovered 'the head and bones of a hippopotamus; the hairy lips of which were still sound and not putrefied'.[10] Although it is safe to assume it was actually the remains of a Dugong they discovered in the shark's stomach, such encounters did little to dispel the view of Dampier and his men that New Holland was a perilous shore.

Although he was better remembered in Europe for his later rescue of Alexander Selkirk (the real Robinson Crusoe) from an island off the coast of South America, Dampier's stories of fantastic encounters with the supposedly miserable natives of New Holland discouraged further visitation. A few years earlier the Dutch Captain Willem de Vlamingh, considered to be the European 'discoverer' of the Swan River, had described New Holland as a 'barren, bare, desolate region'.[11] Following Dampier's voyage of 1699, no major European expedition made its way to Western Australia for nearly a century.

::

It took Captain James Stirling of the British Navy to change Europe's perception of wild inhospitable New Holland.[12] Sailing from Sydney, Stirling arrived off the coast of Western Australia in March 1827 with orders to explore the area around the Swan River. He already harboured ambitions to found a British settlement there. While Stirling was not the first European to explore the Swan (Vlamingh had beaten him to that honour in 1697) he and his men were officially the first Englishmen. On his first excursion into the river Stirling demonstrated his enthusiasm for the wonders of the local environment by shooting dead three black swans. When not gazing down the barrel of a rifle or up to his elbows in blood and feathers, Stirling also had the opportunity to notice the tranquil surrounds. He was mightily impressed. Stirling's exploration of the Swan River resulted in fantastic glowing reports of an untouched paradise in New Holland.[13]

Bizarrely, before Stirling departed Western Australia in 1827 he left 'a cow, two pregnant ewes and three goats' behind on Garden Island, just off the mainland, south of the Swan River. His intention was for them to breed and proliferate, creating a source of livestock returning colonists could potentially draw upon for their survival. Of what became of these animals no one knows. They probably starved or otherwise perished due to the sun or snakes. Certainly when Stirling returned in 1829 there was no sign of his castaway farmyard friends. Along with the black swans shot dead in the river named after them, they constituted the first casualties of British colonialism in Western Australia.[14]

Returning to England, Stirling petitioned the British government to establish a colony at the Swan River. Although a small military outpost had been built at King George Sound (Albany) in 1826, Stirling had in mind a more ambitious settlement based around the Swan River. In 1829 Stirling returned to Western Australia as its foundation Lieutenant Governor. Among the many gifts of European civilisation that he brought back with him were British jurisprudence and the hangman's rope.

From about the tenth century, hanging had developed as the preferred form of legal punishment in Britain. At first, with a simple rope strung from a tree, hanging resulted in death by strangulation. Under this method, death came slowly and agonisingly to the condemned. With time, however, methods of hanging were refined so that with a specialist noose fastened under the chin and a 'long drop' calculated correctly, death was the prompt result of a fracture of the vertebrae (that is, a broken neck) combined with compression of the windpipe. This was considered an appropriately humane form of capital punishment.

Botched hangings were frequent. For example, in November 1740, sixteen-year-old William Duell was hanged at Tyburn, in London, for the crimes of rape and murder. After being declared dead and cut down from the gallows he was to be anatomised in the interests of science. While awaiting the blade it was noticed that the corpse was showing distinctive signs of life. William Duell was revived, declared alive, and promptly returned to prison. The authorities, with a fearful regard for divine intervention, reprieved the death sentence and exiled Duell from England instead.[15] Other victims who became entangled in the hangman's rope during the drop, or whose necks did not break and slowly suffocated, were not nearly as lucky.

English innovation in the construction of gallows eventually allowed for simultaneous mass hangings. Perhaps the largest occurred at Tyburn (now Marble Arch in London) where twenty-four people were hanged at once on a single morning in 1649. All had been sentenced to death for robbery or burglary.[16] Even in cases where a single person was hanged, sometimes crowds of up to twenty thousand people would turn out to watch the execution of a notorious criminal. Public hangings at Tyburn started to take on a carnival atmosphere.[17] Historians Brooke and Brandon have explained:

> The hangman expected his perks from selling the rope and the clothes of the deceased while the physically afflicted in the crowd pressed forward to touch these because it was widely believed that they had curative properties. In later years, fights occasionally broke out as the relatives of the deceased fought those who wanted to take the body away for dissection. The vendors of the felon's so-called 'dying confessions' hawked their wares among the crowd, as did a multitude of prostitutes. Pickpockets enjoyed rich takings. The wealthy hired expensive grandstand seats to obtain the best views at Tyburn Fair. All this etched itself deeply into the popular culture of London.[18]

There were thousands of public executions – including multiple hangings, and executions of children as young as fourteen – in Britain between the sixteenth and eighteenth centuries. Between 1715 and 1783, for example, 2,169 people (including 146 women) were hanged at Tyburn alone. Even during the nineteenth century, at a time when agitation by the novelist Charles Dickens and other social reformers was leading to changes in the imposition of the death penalty, thousands were executed. Historian V. A. C. Gatrell estimates that 7,000 people were hanged in England and Wales between 1770 and 1830. Most of those hanged were poor, many were recent migrants to the cities where they were executed, and almost all were young and male. In the words of Gatrell, the 'more rootless the felon, the more likely the execution'.[19]

Urban density was frantically increasing during this period due to social changes wrought by the industrial revolution. The population of England nearly doubled while the population of London increased from one million to 1.7 million people during the first thirty years of the nineteenth century.

The arrival of industrial capitalism not only created previously unimaginable wealth and economic power, it also led to drastic increases in urban crime and poverty. The British government utilised the hangman's rope to keep this seething and combustible society under control.[20] It was this history, and these legal traditions of death by hanging, that Lieutenant Governor James Stirling carried with him to the Swan River in 1829.

::

In the bold words of Australia's most famous historian, Manning Clark, 'Civilization did not begin in Australia until the last quarter of the eighteenth century'.[21] Although the British founders of a European Australia believed in the innate superiority, benevolence and justice of their civilisation as compared to the 'barbarous savages' whom they encountered, eighteenth-century British justice was magnificently cruel. In the words of one historian, 'men and women dangled outside Newgate prison up to 20 at a time, a sight unknown elsewhere' in Europe. Gibbeting – the practice of publicly displaying the corpse of the condemned in a hanging cage where it would slowly rot – was still widely practised during the 1770s. Indeed, at Hounslow Heath there were dozens of gibbeted criminals at any time and when the wind blew, 'it brought with it a cadaverous and pestilential odour'.[22]

While the number of hangings in Britain gradually declined over the nineteenth century, this was principally due to an increase in the punishment of transportation for what had previously been capital crimes. Transportation to the colonies had restarted in 1786 and 'suited the English authorities because it enabled them to be seen as exercising clemency while getting rid of some of the country's most anti-social elements'.[23] The number of hangings in London-Middlesex declined from 434 between 1784 and 1793, down to 119 for the period from 1804 to 1813.[24] Still, the British legal system remained decidedly homicidal. For example, during 1820 there were forty-two hangings at Newgate prison in London. Twelve of those who died were hanged for forgery, with another seventeen executions for robbery or burglary. Not a single person was hanged for murder.

In 1810 there were still over 220 capital offences in England including sacrilege, stealing letters and stealing from a shop of property worth over five shillings. No wonder that the author Charles Phillips wrote in 1857 with reference to the history of capital punishment in England, that 'every page of our statute book smelt of blood'. Between the 1830s and the 1860s, however, the number of capital crimes in Britain were gradually reduced to two – murder and high treason. Hundreds of people who would have faced the gallows in an earlier century for crimes such as burglary or forgery were transported to Australia instead.[25]

Crime and punishment were central to the colonisation of Australia. New South Wales was, of course, established as a penal settlement, and only one month after the landing of the First Fleet the first public execution took place. Four convicts were caught stealing provisions and on 28 February 1788 they went to trial. British Marine Captain Watkin Tench recorded that of the four 'miscreants':

> ...three were condemned to die and the fourth to receive a very severe corporal punishment. In hopes that his lenity would not be abused, His Excellency [the Governor] was, however, pleased to order one only for execution, which took place a little before sunset the same day. The name of the unhappy wretch was Thomas Barrett, an old and desperate offender who died with that hardy spirit which too often is found in the worst and most abandoned class of men. During the execution the battalion of marines was under arms and the whole of the convicts obliged to be present.[26]

Although Tench describes Barrett as 'an old and desperate offender', some historians suggest he might have been, in fact, a seventeen-year-old boy. Regardless, Barrett confessed to leading a 'wicked life' before he was hanged from a gallows tree conveniently located between the male and female convict camps. Years later Robert Hughes, examining the case for his monumental history of Australia's convict period, *The Fatal Shore*, would wonder, 'how much 'wickedness' could a boy compress into that small span from his birth to the fatal act of stealing some butter, dried peas and salt pork at Sydney Cove?'[27]

Nor did the hanging end there. Two more death sentences were imposed four months later. Again the condemned were convicts, again the crime was theft, the punishment death by hanging. One of the condemned men, twenty-year-old Samuel Peyton, had a fellow convict write a final letter home for him. Dated 24 June 1788 from Sydney Cove, the letter poetically exclaimed:

> My dear mother! with what agony of soul do I dedicate the few moments of my life to bid you an eternal adieu: my doom being irrevocably fixed, and ere

this hour tomorrow I shall have quitted this vale of wretchedness to enter into an unknown and endless eternity… Banish from your memory all my former indiscretions, and let the cheering hope of a happy meeting hereafter console you for my loss. Sincerely penitent for my sins; sensible of the justice of my conviction and sentence, and firmly relying on the merits of the Blessed Redeemer, I am at perfect peace with all mankind, and trust I shall yet experience that peace which this world cannot give. Commend my soul to the Divine mercy. I bid you an eternal farewell.

Your unhappy dying Son,[28]

The hangings and public floggings continued. Tench reported with considerable regret that less than a year later, in March 1789:

Six marines, the flower of our battalion, were hanged by the public executioner, on the sentence of a criminal court composed entirely of their own officers, for having at various times robbed the public stores of flour, meat, spirits, tobacco and many other articles.[29]

And again reported in late 1790 that:

The convicts continue to behave pretty well; three only have been hanged since the arrival of the last fleet, in the latter end of June, all of whom were newcomers.[30]

The frightful practice of gibbeting was also carried to New South Wales. In November 1796 a man called Francis Morgan was hanged and gibbeted on a small island in the middle of Sydney Harbour, much to the horror of local Aborigines. According to Judge Advocate David Collins, the gibbeted corpse caused:

…much greater terror to the natives than to the white people, many of whom were more inclined to make a jest of it; but to the natives his appearance was so frightful – his clothes shaking in the wind, and the creaking of his irons, added to their superstitious ideas of ghosts…all rendering him such an alarming object to them – that they never trusted themselves near him, nor the spot on which he hung; which, until this time, had ever been with them a favourite place of resort.[31]

How truly bizarre and cruel settler society must have seemed to the indigenous Sydneysiders, the Eora – to hang a man's corpse in chains and mock it. The Eora had no more chance of comprehending Europe's 'barbarous ways' than the settlers had of understanding their culture of crime and punishment. Moreover, as in Britain, the Australian system of hanging didn't even have efficiency to recommend it. For example, in 1803 a Jewish convict named Joseph Samuels was unsuccessfully hanged three times in a single day before the authorities gave up and issued him a reprieve instead![32]

On the other side of the continent, following the proclamation of the Swan River Colony in 1829, Lieutenant Governor James Stirling had – like his predecessor in New South Wales – dutifully set about the construction of institutions to manage British law and order. These included the appointment of W. H. Mackie as Chairman of the Court of Quarter Sessions in December 1829, making him Western Australia's first (and for a while, only) judge. During 1830 proper civil and criminal courts were established although significantly, few of Stirling's initial legal appointments (beside Mackie) had any formal training in the Law. While the early Swan River legal institutions may have lacked the ambience of a British (or latter day Perth) courtroom – what Robert Drewe described as 'the powerful combination of law, history, punishment and varnished timber' – they still maintained British justice's 'stern demeanour'. Defendants may not have been 'crushed by important-looking wood', but the legal environment was punitive and ritualistically formal. Ironically, it was under these rudimentary conditions in the remote Swan River Colony that Australia's first jury trial was held in July 1830.[33]

Stirling prided himself on the fact that although the legal system he constructed officially introduced the hangman's rope to Western Australia, it was never used under his governorship.[34] Under the instructions given to him as governor, Stirling was required to refer any death sentence to his Executive Council for consideration before either commuting the sentence, or confirming it and issuing an execution warrant.[35] The fledgling Swan River legal apparatus did not formally impose a penalty of death upon anyone until 30 December 1837 when Richard Reilly was found guilty of setting fire to a house in Guildford. However, his death sentence was commuted to transportation to the penal settlement of Van Diemens Land. In at least one other known case, an Aboriginal man called Helia was sentenced to death during April 1838 for the murder of an Aboriginal woman on the streets of Perth. At the Executive Council meeting of 31 July, however, Lieutenant

Governor Stirling argued against carrying out the death sentence because it was an inter-tribal killing. Helia was exiled to Rottnest Island instead.[36]

The first official hanging did not take place until 10 July 1840 – after Stirling had been replaced as governor and departed from the Swan River – when two Aboriginal men named Doodjeep and Barrabong (or Bunaboy) were hanged on a farm south of York for the murder of a white woman and her baby daughter. The woman, Sarah Cook, had been speared to death during May 1839 while her husband Elijah was away from the homestead. The two Aborigines then set fire to the house, cremating the corpse of the innocent woman and burning to death the baby girl left inside.[37]

The murder gave the colony's fledgling newspaper, the Perth Gazette, opportunity to publicly criticise the 'absurdity' of recently retired Governor Stirling's policy of placing Aborigines 'under the same laws which control civilized beings'. The newspaper was at pains to point out that, among many other contradictions, while Aborigines were protected under British law, 'native evidence' was 'not admissible' in court. The newspaper also warned that settlers might soon take 'the law into their own hands' if Aboriginal offenders continued, as they saw it, to go unpunished.[38]

The alleged reason for the murder of Sarah Cook and her baby Mary was revenge for the imprisonment of the son of one of the Aboriginal attackers on a charge of stealing sheep. Although the local settlers had strong suspicions as to which local Aborigines were responsible for the attack on the Cook homestead (based on information passed on by friendly Aborigines) it took some time to apprehend the killers. Indeed, it was not until June 1840, more than a year after the murders, that John Drummond, the son of a well-known Swan River settler, was sent out as a 'special constable' with two 'native assistants' to hunt down the offenders. Drummond captured both Doodjeep and Barrabong by the end of the month.[39]

Both of the men later admitted (through a court translator) their involvement in the murder.[40] George Fletcher Moore prosecuted the case and spoke of the murder of Sarah Cook as being:

> ...the most wanton and savage [murder] which has been committed since the establishment of the Colony; wanton because it was committed without the slightest provocation on the part of the unfortunate victim, or any person connected with her; and savage because it was committed upon a lonely and

defenceless woman and her helpless infant, under circumstances of the basest treachery and the blackest ingratitude.[41]

Although the trial of Doodjeep and Barrabong was held in Perth, they were transported back to York and then to the charred remains of the Cook family's home to be hanged. The *Perth Gazette* reported that during the journey the condemned and their guards were followed by a group of local Aborigines, and that Doodjeep and Barrabong 'repeatedly asked to be shot or speared' rather than hanged. The soldiers and the condemned men spent one night in York before making the final thirteen mile journey south to where Sarah and tiny Mary Cook had been killed. Finally arriving at the scene of the murders, the death warrants were read out, the two condemned were hooded and placed on the back of the cart (one fainted and had to be revived), and then their executioners 'launched them into eternity'.[42]

The bodies of the two Aborigines were left hanging in chains from the gallows tree so as to provide, in the words of the Protector of Aborigines, 'a terror to evil doers'.[43] The sight of the gibbeted corpses may well have terrified the local Aborigines, but not all the settlers of the region were troubled by the hideous visage. A government official wrote to *The Inquirer* appalled by the fact that at such a scene of 'blighted hopes' where murderers had been launched 'into dread eternity', locals from among 'the lower classes of people' had been desecrating the corpses of the Aboriginal killers:

> The ears of one of these unhappy natives have been cut off, and are now preserved in the house of a small farmer in the district. Others have gone out *and fired at the bodies* – stretching out their legs by the insertion of sticks between them, and committing other disgusting acts of brutality…[44]

It was over a year before there was another hanging in the Swan River Colony. Again the condemned was Aboriginal. Again the crime was murder and the victim a white settler. Mendik was hanged on 14 October 1841 for the murder of John Burtenshaw Cox, a young farm worker who was killed almost two years earlier near the Canning River. There were claims that Mendik later confessed to killing twelve-year-old Cox because white settlers had killed an Aboriginal boy in the area some time earlier. Regardless, Mendik was found guilty of murder and was hanged beside the Canning River at the scene of Cox's fatal spearing.[45]

Aborigines therefore were the first victims of British hangmen in Western Australia. They were condemned by a foreign legal system they neither properly comprehended nor consented to. Another two and a half years passed before someone else was hanged – young John Gavin. Yet despite the fact that no one was officially hanged during Stirling's tenure as governor, life and law in the colony he established were by no means bloodless. Indeed, it was during Stirling's temporary absence from the colony in 1833 that Western Australia's first formal execution took place – the killing of the Aboriginal elder Midgegooroo. It was an affair of dubious legality.

::

James Stirling served as governor of Western Australia for over ten years, from foundation in 1829 until 1839. However, he was actually overseas from August 1832 until June 1834 as he returned to England to report on the progress of the colony. Frederick Chidley Irwin, commander of the military forces in Western Australia, was left in control. However, in February 1834 the two men actually met up in England (leaving the ranking military officer in command of the colony) and Irwin reported to Stirling on the escalating violence between settlers and local Aborigines. At least three settlers had been fatally speared since Stirling had left the colony, leading to an unknown number of Aborigines being killed in revenge. The violence was increasingly blamed on one of the most impressive of the young Aboriginal men known to the whites, Yagan, who became the focus of the fear and loathing of the settlers.

During July 1831 an Aborigine was fatally ambushed at Archibald Butler's farm on the Canning River while taking potatoes from the garden. Aborigines had taken food from Butler's farm on a number of previous occasions and one of Butler's servants had concealed himself and waited for them to approach the garden again. When they did so he opened fire, killing one. It was Yagan and his father Midgegooroo who came to the Butler farm two weeks later and tried to force their way into the house – using their spears to try and hack through the mudbrick walls. Although Butler was absent from the farm at the time, a servant of his called Entwhistle and his two young sons were inside the house. Entwhistle (who had not been involved in the original incident) pleaded with Yagan and Midgegooroo, but was eventually speared to death. The two Entwhistle children escaped detection and possible death themselves by hiding under a bed.[46]

13

The following June William Gaze, another of Butler's servants, was working with another man along the Canning River around Kelmscott when Yagan and some other Aborigines emerged from the nearby bush. Obviously frightened, one of Butler's servants escaped, but Gaze tripped in the thick scrub along the riverbank and was speared to death.[47] In October 1832 Yagan was captured and imprisoned on Carnac Island after being led in chains through the streets of the settlement. Two soldiers and the gentleman scholar Robert Lyon (who had been so convincing in arguing Yagan's defence that he had succeeded in having him exiled to Carnac Island rather than executed) were sent to guard him. Lyon hoped to use this as an opportunity to teach Yagan about European culture. Yagan apparently had more pressing concerns as he escaped from the island instead. His fearsome legend grew.

In February 1833 one of the soldiers who had guarded Yagan on Carnac Island, Private Jenkins, was speared and nearly killed. The *Perth Gazette* described Yagan as a 'determined villain' and speculated that he was probably involved in the attack.[48] Two weeks later, however, Yagan was present at a remarkable 'Native Corrobory' held in 'Mr Purkis's yard' and attended by numerous Swan River and King George's Sound Aborigines, along with the Acting Governor, and the assembled ladies and gentlemen of the colony. Bizarrely, the *Perth Gazette* reported that, 'Yagan was the master of ceremonies, and acquitted himself with infinite dignity and grace'.[49]

Despite these entertaining distractions, the violence continued. At the start of April, Yagan was in trouble again for allegedly threatening settlers in Perth.[50] On 29 April, Domjum, a brother of Yagan, was shot dead near Cliff Street in Fremantle while breaking into a store. The following day Yagan and his father, Midgegooroo, as well as Munday (an important elder) and at least a dozen more Aborigines, attacked a wagon on a road outside Fremantle and killed John and William Velvick in revenge.[51] Irwin issued a proclamation on 4 May declaring Yagan an 'outlaw' and offering a reward of 30 pounds for him to be captured 'DEAD or ALIVE'. He similarly declared:

> AND whereas there is every reason to believe that two other Natives well known by the names of Midgegooroo, and Munday were present, aiding and abetting the said Yagan in the perpetration of the said Murder; – I do hereby further proclaim the said Midgegooroo and Munday to be outlaws, deprived of the protection of British Laws – and I do hereby offer a reward of TWENTY

POUNDS for the apprehension of each of them, the said Midgegooroo and Munday, dead or alive.

GOD SAVE THE KING![52]

The hunt for Yagan and his accomplices continued until 18 May when it was announced that Midgegooroo had finally been captured.[53] Leading figures within the colonial establishment were divided over a suitable punishment. George Fletcher Moore (who was later to prosecute the killers of Sarah Cook and her baby) wrote in his diary that Midgegooroo, 'has been taken, and there is great perplexity as to what should be done with him: the populace cry loudly for his blood; but the idea of shooting him with the cool formalities of execution, is revolting: there is some intention of sending him into perpetual banishment.'[54]

On 21 May depositions were given before Irwin and the Executive Council with regard to the alleged crimes of Midgegooroo. He was blamed, along with Yagan, for many of the attacks by Aborigines over the previous two years. Six white witnesses gave evidence against him. One was young Ralph Entwhistle, who had hidden under the bed while his father was murdered nearly two years earlier. Ralph was only twelve-years-old when he testified against Midgegooroo and his life had been one of seemingly unending misery. His mother had died during the passage to Western Australia and all the family's possessions had been lost at sea. At Butler's farm, Ralph and his younger brother Enion had hidden as their father was speared to death. The poor destitute boys, now orphans, became beggars in the Swan River Colony. Enion died of starvation before Ralph finally got work on Morgan's farm, near where the Velvick brothers were killed.[55]

Young Ralph Entwhistle's testimony was as unreliable as it was compelling. His employer, John Morgan, believed Midgegooroo to be responsible for the deaths of white settlers and wanted to see him punished. At the height of the crisis Morgan informed the *Perth Gazette* that he had rifles and ammunition available for anyone who was under attack from Aborigines. Morgan was also all that stood between young Ralph Entwhistle and a potential return to destitution. Nevertheless, it was this same John Morgan who, as Resident Magistrate, announced the death sentence to Midgegooroo. Midgegooroo had not had the benefit of a trial in any real sense. He was not brought before his accusers, nor given a chance to defend himself. Following the proclamation of a death sentence, Midgegooroo was simply taken into the yard of the Perth Barracks and shot by a firing squad composed of British soldiers. Irwin oversaw the execution while Midgegooroo's five-year-old son, who was captured with him, was removed to Garden Island.[56]

The *Perth Gazette* of 25 May, reporting on Midgegooroo's execution, commended 'this prompt and decisive measure'. It also claimed that after reading the death warrant, 'Midgegooroo, on seeing that preparations were making to punish him, yelled and struggled most violently to escape'. However, 'in less than five minutes he was pinioned and blindfolded, and bound to the outer door of the jail'. Irwin signalled for the firing squad to shoot.[57] The newspaper commented that:

> A great number of persons were assembled on the occasion, although the Execution was sudden, and the hour unknown. The feeling which was generally expressed was that of satisfaction at what had taken place, and in some instances of loud and vehement exultation, which the solemnity of the scene, – a fellow being – although a native – launched into eternity – ought to have suppressed.[58]

When Irwin reported the execution to the British Colonial Office he took care to report on the deliberations of the Executive Council (the governor's advisory committee) prior to deciding to end Midgegooroo's life. According to Irwin the Executive Council had been:

> ...convinced of its necessity founded on a knowledge of the character and disposition of the aborigines, after nearly four years intercourse. The previous lenient measures and forbearance of the Government, after they had with impunity murdered several of the settlers, having been considered to have had an injurious effect in causing the natives to believe the course pursued to be the result of fear of their superiority.[59]

Interestingly the Colonial Office disagreed, indicating that they would have preferred to have seen Midgegooroo locked up, rather than put to death.[60] To make matters worse, Yagan was still at large and it was feared that upon learning of his father's death he would wreak vengeance upon the colony's isolated settlers.

Yagan remained free – the colony's most feared 'outlaw' – for two months. The price on his head, thirty pounds, was equal to a year's pay for a British worker. As he continued to evade capture, Yagan was blamed for a number of attacks on remote farms, although it is unclear just how many of these he was genuinely involved in. Yagan was finally killed on 11 July 1833 near Guildford after two teenage shepherds, the Keats' brothers, had feigned friendship, before one of them shot him in the head with a rifle. In the melee that followed another Aborigine, Heegan, was also mortally wounded and the older of the Keats boys, William, was chased down and speared to death by Yagan's companions. Blood for blood.[61]

Nervous settlers, returning to the scene of the killings, found the corpse of young William Keats on the riverbank. His body had been speared many times and his skull smashed open with the rifle he shot Yagan with. According to one witness, Keats's gun 'lay broken beside him smeared with hair and blood'. About 300 yards away the bodies of Heegan and Yagan also lay in the dirt. Heegan was moaning, still barely alive. One of the armed settlers 'put him out of his misery'.[62] Yagan was dead. He was beheaded by the settlers and had the skin taken from his back, to preserve his cicatrise markings. Whether this was a sick trophy, or for reasons of anthropological curiosity, is debateable.

Bizarrely, Yagan's head was preserved and sent back to England on the same ship that carried Irwin back to the centre of the British Empire. Yagan's head was displayed in London's Saville Row for a while, with a Perth newspaper reporting that, 'His features are well preserved, his skin is a deep jet black, and the hair on his chin very crisp.'[63] Yagan's preserved head eventually ended up in the Liverpool Museum and was then buried in an unmarked grave during the 1960s. Tragically, it was not until 1998 that Yagan's skull was disinterred before finally being returned to his people and the land of his dreaming in Western Australia.

::

The place where Elijah Cook built his homestead, roughly three miles inland from Fleay's station and thirteen miles south of York, was wild and remote in 1839. A brook snaked its way through the southern edge of the property, with thick thirsty gum trees growing along its banks. It's not hard to see why Elijah and Sarah chose to live there. It was a place of hot brown rolling hills and wide open blue skies completely unlike the old world of Britain, from where the first settlers had come to York less than ten years earlier. The chimney and walls of the house were built of hard rusty brown stones held together with mud. It must have been sweaty back-breaking labour to build the place under an Australian sun. Elijah and Sarah Cook, with their child Mary, obviously intended to live there for a while. The stone cottage was built to stand against time.

Elijah had arrived in the Swan River Colony during 1831. He had been in the colony almost nine years at the time of his wife's and daughter's murder, three years in the York district. After he met Sarah he had gone into business as a sheep farmer, and had built the stone cottage himself. According to the Advocate-General, George Fletcher Moore, Elijah tried to cultivate friendly relations with local Aborigines and although the cottage was 'retired and solitary', Elijah's 'whole hopes and prospects' were his farm and family.[64] While prosecuting Doodjeep and Barrabong for the murder of Sarah Cook and her baby, Moore tried to give a sense of the rising horror experienced by Elijah as he returned home that fateful day, riding over the gentle hills to first see that the wooden roof of his distant cottage had been collapsed by ravenous fire. Cook galloped on towards the smoking ruin of his homestead and frantically dismounted, calling out for his wife, only to discover her charred corpse near the doorway. It was a terror from which no man could ever rightfully be expected to recover.[65]

No one ever rebuilt the Cook homestead after Sarah and baby Mary were brutally murdered there in 1839. It wasn't just that the place had been set on fire by the Aboriginal killers, but the fact that those same killers had also been hanged on the property during July 1840. One suspects that there was simply too much death about the place. Certainly Elijah Cook, who buried his wife and child, never returned to try and rebuild the house on the hill, above the brook, just three miles ride from Fleay's station. The blackened ruin was left to the silence of the years, interrupted only by the cawing of crows and the creaking of the gallows tree where the gibbeted corpses of Doodjeep and Barrabong had hanged.

It must have been quite a scene to pass the ruined homestead in 1840. The gallows tree and the ruined stone cottage must have created an atmosphere of lingering evil. Remarkably, the remains of the Cook homestead are still standing over 165 years later. Driving down the 'Old Scenic Road' from York to the rural township of Beverley, the remains of the stone chimney and crumbling walls are still clearly visible. Pulling the car into the gravel at the side of the road there is only a small wire fence and a dusty paddock between yourself and the scene of the Swan River Colony's first 'most dreadful' crime. A double murder followed by a double hanging.

Today the Cook homestead appears like a dignified rustic ruin, perfect for a postcard of the rugged Australian landscape, rather than a place of misery. The crows still caw, the summer heat is thick with the buzzing of locusts, but otherwise there is nothing inside the ruined cottage to act as a historical monument to the violence that occurred there. Even the gallows tree is gone now, wiped clean from this farming landscape. Walking back to the car there is only the occasional crunching of bleached sheep bones underfoot to remind you that this is still a place of occasional death.

Thomas Paine, the incendiary polemicist who helped inspire the American revolution, once wrote that 'When, in countries that are called civilised, we see age going to the work-house and youth to the gallows, something must be wrong in the system of government.' He wrote those words in revolutionary Paris during 1792. He was thinking of crime and punishment in England, but his piercing critique was just as relevant to the British penal colony then being established in Australia. The society that killed Barrabong and Doodjeep, the society that Captain James Stirling inaugurated in 1829, although built during Paine's great 'age of reason', still rested firmly upon the gibbet, the hangman's noose and the gallows tree.

2

Edward Bishop and the Convict Stain, 1854

A 'Chinaman' is murdered in York and a man is sentenced to death. The first convict transportee is hanged in Western Australia. There is fear that convictism will permanently stain the fabric of society.

In the grainy morning light the murderer dragged the body of the Chinaman down to the edge of the Avon River. He must have been frightened, knowing full well that if he were to be detected now, he would surely hang for it. The hatchet had left noticeable wounds on the face of Ah Chong, the Chinese carpenter. The murderer needed to dispose of the corpse before any of the local workers came down to the river to wash. Dumping the body into the river he assumed it would be taken downstream, to be swallowed into the murky underwater darkness. He threw the Chinaman's washing-up bucket into the water for good measure, so as to give the impression the Chinaman had fallen into the river, drowned and floated away. The murderer stopped momentarily to clean the blood off himself and then left the riverbank. What he did not notice was that Ah Chong's body did not wash away. Instead it travelled a short distance downstream before becoming entangled in the roots of trees and trapped near the river's surface.

On that same morning of 20 August 1854, William Voss, formerly prisoner 1388, who had been transported to the Swan River Colony and then given work as a Ticket of Leave man on Meares's farm in York, was disturbed by another freed convict, Edward Bishop. Bishop was only twenty-three but had been doing hard manual labour since he was eight, when he had started work as a miner in England. In 1849 he had been convicted of burglary and sentenced to ten years. He was transported to Australia and arrived in Fremantle on the

Dudbrook during February 1853 as prisoner 1695. He was twenty-one years old. Perhaps because he displayed initiative – in prison he had learnt to read and write – Bishop was immediately granted a Ticket of Leave. He too found a job on Meares's farm. His personal details, as recorded when he arrived as a convict, listed him as single, without children, five foot seven and a half, with light hair, grey eyes and of 'robust' build. He had 'e.x.b' tattooed on his left arm.

Bishop came into Voss's hut, disrupting his breakfast, to tell him that the Chinaman, Ah Chong, with whom Bishop had been sharing a bed in a workers' hut nearby, was missing. Quickly the men went outside where a small search party was assembling. River accidents were common in the early days of the colony, many people could not swim, and Voss told Bishop he feared the Chinaman may have fallen into the river and drowned while washing. This was already the belief of Ah Chong's brother, the farm cook, who had noticed his brother's bucket floating in the water. Earlier an Aboriginal farm worker, 'Jimmy the Native', had heard screams and had gone to fetch the brothers William and George Meares, who owned the farm. They too feared for the life of Ah Chong.

The Meares brothers, Jimmy the Native, Voss, Bishop and another man, Charles Claydon, split up to search for Ah Chong. William Meares told Voss to 'look up and down the river'. Voss, scouring the riverbank with Charles Claydon, noticed something near the surface of the water and with the assistance of a 'crook', he was able to pull it to the shore. Voss and Claydon pulled the dead body of Ah Chong from the river and lay it on the bank. Voss immediately noticed 'several cuts about the neck and face and one on the mouth'. As the others arrived there was already talk that the Chinaman had been murdered. Suspicious glances were directed at the former convict, Edward Bishop. One of the Meares brothers sent for the police.[1]

::

In J. S. Battye's famous 1926 history of Western Australia, the state's most esteemed librarian wrote that it was an indisputable fact that West Australian history had been 'tainted by the convict period – and no material prosperity that ensued at the time will ever efface the stain'.[2] Battye was acutely aware, of course, that Western Australia was not supposed to be a convict colony. The investors and speculators who originally settled the Swan River saw themselves as gentlemen farmers. They aspired to live as a landed gentry with paid servants. Rustic indentured labourers, imported from Britain, would work their extensive land holdings for them. Or as Tom Stannage wrote of these founding gentlemen settlers:

> Their milieu was that of Jane Austen: indeed all of them could have walked out of one of her novels. They valued, above all things, 'respectability and comfort', and lacking an independent income in England sufficiently large to ensure this, they sought placement in a society which they could shape in their own image.[3]

Such gentlemen never imagined that their precious Swan River Colony would sink to such desperate economic depths that it would require the importation of penal labour in order to prevent its expiration.[4]

The notion of ungrateful, slothful servants was a recurring theme in the letters of the early wealthy settlers. George Fletcher Moore, the Advocate General and a leading agriculturalist, complained that workers who 'but seldom taste meat at home, demand it here three times a day'.[5] In a December 1832 letter to England James Purkis similarly complained that the 'English servants we brought here are not worth much; we find that the Lascars, Javanese, and Chinese, who have emigrated here, are much better labourers.' Purkis had a native Hawaiian working for him.[6] There were simply not enough cheap non-European labourers, however, to meet the needs of the colonists. In 1833 William Tanner, a respected Swan River landowner, wrote to his family in England complaining about the servants of the colony. Tanner particularly resented 'the scarcity and consequent badness' of the servants, commenting that this was 'the greatest drawback to our comfort'.[7]

Another leading settler, Thomas Brown, similarly complained in a letter sent to England in July 1843 about the extravagances of farm labourers who consumed far too much meat, flour, sugar and tea for people of their social status. The reason for such extravagance was the 'scarcity of labour' and Brown commented that the Swan River Colony desperately needed 'a few hundred good labourers and shepherds sent out free of expense'.[8] One way to get these cheap labourers, of course, was to simply have the British state send them as convicts.

Between 1850 and 1868, long after convict transportation had ceased on Australia's eastern seaboard, forty-three convict ships sailed to Western Australia to deliver up the flotsam of the British legal system. The first convict transport arrived in June 1850. In October another convict ship appeared off the coast of Fremantle, followed by three ships in 1851, four in 1853 and so on. In all, 9,669 male convicts were transported (no female convicts were sent), with about 150 dying during the journey.

Statistically, Western Australia's convicts were somewhat different from their counterparts in the eastern colonies. In a sample study of the convict population it was estimated that 13 per cent were transported for 'crimes against the person' and 19 per cent for 'burglary (usually with violence)'. Although 'simple larceny' remained the most common offence, the number of violent offenders was comparatively higher. About 73 per cent of Swan River convicts were urban labourers or artisans (in the east there was a higher proportion of agricultural workers) and 34 per cent were literate. About 72 per cent of those transported were single, more than half were between twenty and thirty years of age, only 19 per cent were Catholic, and the most common sentence (44 per cent) was for eight to fourteen years. This meant the convict population of the Swan River was generally less Irish, more urban, younger and more Protestant than convicts in New South Wales. Prior to transportation their occupations included everything from doctors and school teachers, to carpenters, miners, stonemasons and even one rat catcher.[9]

While the Swan River profited from the convicts' enforced labour, society gentlemen worried about the moral welfare of the colony. For example, the 1855 report of the Colonial Chaplain regarding the reading habits of convicts revealed that:

> Among the most depraved there is a morbid taste for narratives of the Great Rebellion, the French Revolution, &c. I shall be pardoned in expressing my opinion that such books should rarely if ever be admitted into the libraries of convict prisons...the men who most covet their perusal within the walls of a prison have their moral sense blunted, and cannot appreciate the better part. They gloat only over the crime and licentiousness laid open to their view.[10]

By the time transportation ceased, convicts and their descendants were nearly half the white population of Western Australia. Together with the free settlers and soldiers, they constituted a fledgling European population of merely 22,000 people perched on the edge of the Indian Ocean and surrounded by what they perceived as an inconceivably vast and inhospitable expanse of desert.

The world the convicts created did not always match the aspirations of Captain James Stirling and the gentleman founders of the Swan River Colony. According to that doyen of Australian history, Manning Clark:

> As in the eastern convict colonies, the bond were accused of living without any regard for the observances of religion; drunkenness was universal among them, and most of them were strangers to the refining influences of female society. Bush barbarism, it was said, was spreading over the red sandy deserts of the inland; the moral sewage of Great Britain had once more been let loose in the Australian wilderness, corrupting and still further degrading the Aborigine, and making life in white society hideous.[11]

The colony had started out, from the point of view of the British, honourably enough. On 2 May 1829 Captain Charles Howe Fremantle had landed at the Swan River and established a beachhead for colonisation. He raised the British flag on the banks of the south side of the river, toasted the King and had his men stand sentry nearby. The settlers, under Stirling's command, arrived four weeks later. However, at the moment of his triumph Stirling's over-enthusiastic arrival nearly resulted in his sinking his own ship on a sandbank in Cockburn Sound. Most of the settlers were eventually resettled aboard Fremantle's ship, although a group of twenty-eight women and children were marooned for five days on Carnac Island in lashing rain with only a single knife, one mug and some salted beef and sea biscuits to sustain them. Clearly not all colonists were equal.[12]

On 12 August 1829, the King's birthday, Lieutenant Governor James Stirling formally assembled the leading officials of the Colony in the bush further down the Swan River (the site is near contemporary Barrack Street). They were joined by a frugal contingent of British soldiers in full ceremonial dress. Stirling asked Mrs Dance, the wife of a naval officer, to deliver a blow with an axe to a nearby tree. With this blow, 'chivalrously guided by Captain Stirling' in the words of Manning Clark, the site of Perth was proclaimed. According to Stirling's biographer, the soldiers then fired 'a *feu de joie*, and all present gave three hearty British cheers'. The colony seemed to be proceeding to plan. Three more ships arrived from England soon after, leaving the combined population of Fremantle and Perth at '200 settlers, 35 horses, 17 cows, 3 bulls, 25 draught oxen, 10 calves, 200 sheep, 100 pigs and hogs', and a 'large stock of poultry'.[13]

Captain Charles Howe Fremantle, after whom the port settlement at the mouth of the Swan River was named, was also present at the foundation of Perth. His father had been a hero of the battle of Trafalgar and Charles had joined the Navy at age eleven.[14] Fremantle accompanied Stirling, the Dances, and the assembled soldiers and officials into the bush above the Swan River. The decision to cut down a tree was apparently the result of there 'being no stone contiguous for our purpose.'[15] One can almost imagine Fremantle's tight-lipped displeasure as he stood in formal naval dress while Dance's wife (whom he disliked) was given the honour of felling a tree. Fremantle departed from the Swan River Colony soon afterwards.[16]

Notwithstanding felling trees and rampant diarrhoea, progress of the colony turned out to be excruciatingly slow. Although eighteen ships arrived at the Swan River during the first six months of the settlement, due to bad publicity in England the number of new settlers slowed to a trickle.[17] Stirling, in particular, was blamed for either terribly misjudging the quality of the land, or deliberately deceiving prospective settlers. His prophesies of an antipodean Garden of Eden proved false. For example, in a letter home to England (and the newspapers) while enroute to the Swan River, Stirling wrote that:

> Various exploring parties will be sent out. We expect the discovery of a large river, and of a range of snow capped mountains... So large a portion of inhabitable country, without a large river, is unknown in any other quarter, and contrary to the received rules of nature, and as yet all attempts to find one have proved vain.[18]

Similarly, Harrison Collins Sempill, who chartered a ship to take settlers from England to the Swan River, needed to fill it with passengers. His solution was to publish a pamphlet that further contributed to the false expectations of prospective Swan River settlers.

> The Emigrant will not have to wage hopeless and ruinous war with interminable forests and impenetrable jungle, as he will find prepared by the hand of Nature extensive plains ready for the ploughshare. He will not be frightened from his purpose by beasts of prey and loathsome reptiles. He will not be scorched by tropical heat not chilled by the rigours of a Canadian winter.[19]

With the arrival of the settlers' first Australian summer at the end of 1829, the dizzy optimism died. Even by January 1830 some newspapers in England were actively discouraging migration to the Swan River, with one claiming that the settlers would have been better off if they had 'gone to Ireland and cultivated the bogs'.[20] Another report written by a recent visitor to the Swan River and published in South Africa during July 1830, reported that:

> The Water is bad tasted; there is not yet a good house erected, for everything seems in a state of uncertainty. Many people are leaving for Van Diemen's Land. It rained for nearly three months in torrents, and almost drowned the Settler and his goods; the greater part of the town of Freemantle [sp] was ancle-deep [sp] in water. There is scarcely a garden to be seen in the whole Colony; people are subject to bad eyes, and bowel complaints; and there are myriads of fleas.[21]

No wonder that George Fletcher Moore, writing about conditions in Fremantle at this time, described 'our colony, a few cheerless dissatisfied people with gloomy looks, plodding their way through the sand from hut to hut to drink grog, and grumble out their discontents to each other'.[22]

Some Swan River settlers abandoned the colony for the East Coast. Local Aborigines harassed those who remained as they intruded upon their hunting grounds. Livestock died. The sun withered crops. By 1837 there were only 2,032 settlers in the colony – nominally covering the entire western third of the continent. Of these two thousand whites about 590 were clustered in Perth, 524 in the Swan River farming district, 387 in Fremantle, 65 at York and others scattered in small pockets across the south-west. They were protected by 185 British soldiers. It is therefore perhaps not surprising that in May 1830 one settler wrote to the London *Times*, claiming that, 'We have been duped,' and that the entire colony was both literally and figuratively built on sand.[23]

In 1845 no new immigrants arrived. The colonists became frantic and no less than three petitions were organised calling upon the British government to save the Swan River Colony. The settler population was still only 4,290 and the economic situation was perilous. Key businessmen urgently petitioned for convict transportation.[24] While this seemed to contravene the settlers professed pride in the fact that their colony had been founded as a private enterprise, rather than a penitential outpost, important backers of the colony back in England, including James Stirling himself, supported the idea of an injection of convict labour in order to save the colony 'from utter ruin'.[25]

Which is not to say that convict transportation did not have its detractors. On 16 November 1849, following the announcement of the British government's decision to send convict labour to Western Australia, the *Perth Gazette* published a poem predicting dire consequences:

The convicts are coming – what capital sport,
The road to the gallows made easy and short,
And long will the Swanites remember the day,
When the convicts were sent to their shores by Earl Grey.

Conversely, supporters of transportation argued that the convicts would build the infrastructure necessary to make the Swan River Colony viable, would significantly expand the white population base, and could be used to drive down the price of wages. (On the last point they were certainly correct. Some historians claim the arrival of convicts cut labourers' wages by as much as 60 per cent).[26] It was simply a question of economic pragmatism. The real challenge, everyone agreed, was to make sure that the convicts did not poison colonial society with their criminality.

::

Colony of Western Australia
to wit}
The Jurors for our lady the Queen upon their oath present that Edward Bishop late of Hawkhurst in the Colony aforesaid laborer not having the fear of God before his eyes but being moved and seduced by the instigation of the devil on the Twentieth day of August in the year of our Lord one thousand eight hundred and fifty four with force and arms at in Hawkhurst aforesaid in the colony aforesaid one Ah Chong in the peace of God and our said Lady the Queen then and there being did feloniously wilfully and of his malice aforethought kill and murder against the peace of our Lady the Queen her crown and dignity.

The documents for the case of Regina versus Edward Bishop are carefully folded and tied with a ceremonial ribbon. They consist of twelve handwritten pages in elaborate, barely readable script relating to 'Proceedings of a Court of hanging' regarding the murder of 'A Chong a Chinaman who was found dead in Avon on Sunday evening the 20th August 1854'.[27] Prior to 1855 in Western Australia all relevant evidence in criminal cases was first presented to a Grand Jury who would reach a verdict regarding whether to proceed to a trial. After 1855 this practice was taken over by the Public Prosecutor in Perth.[28]

Edward Bishop's case, therefore, was one of the very last to be submitted to a grand jury in Perth.[29]

According to Edward Bishop's deposition, he 'slept in the same room with Ah Chong on Saturday night', the 19th of August, and 'left him in bed at daylight on Sunday morning'. Bishop testified that he 'got up to feed the horses' and then came over to the hut of Voss 'as I do every morning' for breakfast. He went on to claim that when he went to the river to have a wash he had heard screaming but could not tell where it came from. When asked about the scream he heard, Bishop said it sounded 'like the cries of a native woman' but he did not 'see anyone about'. Bishop claimed he later went back down to the river to discover the Chinese cook, Ah Chong's brother, sitting by the river's edge. The Chinese cook told Bishop that his brother was clearly drowned because he could see Ah Chong's bucket floating in the water. Bishop said that he walked to the water's edge but could see nothing. So ended Bishop's testimony.[30] The literate ex-convict signed his statement.

Bishop's ex-convict friend, William Voss, was the next to be called to give evidence. Voss claimed he had not heard any cries on Sunday morning. Instead, Bishop came and got him in the morning and said 'the chinaman was lost'. Voss then went down to the river where he met Mr William Meares and was told to 'look up and down the river' with Charles Claydon. It was Voss who spotted something in the water and with the assistance of Claydon, he fished out the body of Ah Chong. Voss also signed his own statement.[31]

Voss's evidence was followed by Charles Claydon who mentioned that he heard a scream on Sunday morning and that, like Bishop, he thought it was 'the voice of a native woman'.[32] The court then heard from Ah Chong's brother, described in the record only as 'Meares's cook'.[33] Ah Chong's brother stuck closely to the established facts, adding only that on the morning of the murder he got up early to make bread, which explained his presence around the river and his brother's hut. He testified that he 'heard the cries' of his brother 'before I saw Bishop'. This was a disturbing and important piece of evidence. The cook had heard his own brother's death cries as he was being murdered with a hatchet, although the cook did not recognise them as such at the time. This testimony also established that Bishop was not with the cook at the time, or just after, the screams were heard. Bishop had testified that he saw the cook right after the screams, implying that he could not have murdered Ah Chong, dumped his corpse in the river, cleaned himself up, and then run into the Chinese cook within such a narrow corridor of time.

As for whom he believed to be responsible for his brother's death, the 'Chinaman' did not hesitate in saying, 'I think that Bishop knows all about it.' He also alerted the court to the fact that his brother Ah Chong had 'accused Bishop of taking his boxes of matches' a few days prior to his murder. He added that his brother also 'had two pounds in money about him'. Ah Chong's brother, trying to establish motive, stated his belief that Bishop killed Ah Chong because he had accused him of stealing his money. Damningly, the Chinese cook identified a piece of 'cord' produced in court, and found on Bishop, as being 'what my brother used to fasten his little bag to with his money'. Having fulfilled his task in trying to condemn the man whom he believed killed his brother, the Chinese cook stood down.

One of the more controversial aspects of the evidence collected against Edward Bishop was that the legal authorities relied on the testimony of non-Europeans – Ah Chong's brother, the seemingly nameless Chinese cook, and an Aboriginal farm worker known by the other witnesses as 'Jimmy the Native'. During the early part of the nineteenth century many Australian colonial courts prohibited Aboriginal evidence with the justification that 'Natives' were unable to take a Christian oath to tell the truth. Nevertheless, Aboriginal evidence 'on affirmation and without oath' had been legally permitted in Western Australian courts since 1841, and the authorities formally recorded the Aboriginal witness's name as Jimmy Gubau, a 'native boy long in the service of Capn Meares'. After 'being cautioned to speak nothing but the truth', Jimmy's statement was duly recorded.[34]

Jimmy gave evidence that he 'slept in Black Harry's hut on Saturday night' – the home of another Aboriginal farm hand working for the Meares brothers. Jimmy got up early on Sunday morning to 'go milk in the stock yard', when he 'heard some cries' coming from the area near the huts of the white farm workers. He went to investigate the origin of the cries and saw both Bishop and Voss inside one of the huts (this corresponded with Voss's evidence that Bishop had come to get him after the cries were heard in order to tell him the Chinaman was missing). Jimmy saw the two men together in Voss's hut, but did not speak to them. He returned to his work.

Asked further about the cries he heard – the timing of which now seemed to be crucial to determining Bishop's fate – Jimmy testified that, 'The sun was an hour high when I heard the crying'. However, Jimmy also added that around the time of the cries he saw Bishop down at the river. According to Jimmy, when he saw Bishop he was 'washing at the place on the side of the river where the water is usually taken for house work'. This was very important evidence as Jimmy was the first witness to actually place Bishop at the river's edge at about the same time as the cries. The fact that Bishop was washing where water was 'usually taken for house work' was circumstantial evidence that he was up to no good – the presumption was that he was washing blood off his hands. However, there appeared to be a contradiction in Jimmy's evidence. Jimmy said he saw Bishop at the river and in Voss's hut at around the same time – 'after the cries'. Jimmy was asked to clarify the precise timing of events. He replied that, 'I heard the noise and I saw Bishop washing at the river not a minute after'.

Jimmy's statement was signed with an 'X'. A note underneath explained that, 'This evidence was taken immediately on Jimmy's arrival from the sheep station.' This was so as to 'prevent his being spoken to by any person'. Jimmy Gubau, the 'native boy', was the only witness to be treated in such a way.[35] The grand jury now had to decide whether the evidence of such a witness could be used to send a white man to trial in a capital case.

::

Prior to the importation of convicts the Swan River settlers had tried to coax Aborigines into doing their menial labour for them. The Brown family, who were farmers in York, had several 'natives' employed around the farm, although they complained that it was hard to stop them from leaving when they got bored with the work, or when they had been paid enough flour or sugar to satisfy their short-term needs. Still, in an October 1843 letter to her family back home in England, Eliza Brown mentioned that an eleven-year-old 'Native boy' called Corell, 'and a fine interesting fellow he is', had been working as a shepherd for them for several months and had 'fine romps' with the Brown children.[36]

Yet, the determination of most Aborigines to maintain their traditional lifestyles, where possible, prevented wider employment of 'natives' at the Swan River. Even when they were employed by whites their unwillingness to break entirely with Indigenous culture could often complicate relationships. For example, in the same 1843 letter home Eliza Brown complained to her family about an Aboriginal worker called 'Tom' – 'I forget the Native name of the man,' – and his wife Biedan. Due to a dispute between Biedan and another Aboriginal woman, Biedan was speared in the kitchen of the Brown's home. Biedan ran into one of the Brown girl's rooms for protection and was bleeding profusely from a leg that was 'frightfully lacerated from the hip joint down to the knee' when Eliza Brown found her.[37] Such incidents could hardly inspire confidence in the minds of the settlers that Aborigines might become a dependable labour force for the Colony.

Although she did not mind employing Aborigines, Mrs Eliza Brown did write home to her family in April 1851 regarding her embarrassment over the Swan River being turned into a British penal settlement:

> I am afraid you look down upon us with contempt since we have harboured convicts. I must own that my pride is taken down a few notches, perhaps it will prove a wholesome castigation.[38]

But what choice did they have? Even by 1839 Nathaniel Ogle, in his *Manual for Emigrants*, was already referring to 'the neglected colony of Western Australia' and pointing out, rather too desperately, its 'advantages'. Included in these was the fact that the westernmost third of the continent was 'happily without the taint of a penal colony'. Ogle believed that Western Australia could 'never be made a penal settlement' and that as a result, no 'polluting example derived from convict servitude or society, exists'. He also quoted approvingly from a report by Sir James Stirling from 1838 which pointed out that at the time of writing, 'the law has not found occasion to execute sentence of death upon any individual' – the case of Midgegooroo obviously not being considered worthy of mention. For men like Nathaniel Ogle, this was proof positive that the free settlement of the Swan River had bred an altogether more law-abiding, righteous and godly community of settlers than existed on the Australian eastern seaboard.[39]

However, Ogle was also concerned by the fact that too many labourers 'who reach these new colonies see that their labour is necessary, and cannot, in case of misconduct, be readily replaced; and taking advantage of their relative positions, create mistrust, vexation, and injury'. Or in other words, the poor did not accept their poverty. They did, however, take to the bottle, with the imbibing of 'intoxicating liquors' being, in Ogle's opinion, a true Western Australian working class 'evil'. It was a view apparently shared by Stirling who, according to Ogle, 'with candour laments the propensity to intoxication among the lower classes'.[40]

Ogle was also aware that among the Swan River colonists themselves there were a growing number of advocates for convict transportation. Addressing these 'inconsiderate individuals' he reminded his readers that convictism would lead to colonists' wives interacting 'with the lowest prostitutes and abandoned thieves, swept from the sinks of iniquity of a great metropolis'. Moreover, their children would be corrupted by sinners and felons. Instead Ogle hoped that 'Western Australia will never again be disgraced by proposals' for convict transportation which were 'branded with the marks of either infamy or ignorance'. There should be no more attempts to 'pollute their new and beautiful country' with convicts, and those who thought otherwise should simply relocate to Van Dieman's Land.[41]

Unfortunately, history does not record what Nathaniel Ogle thought of Edward Bishop. One suspects, however, that he would have seen him as confirming his worst suspicions about convict pollution.

::

According to George Meares, one of the two brothers who owned the farm on which Edward Bishop worked, he was at his property on the Sunday morning that Ah Chong was murdered when suddenly, 'Jimmy the Native called my brother William out and I heard him say I think the China Man is drowned'. George went out 'directly' and then the two Meares brothers and Jimmy went down to the riverbank where the water for housework was drawn. While walking there they questioned Jimmy. Jimmy told George Meares that 'when he was getting up he heard someone cry out four times' and that he, Jimmy, 'ran down to the fence' to try and see what was happening. When called to give evidence in court, George Meares' testimony was supported by his brother William.[42]

Interestingly, another Aborigine, 'Black Harry', was then called. 'Jimmy the Native' had told the court that he stayed in Harry's hut the night before the murder. Harry confirmed this and also testified that Bishop had told him, 'he did not like the China man at all'. And then, remarkably, Mary Mitchel, Black Harry's wife, gave evidence, although she was not recorded in the official list of witnesses. She revealed that she had actually gone with Jimmy down to the fence when they first heard 'the cries' of, they now knew, Ah Chong being murdered. However, Mary and Jimmy couldn't see anything suspicious from the fence and so Jimmy 'said he would ask about the noise from the white fellows'. She added that Jimmy later told her that Bishop had told Jimmy 'that drunken men were passing by who made the noise'.

This was the first the court had heard of Black Harry's wife Mary accompanying Jimmy to the fence at the time of the cries, and the first the Grand Jury had heard of Bishop's explanation to Jimmy that the cries, which had disturbed everyone's peaceful morning, were just drunken passers-by. 'Jimmy the Native' was recalled by the court. He confirmed that it was himself and Harry's wife who ran to the fence when the first cries started. He added that when the cries stopped he went back down to the house for a bucket to do the milking, 'and saw Bishop go in to the hut with a jacket in his hand'.

So what was in the jacket? The murder weapon (a sharpened hatchet) perhaps? Some of Ah Chong's bloody clothing? Or Bishop's own blood splattered clothing which he wanted to wash and hide away? Perhaps only an innocent jacket after all? The Jury clearly could not decide, even though the records reflect that they believed Ah Chong's death to be the result of malfeasance. Not least of all because the doctor had officially testified that the 'the Chinaman' was murdered with a hatchet and then dumped in the water. But by whom?

One of the frustrations that seemed to pulse through all of the Jury's handwritten notes was that this 'native boy', Jimmy Gubau, was not a reliable witness. He was Aboriginal after all, and therefore, according to the prejudices of the age, he could easily have been convinced to lie. And yet, it was his evidence upon which Bishop's fate seemed to hinge. He was the only witness who could place Bishop at the riverbank just after the murder. The Grand Jury obviously thought this was not enough. It was recorded that, 'The jury are of the opinion that A Chong the China Man met his death from having been murdered by some person or persons unknown.' They suggested a public reward of twenty pounds be offered for evidence leading to the arrest of Ah Chong's murderer. Edward Bishop would not face trial for murder.

::

Edward Bishop nearly escaped the hangman's noose. And then new evidence was offered on 2 September 1854 by Sophia Doncon, the wife of a York publican, who signed her name with a simple 'X'. She stated that she met up with Bishop after he left the employment of the Meares brothers. He came to the pub owned by her and her husband to drown his sorrows. With drink taken, Bishop revealed to Sophia much about the case. 'He told me' that the Meares brothers, 'did not want him any longer', presumably because although the grand jury had found him not guilty, the Meares brothers and all of his co-workers assumed that he was the violent hatchet killer of Ah Chong. Bishop was dismissed. Sophia then told the court that Bishop had told her that he 'and the China Man slept in the one room together'. Conditions were cramped. They got on each other's nerves. On the night before the murder Bishop went out and got drunk in the house of a nearby settler. The next morning, with Bishop hungover, a fight broke out between the ex-convict and the Chinaman. Bishop killed Ah Chong.[43]

On the basis of the new evidence Edward Bishop was committed to stand trial for murder. The trial opened with the Advocate-General dramatically emphasising the heinousness of Edward Bishop's crime, along with the racial dimension to the proceedings:

> The solemn investigation which is now to occupy us, is in some measure enlivened and ennobled by the exercise of the higher qualities of our nature. It is to inquire into the death of one under the Queen's protection – neither a countryman nor even a European, but a native of a land which we, I know not how justly, deem our inferior in civilization, and especially so in jurisprudence. Without our boasting of what is our simple duty, I am sure you will agree with me that high and honourable feelings blend with our usual horror of bloodshed, and share my desire to show the friendless foreigner that our laws protect his life and visit his death equally as effectually and as earnestly as the most honoured of our countrymen.[44]

Sophia Doncon's evidence was supported by testimony from Robert Viveash, the Surgeon at York, who claimed that a 'monkey jacket' worn by Bishop on the day of the Chinaman's murder was stained with blood and that someone had tried to wash it off the left sleeve. Moreover, Thomas Martin, who lived with one of the Meares brothers, also claimed that he had been drinking with Bishop at the Doncon's pub on 27 August 1854 – a week after the murder. Later, while walking, Bishop allegedly asked Thomas whether, 'if you were to kill a man and no one saw you do it, would you be hanged?' Almost a week later Bishop and Martin were again walking together when they passed a local settler, George Wall. Apparently Wall remarked, 'they haven't hung you yet Bishop?' To which Bishop replied, 'No,' before muttering to Martin, 'they must prove me guilty first before they can hang me'.[45]

Regrettably, although part of the court record is now lost, one final official statement provides a summation of the evidence against Bishop. The speaker noted that 'we always find the Chinese naturally of a very quiet unobtrusive disposition we don't find that this poor A Chung', meaning Ah Chong, 'offended any human being'. The statement goes on to say that the evidence suggests, 'that Bishop did not like the Chinese and wished they were gone' from Western Australia. On the night before the murder Bishop drank a bottle of rum. He was a man 'not in the habit of drinking regularly' and 'it affected him'. However, 'we find by Bishop's own statement' that he and Ah Chong 'went to bed together and got up together – we know that men who drank over nights do not rise in very good humours'. Then the Court speculated: '[W]as there a quarrel in the morning and might an affray have taken place and might a blow have been given with the back of the axe?' The speaker noted that a doctor had testified that 'the first blow given was with the back of the axe on the left temple'. After death, the body of Ah Chong 'was thrown in the water, in 20 feet of water, and that the murderer had good cause to assume it would be washed away'. Instead, 'it got tangled in the roots of trees'.

Going back to the basics of the case, motive for murder was established. It was stated that at the time of the murder the Meares brothers had two 'ticket of leave men' (convicts on probationary release) in their employ – Voss and Bishop. Initially Voss and Bishop slept in the same hut and Ah Chong and his brother shared a hut. However, Ah Chong, the farm carpenter, was working on the other side of the river. Ah Chong did not want to sleep there alone and so Bishop was sent over to share the hut with him. Each morning Ah Chong's brother, the Chinese cook, would send his brother food scraps. Bishop objected to this preferential treatment and said he would 'chuck the Chinaman's bloody things into the river'. Ah Chong, in turn, accused Bishop of getting him drunk and stealing from him. It was pointed out that Ah Chong's hat had been found with blood stains on the inside. The hat, discovered inside the hut Edward Bishop and Ah Chong shared, had been put near some mutton so as to appear that the blood was from butchery rather than murder. A bloodstained axe was also found inside the hut. The conclusion drawn was that this fateful hungover argument between Ah Chong the Chinaman and Edward Bishop the English ex-convict had turned violent. Bishop had hit Ah Chong with the axe and killed him.

::

It took the jury in the criminal trial just twenty minutes to decide Edward Bishop was guilty of murder. He was sentenced to death, with the judge donning the black cap and urging Bishop to atone for his sins in front of God. On 11 October 1854 *The Inquirer* notified its readers that:

> The fate of Edward Bishop is decided, and he is to die tomorrow. The time of his execution will doubtless be early in the morning, and the place is fixed at some distance (about one and a half mile) beyond the causeway bridge. We hope that measures will be taken, by placing policemen on the bridge, to prevent women and children passing over to be present at the execution.[46]

Edward Bishop maintained his innocence until the bitter end. Through *The Inquirer* he gave an overview of his life and struggles, relaying that he had been born near Bristol in England in 1831 – 'My father is a farm labourer, my mother is dead, and I have three sisters and two brothers,' family that he was never to see again. Bishop was, according to his account, 'never sent to any day school' and went to work when he was eight. He first came to the attention of the law when he was convicted of housebreaking at age eighteen, although in his account, he was simply trying to get 'out of the rain'. He learned to read in prison. He was sent to Western Australia and immediately given a ticket of leave. He worked hard. He was falsely accused, wrongly condemned and asserted his innocence, 'in the prospect of death, and do it as if it were done in the presence of God'.[47]

God or not, Bishop was to hang. *The Inquirer* asserted there was 'no shadow of doubt' as to his guilt. *The Inquirer* was also appalled to report that people had placed bets on whether Bishop would be given a last minute reprieve. As things turned out, on the morning of 12 October 1854 at eight o'clock, two carts set out from the prison – the first carrying a coffin, the second carrying Bishop, accompanied by some soldiers. Bishop remained calm as he passed through the streets of Perth:

> Through the whole passage to his execution, the wretched man seemed perfectly composed, and impenetrable to any feeling of fear at his fate, showing no remorse at the conduct which brought him to such an untimely end.[48]

Arriving at the site on the road outside Fremantle chosen for his execution, Bishop had his handcuffs removed and was pinioned. The death warrant was read and prayers muttered over. Asked if he had any final words, Bishop declared his innocence before God. The assembled crowd then watched as 'with hardly a struggle the soul of the murderer was sent to meet his Judge Eternal'.[49]

Altogether, *The Inquirer* was lacklustre in its support for Bishop's hanging. Indeed, the newspaper went so far as to argue that the entire event reeked of England's most notorious site for public executions:

> The days of Tyburn are past; we call upon our Government to do away with the existing practice of parading a condemned malefactor through our principal street, with the church-bell ringing in his ears, and harrowing up the feelings of every right-minded inmate of those dwellings before which the criminal may be escorted.[50]

Private execution was still some years off, but *The Inquirer* suggested that hangings possibly take place 'on the other side of Perth Water', and that only required attendees, as opposed to a mass of spectators, be taken in boats to the site of execution. Obviously troubled by the meaning and implications of Bishop's crime and death, that day's editorial boldly called for greater religious instruction for convicts in order to keep them on the moral path.[51]

::

Edward Bishop was the first transported convict to be hanged in Western Australia. However, three former convicts were hanged the following year, two in 1856, and two more in 1857. After a year without the need for legal execution, another was found guilty of murder and hanged in 1859. Indeed, these eight former convicts were the only white men hanged in Western Australia between 1854 and 1859. Although this did not bode well, *The Inquirer* tried to reassure its readers that there was little danger of Western Australia developing into a criminal confederacy. The newspaper approvingly reported the Governor's speech to the Legislative Assembly on 22 October 1859 where he had congratulated the colony on the relative absence of misery and malfeasance.

> And yet Western Australia, almost free from crime and pauperism, is a convict settlement, where the adult male population is nearly equally divided into free and bond.[52]

The Inquirer agreed:

> In no part of the empire are life and property more secure than here, in no part
> is there a smaller ratio of crime in proportion to the population, and never in the
> history of man has a system of reformation of the criminal been so successfully
> carried out, or has produced so good an effect, as that now in force in Western
> Australia.[53]

Not everyone was convinced. The idea of the convict stain remained in
the minds of many colonists. They feared that they were importing the
dregs of British society and were in danger of creating – like New South
Wales or Tasmania – a drunken and homicidal commonwealth of thieves.
Transgressions by freed convicts seemed to confirm the dismal prospects for
a country imprinted with criminality.

William Voss, who had discovered the body of Ah Chong in 1854 and
who had given crucial evidence at the trial of his fellow ex-convict and friend
Edward Bishop, must have read these debates with interest. He had been given
a conditional pardon in March 1857. Voss was already in his thirties when he
arrived in Fremantle and transportation to Australia had rescued him from his
previous life of poverty and prison. After Bishop's trial he continued to work
on the Meares' farm and found a wife, Mary Moir. Then on 11 November 1861
Mary suddenly disappeared.

That night Voss went to the huts of several local workers, and of his
employer, looking for Mary. After searching the farm and surrounding
bush with Meares and some others, Voss voiced his opinion that his wife
had either been kidnapped, or 'she might have been bitten by a snake'.[54] The
search continued until about three in the morning when rain, poor light and
exhaustion forced a halt.

The search resumed at dawn – although this time Voss did not join the
party – and Mary's corpse was discovered under a large gum tree shortly
afterwards. According to Meares' evidence at a later trial:

> I saw something on the ground ahead, and on going up to it found it to be
> the body of Mrs Voss with the head all chopped…The body was lying on the
> right side with the arm stretched out…she had on boots, no stockings, and a
> red petticoat, her hood was lying on the ground saturated with blood, of which
> there was also a great quantity on the ground, and the marks of a scuffle…[55]

With the help of an Aboriginal tracker it was pointed out to the police, and Meares, that whomever had killed Mary Voss was wearing boots that had a sole held together with nails of two distinctly different sizes. The murderer had also stepped on Mary when she was on the ground, possibly to deliver a final fatal blow, leaving a boot print on her corpse. The position of the corpse indicated that a significant struggle had taken place. Mary's attacker had almost certainly hit her in the face several times with a small axe before finishing her off as she lay on her back on the ground.

Returning to Voss's hut, the news of the grim discovery was broken to the former convict:

> Mr Bailey said, 'Voss, we have found her'. Voss asked if she was dead. Mr Bailey replied that she was; he cried out and leaned against the fence, and then asked where she was and if she was hurt, threw himself upon the ground and made a great noise... 'I did not see him shed any tears; he said they had never had a wrong word...'[56]

However, Meares' attention was drawn to Voss's boots and he 'saw they corresponded with the foot track found by the native'. William Voss was arrested and charged with murder. Voss told Sub-Inspector Tymperly that he was not guilty.[57] At the lock-up Tymperly removed Voss's incriminating boots and later matched the heel to the distinctive bruise left upon Mary's dead body. When Mary Voss's autopsy was carried out on 12 November by Dr M'Coy, the Colonial Surgeon at York, he discovered that both her clenched hands 'were stained with blood and in the palm of the right there was some soil with a few hairs'. In the learned doctor's opinion, these hairs matched the 'whiskers' of Voss and had probably been taken, in violence, as Mary fought for her life.

When the case came to court in January 1862 *The Inquirer* reminded its readers that:

> Voss, it may be recollected, was one of the witnesses against Bishop, who was executed in October, 1854, for the murder of a Chinaman, and who declared his innocence to the last. As these two men lived in the same hut shortly before that murder, and were intimates, it is possible he may throw some further light on the affair, in which, it is not altogether impossible, he might have been concerned.[58]

Indeed, as the case progressed it became plausible to suspect Voss may have actually been Ah Chong's murderer in 1854. In court Voss's employer, S. G. Meares, testified that Voss had, 'the character of being a very violent man; during the sheep shearing he kicked one of the sheep so that it was crippled and obliged to be killed, and it was then found that its entrails were burst'.[59]

There was also much that was superficially similar in the Ah Chong and Mary Voss murders – the futile search for a missing person; the murder weapon being a small axe; the murder resulting from a presumed fit of violence rather than premeditation; and so on. Was it possible that Voss had actually framed Edward Bishop for the murder of Ah Chong in 1854? That he had allowed his friend Bishop to go to the gallows for a crime that he, Voss, actually committed? Or had Voss simply killed Mary in a rage and then, in desperation, attempted to cover up the murder by resorting to his knowledge of the Ah Chong case, where Bishop had almost escaped justice? We will never know.

In court Voss's lawyer, Mr Howell, addressed the jury and half-heartedly pointed out that the case against Voss lacked a motive for murder. He conceded, however, that if 'the Jury should come to the conclusion that the wounds had been made by the prisoner, he would urge upon them the consideration' that they were probably 'the effect of a gust of passion, and that he had no intention of killing the unfortunate woman'. The Jury was unconvinced. William Voss was found guilty and sentenced to death. Although Voss, like Bishop before him, persisted in his claim that he was innocent, he was hanged on the morning of 10 January 1862. The convict stain proved resilient.

3

Richard Bibby and the Law of the Frontier, 1859

The first white man is hanged in Western Australia for the murder of an Aborigine, leading to a major public debate on issues of law and justice.

When Captain James Stirling officially established the new colony of Western Australia on 18 June 1829, he was conscious of the Aboriginal people whose country he was occupying in the name of the British Empire. While he had not paid the local Aborigines any money for the land, nor made any treaty with them in which they ceded sovereignty, he did not entirely ignore their presence:

> I do hereby give Notice that if any Person or Persons shall be convicted of behaving in a fraudulent, cruel or felonious Manner towards the Aborigines of the Country, such Person or Persons will be liable to be prosecuted and tried for the Offence, as if the same had been committed against any other of His Majesty's Subjects.[1]

Such words were intended to convey Lieutenant Governor Stirling's belief that the 'Swan River natives', as the settlers called the Aborigines, would be treated with fairness and justice during his rule. Nevertheless, Stirling's words left him caught in a historic contradiction not of his own making. A generation earlier when Captain Cook had set out on his epic journey of exploration he had been given instructions that stipulated that if he was fortunate enough to discover the eastern passage to the Great Southern Land he was to:

> ...observe the Genius, Temper, Disposition and Number of the Natives, if there be any and endeavour by all proper means to cultivate a Friendship and Alliance

with them, making them presents of such Trifles as they may Value inviting them to Traffick, and Shewing them every kind of Civility and Regard...[2]

The historically crucial part of his instructions, however, concerned the actual protocol for the acquisition of land.

> You are also with the Consent of the Natives to take Possession of Convenient Situations in the Country in the Name of the King of Great Britain: Or: if you find the Country uninhabited take Possession for his Majesty by setting up Proper Marks and Inscriptions, as first discoverers and possessors.[3]

Arriving off the coast of Australia in April 1770 Captain Cook became aware of the presence of Aboriginal people, and even interacted with some of them as he sailed north along the coast stopping off in what is now New South Wales and Queensland. Heavily influenced by William Dampier's earlier reports regarding the 'wretched' natives of New Holland (although Cook conceded 'in reality they are far more happier than we Europeans') Cook reached a number of hasty conclusions that were to have far-reaching implications. Included among these was the idea that Aborigines had 'no fix'd habitation but move about from place to place like wild Beasts in search of food', and that 'these people live wholly by fishing and hunting, but mostly the former for we never saw one Inch of Cultivated Land in the Whole Country'.[4]

Despite the fact that he had not been given 'the Consent of the Natives to take Possession of Convenient Situations', Cook nevertheless claimed the entire eastern coast of Australia in the name of the British Crown. Interestingly, when he had his ship's name and the date of his 'discovery' of eastern Australia cut into a tree, he made sure the inscription faced the sea. It was intended for other European seafarers to read. The people who had the greatest chance of actually stumbling across the inscription, local Aborigines, were not the intended audience.[5]

When the First Fleet, laden with the penal refuse of Britain, arrived at Botany Bay in January 1788 they scarcely knew anything about the country they were about to settle. No formal reconnaissance had been carried out since Cook's initial voyage eighteen years earlier. Even Sydney Harbour, the entrance to which Cook had sailed past, was unexplored. In the words of Robert Hughes in *The Fatal Shore*, 'Never had a colony been founded so far from its parent state, or in such ignorance of the land it occupied.'[6]

The men and women of the First Fleet quickly became aware of the inaccuracy of Cook's judgement that Australia was largely unoccupied. The talented Watkin Tench, a British Marine Captain whose first-hand account of the early years of the Sydney settlement remains essential reading for any enthusiast of Australian history, wrote candidly about the first tentative explorations of the area around Botany Bay.

> We found the natives tolerably numerous as we advanced up the river, and even at the harbour's mouth we had reason to conclude the country more populous than Mr Cook thought it.[7]

Tench records that a group of about forty Aborigines observed the British ship *Supply* from the beach on the south shore of Botany Bay after its arrival on 18 January 1788. The Aborigines shouted at the ship and made 'many uncouth signs and gestures' – presumably an attempt to ward off such an unnatural visage. When a smaller group of about six Aboriginal men appeared on the north shore of Botany Bay, 'the governor immediately preceded to land on that side in order to take possession of his new territory and bring about an intercourse between its old and new masters.'[8] And so the legal fiction of British rights to newly discovered territory was conjured up before Aborigines for whom this was just a bewildering performance by strange white spirits who had arrived without warning upon their ancestral lands.

Moreover, despite the fact that his own experience of the Sydney area directly contradicted Cook's assessment of unoccupied (or at least, under-occupied) land, even a sharp observer like Tench clutched to the idea that the country was free for the taking.

> I have already hinted that the country is more populous than it was generally believed to be in Europe at the time of our sailing. But this remark is not meant to be extended to the interior parts of the continent, which there is every reason to conclude, from our researches as well as from the manner of living practised by the natives, to be uninhabited.[9]

Even the erudite Watkin Tench, a representative of a colony that had barely explored beyond Parramatta and was wholly ignorant of the actual circumstances in the 'interior parts of the continent', could not conceive of the cultural diversity and ecological mastery that allowed significant numbers of

Aborigines to exist in even the driest and most inhospitable parts of Australia. Overall, the British occupation of Australia depended upon a complex fiction that ignored, diminished and eventually eradicated Aboriginal sovereignty. In the words of historian David Day:

> The British invaders did not consciously come as invaders of what Cook had styled New South Wales. Instead, they came flourishing a legal claim based upon Cook's supposed discovery. This was backed by an effective claim based upon their occupation of Sydney Cove and their exploitation of its immediate hinterland. And overlaying it all was a moral claim based upon the 'gifts of European civilisation' which they were about to bestow upon the Aborigines and their fulfilment of their God's injunction to make the earth fruitful.[10]

However, by 1829 when James Stirling embarked upon the colonisation of the Swan River, it was abundantly clear that contrary to the assertions of Captain Cook or Watkin Tench, Australia was extensively occupied. Moreover, Aborigines were not restricted to the coastline, and in small numbers, as Tench, Cook or the famous botanist Joseph Banks had believed. Their mistake had been, essentially, an environmental one. Given its aridness and based on earlier reports from Dampier regarding the north-west coast of 'New Holland', Cook and Banks believed the Australian environment to be incapable of producing enough food to sustain human life away from the sea.[11]

In addition, despite an enduring belief that Aboriginal people were nomads without a particular connection to any specific tract of land, they were arguably much more intimately connected to their environs than Europeans. The white settlers had come in ships across the ocean to make a new life for themselves on the other side of the world. To Aboriginal people such a journey was both technologically and spiritually inconceivable. To local Aborigines the European concept of land ownership was as alien and offensive as suggesting to Europeans that they could somehow sell the sky to one another and accuse people of trespassing under it. Aboriginal people believed they belonged to the land, not the other way around.

When European settlers first came into contact with Aboriginal people they also found it difficult to understand their social structures. Europe of the eighteenth and nineteenth century was highly stratified with most Europeans being ruled by Kings and Queens who derived their position from hereditary privilege. Aboriginal society, by contrast, was reasonably free from disparities of wealth and power. People starved and prospered together. Elders were respected, Aboriginal cultural law was rigorously enforced and there was a gender-based division of labour. Brute exploitation and despotic rule, however, were generally alien to traditional Aboriginal society where collective welfare predominated over the rights and power of any one individual. Most European settlers could neither respect nor truly comprehend these forms of social organisation.

These differences regarding concepts of life, society and land ownership made some sort of clash on the Australian frontier highly likely, if not inevitable. Conceptually, the British believed that Cook had taken legal possession of the whole eastern coast of the continent in 1770. Proclamations, like James Stirling's of 1829, were all that was required to expand the European settlement. And yet the awful truth, which became apparent to some of the settlers, was that Aborigines did not recede into the uncharted wilderness with the arrival of whites. Aboriginal people continued to roam their traditional lands and they continued to hold on to their traditional ways of life.

When Stirling wrote a dispatch to the Colonial Office in 1832 he reported that the tiny West Australian settler population of 1,497 people (including 400 in Fremantle and only 360 in Perth) were spread over thirteen locations in the south-west of the colony. He noted, however, that 'the Aboriginal tribes' were 'pretty equally spread over the whole surface of the country on the conjectural average of one to each square mile'.[12] Similarly, after visiting Western Australia one Quaker missionary commented in 1838 that the Aborigines 'from the Swan River to King George Sound, recognise their distinct hunting grounds as the private property of the different families, and that the boundaries are clearly defined'.[13] George Fletcher Moore, one of the more enlightened and influential settlers of the early Colony, similarly wrote of the Aborigines, 'It seems that the land is all parcelled out into districts among themselves, and that they rarely travel far from their own homes.'[14]

In North America, Southern Africa and the Pacific Islands (including New Zealand) the British had generally acknowledged pre-existing indigenous land rights. In some places this had taken the form of a land sale, or of treaties that formally transferred sovereignty to the British colonisers (usually following a war of conquest). By contrast, in Australia the British clung tenaciously, despite all the evidence to the contrary, to the legal fiction that Australia had not been meaningfully occupied until the arrival of the First Fleet in 1788. Those Aborigines they did encounter were legally considered to be fellow

British subjects, not sovereign peoples. Therefore, no land sales were to be negotiated with Aborigines and no treaties signed. In the few instances where settlers proposed such things this was rejected. John Batman, for example, initially negotiated to buy the land around Melbourne for an annual rent of 100 blankets, 100 knives, 100 tomahawks, 50 suits of clothing, 50 'looking glasses', 50 scissors and five tons of flour. This was officially overturned.[15]

The diverse groups of Aborigines who inhabited the land around the Swan River shared a common language in which the word *nyoongar* (also *nyungar* and other spellings) meant person. Today the word *Nyoongar* is commonly used as a collective noun to describe their descendants. At the time of Stirling's arrival in 1829, however, there were many sub-groupings who hunted, struggled against the elements, lived and died within the specific boundaries of traditional lands that they were supposed to protect and maintain. The *Juet Nyoongar*, for example, were custodians of land to the north of the Swan River while the *Whadjug Nyoongar* (or *Whadjuk Nyungar*) lived south of the river around Fremantle, in country they called *Walyalup*. It was estimated that several hundred *Whadjug Nyoongar* lived in different groups around *Walyalup* in 1829. There were also many sub-tribes in the area around the Swan and Canning Rivers, including the *Mooro*, *Beeliar* and *Beelu Nyoongar*. They observed, interacted and sometimes battled with the European newcomers.

On the other side of the frontier, settlers lived in a colony where British law and order was paramount. Or as Lord Goderich put it in a 1831 letter to Stirling explaining the legal parameters of his commission as Lieutenant Governor of the Swan River Colony:

> It may be proper to notice that Western Australia being a Territory acquired by mere right of occupancy, & not by conquest, the King's subjects residing there are, by general principle of Law, entitled to all the Rights & Privileges of British subjects, & carry with them the Law of their Native Country, so far as it is applicable to their new situation and circumstance.[16]

Yet, some settlers remained troubled by the unstable fiction of a continent for the taking. On 17 September 1836, seven years into the colonial project, the *Perth Gazette* revealed that Francis Armstrong, the 'Native Interpreter', had on the orders of Lieutenant Governor Stirling made contact with local Swan River Aborigines in order to negotiate the purchase of their land. In the minutes of an important meeting of Stirling's Executive Council earlier on 13 September it was recorded that Armstrong had reported that some local Aborigines were prepared to sell the lands already occupied by whites in return for food, clothing and 'provided they were allowed free access to such parts as were not enclosed'. Stirling declared his support for the plan but this was opposed by the majority of the Executive Council who argued – in one of the most remarkable statements in the Colony's short history – that it was better to:

> Inform the Natives that it was not the wish of the Government to deprive them of any part of their land, beyond that which is, or maybe required by the White Inhabitants of the Territory, and upon which they are not to trespass or commit any theft on pain of forfeiting the goodwill shown, and the protection afforded by the Local Government.[17]

Stirling realised he was in a minority. Thus, like Batman's bold initiative in Melbourne, the proposed Swan River land treaty was quashed and nothing more was heard of it.

While the settlers were prepared to admit that Aboriginal people existed, they insisted that the 'primitive state' of Aboriginal society at the time of initial settlement rendered Indigenous sovereignty null and void. Or as one Swan River settler explained in an 1832 letter to his family back home in Britain:

> Now for the natives, here we have nature in its pure and unadorned state…They are probably the furthest removed from civilization of any human creatures on the globe, for they have neither religion, laws or government, houses nor clothing, none worthy of the name, and yet they do not appear stupid. It seems to me that their principal mental deficiency is total absence of what we call taste, or the capability of perceiving what is beautiful…[18]

Given such ignorance of Aboriginal culture it is no wonder that many among the settler population were therefore generally unconcerned by the dubious legality of the British colonial project. As Edward Landor, a much respected West Australian lawyer, argued in 1847:

> Why not say boldly at once, the right of power? We have seized upon the country, and shot down the inhabitants, until the survivors have found it

expedient to submit to our rule. We have acted exactly as Julius Ceasar did when he took possession of Britain. But Ceasar was not so hypocritical as to pretend any moral *right* to possession.[19]

But what to do with the remnants of Aboriginal society? What were their rights and priviledges? Did British Law apply to Aborigines who had, to one degree or another, come to an accommodation with white colonial society? Stirling's proclamation of 1829 – coming forty-one years after the First Fleet sailed into Sydney Harbour – had been his attempt to anticipate some of these issues. Stirling had declared that Aborigines were subjects of His Majesty and would be treated the same as any white settler. While any attempted hostile 'invasion' (Stirling's words) of the colony by Aborigines would be resisted, those settlers who behaved in a 'fraudulent, cruel or felonious Manner' towards the Aborigines would be punished. In 1829 this must have sounded like noble sentiment. But such ideas were yet to experience the test of history.

One such test came during April 1838 when an Aboriginal man called Helia was tried and sentenced to death for the murder of an Aboriginal woman in Perth. At the Executive Council meeting of 31 July, Governor Stirling argued against carrying out the death sentence, insisting that 'to apply strictly and impartially the British Law to this particular offender would be to pass a sentence of death upon the whole race'. Stirling was supported on the Council by George Fletcher Moore who similarly argued that, 'it would be cruel to take away his Life for acting amongst his own people, in a manner sanctioned and recognised as right by them', even though, 'that conduct be in contradistinction of our own Law'.[20] The death sentence was commuted and Helia was exiled to Rottnest Island instead.

The following year, after a number of attacks by Aborigines upon other Aborigines working for white settlers, the governor produced a proclamation to be read in *Nyoongar* to whatever local Aborigines could be compelled to listen. It was also published in the *Perth Gazette*, with an adjoining text that explained:

> The substance of the above is, that if a Native residing with, and under the care of a European, is killed by a Native, the Governor will immediately have the murderer apprehended and punished in precisely the same manner as if the murder had been committed on a white person.[21]

But what if a settler murdered an Aborigine? Would British Justice prevail over the unwritten law of the frontier where, in the words of one Swan River colonist in 1832, it was a simple case of 'blood for blood'?[22] Could Aborigines seek justice under 'white man's law'?

::

Western Australia. Champion Bay. Evidence of Ginbaroo, an Aboriginal Native, given on this 27th day of June 1859.
Saith, about three months back, I was sleeping at a Native camp on the Upper Irwin about forty yards from Mr Davis's shepherds huts where Richard Bibby was hut keeper, one morning about daylight Dicky, that is Richard Bibby, and Ned, that is Edward Cornellie, came to the Native fires, Dicky had a pistol, Ned had no gun or pistol, Dicky or Bibby went up to the fire where a Native named Bil-a-mar-rah was sleeping, he called him and told him to get up, the Native he was sick and could not get up. He again told him to get up. Bil-a-mar-ra then stood up and as soon as he did Richard Bibby or Dicky fired the pistol at him and shot him with one ball through the forehead and out at his pole, he at once fell down dead, he never spoke or moved.[23]

The above was the official translation of the story told by Ginbaroo, who had watched the shooting of Billimarra. After witnessing this murder Ginbaroo went up to Richard Bibby, the white shepherd he called 'Dicky', and asked why he had killed Billimarra. Bibby simply turned and walked back to his hut. Billimarra lay dead at the campfire with 'a big hole in his forehead' and blood seeping into the dirt. Ginbaroo was asked by the legal authorities why he thought Bibby might have wanted to kill Billimarra. Ginbaroo said that 'Bil-a-mar-ra had a young woman and Dicky wanted her, she ran away into the bush when the shot was fired, and Dicky told me to go and fetch her back, I told him that she was gone far away.'[24]

Motive having been established, Ginbaroo was asked what happened after the killing. Ginbaroo told how he had followed Bibby to his hut and asked him for a shovel to bury Billimarra with. According to Ginbaroo, 'he gave me a shovel and I and two women buried the body.' It was also recorded that Billimarra was Ginbaroo's uncle. His interview concluded, his role in a monumental moment in Western Australian legal history complete, Ginbaroo signed his statement with an 'X'. It was noted the X represented

'Gin-ba-roo, alias Monkey', the complainant in the case of the murder of Billimarra, 'a native'.[25]

::

In 1859 Western Australia was still an overwhelmingly agrarian society. An estimated 49.3 per cent of the European workforce laboured on the land, and while rural settlements like York (to the east of Perth) attempted to recreate the villages of Britain, many farm workers lived in remote isolation.[26] It was often a lonely life, with only a few scattered whites for company. On the frontier the line between white and black was, theoretically, clearly defined. However, white farmers were often left to fend for themselves on remote stations where they were surrounded and outnumbered by Indigenous Australians. Isolation, ideas of racial superiority, sexual impulses and the struggle for physical control of the land created frightening and exciting new worlds on the margins of colonial life. The theme of romantic inclinations across racial boundaries, of sexual taboo, became a feature of some of Australia's most audacious creative writing. For example, Bruce Bennett compares E. L. Grant Watson's outback fantasies to Conrad's *Heart of Darkness* where the emphasis is similarly on white men living at the outer limits of European society and morality.[27]

There was undoubtedly a sexual tension that was part of the experience of the Australian frontier. Sometimes this tension resulted in romance and love that defied the conventions of the age. For example, George Fletcher Moore wrote in his diary about a case in February 1838 where:

> A native came to complain of a white man having stolen his wife. He was very angry and threatened to spear the person. The Governor referred the case to me, and I had no small trouble in settling it to the satisfaction of all parties, which was done principally by way of damages, and accepted, after some demur, as a peace offering.[28]

Similarly, the *Perth Gazette* of 8 March 1845 reported 'the first instance of a matrimonial union between an Aboriginal and a European', when a 'native girl' married one of the settlers in a solemn ceremony at the Wesleyan Chapel in Perth. Given the uniqueness of the occasion, 'considerable interest was excited, and a number of spectators assembled' in the church to witness the proceedings. It was noted that, 'for a length of time mutual attachment has been apparent to those who had charge of the bride' and that, 'after giving them six months to reflect, they consented to the union'. [29]

Other times the sexual tension resolved itself in rapine and violence. In a colony where white women were scarce, colonists and convicts often saw Aboriginal women as an exploitable natural resource. The consequences of this sexual frontier between white and black, even when based on mutual consent, could often be deadly. For example, in July 1845 a young man named Johnston Drummond was speared to death by an Aboriginal man called Kabinger on the Victoria Plains. Johnston was the son of the Swan River's government botanist, and had been secretly sleeping with Kabinger's wife. Under Aboriginal law Kabinger was permitted to take violent revenge upon the man. However, Johnston's bereaved brother, John, happened to be a police inspector in the York-Toodyay area. He tracked Kabinger down and two weeks after his brother had been killed, John Drummond shot Kabinger dead. For reasons of propriety John was fired from his position as a police officer by the governor, but he was never brought to trial for murder. Indeed, Drummond was later reinstated and ended his career in Champion Bay (Geraldton) as Deputy Superintendent of Police. [30] Frontier justice.

::

Edward Cornellie was an employee of Mr John S. Davis of the Upper Irwin, for whom he minded ewes and lambs. Cornellie, who was no more than seventeen years old, had never been to Perth, could not read nor write, and had been living in a shepherd's hut over fifty miles from the nearest settler's house. Cornellie worked with Richard Bibby, an ex-convict transported to the Swan River for violent robbery. The two white men, under George Coates the chief shepherd, resided near a 'native camp'. Some time around March of 1859 Coates left the camp for two weeks to hunt for kangaroo skins. During that time, according to Cornellie, 100 lambs 'dropped' and, as he later proudly told the court, he never lost a single one. [31]

Then, 'one morning after daylight Bibby got up and took a pistol and said to me I will cop that bugger now, meaning the native Bil-a-mar-ra, he had said overnight that the pistol was loaded with ball and that he would cop him, Bil-a-mar-ra, in the morning'. Bibby told Cornellie he was going to kill Billimarra because the Aborigine had been stealing ewes. Cornellie stated, 'I never knew of his stealing any sheep or lambs, nor did I suspect him for it.' Cornellie did, however, tell the court that Bibby had been chasing 'a young Native girl at the Native camp', but that she had 'bolted'. The 'native girl' was attached to Billimarra.[32]

According to Cornellie, early in the morning Bibby 'got the pistol, he left the hut, and walked on the tip of his toes to the Native fires'. Cornellie quietly followed. The Aboriginal camp was about fifty yards from the whitemen's huts. Despite his stealth, Billimarra saw or heard Bibby coming and 'raised himself up on his knees'. Cornellie could see spears around the campfire but Billimarra was unarmed. Cornellie watched Billimarra and Bibby stare at each other across the campsite before Bibby fired. Cornellie was close behind Bibby when he shot Billimarra. Cornellie saw Billimarra fall dead into the dirt.

Turning from the scene of the crime, Bibby noticed Cornellie standing nearby. The two men walked back to their lodgings and once back in the hut Bibby told Cornellie, 'I have cooked the bugger's goose, he will never steal any more sheep'. Cornellie then walked back to the native campsite and was there when Ginbaroo dragged Billimarra's body away and buried him, with blood still running from the bullet wound in his head. Deeply disturbed by the murder and by Billimarra's hasty burial, Cornellie returned to the hut and told Bibby that, 'you are a ticket man, you will be in for it'. The ex-convict Bibby seemed unconcerned, he told Cornellie that he would send a note to their 'master', Mr Davis, explaining that Billimarra had been stealing sheep. Everything would be fine. No one would miss a black sheep-thief.

When Coates returned from his kangaroo hunt three days after the murder he sent a note to their employer explaining that one of the workers had shot dead a native for stealing sheep. Cornellie was told by Bibby to keep quiet about what he had seen that fateful morning. None of the three white men ever expected to hear about the matter ever again.[33]

::

When Europeans arrived in Australia their first contact with Aborigines was often curious and confusing. During his initial 1827 exploration of the Swan River, for example, Captain James Stirling had been yelled at by a small number of Aborigines on the river bank. They appeared perturbed by the ghostly figures gliding up the Swan River in their strange craft. In response Stirling threw a black swan he had shot to the riverbank, much to the happiness of the Aborigines to whom it must have seemed like a wonderful gift hurled to them by visiting aliens.[34]

Captain Charles Howe Fremantle, establishing a small military outpost in early 1829 to assist in the impending British colonisation of the Swan River, was similarly approached by Aborigines along the riverbank who were, as he recorded in his diary, 'very loud and appeared to cry out, "Warra, Warra", which I supposed to be "go away"' (Warra was actually the word for 'bad'). Exploring the Swan River in a rowboat, Fremantle and his men met other Aborigines with whom they shared food, exchanged articles of clothing and tried to establish friendly relations. The Aborigines followed the boat of these strange men, whose presence they were later to rationalise as djandga – the returned sprits of the dead – until Fremantle had his men row out towards deep water.[35]

It was during April and May of 1829 when these first curious encounters took place. Stirling's ambitious settlers were still at sea on their way to the Swan River and Captain Fremantle and his men were alone, encamped on the edge of the continent. Fremantle (who was only twenty-nine at the time) was as fascinated by Aborigines as they were with him. On May 26 he recorded that he came across a group of 'natives' who started imitating the European manner of walking and talking. The Aborigines followed the Europeans to their tents. Each group seemed ridiculous to the other. Fremantle and his men laughed at the 'indecency' of the Aborigines, who were naked, and they in turn laughed at the clothing of the Europeans. Fremantle records a wonderful moment of discovery as the Europeans revealed themselves (literally) to the 'Swan River Natives':

> I made some of our men strip and shew their Arms, the Size of which astonished them very much & they could not refrain from feeling them & in fact were not satisfied without seeing all the parties', then our legs which excited more surprise than our Arms; & well they might as I think the limbs of some of our people would make three of some of theirs. I have a couple of good looking young lads in my Gig, whose chins happened to be particularly smooth, & they evidently believed them to be women, also the Youngsters with me, & I do not think that they would be brought to believe the contrary. They wanted the men to take off their trowsers after the shirts, but Jack had too much decency to think of satisfying their curiosity in that particular.[36]

There were other issues separating the two peoples. The Aborigines carefully managed local natural resources so as to maximise their ability to survive and reproduce. This stood in stark contrast to the newcomers who saw flora and fauna as potential commodities to be exploited without much thought for the future. In his diary for 28 April 1829, for example, Captain Fremantle casually relays his crew's exploration of Garden Island:

> Found nothing on the Island but seals; killed three or four; they took to the shore from the water & the boats. Crew with Tomahawks had a capital hunt after one, which they succeeded in killing with the assistance of two or three shot through him. An immense monster, so large that the four men could not carry him onto the boat; most likely a Sea Elephant…Dined late on board after our seal hunt, great fun.[37]

When Captain Fremantle said he found nothing on the island but seals, what he meant was that he found nothing a nineteenth-century European might eat, or place a commercial value upon, except seals. A local Aborigine, scouring the same island, would have found various 'bush tucker' as well as valuable plants used in traditional medicine. Moreover, the island had a spiritual significance for local Aborigines that transcended its short-term utility as a provider of seal meat.

Less than two weeks after the account of the seal hunt we find the following sad entry in Fremantle's diary for 6 May 1829:

> The shore quite hot & fatiguing walking; very few shells on the beach, & the Seals have nearly disappeared, the men having attacked them so violently. We made oil from them, but not more than 5 gallons although 20 seal; they are the very worst kind.[38]

Unlike the first seal hunt, where his men had killed 'an immense monster' of the sea, after a few weeks Fremantle's crew were already reduced to killing orphaned seal cubs.

It was this sort of reckless over-hunting that placed such immense pressure upon the food resources that Aborigines depended upon for survival. The settlers killed for sport, for survival and for profit. They over-hunted kangaroo, shot swans by the dozen and when they got the chance, even started whaling off the coast. The net effect was to seriously deplete local food supplies. In return, it only seemed fair that Aborigines should be able to hunt and spear the strange animals which the *djandga* brought with them – cattle, sheep, goats, chickens, horses and pigs, all of which, the Aborigines quickly discovered, were good eating. Unlike Europeans, Aborigines did not differentiate between animals of 'nature' (upon whom it was open season) and domestic animals (which were private property). It was differing cultural attitudes to the environment and food, as much as any other issue, which poisoned relations between 'settler' and 'native' at Swan River. Captain Fremantle's harmless semi-naked show-and-tell session with curious laughing Aborigines eventually gave way to bloody spears and the fatal cough of muskets.

When Captain Fremantle returned to Swan River in September 1832 he was generally disappointed by the state of the colony. Perth did 'not appear to have made much progress, very few houses having been built, and many of those scarcely worthy of the name'. He now felt that the Swan River Colony's only salvation lay in becoming a penal outpost of the British Empire. Fremantle was especially concerned by the degeneration of relations between settler and native, writing:

> I was sorry to find that there was a very bad understanding with the Natives, who were most troublesome & did much damage, spearing the sheep, pigs, &c. in great abundance. Many deaths have also been occasioned by them & in return many of them have been killed. I am induced to believe that amongst the lower Classes it has almost amounted to a war of extermination & they are shot whenever they are fallen in with; indeed it is considerably dangerous to move about unarmed or alone. It is laughable to see a Shepherd with a Musket instead of a Crook, & every flock is obliged to have two if not three men guard it.[39]

Captain Fremantle despaired for the future, contemplating ways in which a 'better understanding' might be re-established with the Aborigines and suggesting that they might be removed to 'some Island or distant part of the Country not settled'. His half-naked encounter in the tent three years earlier must have already seemed a world away. Fremantle confided in his diary that:

> There is much to be said & allowed for the poor Savages. We take possession of their Country, occupy the most fertile parts, where they are in the habit of resorting to for nourishment, destroy their fishing & Kangaroo, & almost drive them to starvation, & they naturally consider themselves entitled to our Sheep & Stock whenever they can get hold of them; they lately took from Mr Bull's

farm upwards of 70 sheep & destroyed them; at another time they took from Mr Brown 40; they approached the shepherd calling out 'Kangaroo', & when he turned his head round to look the way they pointed, the Savages knocked his brains out with Clubs after spearing him; they then drove off the Sheep.[40]

Still, Fremantle's pessimistic conclusions betrayed his loyalties.

I believe one tribe was nearly exterminated by two or three Soldiers who followed them after they had stolen some sheep, & coming upon them unawares the Natives were nearly all bayoneted. This is really a most awful warfare, but I am sorry to think it at present necessary.[41]

This was a view widely held by the early settlers. And as the spearing of livestock developed into a form of Aboriginal resistance, as well as a method of survival, it became widely accepted that settlers had the right to shoot at Aborigines 'trespassing' on their farms. In 1847 the Legislative Council actually passed a law empowering rural police to do away with trials for some Aborigines, allowing them to 'summarily convict and punish native offenders' instead.[42] The main target of the law were Aborigines accused of stealing or trespassing upon land that had been their people's for countless millennia. Most Aborigines captured or arrested under this law were flogged or chained up as punishment. Given such an approach to justice on the frontier, it's no wonder some settlers felt emboldened to dispense punishment, and bullets, to Aborigines as they saw fit.

::

Joseph Watson was a Mounted Constable stationed at Champion Bay (Geraldton). Watson was first informed about the killing of Billimarra by local Aborigines.[43] Troubled by the account he had heard, Constable Watson decided to make the long journey to Davis's farm to find out more. Watson was informed by Mr Davis that 'a Native had been shot on the Upper Irwin at his station by one of his men', and 'that it was done in self defence protecting his property'. Interestingly, Davis had not bothered to report the fatal shooting prior to Constable Watson turning up at his farm.[44]

Mr John S. Davis was one of the pioneer pastoralists of the Victoria District, inland from Geraldton. He had originally moved into the region around 1850 as an employee of Thomas Brown (formerly of York). By March 1852 he and two other young ambitious pastoralists, Walcott and Logue, had gone into business on a combined lease of more than 16,000 hectares. Davis's property, which he named Tibradden, was home to both *Nhanhagardi/Wilunyu* and *Wajarri* Aboriginal people. In particular, the *Nhanhagardi/Wilunyu* had been heavily affected by earlier contact with white settlers and many had been displaced from traditional lands – they were now moving eastwards across Davis' station into bordering *Wajarri* country, or living on the fringes of other nearby white-owned farms. In 1858 two of Davis's shepherds, minding sheep at an outlaying camp, had shot and killed several Aborigines for spearing livestock. The men were arrested but the court later dismissed the charges. Beside the murder of Billimarra in 1859, several more killings took place (with lives lost on both sides) on Davis's property in 1862 and 1864.[45]

Mr Davis clearly saw local Aborigines as a menace to the economic profitability of his station. It is not surprising, therefore, to discover that Mr Davis did not bother to report to the authorities that one of his men had, once again, shot an Aborigine for stealing sheep. Nevertheless, Constable Watson persisted with his investigation. Six weeks after his meeting with Mr Davis, Watson met up with 'Dan-daragon Charley' who, according to Watson, was 'a civilized Native who had been assistant Constable in the Police at Champion Bay for some time'. Dan-daragon Charley told Watson that according to local Aborigines Billimarra had been murdered by Richard Bibby. Watson started to seek out Aboriginal witnesses to the alleged crime. About a month later Watson finally met up with Ginbaroo who personally told Watson all about the bloody incident around the 'native campfire' near the shepherds' hut. Watson then located Bibby and arrested him for murder.[46]

With Bibby under arrest Watson then went with Ginbaroo to the shallow grave of Billimarra and dug up the corpse. According to Watson:

> I found a body in a state of decomposition. I examined the head, which I took out of the grave and laid on the surface. I took the hair off the skull and left it perfectly bare, there was a hole about the size of a shilling in the left side of the head above the ear and on the opposite side of the head there was a piece blown out leaving a hole about the size of a half crown.[47]

Watson also noted, perhaps unnecessarily, that 'there was a bad smell from the body'. His rudimentary forensic examination complete, the bush policeman reburied the skeleton. In the company of Ginbaroo he then proceeded to the site of the old campfire where he also found evidence of a pool of Billimarra's blood – 'it was coagulated and quite hard'. Watson's evidence, later offered to a court of law, helped seal Bibby's fate.

All of this must have seemed faintly familiar to Bibby who, after all, was in Western Australia in the first place because he had committed 'robbery with violence' in England. He had been found guilty and was transported to Fremantle in 1854 as convict 3134. His convict record described him as having dark hazel eyes, a long face and a scar under his right eye. However, standing again before a British court of justice, only five years after he had been exiled from England, Bibby never suspected his jealous murder of an Aborigine would lead him to the hangman's noose.[48] Richard Bibby was tried for 'murder of a native' in front of Judge A. McFarland on Wednesday 5 October 1859. Bibby claimed that Billimarra was a sheep thief and that he had killed the man in self-defence. Nevertheless, it took the jury only thirty minutes to find him guilty. Judge McFarland sentenced him to death the following day.[49]

Richard Bibby was hanged on the morning of 15 October 1859. Although the *Perth Gazette* later reported that, 'some bungling took place' regarding the placement of the noose, the newspaper was still confident that 'life was extinct almost immediately upon the fall of the drop'.[50]

::

George Fletcher Moore was among the most educated, talented and empathetic of the early settlers of the Swan River Colony. Born in the revolutionary year of 1798 in County Tyrone, Ireland, he was of solid Anglo-Irish stock – that is to say, his family were part of Ireland's colonial Protestant ascendancy. He studied Law at Trinity College, Dublin, and was admitted to the Bar. Despite a life of privilege, Moore felt the pull of adventure and possible rapid career advancement in Britain's antipodean possessions. He came to Swan River in 1830 with four servants. In 1834 he became Advocate General of the Swan River Colony and as such, he sat as one of the four members of the Executive Council which served as the Colony's embryonic government under Governor Stirling.

Moore established a farm on the Upper Swan that he first named 'Hermitage', but later called by the *Nyoongar* name for the area, 'Millendon'. Moore was fascinated by the Aboriginal society that the Swan River Colony was displacing. Moore developed a basic *Nyoongar*-English dictionary, studied

Aboriginal customs and attempted to converse with local Aborigines in their own language. Nevertheless, in his book about his time in the Swan River Colony Moore wrote that, 'The Aborigines, when we first came in contact with them, had no knowledge of a GOD, no worship, no object of worship, no ideas on the subject.'[51] Despite breaking bread with Yagan, Midgegooroo, Munday and other leading *Nyoongars*, Moore remained profoundly ignorant of the deep spirituality inherent within their culture.

Moore's diary of his time at Swan River was also full of references to the developing conflict between settler and native over food resources. He appeared torn between his intellectual understanding of why Aborigines were attacking the settler's livestock, and his own personal frustrations:

> The wretches have destroyed £3 worth of my swine's-flesh altogether; but after all, perhaps these uninformed creatures think that they have as good a right to our swine as we have to their kangaroos; and the reasoning, if such there be, may be plausible enough: however, if we had caught them, *flagrante delicto* – in the act of slaughtering them – I would not answer for the force of it.[52]

The following month he wrote that the governor's pigs had also been speared by Aborigines and that, 'there have been nearly as many killed as would have supported the whole colony during the winter; and now we have no meat'. Nine days later he reported that a soldier had been speared by Murray River Aborigines, 'in a very treacherous way', and, 'It is said that the natives have had a severe retaliation, five being killed and many wounded.'[53]

Moore feared an all-out war between settler and native. He wrote about Yagan's violent conflict with settlers, of the innocent blood shed by both sides, and his uneasiness with the state of relations between Indigenous and newcomer. At times it appeared that Moore reviled and admired the *Nyoongar* in equal measure. Even as the colony convulsed with violence, he still found time to record in his diary that one of the Aborigines who visited his farm carried a number of frogs with him, 'nicely packed up in the bark of the tea-tree, and tied with grass; these he signified they roasted for food, with a long white root, growing like a parsnip, which they dig up in wet weather.'[54] Such respectful curiosity did not, however, prevent Moore from later rejoicing in Yagan's death, or Stirling's punitive expedition to Pinjarra.[55]

Perhaps the most interesting part of Moore's diary is his now famous debate with Yagan outside his farmhouse in May 1833. Moore, recognising

Yagan in the group of Aborigines who came to his house, called him by name. At the time Yagan was the most wanted Aboriginal outlaw in the Swan River Colony. According to Moore, Yagan simply 'came forward, avowed himself, and entered into a long argument and defence of his conduct, in a way I can hardly make intelligible to you; and I confess he had almost as much of the argument as I had'. In particular, the two men debated the issue of Aborigines killing settlers' livestock. Moore implored Yagan, and the other Aborigines with him, not to steal livestock and they would not be shot at, but rather, settler and native could all remain friends.

In response, with his hand 'leaning familiarly' on Moore's shoulder and 'looking earnestly' into his face, Yagan said to Moore:

> You came to our country; you have driven us from our haunts, and disturbed us in our occupations: as we walk in our own country, we are fired upon by the white men; why should the white men treat us so? [56]

Yagan then enquired after his father, Midgegooroo (who, unbeknownst to Yagan, had been executed). Yagan said, 'with extraordinary vehemence of manner, distinctness of utterance, and emphasis of tone', that he would kill three whites if Midgegooroo was killed. Moore replied that if Yagan did so, every settler in the colony would hunt him down, a comment to which Yagan responded 'with an air of ineffable contempt'. The two men separated on reasonably friendly terms, with Moore later referring to Yagan in his diary as, 'the "Wallace" of the tribe' – a complimentary reference to the fierce Scottish warrior, William Wallace. [57]

Less admired by Moore were the Aborigines who continued to kill his livestock. After losing another pig, Moore, a man of the Law, commented, 'I wish it was either peace or war between us; but now we must not touch them, for by proclamation they are declared under the protection of the law, as British subjects.' He also remarked that the Colony needed to 'come to a friendly understanding and arrangement' with local Aborigines, otherwise:

> ...they will annoy us, for we are not able to drive them away so as to secure ourselves, without their extermination. Each tribe has its distinct ground; and they will, of course, rather adhere to it, dispute its possession, and take their revenge on the intruders, then fall back on other tribes of their own countrymen, and fight their way inch by inch with them. [58]

Still, understanding the plight of the Aborigines did not necessarily begat compassion. Following the death of 'the "Wallace" of the tribe', Moore wrote:

> On Saturday I saw at Mr. Bull's the head of Ya-gan, which one of the men had cut off for the purpose of preserving. Possibly it may yet figure in some museum at home. I should have been glad to get it myself, as the features were not in the least changed. [59]

In May of 1835 George Fletcher Moore, the Colony's paramount legal mind, continued to struggle with the legal position of Aborigines as British subjects entitled to full protection (and prosecution) under British Law. In his diary Moore wrote about a particularly challenging case where a Perth shopkeeper had had his store robbed by Aborigines. The shopkeeper set off with a gun to where a number of Aborigines were camping nearby. After a scuffle his gun accidentally discharged, seriously wounding a young Aboriginal 'lad'. According to Moore:

> They [the Aborigines] wanted to take summary vengeance, and were with difficulty persuaded to let our law take its course. They have been pacified in the meantime by seeing him sent handcuffed to gaol to await the event, if the boy should die. They wished to be allowed to spear him in the leg, and said if he gave some bread they would only spear him a very little. If the boy dies they say that they will kill the guilty man who stole the flour, as he was the cause of it, but they expect that the white man will be killed by us if Gogaly [the boy] should die. [60]

By 28 June Gogaly was dead and Moore's legal headache had intensified:

> We are in a dilemma about the trial of the settler for the murder or manslaughter of the native boy named Gogaly. The natives are desirous of seeing him severely punished, and if he be acquitted they will take revenge. It is a most extraordinary thing that we are not furnished here with the Acts, or amendments to the laws, which are taking place every day at home. How we are to know anything about them is difficult to conjecture. Yet we are bound to act according to the law of England. [61]

What to do? The shopkeeper was eventually banished from Perth and the rage of local Aborigines was contained. This was a special case but there were general principles at stake. Should settlers be punished for defending themselves against thievery and for committing violence against Aborigines? And how to get the 'natives' to appreciate the majesty of British justice? How to do justice to their right, under British Law, to be protected from harm? These were questions that not only plagued George Fletcher Moore, but challenged the legal foundations of the entire Swan River Colony. Another twenty-four years would pass before a white murderer of an Aborigine would finally have to face the hangman for his crime.

::

Richard Bibby was the first white man ever to hang in Western Australia for the murder of an Aborigine. In the aftermath of Bibby's botched hanging, the newspapers attempted to come to terms with the implications of the case. As *The Inquirer* reported:

> The wretched man, Richard Bibby, condemned to death at the recent Quarter Sessions for the murder of the native Billimarra, was hung at the Perth gaol on Monday. He apparently fancied to the last that he would be reprieved…The unfortunate man struggled much, the rope having been unskilfully adjusted. It is said, however, that his neck was dislocated the instant after the drop was drawn and that his struggles were muscular only. Let us hope it was so.[62]

The case was, of course, unique not least of all because of the willingness of two white witnesses (Cornellie and Constable Watson) to testify against the white killer of an Aborigine. Or as *The Inquirer* saw it:

> The peculiarity in this case was that it was the first execution in the colony of a white man for the murder of one of the aboriginal population. Many thought the man's life would have been spared, and very strong intercession was made, but the cool deliberate way the murder was committed, and the previous antecedents of the condemned, he having been transported for robbery with violence, after a long career of crime, was a bar on the exercise of mercy in this case.[63]

Still, the fervent opposition of a great many settlers to Bibby's hanging prompted *The Inquirer* to publish a follow-up editorial in the next week's edition. *The Inquirer* announced that, 'It is not our general custom to give prominence to events such as that which ushered in gloom the past week, but the amount of public debate warranted a response:

> If the deceased [Billimarra] had been a white man nothing would have been said, the condemnation and execution of the murderer would have been taken as a matter of course…The degraded position of the aborigines, the lowest in the scale of human kind, rather invites our compassion and demands our protection than the reverse.[64]

Indeed, *The Inquirer* pointed out that the Aborigines were, 'recognised as British subjects', and 'amenable to British laws'. What was really bothering *The Inquirer*, however, was the claim that Bibby was a frontier martyr:

> But another and more serious objection has been advanced against the extreme punishment of Bibby, namely, that he was made the scapegoat, and sacrificed for the crimes of others not under the ban of the law, and many of them moving in a respectable circle. It is said that the shooting of natives is common in the Victoria district, and that amateur homicides are in the habit of boasting of their prowess. Bibby, it is alleged, did but follow the example set him by his betters.[65]

While reminding the 'talkers' and 'boasters' that 'their own safety' depended 'upon silence', the newspaper offered its final word on the matter:

> In conclusion, we would entreat those who have the making of our local laws to protect the white man as well as the black and, by ensuring a speedy and sure execution of justice upon native offenders – who, by wholesale robbery of the settlers, excite them to revenge, – prevent that reliance upon self for protection which has been the cause of the loss of life among the aboriginal race, and will, we fear, if no such step be taken by our Legislature, be the cause of the sacrifice of other lives by judicial sentence than that of the criminal who so lately terminated his unrighteous career on the scaffold.[66]

Somehow, in death Richard Bibby partially succeeded in becoming the victim. Yet, neither his infamy nor his status as a frontier martyr were to last. These days Richard Bibby's name and significance are largely unknown. Despite his role in such a tragic and significant moment in Western Australia's legal history, both Bibby and Billimarra are gone and forgotten.

4

'Great Is Our Sin': Rape, Sodomy and the
Hanging of Joseph McDonald, 1861

A woman is raped, a heinous crime for which a former convict is sentenced to death.
The colony struggles with sex crime and sectarianism.

The ship Joseph McDonald arrived on, the *Phoebe Dunbar*, had carried 286
Irish convicts across the seas to Western Australia, arriving on 30 August 1853.
It was the last ship to carry convicts to Swan River directly from Ireland. The
voyage took almost ninety days. Eight men died during the journey and two
more perished soon after the ship arrived off the coast of Western Australia.[1]
The surviving convicts entered a colony increasingly concerned about the
moral stain of convictism and nervous about the morality and 'breeding' of
Irish Catholic prisoners of the British Empire.

After the completion of the Perth Gaol in 1856, it became the most
common site for legal hangings in Western Australia. Although some people,
especially Aborigines, were still executed at the scene of the crime or at a local
gallows, most offenders were brought to Perth. This did not change until 1888,
by which time public execution had been abolished (except for Aborigines),
and Fremantle Prison became Western Australia's exclusive 'hanging prison'.
In 1861 the Civil Court and the Court of Quarter Sessions were amalgamated
into a Supreme Court.[2] It was in front of the bench of the Chief Justice that
most capital cases continued to be heard.

Despite the growing numbers of convicts in the colony, capital cases were
still relatively rare. For example, during the period from 1856 to 1861 there
was an average of less than three hangings a year.[3] When they did occur, and
particularly when the condemned was white, the press generally paid close
attention to the court proceedings. It is therefore somewhat surprising that

transported convict Joseph McDonald's trial received only the briefest mention in *The Inquirer's* court report for Friday, 4 January 1861:

> *Joseph McDonald*, charged with rape at Toodyay was found guilty, and sentenced to death. The prisoner was undefended.[4]

Similarly, while the *Perth Gazette* published ten full columns of proceedings from recent court cases, if offered only thirteen brief words regarding the fate of McDonald:

> Friday, Jan. 4.
> *Joseph McDonald*, was found guilty of rape, and sentenced to Death.[5]

By comparison to McDonald's thirteen words, a case involving the theft of two cows received three full columns of newsprint. The following edition of the *Perth Gazette* was similarly succinct in reporting the hanging of McDonald, noting simply that 'The unhappy convicts Clancy and McDonald suffered the extreme penalty of the law on Tuesday last.'[6] Nothing more was written on the topic.

McDonald, an Irishman and former convict transportee, was sentenced to die as Western Australia was about to enter its eleventh year of convict transportation. Although historians would later claim that in Western Australia convicts did not endure the same 'widespread sadism and unscrupulous exploitation' as New South Wales or Tasmania, conditions remained tough. For example, Frank Crowley claimed that 'between 1850 and 1863, 119 convicts were tied to the triangles and flogged on the back with the cat-o'-nine-tails, receiving between them 6,209 lashes.'[7] The punishment ground at the Fremantle Convict Establishment may not have been as blood splattered as its Sydney or Hobart counterpart, but it was certainly not unblemished.

Into this world came Joseph McDonald. He had arrived at Swan River in August 1853 as prisoner 2466. McDonald was listed as 'unmarried', and his occupation was given as 'Labourer'. His transportation details also recorded that he was literate and an 'RC', a Catholic. He was five-foot-nine-inches tall, with brown hair and blue eyes. In 1850 he had been given a ten-year sentence for sheep stealing at Kildare in Ireland before being transported to Swan River. Less than a year after he arrived he was given a ticket of leave and released from penal servitude. He was twenty years old when he arrived in Fremantle, twenty-eight when he was sentenced to death for rape.[8]

::

Until the twentieth century, Christianity was central to European politics and culture. As John Gascoigne has argued, 'Civilisations like to create monuments in stone but what sustains and shapes them are edifices of the mind.' Gascoigne argues that the convicts and guards who waded ashore at Sydney during January 1788 understood and explained their world 'by recourse to religious language':

> Protestant Britain might have dispatched them unceremoniously forth but it still shaped their lives in this distant place. For the chiefly Irish Catholics the hand of Protestant England was no less obvious, as they defined themselves in opposition to it.[9]

There were Irish among the first convicts ever sent to Australia, with the First Fleet in 1788, and Irish were heavily represented among the very last convict shipment to Fremantle in 1868. The Irish government estimates that 30,000 men and 9,000 women were transported directly from Ireland to Australia between 1791 and 1853. Tens of thousands more Irish convicts were transported from Scotland and England.[10] The first direct transportation from Ireland arrived in Sydney aboard the *Queen* in September 1791. The youngest among the 133 male convicts and 22 females was David Fay of Dublin – exiled to Australia at the tender age of eleven. However, old age was not spared this indignity either. The oldest convict aboard, Patrick Fitzgerald, was a well-weathered sixty-four.[11]

Watkin Tench, a Captain in the British Marines who sailed to Botany Bay in 1788 with the First Fleet, relayed 'a very extraordinary instance of folly' that November. A group of twenty male convicts and one pregnant woman escaped from Rose Hill and set out to walk to China. After a week most had returned to the colony half starved. One had been killed by Aborigines. Under questioning the convicts revealed their belief that China was about 100 miles from Sydney and that only a river separated the colony from the ancient Asian civilisation. Tench, an otherwise compassionate and enlightened man, could hardly contain his amusement:

I trust no man would feel more reluctant than myself to cast an illiberal national reflection, particularly on a people whom I regard in an aggregate sense as brethren and fellow-citizens…But it is certain that all these people were Irish.[12]

Tench's restraint was not matched by some of his establishment peers for whom Irish convicts were wretched, treacherous, violent people of feeble mind and poor breeding. Judge Advocate David Collins treated the convicts' 'chimerical idea' of walking to China with contempt.[13] He also described the Irish as having 'natural vicious propensities', and complained that by 1798 the Irish convicts had 'become so turbulent and refractory, and so dissatisfied with their situation that, without the most rigid and severe treatment, it was impossible to derive from them any labour whatever'.[14] If nothing else the attempt by Irish convicts to walk to China revealed a deep longing for freedom and an unwillingness to passively accept their servitude. This was overlooked or ignored by establishment figures at the time.[15]

If Watkin Tench reflected some of the best qualities of the British mind in 1788, Judge Advocate David Collins sometimes represented the imperial mindset at its most inflexible. The Irish, in particular, appalled him. Describing them as 'nearly as wild themselves as the cattle' he believed that their ignorance made them generally undeserving of 'the appellation of men'.[16] He was not alone in holding such views. For example, the Reverend Samuel Marsden strenuously opposed the legal toleration of Catholicism in New South Wales. Writing in 1807, Marsden's fear and hostility boiled over:

The number of catholic convicts is very great in the settlement; and these in general composed of the lowest class of the Irish nation, who are the most wild, ignorant and savage race…men that have been familiar with robberies murders and every horrid crime from their infancy…governed entirely by the impulse of passion and always alive to rebellion and mischief they are very dangerous members of society…and was the catholic religion tolerated they would assemble together from every quarter not so much from a desire of celebrating mass, as to recite the miseries and injustice of their punishment, the hardships they suffer, and to enflame one another's minds with some wild scheme of revenge.[17]

Marsden argued that simply to allow Catholic mass to be practised would mean that, 'the colony would be lost to the British empire in less than one year'.[18]

Faced with the Irish, some colonists believed the Aborigines to be cultured and intelligent by comparison. Indeed, specific comparisons between the 'native Irish' (meaning those who were Gaelic and Catholic) and the 'uncivilised' Aborigines were not altogether unknown. George Fletcher Moore, the Anglo-Irish settler and Advocate General of the Swan River Colony, described Aboriginal mourning rites as reminding him, 'of the Irish *keen*, as a sort of address to the departed'.[19] Anthropologist Daisy Bates, famous for her work with Aborigines, described Aboriginal people as possessing, 'many of the characteristics of the Irish'. Bates felt that Irish and Aboriginal people were similarly hospitable, suffered 'profound begrudgery' and shared a strong and irrational belief in magic. The wailing of mourning Aboriginal women also reminded her of the 'keening' of the Irish. According to Bates she publicly presented her views on the similarities between the Irish and Aborigines during a talk to the shocked ladies of the Karrakatta Club in Perth during 1907.[20] Ironically, Bates also regularly denounced miscegenation, an occupation, historian Bob Reece notes, 'in which her Irish countrymen distinguished themselves'. Although the evidence is mainly anecdotal, Reece and others claim that, 'the Irish seem to have been rather exceptional in early Australian-European society in their preparedness to accept Aboriginal women as something more than casual sexual partners'.[21]

All that, however, was still to come. In April 1829, the very same month that Captain Fremantle's men built their rudimentary fort at the mouth of the Swan River, back in England royal assent was given to the Catholic Relief Act which finally repealed the prohibition on Catholics sitting in the British parliament. And while the Swan River Colony was free (at least until 1850) from the political and social threat of Irish convicts, it was not free from inherited ideas about the alleged criminal propensities of the deranged sons and debauched daughters of Ireland.

Nor was it free from the sectarian baggage of several hundred years of British legal history. For example, when an acting Lieutenant Governor was sworn in during October 1834, he was compelled to utter the oath that:

> I do solemnly and sincerely in the presence of God testify and declare, on the true faith of a Christian, that I will never exercise any power authority or influence which I may possess by virtue of my office and truth as Lieutenant Governor and Commander in Chief of this Colony of Western Australia to injure or weaken the Protestant Church as it is by law established in England.[22]

What Irish Catholics lacked in institutional power they sometimes made up for with their own sectarian passions. In 1854 the Catholic prison chaplain in Fremantle, Father O'Neil, was suspended from office after the Irish priest had denounced his Protestant counterpart as 'an Agent of the Devil'. After he was suspended a small riot broke out among Catholic prisoners at Fremantle Prison and five men were publicly flogged.[23] Notwithstanding such momentary lapses into sectarianism, concepts of race, evolution and social Darwinism were to gradually displace religion at the ideological centre of colonial Australia. In Australia and throughout the British Empire, there was an enduring perception of the Irish as being an inferior people. A prejudicial corollary of this was the lingering suspicion that the innate criminality of Irish men was matched by the wanton promiscuity of Irish women.

::

The former Irish convict Joseph McDonald was accused of raping an Irish female settler, Ellen McMahon, at Toodyay outside Perth. He stood trial at the January 1861 Quarter Sessions. Four witnesses appeared in the case, including Ellen McMahon. Ellen testified that on 23 December 1860 she and her husband were having breakfast when McDonald came to McMahon's home in the company of another man in order to let Ellen's husband know that 'a ship had come in'. Ellen's husband left to see if he could get some work unloading the ship. Later, when she was out walking (intending to visit her sister), Ellen noticed that McDonald was following her. He eventually caught up with her and the two walked together for a while, before Ellen parted company with him.[24]

Further along the road McDonald again caught up to Ellen. According to Ellen, McDonald offered her a piece of gold as a present, which she declined. After several attempts to get rid of McDonald, and similar unsuccessful attempts to find a male friend in the area who would walk her home, Ellen reluctantly continued walking alone. On an isolated pathway nearby, McDonald finally set upon Ellen McMahon and raped her. Distraught while retelling her tale for the court, Ellen commented that she was 'a good deal bruised about the body' after McDonald had assaulted her and that 'when the prisoner was having connection with me there was an emission of semen from him – my clothes were stained in the same manner as if I had been with my husband'. Illiterate, Ellen McMahon signed her witness deposition with a simple 'X'.

Appearing for the prosecution, Robert Waters claimed that he had witnessed McDonald and Ellen McMahon walking together (although they had not seen him) and that a short time later he had heard Ellen screaming. Standing at some distance, Waters, who was eighteen, had seen McDonald throw Ellen to the ground. He could clearly see McDonald on top of Ellen. She was fighting and screaming for someone to come help her. Soon after, McDonald got up and came back up the path past Waters. Under cross-examination, young Robert Waters swore that 'the woman' appeared to be struggling to get away and that 'the prisoner', McDonald, was holding her down. Asked why he didn't help rescue Ellen McMahon from her attacker, he commented only that he 'was frightened' and that 'a feather would have knocked me down'.

Joseph Alkinson, who was present in a house where Ellen had earlier stopped and made an unsuccessful attempt to get rid of McDonald, testified that he had heard Ellen tell McDonald to 'be off about your business'. Later, after the rape, Ellen made her way back to this house and was let inside. She said she wanted to see her husband immediately, and Alkinson agreed to walk her home. Remarkably, she was again to be confronted by McDonald, who came to the door and proclaimed that no matter what the woman might be saying, he never touched her – 'So help me God I never touched the woman, but I only put my hand on her shoulder.' From inside Ellen asked, 'Who ripped my bonnet then?' To which McDonald proclaimed that she had ripped it herself. Alkinson, who testified that he thought it unlikely a woman would rip her own bonnet, told how 'Mrs McMahon' then threatened McDonald with a stick to get rid of him.

After testimony from Martin McMahon, Ellen's husband, who said that his wife was traumatised and dishevelled when he returned that evening (he also mentioned that McDonald was hanging around outside his house), and from the Medical Examiner, the evidence ended. Joseph McDonald was found guilty of rape and sentenced to death. However, unlike twelve other cases of rape resulting in a similar sentence during the nineteenth century, McDonald's death sentence was not commuted. McDonald was hanged on 4 January 1861. He was one of only six people in Western Australia ever to be hanged for the crime of rape.

::

At the time of the arrival at Swan River of Joseph McDonald and the other Irish convicts of the *Phoebe Dunbar*, Ireland was still recovering from the potato famine of 1845 to 1851 in which a million Irish perished, and millions more set sail for America, Canada and Australia. *The Perth Gazette*, relaying news from the Irish newspapers, reported as late as 1853 that:

> The Irish Exodus was still on the increase. It is mentioned as a fact in several instances, parishes which five years since numbered 5000 inhabitants have now dwindled down to 7 or 800. Great numbers of Roman Catholic chapels are entirely without a congregation and the Priesthood of that communion are in great distress.[25]

The information was months out of date but it was still news in Western Australia. Meanwhile, despite earlier controversy, it was clear that the arrival of convicts – even Irish ones – had done much to contribute to the burgeoning economy of the Swan River Colony. Or as *The Perth Gazette* celebrated in the same 1853 edition:

> TRANSPORTATION TO BE CONTINUED TO WESTERN AUSTRALIA!!!
> By the arrival of the *Phoebe Dunbar* we have English intelligence to the 3rd June...The most important intelligence is that giving us assurance of the continuance of transportation to this colony...we have the greatest pleasure in giving publicity to this gratifying intelligence, which will reassure our brother settlers, give an immense impetus to trade and improvements, and increase the value of all kinds of property, since we may now rest assured that the future prosperity of the colony is secured against all risk.[26]

The Inquirer remained less enthusiastic, although ultimately pragmatic, in its analysis of the same May 1853 debates in the British House of Lords with regard to the future of convict transportation to Western Australia:

> It does not appear that there is any intention to discontinue transportation to this colony. On the contrary, it is evident that Ministers will be too glad to avail themselves of a colony which will take some of their worst-class convicts.[27]

However, by 1865 the British government had made it clear to the Western Australian authorities that transportation was going to end, a decision that prompted the Perth Chamber of Commerce to demand compensation and assisted migration from the British government. Some politicians and local newspapers mocked the Chamber of Commerce, arguing that, 'Of course it is very sad to lose a goose that has laid so many golden eggs,' but that the claim for compensation was nonsense.

> The real state of facts, as between the Colony and the Mother Country, is merely this: In 1849 there was not a spot on the face of the earth to which Great Britain could send her convicts. The older colonies – New South Wales and Tasmania – had thriven on the abuses of the old system, and the old system had, in its turn, produced such a heap of wickedness and corruption, that humanity could endure it no longer, and with one voice they honestly and fairly shook off their incubus.[28]

The author was keen to point out that convicts were sent to Western Australia under an entirely different system from that in New South Wales and Tasmania – meaning that Western Australia had not been corrupted by vice and degeneracy. No incubus here. Later generations of historians would point out that the statistics did not support this view:

> Far from convictism not leading to a marked increase in crime, it can be shown that between 1850 and 1860, 40% of the cases heard before the Court of Quarter Session involved convicts and ex-convicts as defendants; this rose to 72% of cases heard by the Supreme Court between 1861 and 1870; 65% between 1870 and 1880; and as late as 1880 to 1890 still 40%. Charges heard, per head of population, doubled after 1850. ...(I)n 1881 Western Australia had the highest crime rate of all the Australian colonies.[29]

Joseph McDonald was part of this crime wave. In 1865, however, *The Inquirer* would not countenance suggestions that the importation of convicts had been anything but a success story:

> If Western Australia has received these convicts, the colonists have had much to be thankful for...The convicts have supplied the labour market. Providence and Downing Street have done their part...What did the Colonists lose by the Convict system? Nothing. It was all clear gain to them.[30]

And yet the general public remained nervous about the potential negative social impact of convict transportation. In 1861, fearing the possibility of a convict uprising, free settlers had formed the Fremantle Volunteers and organised military drilling. Constant newspaper reports of crimes committed by convicts, or recently released 'bond men', seemed to confirm their worst fears. *The Inquirer* had reported in July 1854 that:

> The number of conditional-pardon men who have been committed at the late [Court] Sessions is but a bad presage for the future. It would appear as if many of them only waited to when they became free from coercion, to return again to their old habits...[31]

By 1859 there were 487 convicts (not counting ticket-of-leave men) in the small port town of Fremantle, 260 in Perth and several hundred more scattered across the south-east of the colony. In Fremantle each night a soldier would walk the streets asking men if they were 'Bond or free?' – checking to see if they were convicts breaking curfew.[32] Such measures were considered necessary in a colony with such a small female population. With so many miscreants around town, gentlemen were particularly nervous about the safety of their wives and daughters.

::

Convict transportation may have temporarily solved the labour shortage in Western Australia, but it only added to the gender imbalance. Moreover, in an economy that was structured around gender, there were insufficient domestic servants and working class women. Therefore, for a range of social and economic reasons the colonial establishment desired greater numbers of female immigrants. One solution, obviously, was simply to import female convicts to the Swan River Colony. It was hoped that these women could wash the clothes, cook the meals, and help raise the children of middle-class families. With time (and tickets of leave) they could also become potential spouses for the sex-starved male convicts.

Public meetings and petitions both in favour of, and in opposition to, the proposed introduction of female convicts were held throughout the settled districts of Western Australia during 1854. The debate also spilled over into the press.[33] Much of the discussion focused on the painful shortage of female labour and the fact that previous government-assisted single female migration to the Swan River Colony had been disproportionately Irish in its composition. *The Inquirer*, reporting on the public meetings, paraphrased the speech of Mr Clifton, soon to become the colony's Advocate General, speaking in Perth during May 1854:

> He deprecated in firm terms the course now pursued by the Home Government of sending such a class of female immigrants, the great majority of whom were Roman Catholics, and argued that the introduction of so many of that creed was unfair to the settlers, as tending to destroy the Protestant character of the colony. Personally he had no objection to Roman Catholics, but he asserted that society here wanted protestant wives for protestant husbands, and that Roman Catholic servants were not required, and that continuance of such a course as now pursued would cause serious evil to the colony.[34]

Significant figures inside the colonial establishment concurred. For example, Governor Fitzgerald had written to the British government in September 1853 opposing the high numbers of single Irish migrant women being brought out to the colony to work. Fitzgerald wrote that 'Irish Roman Catholics are not so likely to be absorbed as English Protestants', and that most settlers 'prefer taking into their families servants of their own persuasion'.[35]

However, Catholic settlers already in the Colony were unprepared to tolerate such naked sectarianism. For example, in response to one of Clifton's 1853 speeches opposing further Irish Catholic female migration, several letters were written to *The Inquirer*. Clifton's real objection, one author suggested, was that the Irish female servants were possibly 'endangering colonial Protestant ascendancy'. As a result, Clifton was accused of trying to 'kindle the flame of religious dissension in our hitherto peaceful community'. The author also suggested that Clifton would prefer English female prostitutes, or even 'a shipment of square-headed Chinese', to wholesome 'Irish Roman Catholic girls'.[36]

Meanwhile 'Grandmama', a columnist in *The Inquirer*, wrote of the 'Roman Catholic Irish girls':

> ...I cannot help saying that if these people are allowed to come into the colony, *we are not SAFE*. People may laugh now, but they will not laugh some night when these girls shall rise as a body, rekindle the fires of Smithfield, and burn all the Protestants in the place.[37] [Emphasis in original]

While newspaper writers routinely employed sarcasm, humour and exaggeration to make their points, there is no mistaking the seriousness of the issues involved. Interestingly, these articles and 'letters to the editor' were published at a time when the matter of 'mixed-marriages' between Catholics and Protestants was also being carefully debated on the pages of *The Inquirer*.[38]

Despite these skirmishes, more than 2,000 Irish servant girls were eventually imported into Western Australia. Indeed, by 1861 Irish-born women like Ellen McMahon formed 22 per cent of the female population of the colony.[39] Despite the objections of occasional demagogues, these Irish women – 'servant girls', farm hands, nannies, potential wives – were probably the principal reason why Western Australia never resorted to female convict transportation.[40] However, their poverty and social vulnerability often resulted in them being victims of violent crime and sexual assault.

::

Sex crime posed particular problems for 'Britishers' of the Victorian Age. For example, drawing on Christian traditions going back to Thomas Aquinas, and relying upon English laws dating from 1533, sodomy (or 'buggery') was considered an 'unnatural act' regardless of whether it occurred between a man and a woman, two men, or a man and 'beast'.[41] In Colonial Australia – as elsewhere within the British Empire – sex was supposed to be for procreation and was only meant to occur between a man and his wife. Any other acts were tantamount to perversion. The basis of this belief, which was reflected in the Law, was Christian theology that condemned adultery, sodomy, bestiality, incest and rape. On this issue, at least, both the Catholic and Protestant churches were in agreement. Pragmatism also played a role; Australia needed population growth. Sexual deviancy, therefore, carried harsh penalties under colonial law, although these were rarely carried out. The purpose was to intimidate the public into sexual propriety. So, for example, the Western Australian legal system maintained rape as a hanging offence even after it ceased to be a capital crime in England.[42]

The courts struggled with sex crime in a way that is deeply shocking to those of us living in another age. For example, during the nineteenth century defence lawyers in rape cases were allowed to attack the moral virtue of female witnesses. Take, for example, Richard Haynes, who acted as defence counsel in four rape cases in Western Australia between 1880 and 1897. In all these cases Haynes attacked or denigrated the victim. In one particularly unedifying example he defended a man named (ironically) James McDonald who was accused of raping an Irish girl in his care, Florence O'Brien.[43]

In the newspapers James McDonald was described as 'a middle-aged man, of respectable appearance'. It was explained by the prosecution that Florence O'Brien, meanwhile, was originally from Queensland and had lived with McDonald and another woman who was not her mother for some time. Haynes, defending McDonald, argued that O'Brien was actually 'an abandoned little wretch, who had been demoralised almost from her infancy'. Haynes called on the jury to place 'no reliance whatsoever' on her testimony as she was deliberately mischievous and 'utterly untrustworthy'. All this despite the fact that Florence O'Brien was only nine years old.[44]

During the trial the defence produced a doctor who testified that he had examined Florence O'Brien:

> The conclusion he arrived at, after questioning the child for the purpose of testing the condition of her mind, was that she was obstinate, that she was sullen, that she was unchaste, that she was immoral, but that she was not insane. When he saw her, her ankles were tied together with a thick string or rope, which he understood had been done in order to prevent her leaving home for purposes of immorality.[45]

Young Florence O'Brien was undoubtedly a victim of sexual abuse – although approximately nine years old, no one disagreed that that she had already had many sexual encounters with numerous men 'on the jetty' in Fremantle and elsewhere. It was also stated in evidence that O'Brien's mother, whom she no longer had any contact with, had used her since about the age of six, 'to decoy men into the house for purposes of prostitution'.[46]

Nevertheless, in defending McDonald against the charge of rape it was perfectly permissible to denigrate the young victim. The defence case focused upon that fact that O'Brien was a street 'urchin', that it was not even clear that Florence O'Brien was her real name, that no one was sure of her age (nine was a guess), and that she had been living on the streets, and with men like McDonald (who had, essentially, adopted her for sexual purposes), for years. Although McDonald was found guilty of the rape of Florence O'Brien and sentenced to death, the sentence was commuted to penal servitude instead.[47]

Florence O'Brien was a sexually abused child and yet the Law, while puritanical in its condemnation of 'unnatural' sex acts, struggled to come to terms with incest, carnal knowledge and other forms of sexual assault against children. Notwithstanding the prejudices of the age, this is perhaps not that surprising given how thoroughly unsuccessful the state was in maintaining sexual boundaries between adults in the remote conditions of Australia. The legal prohibition of sodomy, for example, did little to curb clandestine homosexual encounters among men. This, in particular, terrified the establishment.[48]

Although no convict was officially charged with the crime of sodomy in Australia until 1791, homosexual encounters, both consensual and coerced, were a regular part of prison life on the transportation ships and in convict barracks. Sex between men was a secret, illegal activity liable to punishment. It was also extremely difficult to catch consenting couples in the act. Nevertheless, over the six years between 1829–35 about twenty-four convicts were sent to trial for 'offences against nature' in New South Wales and Van Diemen's Land. Half were convicted and one was hanged.[49]

Such was the official abhorrence of homosexual sex that Governor Arthur Phillip, the founder of Britain's first Australian colony, New South Wales, apparently wanted to give 'sodomites' to cannibals to be eaten.[50] What was at stake was the entire moral and spiritual future of the Australian colonies. During the 1840s the Bishop of Van Diemen's Land wrote to the British Colonial Secretary, Lord Grey, complaining that 'unless sternly arrested in its growth', the propensity of unnatural acts among the convicts would 'not only ensure the moral degradation of the colony, but draw down divine vengeance upon it'.[51] In his mind Australia had already become a Sodom of the south-seas.

Regardless, the convicts continued in their 'evil ways'. The Female Factory at Parramatta in Sydney was said to be a hotbed of convict lesbianism with many long-term couples.[52] Robert Pringle Stuart, a magistrate on Norfolk Island, similarly described how male convicts sometimes paired off as 'man and wife' and that the 'natural course of affection is quite distracted, and these parties manifest as much eager earnestness for the society of each other as members of the opposite sex'.[53] Although genuine loving relationships sometimes developed, there also continued to be many guilty fumbling secret encounters among the male convicts. Young convicts were also susceptible to sexual assault. In 1846 Stuart reported that inside the locked men's barracks on Norfolk Island:

Atrocities of the most shocking, odious character are there perpetrated, and that unnatural crime is indulged in to excess; the young have no chance of escaping from abuse, and even forcible violation is resorted to. To resist can hardly be expected, in a situation so utterly removed from, and lamentably destitute of, protection. A terrorism is sternly and resolutely maintained, to revenge not merely exposure but even complaint.[54]

Related to this is the fact that the current notion of homosexuality as a distinct sexual orientation is a late nineteenth-century invention. Michel Foucault, in *The History of Sexuality*, claims that the 'medical category of homosexuality' did not even exist until 'Westphal's famous article of 1870 on "contrary sexual sensations"' turned sodomy from an incidental 'unnatural act' into a sexual lifestyle. After 1870 homosexuality was considered an inversion of 'the masculine and the feminine in oneself'. Foucault summed up the resulting transition – 'the sodomite had been a temporary aberration; the homosexual was now a species.'[55]

Colonial Western Australia did not escape the so-called curse of Sodom. One study claims that at least twenty-five of the convicts transported to Western Australia between 1851 and 1863 were exiled for 'buggery' or the commission of some other 'unnatural' sexual activity. *The Adelaide*, which arrived in Fremantle during July 1855, carried no less than six men convicted of 'buggery' or 'attempted sodomy' with each other. All were single men with no children. Their sentences ranged from twenty-one years to life.[56]

In Western Australia sex crime provoked moral outrage and self-censorship. For example, as Jill Bavin-Mizzi has written with regard to newspaper coverage of sodomy offences in Western Australia during the nineteenth century:

[The] language was far more dramatic, more morally outraged, than any used in rape or carnal knowledge cases. It suggests that forcible sodomy was 'unnatural' in some way that heterosexual assault was not.[57]

On 5 July 1854 Edwin Gatehouse, a labourer, was brought before the Western Australian court. It was alleged that on 23 May, Gatehouse, 'with force and arms', had raped and sodomised a man at Guildford. Or in the words of the court record, Gatehouse:

...did make an assault and then and there feloniously wickedly and against the order of nature had a venereal affair with the said George Jewbo-it and then and there feloniously carnally knew him the said George Jewbo-it and then and

there feloniously wickedly and against the order of nature with the said George
Jewbo-it did commit and perpetrate that detestable crime of buggery (not to be
named among Christians) against the form of the statute in such case made and
provided and against the peace of our Lady the Queen and Dignity.[58]

Three witnesses appeared to testify against Gatehouse, one of whom was
the Aboriginal man, George Jewboit, whom Gatehouse had been accused
of sexually assaulting. The other two witnesses were Europeans. Although
on trial for his life, the court records in the Gatehouse case have not been
preserved. The crime – 'not to be named among Christians' – was simply too
heinous to maintain record of. All that remains is the case summary quoted
above.

In due course Edwin Gatehouse was sentenced to death, although his
sentence was later commuted to transportation. *The Inquirer* reported briefly
on his case in its 12 July edition:

> We understand that Edwin Gatehouse, who was condemned to death at the late
> sessions for an unnatural crime, is not to suffer the extreme penalty of the law for
> his offence, His Excellency the Governor having decided this important point
> by and with the advice of the Executive Council. This determination has, we
> believe, been come to from the fact that the only evidence affecting Gatehouse's
> life was totally and entirely that of an aboriginal native.[59]

The minutes of the Executive Council meeting for 10 July 1854 offer little
additional insight, mentioning only the briefest details about the case and
recording that the 'Council having taken under their grave consideration
whether the sentence of death over the criminal should be carried out', had
decided instead to commute the penalty to 'imprisonment for life, with one
year's solitary confinement and hard labor in irons.'[60]

The brevity of the newspaper account was not unusual for sodomy cases.
As Bavin-Mizzi argues:

> Almost all of the articles dealing with sodomy in late-nineteenth century
> Western Australia noted only the names of those involved, the verdicts found,
> and the sentences passed. Indeed, the censorship was a moral statement, a
> judgement about the act of sodomy itself. The newspapers repeatedly declared
> the details of the offence 'unfit for publication.'[61]

Edwin Gatehouse was the only person to be sentenced to death for sodomy in Western Australia's history.[62] Ironically, that Gatehouse was ultimately saved from the gallows seems to have had more to do with nineteenth-century racial prejudice than anything else. Like James McDonald, who had sex with a nine-year-old girl, despite being found guilty Gatehouse was able to escape the hangman's rope. Irish man Joseph McDonald, who assaulted and raped a respectable working man's wife rather than an 'aboriginal native' or a 'street urchin', was not nearly so lucky.

::

The rapist Joseph McDonald was not the last former convict to hang in Western Australia. Although transportation ended in 1868 (with a final batch of Irish Fenian rebels), until the 1890s there were still cases of former convicts appearing before the courts. In December 1894, for example, *The Inquirer* reported the trial of James Jones, 'charged with committing a breach of the ticket-of-leave regulations, and with giving the police a false name'.[63] Western Australia also continued to severely punish sex criminals. In 1865 the death penalty was revoked for sodomy cases, but the maximum penalty continued to be life in prison.[64]

There were twelve Supreme Court indictments for sodomy between 1880 and the end of the century. Interestingly, however, seven of the accused sodomites were consenting males, while five were cases involving male rape. Although it was not considered an 'unnatural act', rape of women continued to be punishable by death. Interestingly, between 1880 and 1900 the conviction rate for sodomy (50 per cent) was much higher than that for rape (31 per cent). Most convicted 'sodomites' were sent to prison for at least ten years.[65]

There were also issues of blackmail, entrapment and voyeurism to consider. In at least one known case an English convict had been transported to Australia for life for the crime of extorting money from a man by accusing him of being a sodomite.[66] Similarly, Richard Bibby (the first white man to be hanged for murder of an Aborigine in Western Australia), had 'conspired with another convict to bring a charge of "an unnatural crime against a police officer"'.[67] In another case during 1894 a man secretly followed two men into a park in Coolgardie on suspicion that they might be about to commit an 'unnatural act'. After watching the two men have sex with one another, he reported the matter to the police. When asked in court why he had followed the two men in the first place, the witness replied that he did so because he had 'heard they might do something like that'.[68]

Newspaper self-censorship and moral outrage also continued to be features of the reporting of sex crimes. For example, when John Fleming, 'a young man', was put on 'trial in 1895 for having sex with a horse, the *West Australian* reported – under the headline, 'Unnatural Offence' – that the 'details of the case are unfit for publication'. The date of the crime, defendant's name and the name of his lawyer were mentioned. It was reported that the jury deliberated for twenty minutes before finding Fleming guilty of the lesser charge of 'attempt'. It was not mentioned, however, that Fleming's offence was bestiality rather than sodomy, 'unnatural offence' being used as a euphemism in both circumstances. This was no journalistic slip. Female rape was contemptible, but natural. Sodomy, whether forced or consenting, was considered to be – like bestiality – an unmentionable crime against nature itself.[69]

Meanwhile, many sexual predators of women and girls continued to go unpunished. Part of the problem was an ongoing debate about where childhood ended and consenting adulthood began. For example, in January 1883 a man named Jeremiah Condon appeared before the Supreme Court charged with carnal knowledge of a twelve-year-old girl in Fremantle. Previous British Law had restricted the age of the victim in a crime of carnal knowledge to between ten and twelve. Although this had recently been extended to thirteen in Britain, the law in Western Australia had not been amended. As a result, the accused was set free, but not before the judge had opportunity to tell him that he was 'a disgrace', that he had committed an 'abominable offence' and that he ought to be sent to prison for the rest of his life. Before releasing him, the Chief Justice of Western Australia told Condon that:

> I hope the police will watch you, and if ever you come before this court again I have not the slightest doubt, whoever may be the presiding judge, you will receive the punishment you richly deserve. You are a bad fellow – a bad member of society. Go away.[70]

Contemporary sociologists, criminologists and psychologists continue to argue about the importance of social background and other factors in influencing rape and sexual assault. While some assert that all rape is fundamentally about physical and psychological power, there are many that believe that sexual frustration and/or gratification are major contributing factors. However, such a dichotomy can sometimes be a barrier to our understanding of the history of sex crime.[71] Where poverty and hopelessness are greatest, so too is the frequency of alcoholism, violence, assault and sexual molestation.

Which brings us back to the Irish. It is true that Irish people, as convicts and free migrants, endured tremendous prejudice under the British colonial authorities and that to the Irish goes the honour of bringing some important aspects of the democratic tradition to Australia.[72] However, there is a dark side to the Irish experience in Australia as well. Although there were many Irish success stories (including former convicts), Irish people of the nineteenth century were disproportionately represented in the poor houses, prisons and mental institutions of colonial Australia. Throughout Australia, Irish women continued to be seen as being more sexually promiscuous and prone to drunkenness and madness, while Irish men (especially former convicts) were considered to be susceptible to crimes of violence and passion.

The evidence could be viewed simply by visiting the local prison, poorhouse or lunatic asylum. Five of the first seven women to be hanged in Victoria for capital crimes were Irish (three cases involved children born outside marriage). Between 1856–61 Irish women made up 19 per cent of the population of Victoria, and 44 per cent of the population of Melbourne Women's Gaol. Similarly, in New South Wales between 1868 and 1872 Irish women were 45 per cent of the inmates of the Gladesville Asylum, while only constituting about 14 per cent of the general population. In 1871 Irish women made up nearly half the population of the Woogaroo Mental Institution near Brisbane. While Irish women weren't as highly represented in the poor houses, asylums and prisons of Western Australia, their presence was still alarmingly disproportionate. Or as one historian has written, 'Irish woman in Western Australia were vulnerable to social dysfunction.'[73]

Western Australians continued to struggle to understand sex crime, social alienation and the consequences of convict transportation during the second half of the nineteenth century. They argued over the extent to which the remoteness and isolation of Western Australia contributed to the frequency of sexual assaults. Some scholars and newspaper editorialists publicly argued that it was 'breeding' that created the degradation and debaucheries associated with the 'lower classes'. A belief that the poor were born wretched certainly dampened the compassion of many middle-class gentleman, and seemed to be confirmed in the daily parade of miserable impoverished malefactors in front of criminal courts. Those who committed crime (including sex crime) were usually poor, often drank too much, were prone to violence, and were disproportionately Irish. It appeared to be a simple question of biology.

However, a concerned minority worried that all this 'diabolical wretchedness' might not be innate after all, might not be a birthright, but might flow instead from the grim poverty and tough circumstances of life in a remote colony. They feared that the cause of crime and sexual deviancy (rape, carnal knowledge, sodomy) might be social rather than biological. Even Charles Darwin, who briefly visited Western Australia, had his own doubts. In *The Voyage of the Beagle*, his account of his travels around the world, Darwin once wrote that, 'if the misery of our poor be caused not by the laws of nature, but by our institutions, great is our sin'.[74] Great indeed.

5

Vengeance Is Mine Saith the Lord, the Law and the 'Treacherous Natives', 1865

Aboriginal prisoners face the hangman's rope for violence against settlers and for participating in tribal killings. Aborigines are given 'special treatment' under the Law.

On a remote stretch of the Mingenew-Mullewa road running through the middle of the dusty yellow wheat-belt of Western Australia, is the former site of Butterabby station. A simple roadside marker indicates 'Butterabby Gravesite' and a dirt track to the left. Driving down the red dirt road for two kilometres, the track runs beside a dry creek bed before suddenly turning to the right. A few trees litter the scrubby landscape. Dried sheep and kangaroo bones are scattered here and there, reminding you that this is drought country. A small embankment rises above the cracked dusty creek bed. And there, in the middle of nowhere, is a small historical monument: four simple stones pegging out the location of a long since collapsed settler's hut and three simple mounds of reddish dirt, each covered in bleached white stones and representing the final resting place of six men killed while fighting over possession of this seemingly desolate corner of wilderness. For the Aborigines this was ancestral land, but walking around Butterabby it is hard to imagine why any European settler would come from the other side of the world to kill or die for it.[1]

On 4 January 1865 five Aboriginal prisoners – Garder, Wangayakoo, Yeunmacarra, Charlacarra and Williakarra – appeared before the Supreme Court in Perth charged with murder.[2] The five men were accused of killing Thomas Bott of Butterabby, a pastoral station near Mullewa, more than three hundred kilometres north-east of Perth. A former convict turned farmer, James Rudd, and a convict labourer, Thomas Bott, had been living and working at Butterabby. Their humble hut was shared with a widow, Mrs Jane Tunstill, and her five-year-old daughter, also named Jane. Their only modern convenience was a small well built on the bank of the nearby creek.

Butterabby lay on the westernmost fringe of the country of the *Wajarri* Aboriginal group. The *Wajarri* were aware of the presence of these four white newcomers, and must have marvelled at the utilisation and destruction of the local environment as Rudd and Bott cut down trees, drew precious water from the well and tried to build the fledgling 'station' into a viable economic unit. Butterabby was less than seven kilometres from Kockatea, a remote outstation of John S. Davis's vast pastoral holding. The *Wajarri* and their western neighbours the *Nhanhagardi/Wilunyu* had been involved in several known violent clashes with Davis's shepherds in 1858, 1859, 1862 and 1864. At least four lives, both Aboriginal and white, had already been lost prior to the arrival of James Rudd at Butterabby in mid-1864.[3]

Around 20 August 1864, while working, Thomas Bott was suddenly attacked and speared more than a dozen times by Aborigines. Or in the words of the sensational report in the *Perth Gazette*, Bott:

> ...while engaged in grubbing up a tree, received a shower of spears, some of which took effect, one in particular entering the back and proceeding towards the mouth, and then was attacked with dowarks and kileys by about ten natives, who beat him about until they supposed he was dead, they then went away, and Botts [sp] managed to get to the hut, where he was afterwards succoured by the Police...[4]

Bott was working alone about 100 yards from the hut when he was speared. He lay still, pretending to be dead as his Aboriginal attackers plundered the shack. Although bleeding from multiple spear wounds, Bott later managed to crawl on the hard gritty soil back to the hut. There he lay, until Rudd discovered him. It seems that Bott was then left in the care of Mrs Tunstill and her daughter while Rudd set out on horseback for Champion Bay (Geraldton) for help. Lord only knows how frightened Mrs Tunstill and her daughter must have been as they tended Bott's wounds and waited. Days passed before Rudd made his way back to Butterabby with a doctor and an armed police constable. Remarkably, Bott was then taken back to Champion Bay (about 130 kilometres away) on the back of a bumpy cart. He lingered until 18 September – four weeks after the attack – before dying of his wounds. With death approaching,

Bott had dictated a letter detailing the circumstances of the attack on him and claiming that although he had worked at Rudd's for three months he had never seen any Aborigines in the area until the day of the attack.[5]

While a police search party was sent out after the attackers, Mrs Tunstill and her daughter were evacuated to Champion Bay. Only James Rudd remained at Butterabby.[6] Rudd was obviously determined to defend his farm and it must have been a lonely, frightening time standing as a lone sentinel in this most remote corner of the British Empire. No additional soldiers or police came to join him. The nights must have been long and restless. God only knows how many times he awoke to noises in the bush and imagined that 'the natives' were encircling his hut, coming to kill him. The days passed without any sign of the police and no news of the apprehension of the men who had speared Bott.

Unbeknownst to James Rudd, Bott's alleged killers were captured on 29 September. They had been tracked by Joseph Watson, the same police constable who had arrested Richard Bibby in 1859. Watson later testified that about three miles to the east of Butterabby he and the rest of the Police search party found a native camp and that he arrested the Aboriginal defendants there. According to Watson all the men except Wangayakoo immediately confessed to 'having killed a white man at Rudd's'.[7]

::

As Constable Watson and his captives trudged across the dry sunburnt soil back towards Butterabby, three hundred kilometres to the south-west of them lay Perth, the political and economic centre of the colony. During the 1860s Perth was a world away from settlers on the frontier. In just a few decades the authorities had turned this modest outpost of the Empire into a miniature British capital. Churches, courts, prisons and various businesses had been established. English-style homes lined the wealthier streets. Numerous roughly built pubs and other 'houses of ill repute' were poked away in the back alleyways of the working class sections of the town. Strange imported animals – chickens, cows, pigs and sheep – were kept in and around the town. Horse drawn carriages pulled goods and people up and down the dusty roads. And despite the heat, the settlers continued to wear heavy clothes designed for the colder European climate. The Aborigines who still occasionally camped on the hill the settlers called 'Mount Eliza' must have been amazed as they looked down upon this scene. This small patch of land beside the Swan

River had been utterly and irrevocably transformed by the arrival of the pale newcomers.

It is hard for those of us accustomed to the concrete, steel and glittering glass architecture of contemporary Perth to imagine just how unbroken, wild and wonderful the land it rests upon must have appeared in 1829. The spot where Stirling proclaimed the colony, for example, was a stretch of rugged bushland squeezed between the banks of the Swan River and the small freshwater lakes and swamps to the north. Boats connecting Perth and Fremantle, twelve miles down the Swan River, were the small town's psychological lifeline, as well as providing the European settlers with most of their essential supplies. In Fremantle meanwhile, the settlers had seized Arthur's Head – which local Aborigines called 'Manjaree' – and used the prominent hill, with its blinding limestone cliff face, as a legal centre for their transplanted civilisation. The dominating Roundhouse Gaol was built on land that was rich in meaning for local Aborigines, being a place where they believed the *Wagyl* had rested during the Dreamtime, following the creation of the nearby Swan River.

The Swan River settlers knew they were not alone. From the earliest days they were keen observers of the 'manner and temper' of the Aboriginal people of the area. For example, in September 1829, only a few months after the arrival of the first colonists, John Morgan wrote to England remarking that the 'natives are queer fellows, far different from the Aborigines on the other coast'. The most important difference, according to Morgan, was that 'these fellows may fight, if they are put to it, or imposed upon'.[8] The settlers also ventured out into the wilds. In April 1831, two years after the first settlers had set up camp on the sandy fringes of Western Australia, the first issue of *The Fremantle Observer* boldly proclaimed that:

> In a country so recently become the habitation of civilized man, many new and interesting facts in Science and Natural History will doubtless be observed, these observations we shall be proud to diffuse, as we are aware that they will give a greater worth to our Western Australian Journal than the mere effusions of the most able and learned Theorist.[9]

Explorers travailed the expanses of the colony collecting specimens, seeking inland seas, chasing phantom rivers and generally acting as the vanguard of western civilisation. Occasionally their imaginations got the better of them.

In November 1829 Spencer Trimmer sent a letter from Fremantle to England claiming that:

> Several persons who have been into the interior of the country amongst the Lagoons, describe an animal which they have seen as being like the hippopotamus: many traces have been seen of a large animal on the banks of the river. [10]

Often the settlers were discouraged by what they found; the revealingly named 'Lake Disappointment' being an obvious case in point. Other times their rampant enthusiasm endangered their lives. For example, in 1837 William Morrison, the Swan River Colony's official botanist, was collecting samples for the Royal Botanic Gardens in England when he became lost in bush to the north of Perth. Colonists feared for his life. Morrison was eventually saved by three Aborigines who found him half-dead in the bush, fed him and carried him back to Perth where they handed him over to settlers. [11]

Most of all, the explorers judged the suitability of the countryside for pastoralism and settlement. Sometimes they died in the process – speared by Aborigines, or dying miserable thirsty deaths under the brutal Australian sun. Some of their stories were truly remarkable. Peter Egerton Warburton explored the deserts of Western Australia in 1873. Accompanied by his son as well as Aboriginal guides and at least one mentally unstable Afghan camel driver, he was 'tormented by ants', nearly accidentally killed himself with his own pistol, and suffered acute thirst. Under a blazing sun some of his camels were shot and eaten by the men they were supposed to be carrying across the burning sands. On another occasion, Warburton had to administer an impromptu enema with a double-barrel shotgun to a constipated camel in order to save it. He described his travels across Western Australia as like being in prison, 'only we are much worse fed'. [12]

Warburton was a success as compared to the ill-fated members of the Calvert Expedition of 1896. The stated purpose of their expedition was to explore the 'last blank spaces on the map of Australia'. In Western Australia's Great Sandy Desert, where Aboriginal people had lived for thousands of years, two of the white explorers died of thirst and starvation. Like Burke and Wills before them, the two explorers were publicly mourned in Perth and Adelaide, with the Reverend at their memorial service lamenting the 'old story of the advance guard of the race, toiling with bleeding feet in the desert ways, and toiling often to death in order that the millions might safely follow'. [13]

However, what the explorers and colonists often failed to notice, despite their curiosity about their new environment, was the extent to which the 'untouched' landscape had actually been cultivated by Aborigines. Many Europeans, for example, failed to appreciate the ecological custodianship inherent in Aboriginal 'firestick farming'. As two historians of the south-west of Western Australia have explained:

> Fire was an important element in Aboriginal culture, and they used it with great skill. Early European arrivals, accustomed to seeing fire as a destructive force, were dismayed at the blackened and burnt landscapes they found. Aborigines saw it differently: these lands were well cared for and managed according to practices inherited from their Ancestors, and which we now know had developed over many millennia. The rules for fire were complex, and burning served multiple purposes…Any fires which did escape control were blamed on the fire lighter, who could expect to be speared.[14]

In February 1833 *The Perth Gazette* reported that, 'The fires kindled by the natives in different parts of the country have spread with alarming rapidity, and presented a grand and interesting spectacle.' With the whole of Point Walter alight, the newspaper claimed it presented 'as splendid a scene as could well be imagined'. The *Gazette* assured its readers, however, that the Aborigines did not light the fires out of any 'malicious intent', but rather speculated that a fire lit in the bush for the purposes of cooking had probably just got out of control.[15]

In some areas carefully managed Aboriginal 'firestick farming' carried out over thousands of years had facilitated the growth of long grass and towering Eucalypts. These extensive pasturelands much coveted by the settlers were actually Aboriginal hunting grounds where the use of fire had kept the regenerative bush healthy. Similarly, the early pathways and roads of the colony often followed tracks along which Aborigines had walked from one camp to another, or to places of spiritual significance, for thousands of years. With time these ancient trails were taken over, altered, or destroyed by the newcomers often without them having any conception of what they were doing.[16] In other words, the lands most sought after by colonists were often the very same lands that were most precious to Aboriginal people. This increased the likelihood of clashes between 'settler' and 'native' as the two societies were incapable of comprehending how the other tried to regulate access to the land.

Western Australia's explorers have been lionised in our history. For example, J. S. Battye, writing in 1924, struggled with the moral issues involved but was still willing to state that:

> Men who undertook the burdens of pioneering and went out into the unknown districts carried their lives in their hands, and to shoot quickly was often their only safeguard. Such men may have been technically guilty of murder, but even that was preferable to being stalked like game and treacherously slain by blood-thirsty savages.[17]

However, a minority of settlers remained troubled by the moral implications of Aboriginal dispossession. Robert Lyon had asked his fellow Swan River colonists in 1833, 'why the sword of the Roman be considered more classical than the spear' of an Aborigine? Yet, his assertion that 'All nations were once barbarous,' was hardly convincing to many settlers.[18] The problem was that the average Swan River colonist was more likely to sympathise with the Romans – whose literature, architecture and history they had been taught to admire – than their own illiterate 'uncivilised' pagan ancestors. Although their imperial benefactors in London were perturbed by the bloodletting, many Swan River colonists considered themselves to be at war with local Aborigines. Nevertheless, Lyon argued that:

> The Aboriginal Inhabitants of this Country, are a harmless, liberal, kind hearted race; remarkably simple in all their manners. They not only abstained from all acts of hostility, when we took possession; but showed us every kindness in their power. Though we were invaders of their country, and they had therefore a right to treat us as enemies, when any of us lost ourselves in the bush, and were thus completely in their power; these noble minded people shared with us their scanty and precarious meal; suffered us to rest for the night in their camp; and, in the morning directed us on our way to head quarters, or to some other part of the settlement.[19]

Many among the *Perth Gazette*'s readership disagreed. Many settlers felt that they, not Aborigines, had been the innocent victims of violence and wrote to the newspaper listing a litany of crimes pertaining to the 'deceit and impertinence' of the indigenes.[20] The Aborigines were, after all, considered to be uncivilised, un-Christian savages. For a people fond of utilising biblical passage in their public discourse, the settlers may well have quoted back to Lyon one of the most famous passages of the bible, Romans 12:19 – 'Beloved, do not look for revenge but leave room for the wrath; for it is written, "Vengeance is mine, I will repay, says the Lord."'

::

When some of the Police sent out to apprehend Bott's attackers returned to Butterabby on 3 October 1864 there was a grim scene awaiting them. Inside the hut they discovered the decomposing corpse of James Rudd. Some time between 18 September and 3 October a family of Aborigines (a man, woman and girl) came to the hut at Butterabby looking for food. Rudd was fetching water at the time and the Aborigines found his rifle beside the door. Alone and alarmed, Rudd suddenly noticed the Aborigines and came sprinting back from the creek. He starting fighting with them for control of the rifle. James Rudd was killed by a single blow to the head from a digging stick during a violent struggle.[21] He was subsequently buried at Butterabby by the police who had discovered his corpse.

Meanwhile the five Aboriginal prisoners accused of killing Thomas Bott were taken to Perth and tried. According to one newspaper account:

> This case occupied the court from 11 ½ am until it rose at 6 ½ pm the whole of the proceedings having to pass through three interpreters, the prisoners belonging to a tribe living upwards of 200 miles in the interior. At the conclusion the whole of the prisoners admitted that they were guilty, and white men were not to blame. The Jury returned the verdict of Guilty, and sentence of Death was passed in the usual manner.[22]

But why did the Aborigines attack Bott in the first place? The court, and newspapers, assumed that savage bloodlust was at play, but surely the 'natives' had some motivation beyond simply the joy of killing another human being? Violence in traditional Aboriginal society was highly ritualised. Such an attack, involving multiple individuals, would have required some sort of cultural sanction. Although the station was called Butterabby by whites, the water spring nearby had been called Kockatea by local Aborigines. It is possible the attack took place because Rudd and Bott were using precious resources (such as water) without the permission of local Aborigines. There had also been a long history of violence between shepherds on Davis's neighbouring station and the *Wajarri*. As such, the attack on Bott may have simply been an extension of longstanding hostilities, resulting in an opportunistic and violent robbery of an unwelcome trespasser.

Elieu, a young Aboriginal boy of about thirteen, called to testify in court about the events at Butterabby, innocently replied 'I know Cockateer, not Butter Abby'.[23] Elieu also said (through a translator) that when he saw the accused men on the morning of the murder they had said they were going out to hunt opossums to the west, near where 'the white people' were. Nothing was said of murder, theft or vengeance. Another Aboriginal witness, who had spoken to the accused shortly after the murder, told the court translator that when the men first approached Bott, 'they had no intention of spearing the white man, but seeing him they determined to do so'. Asked in court if they had anything to say in their defence, the prisoners apparently replied (in translation) that Bott was not to blame and that, 'the anger was all on our side'.[24] No one bothered to attempt to discern what the Aborigines were angry about.

After the trial the prisoners were transported from Perth back to Geraldton. A police and military escort then trekked inland with them from Geraldton, arriving at Butterabby on 27 January 1865. After watering the horses:

> The tree was fixed on, the ropes bent, and the grave dug, within about 150 yards of Rudd's house. During this time the 5 prisoners were in the camp, crying and lamenting in the usual noisy and native fashion...On Saturday, the 28th, at daylight, everyone in the camp was astir, preparing for the solemn duty about to be performed...[25]

At six in the morning 'native no.1' was pinioned by the hangman and taken to a cart placed under the chosen gallows tree. Then the 'culprit stood up, one rope was put around his neck, and a second round his waist, by which he was hoisted about 9 feet' in the air. The Sheriff 'then gave the word to "let go," and at 13 minutes past 6 the first native murderer that was executed in this district hung by the neck until he was dead'. The man was left hanging for about fifteen minutes before being cut down, placed in a grave and the cart returned to pick up the next prisoner. The process was repeated four more times, as each prisoner 'screamed and continued to lament until the fatal drop was given; and it was a sad sight to witness how each of them gave the last despairing look at his chained companions'.[26]

About a dozen local Aborigines had been brought into the camp by the police to witness the hangings. *The Inquirer* reported that:

> No sound was uttered by them, and, after looking at the 5 bodies as they lay in the grave, with the white cap over their faces and irons on their legs, hurried away, apparently horrified and frightened at all they had witnessed. About 20 more natives made their appearance after the execution was over, and it was supposed they had concealed themselves in the surrounding bush for the purpose of viewing the proceedings.[27]

The Inquirer clearly agreed with the way in which the hanging had been conducted:

> On the 28th of January a most salutary deviation from the ordinary course of infliction of capital punishment on natives took place. Hitherto, whether condemned for the murder of blacks or white, the natives have been executed in Perth jail, and the knowledge of their fate has been confined to such of the lowest of the low of the Caucasian Race as generally are present at such spectacles.[28]

By contrast, the '5 native murderers' were taken to the scene of their crime and there, 'in the presence of about 35 other natives, who were made unwilling spectators of the affair, the Law took their lives'. *The Inquirer* commented approvingly that:

> It is believed by those who well know the working of the native mind, that this example will have good results. At all events the natives will know that in this case Public Justice, of which they have some notion, has been the Avenger.[29]

Vengeance is mine saith the law.

::

During the founding of Perth Lieutenant Governor James Stirling had proclaimed that all 'Aborigines of the Country' would receive the same treatment and protection under British law as any white settler. However, the developing conflict between Aborigines and settlers left Stirling divided on the best way to handle cases of violence. For example, after learning of the summary execution of Midgegooroo and Yagan, Stirling initially returned to Perth in mid-1834 desiring that British justice not be besmirched by the homicidal impulses of frightened settlers. But the contours of settler thought regarding Aborigines were slowly changing. Romantic ideas about 'noble savages' were waning even as Captain Fremantle first raised the British flag at the Swan River in 1829. By 1834 the reality of frontier conflict and growing problems between settlers and Aboriginal fringe dwellers in Perth meant that most settlers had ceased to see any nobility whatsoever in the 'savages' whom they had so recently dispossessed.[30]

Indeed, prejudice against Aborigines was hardening. William Dampier's negative view of the Aborigines of the West Kimberly coast had had a profound influence on subsequent European perceptions.[31] During the 1830s and 1840s these subjective biases espoused by visiting Europeans were slowly being transformed into objective anthropological observations that proved the innate inferiority of Western Australia's Aboriginal people.

By the 1860s, concepts of race and biological determinism were ascendant. Charles Darwin's ideas about evolution – as published in his *On the Origin of Species* (1859), and *Descent of Man* (1871) – reshaped the 'commonsense' view of the development of humanity.[32] In its rawest form, Darwin's theory of evolution, including the notion of survival of the fittest, became a scientific rationalisation for European superiority.[33] Races competed with one another (and internally as individuals) for resources, territory and superiority. Breeding was everything. It is not difficult to see how these ideas, applied to the outback of Australia, provided a convenient justification for the armed dispersal of Aborigines. Aboriginal people were increasingly seen as a pest – and a potential racial contaminant – that needed to be removed from around farms and pasture land.

Even during the 1830s many Swan River settlers wanted blood spilled. To them the spearing of livestock by Aborigines was a serious threat to their economic survival and the presence of Aborigines around farms made them fear for their lives and livelihoods. In this context, Governor Stirling had sometimes tried to restrain punitive expeditions against Aborigines accused of spearing livestock. For a brief period he had even advocated a treaty or purchase of land from Aborigines.[34] However, while Stirling was away in England the Acting Governor, Frederick Irwin, had ordered the military to play a greater role in suppressing Aboriginal 'outrages'. Such an approach had met with the general approval of many settlers who applauded the death of Yagan and supported the execution of Midgegooroo. Therefore, upon returning to the colony in June 1834 Stirling was under some pressure to show that he too could be tough on 'the natives'.

In January 1834 George Fletcher Moore wrote in his diary that:

> The natives have become troublesome again, having killed two pigs of Mr Shaw's, one sheep of Mr Brockman's, also attempted (and nearly succeeded) in spearing a shepherd, and on one occasion my old acquaintance Moley, and, in addition stabbed Nat Shaw in the thigh with a spear.[35]

To make matters worse, wrote Moore, 'the country has been fired by the natives, and we have been obliged to use great efforts to save our houses and property'.[36]

Nine months later in October 1834 James Stirling became possibly the only colonial governor in Australian history to directly participate in a military attack on about seventy Aborigines. The local newspapers reported on the 'Battle of Pinjarra' like it was a grand military encounter, complete with a 'gallant little party' of soldiers (led by the governor), pitted against 'atrocious offenders of the obnoxious tribe' in a precise military operation. In reality it was a surprise attack by well-armed and mounted British soldiers against Aboriginal men, women and children camped along a riverbank. As the Aborigines fled they were caught in the withering crossfire of soldiers shooting from the other side of the river. According to a report, 'between 25 and 30 were left dead on the field and in the river'. One soldier, Captain Ellis, died of a spear wound to the head. Soon after, the *Perth Gazette* was advertising 'The Jackets of Green: A New Song, Giving a brief account of the late encounter with the Natives at Pinjarra'. It was available for sale at taverns in Perth and Guildford. Different songs, those of mourning and death, were being sung in Aboriginal camps across the Murray region.[37]

The account of Pinjarra given by George Fletcher Moore, who had not been at the 'Battle' but had heard about it first-hand, included a telling passage where he explained that afterwards Governor Stirling decided to set the surviving Aboriginal prisoners free:

> ...for the purpose of fully explaining to the remnant of the tribe the cause of the chastisement which had been inflicted, and to bear a message to the effect that, if they again offered to spear white men or their cattle, or to revenge in any way the punishment which had just been inflicted on these for their numerous murders

and outrages, four times the present number of men would proceed amongst them and destroy every man, woman, and child.[38]

Or in other words the deaths at Pinjarra would be nothing as compared to the slaughter Stirling was threatening to unleash upon the Aboriginal people of the Murray if they continued to resist white incursions into their ancestral lands. To say the very least, such an approach fundamentally violated British law. For example, as legal scholar Bruce Kercher has explained, 'Under English law, groups of British subjects could not be punished for the actions of individuals, and there could be no corporal or capital punishment without trial except in self-defence or in the heat of battle in a period of martial law'.[39] Historians continue to fight over the meaning and implications of Pinjarra, but part of its significance was that the authorities, including the governor of the Colony, portrayed it as a 'battle'. Were they conceding that the Swan River Colony was actually at war with Aborigines? Were the Murray River Aborigines no longer considered British subjects, but foreign enemies? The inherent contradictions of such an approach could not be legally resolved, and so they were simply ignored.

Although there was unease in London, the general response of Swan River settlers to what happened at Pinjarra was overwhelmingly positive. Ironically, however, afterwards Stirling was determined to once again bring a more liberal approach to relations between settlers and Aborigines. For example, on 17 September 1836 the *Perth Gazette* reported that a settler in York had shot dead an Aborigine after laying in wait in the loft of a barn. Flour had been stolen the previous day and the settler decided to set up a sniper's post and dispense some rudimentary justice. A few days later a different settler was speared nearby in retaliation for the ambush in the barn. In response, British soldiers took 'further punitive action', to quote historian Pamela Statham-Drew. Stirling wrote to the Colonial Office in London detailing his 'displeasure and regret' at the resulting deaths. He also explained that he had not pressed for the legal prosecution of the settler who had conducted the barn ambush, nor had he pursued the settler's Aboriginal killers. He preferred to calm the situation and not get the justice system involved. It was not a view shared by the Colonial Office.[40]

Indeed, during 1837 Stirling was criticised by London for a deficiency of 'precision and formality' in his 'dealings with the natives'. Stirling, attempting to justify his conduct, replied that:

The true cause of quarrel is the invasion by the Whites of the country of a very peculiar race of people who possess, however low they may be in the scale of civilization, qualities which render them extremely formidable.[41]

Despite Stirling's ruminations, many colonists continued to consider themselves to be at war. In July 1837 an alarmist headline in the *Swan River Guardian* proclaimed 'COLONIAL WARFARE BETWEEN THE WHITE AND THE BLACKS':

The blacks are becoming audacious, the Whites are murdered for want of protection, and unless the Home Government interfere, every settler must leave the place.[42]

The newspaper called for more British troops and for 'every householder to provide himself with firearms'. At the Vasse in 1837 growing violence between Aborigines and settlers over food led to several deaths and spiralling revenge killings. After a number of violent attacks local Aborigines succeeded in temporarily driving the settlers from the land – causing them to abandon their farms. After evacuation the Aborigines gathered at the farms with the intention, the settlers believed, of burning them down. A further clash produced three more corpses.[43] The war continued.

::

Mrs Eliza Brown, a settler in York, wrote home to her family in England during December 1850 complaining that:

It appears the Natives are rather troublesome at the Northward which indeed must be expected until they are brought a little into subjection to the laws of God and man. 'Thou shalt not steal' will be a difficult commandment to teach them and I fear they will not be obedient to it without very harsh measures. It is much to be regretted that loss of life should be the consequence.[44]

It was Eliza Brown's son Maitland who, at the age of twenty-two, led the famous 1865 expedition to find the bodies of Frederick Panter, William Goldwyer and James Harding – two policemen and a settler who were speared to death by Aborigines as they explored the north-west frontier to judge its suitability for development by the Roebuck Bay Pastoral Association. The funeral service for the three explorers in May 1865 (six months after they were killed) was the largest that had ever been held in Perth. Bells tolled mournfully throughout the city and all government offices closed. Maitland Brown, meanwhile, became a hero of the wild frontier and his journal of his mission to find the dead explorers was serialised in the *Perth Gazette*.[45]

Two of the dead explorers, Panter and Goldwyer, are still honoured in the West Australian Police's official publication regarding 'episodes' from its history. Inspector Panter, according to the Police historian, 'was not one to antagonise' Aborigines. Indeed, Panter was 'was more likely to negotiate and had given gifts to the Aborigines'. Accordingly, his death at the hands of 'hostile Aborigines' was possibly 'because of Chinese and Kanaka trepang fisherman who were known to raid their camps and carry off their woman'. Certainly the Police historian believes the white men in no way provoked Aborigines, as evidenced by the fact that the explorers were killed in their sleep.[46]

The three dead explorers are also etched in bronze on an imposing stone memorial on The Esplanade in Fremantle dedicated to their public memory. The monument's central plaque venerates the explorers of 'this terra incognita', unknown land, and mourns their deaths at the hands of 'treacherous natives' in the Kimberley. It particularly venerates Maitland Brown; pioneer, politician and 'intrepid leader of the government search and punitive party'. His bronze head graces the top of the monument, curiously gazing out towards the Indian Ocean. The plaque mournfully implores, 'Lest we forget'.[47]

The three dead explorers and Maitland Brown were not forgotten by the thousands of people who came out to see the Monument unveiled in 1913.[48] No mention was made on the monument of the Aboriginal people who were killed by Maitland Brown's punitive party in 1865. Nor did it mention those who died afterwards from disease, from dispersal, or in prison cells where they were locked up for cattle spearing as the Kimberley was 'developed' by pastoralists. Then in 1988 two historians, Bruce Scates and Rae Frances, working with Aboriginal people, began agitating for a second plaque to be placed on the Explorers' Monument detailing the 'right of Aboriginal people to defend their land', and pointing out that the original monument did not mention:

> ...the history of provocation which led to the explorers' deaths. The 'Punitive Party' mentioned here ended in the death of somewhere around twenty aboriginal people. The whites were well-armed and equipped and none of their

party was killed or wounded. This plaque is in memory of the Aboriginal people killed at La Grange. It also commemorates all other aboriginal people who died during the invasion of their country. Lest we forget. Mapajarriya-nyalaku.

Bruce Scates' research contradicts the version of history offered on the original plaque on the monument and still publicised in the 2006 official publication, 'Episodes in Western Australia's Policing History'. Scates points out that Panter wrote to his superiors in October 1864 that, 'I expect before the next ship arrives some of the niggers [will get] a pass to "kingdom come"'. Scates claims that during their exploration, Panter, Harding and Goldwyer allowed their horses to drink a 'native well' dry (clean drinking water being the single most precious resource of the remote north-west) and the men are suspected of unknowingly desecrating a sacred site. This occurred only days before the three explorers were killed.[49]

In early 1865, however, these details were unknown. The three men had disappeared in the remote north of the colony and had not been seen or heard from since 9 November 1864. By February the Perth newspapers were speculating about the men's fate and advising the government on a suitable course of action.

> We trust that no effort will be spared by the Government to ascertain [the explorers'] fate…Two of them were servants of the Crown; one was the servant of a private Company; and all were engaged in a service which must have resulted in vast good to mankind. They are all, moreover, the first sacrifice, which, inexorably exacted from civilized by savage man, in every instance, as the price of the occupation of their territory, our community has made. They have fallen in the service of their fellow subjects, and it is our bounden duty to ascertain how, and where they have fallen; and if by violence, avenge them.[50]

Maitland Brown's expedition set out from Perth on 16 February. Brown wrote that he anticipated that 'the guilty natives' would 'either attack or resist us in such a manner as will of itself justify us in exterminating them'.[51] After arriving in the general area where the men went missing, Brown took several Aborigines captive, chained them to trees and starved them until they eventually led him to the decomposing corpses of the explorers. The two Aboriginal hostages were then, 'shot whilst trying to escape'. On 6 April 1865, two days after the grisly discovery of the explorers' bodies, Maitland Brown and his seven men attacked an Aboriginal campsite. Somewhere between six and twenty people were killed and several more seriously wounded – men, women and children.[52] Brown later wrote in his journal that it was 'the first lesson taught the natives in this district of the superiority of civilized man' and that local Aborigines suffered from 'an insatiable thirst for blood'.[53]

I often visit the Explorers' Monument in Fremantle with my history students. Standing alongside it we discuss the misunderstanding, violence and recrimination that poisoned black and white relations on the frontier. We discuss how explorers were often the vanguard for the sheep, cattle and farmers who came afterwards to seize and transform the land in the name of progress. We contemplate that, similar to Aborigines, white settlers had their own system of 'payback' killings. We discuss how bitter these debates have become in contemporary Australia regarding our frontier history. On our various visits to the monument we have also noticed that the second plaque (the one from an Aboriginal perspective) has been defaced several times and that there has been at least one serious attempt to dislodge it from the memorial. The stone around its edges remains chipped and broken. Meanwhile Maitland Brown continues to stare out knowingly towards the golden arches of McDonald's at Bather's Bay and over the glittering oceanic expanse that brought his pale people and their justice to Western Australia.

::

Five Aboriginal men were hanged at Butterabby in January 1865 for the murder of Thomas Bott. Three months later Maitland Brown's punitive party killed about twenty Aborigines in revenge for the murder of three explorers in the West Kimberley. Yet another opportunity for exemplary justice presented itself in July when two more Aborigines were tried for murder in Perth. However, this time the victim was not a white man murdered on the frontier, but a 'half-caste' girl speared to death at York. The case challenged, once again, the idea of equal rights before the Law. The victim, Martha Garling, was the daughter of a former English convict transported to Swan River in 1851 for Larceny. The mother was Aboriginal. During May 1865 two Aboriginal men, Narrigal and Yandal (also recorded as Narrigalt and Youndal), approached three-and-a-half-year-old Martha, who was playing with several white children at a nearby farm. They grabbed Martha and speared her to death, leaving the other children alone. The reason for the killing was presumed to be a tribal matter, involving her Aboriginal mother and the death of a relative of the killers.

When Narrigal and Yandal were tried for murder in the Supreme Court in Perth the newspapers debated the merits of the case. *The Inquirer*, which had declared its enthusiasm for the public hanging of Aboriginal murderers only a few months earlier during the Butterabby case, now doubted the justice or sense in arresting Aborigines for what was clearly a 'tribal killing', albeit of a defenceless little girl.

> ...the complexion of the crime is, humanely speaking, widely different when a native, in obedience to a custom, which his ancestors have obeyed, puts another to death; not from a spirit of personal revenge, but, as was fully recognized by the Court in one at least of the cases now in question, as *an expiatory rite*. This surely deprives the offence of the technical shade of 'murder'.[54] [Emphasis in original]

Commenting that to treat tribal killings as murder was 'an absurdity', the argument was put that:

> In the case from York, two very intelligent native men having lost relatives, killed a little half-bred girl by driving a spear or dagger into her throat...If these cases had happened among whites instead of blacks, or even if the victims had been white instead of black, the prisoners would have justly merited the sentence of death.[55]

The Inquirer noted that the 'native does what his law compels him to do', for which 'our law hangs him'. As such, 'it becomes very questionable whether to hang natives for these so-called murders is of any use whatever: for we fear that it is admitted that the fear of death by the hands of the white man does not prevent their commission'. Therefore, 'where a jury can save a native from the gallows by a verdict of manslaughter, we should be delighted to hear such verdicts given'.[56] The article concluded by arguing that:

> ...we say that jurors will be justified in drawing a distinction between a crime committed by a savage, in blind deference to a barbarous custom, for mere purposes of expiation, and one committed by a person of a superior race for revenge or passion. If the law is arbitrary on the side of mercy, jurors can be so too; at all events, we hope we have seen the last execution of natives for 'murders *inter se*'.[57]

The Perth Gazette echoed these sentiments, arguing that although the crime was terrible, involving the murder of an innocent little girl, there was 'a general expression of hope that the extreme penalty will not again be inflicted'.[58]

> In each case the culprits spoke very tolerable English, undoubtedly were aware of the penalty exacted by whites for their crime, and yet were unable to withstand the impulse of their aboriginal customs, or their thirst for blood aroused by the death of their relatives.[59]

Similarly, the newspaper's account of the hanging opened by arguing that, 'On Tuesday last a scene was enacted at Perth Gaol which it is greatly to be hoped will never be repeated.' In particular, the hanging of Narrigal and Yandal forced:

> ...upon us the belief that, while we subject the aborigines to all the pains and penalties of British law, considering them responsible for their actions because we suppose they are aware of their consequences, we are, in reality, dealing with people who are but children in reasoning power, moved and swayed by a savage impulse as entirely now as on the day when they first came into contact with the white man thirty-six years ago.[60]

The newspaper reported that all four Aborigines who were hanged that morning (Yandal and Narrigal plus two from another case) had begged for their lives upon the scaffold and had died resisting the supposedly dignified execution that was being imposed upon them. The hangings, moreover, took place in full view of a crowd who had assembled outside Perth Gaol to view the spectacle. Apparently, 'more than two thirds' of the crowd 'consisted of children from 5 to 12 years old, playing, shouting, racing, and making bonfires.'[61] *The Inquirer* could not resist making an editorial comment:

> We trust this is the last of such executions we shall be called upon to record – that of heathen natives of our own soil, who are bound, we believe, by their tribal customs, in some instances, to take the lives of others in propitiation for those who have been slain, in order to retain their own.[62]

What the newspapers did not consider – what white settlers would not contemplate, let alone accept – was the fact that most murders of whites by

Aborigines during the nineteenth century were similarly carried out under tribal law in defence of country, payback for the deaths of relatives, or because whites unknowingly violated local customs. Furthermore, if killing 'by a person of a superior race for revenge or passion' was murder, then under this logic didn't Maitland Brown's violent reprisals against Aborigines for the murder of the three Kimberley explorers constitute the illegal taking of life? Indeed, wasn't it mass murder, given that up to twenty Aboriginal lives had been forfeited as punishment for the deaths of Panter, Harding and Goldwyer? Shouldn't Maitland Brown have been indicted, tried and hanged for murder rather than venerated and commemorated in stone and bronze?

Basically, *The Inquirer* and many West Australian settlers were arguing that Aborigines should be given 'special treatment' under the law. Where they killed their own people for tribal reasons, leniency should be the order of the day. On the frontier where victims were isolated white settlers, however, there was a need for vengeance, punitive violence and hanging.

::

By the 1850s public execution was increasingly criticised in both Britain and Australia for its ineffectiveness. The famous English writer Charles Dickens weighed in on the abolitionist side of the debate on the grounds that public hangings had become an 'odious' occasion of 'ribaldry, debauchery, levity, drunkenness and flaunting vice' on behalf of the spectators.[63] If the intention of public execution was to deter offenders and impress the general population, it had turned into little more than a spectacle that attracted 'the lowest types'. In May 1868 a British newspaper described the lines of working class people walking to Newgate for the last public hanging ever held in England – 'There was the wretched raggedness, there was the dirt, sloth, scurvy and cretinism of rural vagabondage, trooping over the bridge'.[64] Public execution was halted in Britain not because it was cruel, but because the authorities were worried it was entertaining, rather than terrifying, to the 'great unwashed poor' who were supposed to be cowed with dread.

Similarly, in Western Australia when two Aborigines were hanged outside York in 1840 for murder, a government official was sickened to see local settlers from the 'lower classes' using the corpses for target practice, or cutting off the ears as ghoulish souvenirs.[65] In June 1853 the permanent gallows were removed from in front of Darlinghurst Gaol in Sydney and the *Sydney Morning Herald* opined that public executions were no longer useful. As 'far as an example is concerned', the *Herald*'s editor wrote, 'it may be doubted whether the terror they are intended to inflict is equal in force to the disgust or the pity they generate'.[66] Likewise in Western Australia *The Inquirer* declared its opposition to public execution following a triple hanging of two men and a woman in October 1855 that had been viewed by 'many spectators', including 'a not inconsiderable number of women and children'.[67] Public execution was abolished in most Australian colonies during the 1850s.[68]

There was one major exception. In cases where Aborigines were involved the West Australian, Queensland and South Australian authorities reserved the right to execute the perpetrators in public. In the words of historian John McGuire, 'public execution was intended to instruct the Aborigines in the appropriate penalty for serious crime, while concurrently reassuring the settler population that the Aboriginal menace was being met with vigilance'. Western Australia did not abolish public execution until December 1870 – after convict transportation had ceased and the frontier, in the south of the colony at least, had been secured.[69] Even then, the West Australian government continued to view capital cases involving Aborigines as requiring special treatment. The *Capital Punishment Amendment Act*, which had abolished public execution, was amended in 1875. In the words of John McGuire:

> The amended sections specified that, in cases where Aborigines were convicted of capital offences, the governor would appoint the place of execution at his discretion and that '[s]uch executions...shall take place in public'. Unlike the South Australian experience, the sole justification offered for the reintroduction of public hangings was to deter Aborigines from committing outrages upon settlers in remote districts.[70]

While the *West Australian Times* proclaimed in 1876 that in all murder cases 'the law is still the same, and does not change with colour', this was simply not true. For example, in January 1865, at the same time as the Butterabby case, a settler by the name of David Reader appeared before the Supreme Court charged with kicking one of his Aboriginal workers to death. But as the *Perth Gazette* reported:

> Mr. Landor in addressing the Jury for the defence contended that the prisoner in kicking the deceased only intended to rouse him and make him get up, and

cautioned the Jury not to be carried away by too eager a desire for equal justice between white and black...The learned gentleman also urged that there was but little dependence to be placed upon native evidence.[71]

As late as February 1892, twenty-two years after public execution had been abolished for whites, three Aborigines were hanged in public in the East Kimberley. The three Aborigines – Terribie, Corrondine and Tchawada – had been found guilty of the murder four years earlier of a white miner called William Scott. As was often the case, it appeared that issues of access to land and water were the cause of the violence. Nevertheless, in pursuing the murderers the Police tracked a group of Aborigines and shot three dead before the others escaped into the bush. Some time later another expedition captured the three accused and transferred them to Roebourne where they were found guilty of murder.[72] The three were then transported in chains to Eight Mile Creek (near Mount Dockrell), about 90 kilometres south-west of the frontier town of Halls Creek. A crowd of more than sixty Aborigines was assembled before the men were put to death. The *Australian Advertiser* reported that:

> The three little niggers were seated all in a row on the edge of the dray, with their arms tied, and their feet hanging over the pit, and each man had a rope hitched around his neck...[73]

They were hanged together. When their dead bodies were cut down, Terribie, Corrondine and Tchawada were buried with their prison chains still attached. Afterwards the man who hanged the three Aborigines, Overend Drewry, wrote to his superior in Perth commenting upon the fact that there had been some dispute over the legality of the document that ordered the hanging. In Drewry's words, 'I hanged them first and faced the music afterwards, the coroner advised an open verdict, the jury thought otherwise, holding that the natives were legally hanged but I think if anything of the same sort occurs here again it would be as well to send a copy of the warrant of execution.'[74] Such was the precision with which British Justice was applied to Aborigines in Western Australia.

Of the 154 people legally executed in Western Australia between 1840 and 1964, sixty-one (39 per cent) of those hanged were Aboriginal. An additional 296 Aborigines were sentenced to death but had their sentences commuted during the same period.[75] Most of those who hanged had killed whites. Most of those who had their sentences commuted had killed other Aborigines. Western Australia still allowed for the potential public execution of Aborigines in its 1902 Criminal Code (as well as allowing for whipping male Aborigines as a form of punishment). The state government did not repeal the discriminatory sections until capital punishment itself was finally abolished in 1983.[76] Very special treatment indeed.

::

Thomas Bott was speared a dozen times and died a slow agonising death. Of the seven men killed at Butterabby between August 1864 and January 1865 his death seems the most senseless. He was a convict, an unwilling migrant to Western Australia, having arrived aboard the *Lincelles* in 1862. He was forty when he arrived in Fremantle as a convicted arsonist. His occupation was listed as 'boatman' and perhaps it was a love of irony that saw him deployed to the most remote, dry and isolated part of the interior of the colony where the only water he would see would be from the small creek that ran past the hut at Butterabby during winter. According to the Convict Establishment, Bott was single, stood less than five-foot-five inches tall, had a 'long' face, and a tattoo of a woman on his left arm. Of the seven men killed in the conflict at Butterabby, Bott was the only one not to be buried there.

Three graves – simple dirt mounds covered with white stones – still remain at Butterabby. One contains the skeletal remains of James Rudd, whose misfortune it was to try and eke out an existence in this dry quiet corner of Western Australia. The other two graves contain the remains of Garder, Wangayakoo, Yeunmacarra, Charlacarra and Williakarra – Aboriginal men who were all hanged for the murder of Thomas Bott. That they regarded Thomas Bott as an unwelcome trespasser is undoubtable. Still, the execution of the five Aborigines was part of the Swan River Colony's attempted pacification of 'hostile natives' and was supposed to serve as a warning. The white man's law could be every bit as vengeful as that of Aborigines.

At Butterabby a simple carved headstone, made from local rock, marks out the resting places of the six men buried there and tells the story of their deaths.[77] Like everything else around Butterabby, it has been worn by the heat and dry wind. A few paces away is the former site of James Rudd's hut, reminding you that someone once tried to make a life there. A bit further away is the collapsed remains of an old gum tree – big enough and old enough to have possibly been the gallows tree from which the five Aboriginal men were hanged in 1865. Nothing much else remains of this forgotten frontier battlefield where seven lives were needlessly extinguished during 1865, proving that like everything else in the West Australian bush, vengeance is temporal.

6

Bernard Wootton and the Fenian Disease, 1867

Rebellious Irish convicts bring the alleged menace of Fenian terrorism to Western Australia. Fear of bushranging and convict rebellion grips the colony.

When gold was discovered in the south-east of Australia during 1851 the German radical and Manchester factory owner, Frederick Engels, wrote to his intellectual collaborator and lifelong friend, Karl Marx. 'The British will be thrown out,' declared Engels about Australia, 'and the united states of deported murderers, burglars, rapists and pickpockets will startle the world by demonstrating what wonders can be performed by a state consisting of undisguised rascals.'[1] While the future authors of the *Communist Manifesto* did not believe Australia to be ripe yet for proletarian revolution, they delighted in fantasising about the type of undesirable political spectre that might soon haunt Britain's Australian colonies.

Indeed, in the final chapter of his monumental work of political economy, *Das Kapital*, Karl Marx turned his attentions to the situation at 'Swan River, West Australia', where the abundance of land and a shortage of labour had diminished the fortunes and class power of men like Mr Robert Peel, the former British prime minister's cousin. Marx revealed how shortly after arriving at the Swan River Colony Peel's servants had abandoned him, and how the political establishment in Western Australia had failed to recreate the social discipline of Britain's industrial economy. 'Unhappy Mr. Peel,' writes Marx, 'who provided for everything except the export of English modes of production to Swan River!'[2]

Marx finished writing the first volume of *Das Kapital* in July 1867.[3] Although Marx and Engels did not have the opportunity to read the *Perth Gazette*, their premonition of Australia's future as a united states of undisguised rascals may have been partially confirmed by a seemingly disturbing piece of news published that October.

> EXECUTION. The condemned convict Bernard Wootton suffered the penalty of his crimes on Tuesday morning. This man was undoubtedly one of the most desperate and dangerous characters we have been indebted for to the mother country, and continued hardened to the last, rejecting all offers of religious ministrations. On the scaffold his last words were a shout for the Irish republic.[4]

Bernard Wootton, alias MacNulty, convict 4002, had arrived in Western Australia on the *Runnymede* during September of 1856. He was twenty-one years old when he stepped ashore in Fremantle. He was single, a Catholic and Irish. He had been exiled to Australia for the crime of being a pickpocket. Convicted in Stafford, England, during 1854 he had been given fifteen years penal servitude prior to transportation. Being both literate and a tradesman (a mason), however, he was considered a potentially valuable worker. Wootton was given a ticket of leave in February of 1859, having only served three years of his sentence in exile, and went to work in Toodyay. His story seemed, outwardly at least, to be one of integration and reform.

Wootton was given a pardon in December of 1862, but only one month later he found himself back in trouble with the law when he was convicted of larceny. From then on Bernard Wootton's struggle with colonial society entered its terminal phase. He managed to escape from the police and went 'bushranging' – living free from the social and legal constraints, not to mention material comforts, of 'civilised' life. Wootton was eventually recaptured by the police during August 1867. Or as Sergeant John Moyle of York later told the court:

> I remember, in company with a native, on the 18th August, going to capture the prisoner with others, who were all escaped convicts. I went towards a place called Muraramine, in Beverley. I saw the prisoner with another convict in the custody of Constable Barron, about sundown that evening.[5]

Sergeant Moyle and Constable Barron took the prisoners to the home of a local settler to spend the night. After the policemen fed the two prisoners they all retired for the evening, sleeping near each other on the floor of one of the rooms. The two convicts were handcuffed together, a circumstance which made sleeping understandably difficult. Around two in the morning Sergeant Moyle released one of the hands of each of the prisoners from handcuffs so that they could roll over and sleep more easily. This involved significant trust on Sergeant Moyle's behalf, but the prisoners appeared compliant and docile. The night passed without incident.[6]

In the morning Sergeant Moyle, his 'native assistant' Jack Bousher, Constable Barron and the prisoners prepared to face the day. As Sergeant Moyle later told the court:

> At breakfast the next morning the prisoner complained that he could not eat unless his right hand was loosed. He having behaved so well since he was arrested, I unfastened the handcuff.[7]

Nearby was a fireplace with two iron bars used to tend the fire. Wootton, now entirely un-handcuffed, ate his meal and occasionally stared into the morning fire as the police started to pack their possessions.

> After breakfast Barron and I proceeded to roll up the rug. We knelt on the floor, at each end of it. I was nearest the door, my face towards the prisoner. While we were so engaged, I received a blow on the head, and was knocked down. I got up, and received another blow to the top of the head, which knocked me down again.[8]

Wootton had grabbed a hot metal bar from the fire and attacked both Sergeant Moyle and Constable Barron with it. Both were beaten to the ground, Wootton seriously burning his hand in the process. As Sergeant Moyle rose to his feet, blood streaming down his face, he saw that Wootton had hold of the fire iron. Moyle, barely conscious, somehow grabbed hold of Wootton and tried to wrest control of the weapon. With the help of the also wounded Constable Barron they eventually subdued the Irishman and handcuffed him on the floor. Bleeding profusely from the serious head wound, Sergeant Moyle asked Wootton why he had attacked him. 'Would you not have done it,' Bernard Wootton replied in desperation, 'to get your liberty?'[9]

::

In the same edition of the *Perth Gazette* that covered Irishman Bernard Wootton's trial, the newspaper also reported on the fascinating discoveries of the French-American scientific explorer and relentless self-promoter, Monsieur Du Chaillu, in Central Africa. In fact, the two stories ran right next to each other. According to the newspaper, the greatest of M. Du Chaillu's intriguing new discoveries concerned apes. Or as the newspaper explained:

> This journey has added largely to the traveller's knowledge of the Chimpanzee and the Gorilla. M. du Chaillu found both in immense number in the wooded country south-east of the Fernand Vaz. He succeeded in securing several live gorillas, but not one lived in captivity. With great difficulty a photograph was obtained of one grotesque little creature who survived his mother's death for 4 days, and had begun to know his captor.[10]

Two years earlier in 1865 when the first stuffed gorillas had been displayed at Melbourne's aspiring 'National Museum' it had caused a public sensation. While the director of the museum, Professor McCoy, argued that there was no evolutionary connection between the 'monster ape' and humans, others were not so sure. Interestingly, the Melbourne gorillas, the first to ever be displayed in Australia, had been shot and sold to the museum by M. Du Chaillu.[11]

By 1867 Monsieur Du Chaillu's interests had burgeoned beyond the killing of primates for museum collections (and a tidy profit). He also collected human skulls. According to the *Perth Gazette*, the African tribesmen who donated the skulls were 'rather flattered' when M. Du Chaillu informed them:

> ...that many medicine-men in his country believed Negroes to be apes, almost the same as the gorilla, and that he was anxious to send a number of skulls to England, to shew them they were mistaken.[12]

A hundred and forty years later, watching yet another Hollywood remake of King Kong, I was struck by what a poor choice of monster a giant gorilla makes. Gorillas are, for the most part, peaceful vegetarians who live in remote jungle far from humans. The common urban cat, by contrast, is considerably more ferocious. Unlike gorillas, cats are vicious predators and ruthlessly territorial animals that fight and kill regularly. Aside from British comedians The Goodies, however, no one has seriously considered making Kitten Kong movies. For once Hollywood is not to blame for our irrationality. Gorillas captivate our imaginations because of their obvious similarity to humans. King Kong is, essentially, a story about the human struggle between 'primitive instinct' and the modern world. But the origin of our fascination with gorillas as violent monsters can probably be blamed on Charles Darwin and the Irish.

In the words of Peter Watson:

> Modern (scientific) racism stems from three factors. One, the Enlightenment view that the human condition was essentially a biological state (as opposed to a theological state); two, the wider contact between different races brought about by imperial conquest; and three, the application and misapplication of Darwinian thinking to the various cultures around the world.[13]

In 1836, while still developing scientific ideas that would reach their fruition in his book *On the Origin of Species*, Charles Darwin made a famous visit to Australia as part of the crew of the *Beagle*. Although Darwin's oft quoted remark that he left Australia 'without sorrow or regret' is generally taken as an indication of his distaste for the continent, Darwin offered some insights into antipodean nature and society. Arriving in Sydney, Darwin remarked that the town bore 'a close resemblance to England', although 'perhaps the ale houses here were more numerous'. Darwin expressed concern over the future of the Aboriginal population and the corrupting influence of convictism upon the free settlers. In his words, 'how thoroughly odious to every feeling, to be waited on by a man who the day before, perhaps, was flogged, from your representation, for some trifling misdemeanour'.[14]

Twenty-three years later when Charles Darwin published *On the Origin of Species* it ignited one of the greatest international scientific debates of all time. As his biographer Janet Browne has written, Darwin transformed forever the debate on the origins of life on earth:

> At his most determined, he questioned everything his contemporaries believed about living nature, calling forth a picture of origins completely shorn of the Garden of Eden and dispensing with the image of a heavenly clock-maker patiently constructing living beings to occupy the earth below.[15]

His theories regarding the struggle of life and 'natural selection' came at a time when the British Empire was still expanding across the globe. For some people, the new science and politics seamlessly blended.

Those who sought a radically new manifesto for the living world were sure to find it in [Darwin's] words: no one could afterwards regard organic beings and their natural setting with anything like the same eyes as before; nor could anyone fail to notice the way that Darwin's biology mirrored the British nation in all its competitive, entrepreneurial, factory spirit...[16]

However, of all the ideas attributed to Darwin the one that created the most controversy and captured the general public's attention, was the suggestion that human beings and apes have a common line of evolutionary descent. When Darwin innocently scribbled the words 'Man from monkeys?' in the working journal that he would later draw upon while developing *Origin of Species*, he had little inkling of the controversy he was about to ignite. Although Darwin avoided the question of human evolution in *On the Origin of Species*, he did create a theory that other scientists could utilise. Darwin's collaborators, like T. H. Huxley, pushed the evolutionary argument further than Darwin initially dared, arguing that 'the structural differences which separate Man from Gorilla and the Chimpanzee are not so great as those which separate the Gorilla from the lower apes'.[17]

The debate gripped the scientific community, while intriguing and dividing the public throughout the western world. In the words of Janet Browne, 'Apes or angels, Darwin or the Bible, were burning topics for Victorians.'[18] It was for this reason that the hirsute Darwin, the most famous scientist of his century, was often drawn in cartoon form (in *Punch* and other publications) as a bearded monkey man.[19] Scientists, naturalists, theologians and even opportunistic adventurers like Paul Du Chaillu were pulled into the public debate over the evolutionary relationship between man and ape – or more specifically, between man and gorilla.[20]

The first documented discovery of gorillas by Europeans had occurred only a decade before Darwin published *On the Origin of Species*. The 'discovery' was made in Africa in 1847 by the appropriately named Dr Thomas Savage, a missionary. It was for European science, if not for the local Africans who were already aware of the existence of gorillas, a remarkable find. Here was a beast so obviously similar to humans in size, appearance and social organisation that it challenged our very notion of ourselves. Art followed science. When French sculptor Emmanuel Fremiet first displayed *Gorilla carrying off a woman* in 1859 it not only caused a scandal, but opened up an imaginative path that would lead, eventually, to King Kong. Viewed from this perspective, the ape represented our darker, primitive, violent and sexually aggressive self. All this despite the fact that gorillas were neither violent, nor known to have ever carried off naked humans.

Nevertheless, when M. Du Chaillu arrived in London in early 1861 with his first collection of stuffed gorillas from Africa the public debate about the evolutionary relationship between man and beast was at its peak. By 1861 it even appeared reasonable for someone like the eminently pretentious and respectable Professor Richard Owen, Superintendent of Natural History at the British Museum and an acquaintance of Queen Victoria, to lecture on 'The Gorilla and The Negro'. At the populist edge of the debate, *Punch* published a cartoon mocking both the anti-slavery movement and Darwin with an ape asking, 'Am I a Man and a Brother?' There were, however, serious issues at stake. Three years later in 1864 Benjamin Disraeili, the future British prime minister, would publicly ask his audience, 'Is man an ape or an angel?'[21]

At the same time the image of the 'Simianised Celt' – that is to say, the Irish person who resembled a giant ape – was already well established in the Victorian mind. As Britain's first colonial subjects, the Irish were regarded as uncivilised, drunken, violent and backward. The nineteenth-century caricature of 'Paddy the Irishman' was a commonplace racial stereotype.[22] One writer in *Punch* in 1862 argued that the Darwinist 'missing link' between the Gorilla and the 'Negro' was not to be found in Africa, but rather:

> A creature manifestly between the Gorilla and the Negro is to be met within some of the lowest districts of London and Liverpool by adventurous explorers. It comes from Ireland, whence it has contrived to migrate; it belongs in fact to a tribe of Irish savages: the lowest species of the Irish Yahoo.[23]

These ideas did not develop in a political or historical vacuum. The particular threat posed by the armed Fenian movement of the 1860s led to great public fear and loathing in Britain of the 'Irish terrorist menace'. What was particularly worrying, from a British point of view, was that the menace appeared wherever the Irish were present – including the working class slums of London, Manchester, Liverpool and even across the Atlantic in New York and Boston. In these cities there were large and visible Irish populations whose poverty, strange folk customs and Catholic faith, along with their alleged inability to 'assimilate', challenged mainstream society. It was the dregs of this simianised violent race who were also being transported in chains to Britain's final antipodean penal colony at the Swan River.

::

Bernard Wootton was not the only escaped convict 'bushranging' during 1867. Between May and August of 1867 three particularly notorious convicts broke out of Fremantle Prison and went bushranging in the interior settlements between York and Albany. Some of the police pursuing them – Sergeant Moyle and Constable Barron – were the same men who later arrested Wootton. The three escapees robbed local farmers and fought a series of gun battles with police, resulting in one of the bushrangers being shot dead, another being seriously wounded and captured, and the third finally being arrested in the Blackwood district. Western Australia generally prided itself on being free from the sort of violent bushranger gangs notorious in the eastern colonies, and so the legal authorities were keen to use the full measure of the law against recaptured offenders.[24]

It was with the memory of these recent fearful encounters with bushrangers that Bernard Wootton went to trial in Perth. Wootton defended himself in the Supreme Court on 3 October 1867 in front of Chief Justice Burt. He was charged with the malicious wounding of Sergeant Moyle, a crime that carried a possible death sentence. In evidence given in court it became clear that it was the policemen's 'native assistant', Jack Bousher, who actually prevented Wootton's escape. Described in the *Perth Gazette* as 'a very intelligent aboriginal native', Bousher testified that on the morning in question he saw Wootton reach into the fire, grab the iron, and beat Constable Barron and then Sergeant Moyle with it. It was Bousher who leapt to the defence of the two police officers, wrestling with Wootton for control of the fire iron until Moyle got back on his feet and was able to help. It was Bousher who after managing to break Wootton's grip on the iron bar, then hit him over the head with it, making it possible for the two police to subdue and handcuff their prisoner.[25]

In his defence Wootton called Walter Walker, the other escaped convict who had been a silent spectator to the violent drama that morning. Walker claimed he never saw Wootton grab the fire iron. Walker did, however, make some attempt to pin the blame for the violent attack on the two policemen on Jack Bousher, the native assistant, whom he claimed was the only person in the room he had personally seen 'with a bar in his hand striking about from one side to the other'.[26] Walker's words were carefully chosen as he walked a fine line between attempting to create 'reasonable doubt' as to Wootton's guilt and committing outright perjury.

Wootton then had opportunity to address the jury. He admitted that he had attempted to escape on the morning in question, but denied that he had assaulted Sergeant Moyle or Constable Barron. In Wootton's version of events he had simply made a run for the door and had been prevented from escaping by the Aboriginal police assistant, Jack Bousher, who had hit him with the steel bar from the fire. Wootton implied, as had Walker, that perhaps the native assistant had also accidentally hit the two policemen while trying to prevent Wootton from escaping.[27]

Bernard Wootton's defence was unsuccessful. Or as the *Perth Gazette* plainly recorded: 'Verdict – guilty; sentence – Death'.[28] He was hanged at Perth Gaol on 8 October 1867, virtually his last words on earth being to reject the British Empire that had first exiled him and was now preparing to take his life, and to call for an Irish republic.

::

From the outset the arrival of Irish convicts in Western Australia seemed to bode ill. For example, the *Perth Gazette* of 23 September 1853 reported an extraordinary scene of defiance aboard the *Phoebe Dunbar* as it arrived off Fremantle at the end of its long journey from Ireland.

> A disturbance of rather a serious nature occurred on board the *Phoebe Dunbar* on Thursday last week, in consequence of some mutinous conduct of certain Prisoners on board, who, it appears, managed to rid themselves of the irons which had been placed upon them for punishment, and were most abusive and violent towards the Pensioner Guard set over them. One or two of the ringleaders were bayoneted by the Military, and order was partially restored.[29]

Only eleven days before the *Phoebe Dunbar* (carrying the rapist Joseph McDonald among others) had hove into Fremantle to deliver up its Irish penal refuse, another convict ship, the *Robert Small*, had similarly disgorged large numbers of Irish convicts on to the shores of Western Australia. During its voyage to the Swan River at least six convicts aboard had died. An additional eight convicts had perished during the voyage of the *Phoebe Dunbar*. Therefore, among the various dubious distinctions held by the Irish was now this – the transport of Irish convicts aboard the *Phoebe Dunbar* and the *Robert Small* were the two most costly shipments, in terms of lives lost, of all convict transports to Western Australia.[30]

The Irish were not nearly as heavily concentrated in West Australia as in the eastern colonies. For example, in 1837 there were only thirty Irish-born women in the entire Swan River Colony. Although shipments of male convicts increased the numbers of Irish dramatically, they were still a small but significant minority of the population. By 1854 there were 11,976 people in the Swan River Colony, but only about 2,000 were Catholics (the majority of these were Irish).[31] However according to Stannage and Stevenson:

> Despite the fact that less than one thousand Irish convicts were sent to Swan River, they were sufficiently numerous and vocal for a historian to observe that convictism imported the Irish problem to Western Australia.[32]

Not withstanding the minor matter of a few bayoneted convicts aboard the *Phoebe Dunbar*, by far the greatest 'Irish problem' to be imported to Western Australia, in the minds of British people of the mid-nineteenth century at least, was that of 'Fenianism'.

Founded in Dublin on Saint Patrick's Day 1858 and officially known as the Irish Revolutionary Brotherhood (IRB) in Ireland and as The Fenian Brotherhood in America, the Fenians were an armed Irish republican movement dedicated to the revolutionary overthrow of British rule. During the 1860s the movement's ranks were swollen by thousands of immigrant Irish in the United States, many of whom had experienced military service during the US Civil War and who now wanted to liberate their homeland by force of arms.

Prejudice against Irish Catholics was peculiar to the British Empire, with one notable exception. In the republic that had been constructed from thirteen former British colonies and renamed the United States of America, anti-Irish feeling ran deep. Prejudice bred paranoia of miscegenation and malfeasance. For example, during the building of the Brunswick canal in the southern state of Georgia, African slaves and Irish wage labourers were strictly segregated. There was a fear, eloquently expressed in the journal of Fanny Kemble, the wife of a Georgia planter and an actress of some repute, that the Irish and blacks might kill each other, or worse still, find common cause:

But the Irish are not only quarrelers, and rioters, and fighters, and drinkers, and despisers of niggers – they are a passionate, impulsive, warm-hearted, generous people, much given to powerful indignations, which break out suddenly when not compelled to smoulder sullenly – pestilent sympathizers too, and with a sufficient dose of American atmospheric air in their lungs, properly mixed with a right proportion of ardent spirits, there is no saying but what they might actually take to sympathy with the slaves, and I leave you to judge of the possible consequences.[33]

Despite the fears of Mrs Kemble, the Irish in America generally saw blacks, whether slave or free, as economic competitors for jobs. Despite anti-Irish racism, the Irish had the benefit of white skins, a serendipitous biological reality that when combined with the demographic reality of mass Irish migration during the nineteenth century, assisted their gradual integration into mainstream American society. Although they initially competed with African-Americans for the worst work (particularly with regard to labouring or domestic service), they were eventually able to dominate and then segregate many of these occupations.

During the 1860s, however, the Irish were still considered to be an alien people within America. Mass migration created infamous Irish ghettoes in cities like New York and Boston. The Fenian Brotherhood found no shortage of supporters, many of whom had military experience, within the creaking tenements and dirty streets of New York's Five Points and elsewhere. Exiles like Jeremiah O'Donovan Rossa, the notable Irish patriot and leader of the 'dynamite campaign', could find sanctuary and succour in the United States in a way in which he could not in Australia or elsewhere within the British Empire. By 1871 O'Donovan Rossa had become the 'proprietor of a Five Points saloon' and ran as a Republican Party candidate for a seat in the New York State Senate.[34]

The growing 'Fenian menace' terrified the British authorities. A Sydney newspaper from October 1865 reported on a massive Fenian rally in New York where an estimated thirty thousand Irish-Americans (and police spies) had turned out to hear Colonel William R. Roberts proclaim that 'Blood must wash out what blood and crime have stained,' to the booming cheers of the crowd.[35] It was not just empty rhetoric. The Fenians displayed a fearsome readiness to engage in acts of sabotage and violence, provoking British newspapers (along with their offshoots in far off colonial Australia) into fits of vitriolic comdemnation.

For example, on 20 November 1867 (a month after Bernard Wootton's hanging) *The Inquirer* – republishing an account from the *London Telegraph* – reported to concerned readers in Western Australia on the Fenian menace. The language was intentionally viral:

> We have never doubted that Fenianism, though temporarily suppressed, was anything but extinguished – that from time to time the chronic disorder would develop acute symptoms, and that we should see occasional paroxyms of a more or less serious nature. We were not in the least surprised, therefore, to learn the other day that it has broken out in a fresh place. Fenianism is a cutaneous eruption, indicative of morbid humours in the system, and we cannot hope to expel it by external applications. We only drive back it for a while into the blood, to crop up in new developments.[36]

Alas, *The Inquirer* informed its readers, 'the disease has broken out virulently in Manchester'. Indeed, England became the principal battleground between the Fenian movement and the British state.

At Manchester an attack had been made on a police van in September 1867 and some Fenian prisoners freed. In the raid a policeman was shot dead. On 23 November 1867 three Irishmen – known forever after in Ireland as the 'Manchester Martyrs' – were hanged for the murder of the policeman. For nearly two minutes one of the condemned Irishmen, Larkin, could be seen desperately kicking in agony as he dangled from the gallows. His misery was only ended when the hangman grabbed his legs and pulled on them, breaking his neck.[37] Although the British press condemned them as 'terrorists', the 'Manchester Martyrs' were mourned and venerated throughout the Irish diaspora.

By December 1867 even *The Inquirer* was concerned by the climate of violent retribution in the English newspapers, commenting that a 'portion of the press not obscurely threatens the Irish living in England with Lynch law if these "Fenian outrages" are repeated'.[38] They did not have to wait long. After more Fenians were captured by English police, a conspiracy had been hatched to free them from prison. At Clerkenwell during December 1867 Fenian activists attempted to blow a hole in the prison wall and rescue their imprisoned comrades. The size of the bomb caused extensive damage not only to the prison wall but to the neighbouring working class houses as well, resulting in the unnecessary death, maiming or mutilation of more than two dozen civilians.

The last public hanging ever held in England was of a Fenian political prisoner, Michael Barrett, who went to his death on 26 May 1868 after being found guilty of the disastrous Clerkenwell bombing. Barrett's public hanging was a terrible spectacle, with a newspaper later reporting that Barrett's 'protruding tongue and swollen distorted features' had been visible under the white cotton execution hood, 'as if they were part of some hideous masquerading'.[39] He too was mourned in Ireland and throughout the diaspora, particularly as questions were raised about the fairness of his trial.

When convict transportation to Western Australia finally ceased in 1868 it was an infamous batch of Irish Fenians who had the dubious distinction of being among the last shipment of offenders dispatched in chains to the antipodes. The mere idea that Fenians – 'Irish terrorists' – should be sent to Swan River sent shivers down the spines of most West Australians. As they were soon to discover, one of the Fenians sent to Fremantle was none other than the treasonous James Flood, a close friend of the Fenian leader James Stephens and a man who had been responsible for smuggling arms into Ireland. The others were considered to be of a similarly diabolical ilk. Seventeen of the Fenians had served in the British Army and been found guilty of mutiny. Seven of these soldiers who had deserted after their plot was uncovered had been, literally, scarred by the British – they had capital 'D's carved into their chests with an awl. Most of the deserters had been sentenced to death before having the sentence commuted to transportation.[40]

Given the alleged character of such Irishmen, the bitterness and sarcasm of the editor at *The Inquirer* could barely be contained:

> It seems from this that the English Government, fearing that Western Australia may recover too soon from the injurious effects of convictism, are determined to make the last dose of poison the strongest of all. The convicts by this ship are said to be of the worst kind, including, as it will be seen, a sprinkling of the Fenian traitors, to give variety to the ruffianism of Western Australia.[41]

Interestingly, the Fenians – *enroute* to Australia – interpreted their own convict transportation with sarcasm and humour. Aboard the *Hougoumont* the Fenians crafted their own newspaper, arduously hand copying and distributing the publication below deck. In one edition of the Fenian newspaper, John Edward Kelly (an Irish-American) wrote about Western Australia:

This great continent of the south, having been discovered by some Dutch skipper and his crew, somewhere between the 1st and 19th centuries of the Christian era, was, in consequence taken possession of by the Government of Great Britain, in accordance with that just and equitable maxim, 'What's yours is mine; what's mine's my own'. That magnanimous government in the kindly exuberance of their feelings, have placed a large portion of that immense tract of country at our disposal, generously defraying all expenses incurred on our way to it, and providing retreats for us there to secure us from the inclemency of the seasons...[42]

Never in the entire eighty-year history of convict transportation to Australia had felons mocked their dismal penal servitude with such sharp literary resilience.

However, not all the Fenians were impressed with Western Australia. In letters home to Ireland John Casey denounced the 'thick-skulled' and 'narrow minded bigotry of the colonists'. Writing for the *Irishman* on 4 June 1870, during the third year of his penitential exile, Casey shared his view of the Swan River Colony:

'The population of Western Australia may be divided into two classes – those actually in prison, and those who more richly deserve to be there'...What more can be expected from a nation of felons. Murder and murderous assaults are manly sports to the colonists...they live and die like dogs...More real depravity, more shocking wickedness, more undisguised vice and immorality is to be witnessed at midday in the most public thoroughfares of Perth, with its population of 1,500, than in any other city of fifty times its population, either in Europe or America.[43]

Ironically, while the Fenians were still at sea *The Inquirer* had attacked those 'alarmists' among the Fremantle population who were predicting that the feared 'Irish rebels' would be assisted by the 'Yankee brotherhood', who will 'make a raid upon us and rescue them'.[44] History, famously, turned out to prove the alarmists correct and *The Inquirer*'s learned editor wrong, with the 1876 escape from Fremantle of six Fenians aboard the American whaler *The Catalpa* being perhaps the greatest and most dramatic rescue story in all of Australia's penal history.[45]

The escaped Fremantle Fenians were greeted as heroes in America, with their dramatic arrival in Manhattan being reported in the *New York Times*:

The Fenian military prisoners who escaped from the penal colony of Western Australia, on board the bark *Catalpa*, on April 17, arrived in this City at 2 o'clock yesterday morning…The news of their arrival soon spread among all classes of their sympathizing countrymen, and O'Donovan Rossa's hotel was besieged with visitors anxious to congratulate the Irish patriots on their happy rescue from penal servitude.[46]

The *New York Times*, perhaps conscious of the large numbers of Irish-American readers resident in New York, described the Fremantle Fenians as 'fairly intelligent-looking men'. They were certainly not the ape-like terrorist monsters some people imagined them to be, although the *Times* commented that 'their sunburnt, emaciated faces, tell a tale of suffering and hardship'.[47] New York was, however, another world. Even before the *Catalpa* escape the fear caused by 'Fenian outrages' – including assassinations, bombings and prison escapes – caused anti-Irish sentiment, drawing on pre-existing colonial prejudice, to assume monstrous proportions within the British Empire. For example, the stereotypical Irishman became progressively more 'inhuman' in the cartoons drawn in English newspapers, as the Irish started to resemble violent, uncivilised apes in the minds of much of the British public.

The work of John Tenniel, who became chief cartoonist for the popular *Punch* magazine, was particularly influential. Tenniel, who is better known as the original creative illustrator of *Alice in Wonderland*, did not just draw Fenians as Celtic gorillas, he turned them into vile bloodthirsty monsters. For example, in one of his cartoons entitled 'The Fenian-Pest' (published in *Punch* on 3 March 1866) a matronly Britannia protects her frightened sister Hibernia from an ape-like crowd of sinister Fenians. 'What,' asks Hibernia, 'are we to do with these troublesome people?' 'Try isolation first,' responds Britannia, 'and then…' As Douglas, Harte and O'Hara argue in their history of Anglo-Irish relations:

The clue to the advice is in the cartoon title, a play on rinderpest, a disease which was widely prevalent among livestock in the mid-1860s and attracted much public attention. In the case of diseased cattle, the recommended treatment would have been 'isolation' followed by slaughter.[48]

No wonder most West Australians wanted to quarantine their colony from the Fenian disease.

::

In October 1867, the same month that Bernard Wootton appeared before the Supreme Court, *The Inquirer* reproduced an article on 'The Irish Convicts and Their Grievances'. Surveying the Irish mind and alluding to the growth of Fenian sentiments among the Irish diaspora, the article argued that:

> A power of imagination which can at will create a heaven or a hell out of a few wretched rafters and an acre or two, a facility and a power of language which can give force and life and colouring to the finest or the wildest conceptions of the imagination, a wondrous poetry of feeling and expression, have all been lavished on the Irish nation; but they have been neutralized, perverted, and made profitless by the most untoward combination of misdirected views, misapplied energies, and misplaced stubbornness.[49]

While the focus of the article was the most recent 'Fenian outbreak' in England and Ireland, the view of the Irish as wild, poetic and passionate malcontents was a widely held stereotype. People like Bernard Wootton both suffered under, and reinforced, that view. That he went to his death with a 'shout for the Irish republic' was, like his refusal of religious counsel, a deliberate defiance of the British system of justice, government and propriety that was about to hang him.[50] Whether he held genuine Fenian sympathies, beyond his departing republican declaration, is unclear. Nevertheless, such words from the mouth of the condemned man and former 'bushranger' did little to ease the conviction that he was a dangerous villain.

Nor was he alone. Two years earlier another irredeemable Irishman, Thomas Bushell, had also suffered the extreme penalty of the law. Born in Ireland in 1834, Bushell joined the British Army as a young man and served at Malta before being charged with striking an officer in 1856. For this crime he was given a life sentence. He was twenty-two years old at the time of his conviction and served some prison time in England before being transported to Western Australia for the remainder of his life sentence. He arrived in Fremantle during November 1858 aboard the *Edwin Fox* and was sent to work in the prison kitchen. By January 1859 he was in trouble for destroying prison property and was sent to the punishment cells. Following an unsuccessful suicide attempt he was transferred to the Lunatic Asylum and given the, one suspects, rather unhelpful palliative of solitary confinement. After various violent interludes with warders at the Asylum over a period of several months, Bushell was transferred back to prison.[51]

Bushell was constantly at odds with the prison authorities. He was flogged on several occasions (including at least one punishment of 100 lashes), placed in irons numerous times (including one stint of eight months), given a restricted diet of bread and water, and locked in solitary confinement for weeks on end – all to no avail. Finally, during July 1865 Bushell stabbed a warder, stood trial, and was sentenced to death. He was hanged on 12 September 1865. More than a century later historian Margaret Brown was drawn to the story of Thomas Bushell, 'Probationary Prisoner 5270':

> Was Thomas Bushell a tough, determined rebel who refused to be cowed by arrogant men and a brutal system, or a stubborn, violent thug who would not accept the opportunities for a new beginning that the prison and the colony offered, or perhaps a simple man subject to fits of violent insanity? In the final analysis it is only in the terse records of official punishments that he exists at all, and they hardly allow one to choose.[52]

Examining Bushell's records at Fremantle Prison and the nearby Lunatic Asylum, Brown discovered that:

> The page allotted to him in the Character Books is so cramped with entries that they are difficult to read. There was no punishment in the penal repertoire that he did not bring upon himself between July 1859 and his execution, with threats of violence, persistent insubordination, refusal to work and absconding from work depots.[53]

It was only when the Irishman appeared before Chief Justice Burt on 6 September 1865, charged with attempted murder, that he was able to speak publicly in his own defence. As Brown writes, 'It is not the voice of a hardened or brutal man.' Instead Bushell simply told the court that:

> I am sorry for what I have done. I was urged to it by my fellow-prisoners. I have been in Her Majesty's service, and suffered much as a soldier. I was in the Russian campaign, and was wounded there. I was drunk at the time I committed the offence; but I say again I did not intend to kill Warder Hollis.[54]

One can only imagine how the image of a drunken Irish prisoner careering around Fremantle Prison and stabbing a warder with a knife must have appeared to the jury and Chief Justice. In the words of the *Perth Gazette*, although the Chief Justice was still recovering from a severe bout of illness, the presence of a Thomas Bushell inspired him to summon his remaining strength. 'His Honour,' they wrote, 'passed the sentence of Death in a most impressive manner, holding out no hopes of mercy.'[55] Like fellow Irishman Bernard Wootton, it was almost as if Thomas Bushell had been on a suicidal battle of wills with the British establishment. He would not bend, and so they broke him.

::

In 1867 Fenian fantasies and nightmares abounded in Western Australia. Among sections of the colonial establishment, isolation from England and the very remoteness of the colony exacerbated fears of Fenianism. Leading gentlemen like Charles Manning, the wealthy merchant and Captain of the armed Fremantle Volunteers, reported that:

> ...for some time past I have had news given to me of a probable rising among the bond people of Fremantle and inmates of the Convict Establishment, their holding possession of the town for a few hours and seizing vessels in harbour, carrying off what booty they could secure and such women as they might in their raid take a fancy to.[56]

If the image of a Fenian convict takeover of Fremantle – more like a pirate raid, complete with rapine and booty – didn't strike fear into settler hearts, then other images would. George Walpole Leake, the Crown Solicitor of Western Australia, wrote to the governor's military secretary advising him that few, if any, buildings in Fremantle could withstand the impact of a Fenian cannonball fired from the harbour. Indeed, it seemed possible that:

> A Fenian privateer might destroy all the government buildings on Rottnest, sink a merchant vessel or two and destroy all Fremantle without landing or losing a man merely because there is not even a gunboat to prevent her.[57]

Fresh 'outbreaks' of Fenianism continued to be reported in the West Australian press throughout 1867 and 1868. For example, the 17 April 1868 edition of the *Perth Gazette* carried three full columns of news about the latest Fenian outrages, arrests, riots and trials in England, Ireland and Australia – including testimony from the Clerkenwell bombing case in England, and the trial of deranged Henry O'Farrell for the attempted assassination of the Duke of Edinburgh in Sydney.[58]

On 24 April 1868 a large 'Indignation Meeting' was held in Perth, attended by the governor, regarding the attempted assassination of the British Queen's son, who was visiting Australia, by an alleged Fenian. According to the *Perth Gazette*:

> The Court House on Friday last was filled by one of the largest, if not the largest, assemblages of the settlers and inhabitants of the colony that has ever met together in Public Meeting. High and low, rich and poor, all were there, animated with one desire – to take a part in the expression of the feeling of horror and indignation excited by the intelligence of the attack upon the life of the Duke of Edinburgh.[59]

Details of the meeting ran over five columns in the *Perth Gazette*, pushing all other stories aside. The governor, speaking to the packed Court House, remarked that:

> There were a few Fenian convicts now in this colony and they endeavour to call themselves political prisoners, but this was a luxury in which he could not indulge them; they were treason-felony convicts.[60]

Fenianism would not be allowed to take root in Western Australia said the governor. Outrages would not be permitted, and if Fenian terrorism did 'show its face', the governor would ruthlessly and 'speedily stamp it out'. The crowd were in rapturous agreement.[61] Faced with the reality of Fenian convicts in Fremantle, along with the violence of men like Henry O'Farrell or Bernard Wootton, some among the Irish and Catholic communities sought to distance themselves from the Fenians. For example, at the 'Indignation Meeting' in Perth one of the speakers had been 'the very Rev. Martin Griver', the 'R.C. Administrator', who begged the crowd to understand his predicament.

> He trusted that no one would be weak enough to consider all Roman Catholics and Irish as Fenians. All good Catholics and loyal Irish will condemn and

reprobate this vile act. He felt deeply the anguish the Royal Mother would feel on hearing the news...[62]

Despite Fr Griver's actions, objections to Fenianism often continued to be wrapped up in anti-Irish prejudice. For example, in July 1868 a settler had written to the *Perth Gazette* complaining that employers were still not getting the sorts of labourers they required. Above all others, they desired:

> English and Scotch ploughmen and shepherds, instead of Irish spademen, and some decent English and Scotch single women for domestic servants, instead of our usual assortment of the sweepings of Irish poorhouses and English brothels which it has been the pleasure, for some years past, of Mr Walcott and his brother Emigration Commissioners to send us.[63]

While the 'Fenian menace' weakened during the 1870s, the Irish continued to be seen as politically suspect and culturally distant. They also continued to be viewed as a source of potential sedition and discord. In 1897, 1901 and 1904 there were riots in Coolgardie and Boulder, in the Eastern Goldfields, when the sectarian Orange Order organised Twelfth of July commemoration marches, only to be physically confronted by angry Irish-Australians. Miners armed with Gaelic hurleys clashed with Orangemen wielding their ceremonial swords in a most un-orderly fashion. In one case the police had to draw their revolvers to quell the disorder.[64]

The debates around Australian Federation brought eventual respite. People we now call 'Anglo-Celts' became the cultural and demographic core of the new federal Commonwealth of Australia and old divisions ceased to be as polarising as they had once been. Nevertheless, as late as 1919 the parading of Irish-Australians on Saint Patrick's Day was still seen as potentially subversive. That year the Perth City Council placed such strict demands on the Saint Patrick's Day parade's organisers that one of them denounced the 'outbreak of everyday dirty bigotry'.[65] The parade organisers were instructed that the British Union Jack flag must be carried at the head of the procession and there was concern that speeches might contain comments critical of the British military occupation of Ireland. In evidence of changing times, however, the *Sunday Times* mocked the Council, pointing out that if 'seditious speeches are made', then this was a matter 'for the proper authorities and not for the meddlesome supervisors of footpaths and drains'.[66] The 1919 parade went ahead without incident.

Clearly, the Irish were no longer the civil threat that they were once imagined to be. Their alleged inherent political, cultural and religious difference was now to be incorporated and tolerated (even annually paraded and celebrated), rather than suppressed. Although it would take well into the 1960s for the old sectarian animus to truly expire in Australia, men like Bernard Wootton ceased to haunt the colony. The Irish had been mainstreamed.

7

Cannibalism and Stolen Children:
The Strange Case of Mullagelly, 1873

A young boy is cannibalised, a crime for which two men are hanged. The need to protect children attracts the attention of church and state.

In March 1830, less than a year after British settlers had first arrived at the Swan River, a 'golden haired and engaging' young boy of about four years of age, Bonny Dutton, went missing. This was the primal fear of every settler parent in the wilds of Australia – a child lost in the infinite vastness of the bush who would die of thirst or hunger before becoming carrion for the crows. Or perhaps drowned in the Swan River or the gurgling surf that lapped at the dry edges of the continent. Although a search party was organised, weeks passed with no sign of Bonny Dutton the golden haired innocent. It was assumed the child was lost forever.

Then suddenly, miraculously, some Aborigines came into the European settlement accompanied by young Bonny Dutton. He was unharmed and healthy. The Aborigines had come into town for the purpose of returning him. Observing these strange whites now living on their ancestral lands, they had simply 'borrowed' the golden haired boy to 'show to their wives and children.'[1] Unfortunately, time has not recorded Bonny Dutton's own impressions of his childhood adventure as a travelling anthropological curiosity with the *Nyoongar*. One can only imagine.

Thirty-five years later on 5 October 1865 little Francis Dunne, only three months away from his fourth birthday, disappeared at Yanganooka, in the Victoria district several hundred kilometres north of Perth. Francis had been walking back to the family's home after having lunch when he innocently wandered off into the bush. Over two hundred local settlers joined the search party. After a desperate reconnaissance of the area all hope was relinquished for the child's safe return. His family mourned. The white community lamented another young soul lost to the wilderness of Western Australia.[2]

At the time of the search 'native trackers' had followed the footprints of young Francis Dunne (who was without shoes) to a cattle track that led, eventually, to a small spring of water. The boy's hand and footprints could clearly be seen around the spring as he, presumably, stopped to get a drink in the hot sun. The tracks then led off into the bush. In evidence later offered in court, however, Francis Dunne's father Edward claimed that, 'the native trackers declined to proceed further'. The tracks were leading in the direction of 'Megrew Well' but given the distance and heat there seemed little chance the boy could survive. The search party turned back.[3]

A year later Frank Parker was labouring about fifteen kilometres north-east of Yanganooka (where Francis's father, Edward, had been a miner). Parker had been working clearing out Megrew Well when he discovered 'the skeleton of a child's foot floating on the surface of the water'.[4] Parker, horrified with his grisly find, turned his attentions to the dirt he had already dug out of the well. Sifting through he found, 'fragments of a child's straw hat, remnants of a child's frock of the same material, and trimmed with the same peculiar pattern of braid' as worn by Francis Dunne when he disappeared. Parker immediately sent word to Edward Dunne, Francis's bereaved father, who came and collected the grim remains of his son's skeleton and clothing from Megrew Well.[5]

As news of the discovery at Megrew Well spread, suspicions were aroused that the circumstances of young Francis's disappearance the previous year were not so innocent after all. A search party was reconstituted to dig out the rest of the well and search the surrounding bush. More bone fragments were found nearby, including a piece of a child's shoulder blade and the young boy's skull, 'to which was attached portions of hair'.[6]

The renewed search of 1866 yielded no suspects. No one was arrested or charged with responsibility for young Francis Dunne's disappearance or death. Then in July 1873, almost eight years after the Dunne boy first disappeared, two local Aborigines, Mullagelly and Yaradee (also recorded as Muragelly and Garadie), were in the Geraldton lock-up when Mullagelly was observed by a 'native constable' to be crying. After a brief discussion, a white policeman was summoned. A distraught Mullagelly then allegedly confessed to killing little Francis Dunne. Mullagelly said that he and his friends had roasted the child over a fire and eaten him. Indeed, Mullagelly later took Constable Arthur

Patton into the bush to visit the site of the alleged cannibalism, pointing out the remains of the fire and the location of the initial attack on the young child. He then led the Constable and Corporal Sullivan to a gully where some more bones of the child were recovered.[7]

The very worst fears of the white colonists had finally been realised. What a degraded race of people, they opined, could produce savages who would abduct, murder and eat a child – the most vulnerable, innocent and precious section of society.

::

By the early 1870s the white population of Western Australia was around 25,000 people.[8] The south-eastern portion of the colony was settled, although most of the north, along with the central desert regions, still remained largely unexplored and unconquered by Europeans. Nevertheless, British law and order had, for the most part, been successfully imposed upon Swan River and its outlying pastoral satellites. The local press even felt compelled to congratulate the judiciary on its recent dispensation of justice:

> Another session of the Supreme Court in its criminal jurisdiction is ended, and the excitement and bustle consequent upon the administration of justice, the attendance of witnesses and juries, is over once more. Everywhere, at all times, there is something imposing and impressive in the assemblage of courts of law, and the disposal of offenders against the majesty of that law; but the interest is considerably increased in cases where offenders stand at the bar charged with capital crimes.[9]

The Inquirer was worried, however, by the large numbers of cases where the accused did not have legal representation.

> We allude to wretched prisoners charged capitally, and who, friendless and by reason of sheer poverty, are undefended. Surely, it is a painful spectacle to see a fellow creature – for whether white or black, after all, he is a fellow creature – stand charged with an offence for which he is in danger of forfeiting his life, and the unhappy man without an advocate to watch his case or plead his cause.[10]

The newspaper commented that in such cases any accused who attempted to defend himself appeared like 'a fly caught in a cobweb – the more he

struggles, the more hopeless his case becomes.'[11] Of particular concern were
Aborigines on trial for murder. The newspaper, referring to a recent case,
wrote that:

> With all the kindly instincts of our race, with all the Englishman's proverbial,
> not to say boastful, love of justice and fair play, yet here were to be witnessed
> four helpless, friendless savages, with their lives at stake, thrown on their own
> miserable resources for support, while opposed to them was a properly-qualified
> and acute advocate, the law officer of the Crown...[12]

The newspaper was not for a moment suggesting that Aborigines should
not be held accountable for the 'brutal' and 'revolting' crimes they
committed:

> While we admit all this, and while we also admit that no distinction should be
> made between the black man and the white, when placed on trial for offences
> against the law of our land, we must also state our firm conviction that the
> blacks have not, in our courts of justice, those advantages which are possessed
> by the white man.[13]

What *The Inquirer* was arguing for was, essentially, free court-appointed
legal defence for all accused regardless of race. However, the public's view
of Aborigines (as represented in *The Inquirer's* throwaway comment about
'friendless savages'), meant that even where Aborigines did have legal
representation, racial prejudice usually mitigated against the possibility of a
fair trial. In Western Australia when the victim was white and the accused
Aboriginal, white juries did not (with very few exceptions) find Aborigines
not guilty, even when the evidence was scarce and circumstantial. The reverse,
however, was certainly not true.[14]

The commonsense view of Aborigines at the time was that they were lazy,
childlike, treacherous, thieving and barbarous. Around towns where defeated,
dispossessed and partly 'de-tribalised' groups of Aborigines were struggling to
survive, alcoholism was also becoming an increasing problem. The poverty and
violence that was often a feature of life in these precarious camps confirmed
stereotypes. In October 1873, for example, *The Inquirer* railed against colonists
who had, in contravention of a law passed thirty years earlier, provided alcohol
to Aborigines in Perth.

Too often, in days gone by, did our columns bear testimony to gross outrages perpetrated by intoxicated and infuriated natives on unoffending persons, principally women, and it seemed very certain, at one time in our colonial history, that in the neighbourhood of towns where aborigines congregated no man's life was safe, and no woman's honour secure, owing to the foolish and reprehensible practice of giving intoxicating liquor to the blacks.[15]

In the opinion of *The Inquirer*, it was only while under the influence of alcohol that an Aborigine's 'condition of quiet childishness' could be turned into 'demonical fury'. And while some colonists thought it 'fine fun to "make a darkey drunk"', the results were 'scenes of debauchery and savage fighting'. Similar arguments had originally led to the Publicans Act of 1843, which made it illegal for settlers to supply Aborigines with liquor. While condemning 'with what force our feeble pen can command' those who plied Aborigines with alcohol, *The Inquirer* was no more enamoured of tee-totaling Christians working to convert Aborigines. 'We have,' the newspaper wrote, 'very little faith in any kind of missionary work among the Aborigines, unless it leads them to labour for their living.'[16] Basically, Aborigines were considered to be an unredeemable remnant of a defeated people who clogged the courts, and whose presence blighted the streets, but not the conscience, of the colony.

::

During the nineteenth century it was widely believed that Aboriginal people were cannibals. It was assumed that because Aborigines were 'primitive' and 'savage' that they must naturally therefore also eat human flesh. Such reasoning said more about the irrational fears of European settlers than it did about the Indigenous people they encountered. However, only a few months after the arrival of the First Fleet in 1788 British Marine Captain Watkin Tench, writing of his encounters with Aborigines, commented that:

> From their manner of disposing of those who die...as well as from every other observation, there seems no reason to suppose these people cannibals.[17]

Similarly, when Nathaniel Ogle wrote his *Manual for Emigrants* in 1839, he took care to mention that:

> The Aborigines of Australia have been represented so degraded as to scarce deserve to be classed among the human species; and that has been given

as a reason for their indiscriminate extermination. The charge is false: they are not known to be cannibals; they neither scalp, nor roast or torture their captives.[18]

In fact, there is no credible evidence that any group of Australian Aborigines commonly practised cannibalism. The most that could be said is that, as Katherine Biber put it, 'in some areas, in rare circumstances, and in the conduct of rituals', some Aboriginal people 'practised some forms of anthropophagy, notably mortuary cannibalism'.[19] This, however, was a very different and restricted practice as compared to the murderous feasts of flesh imagined by colonial authors and aspiring anthropologists alike. There was certainly no tradition anywhere in Australia of Aborigines eating Europeans.

Nevertheless, the widespread and disorienting fear of cannibalism persisted. For example, on 23 December 1826 a white shepherd named Henry Preston, and his loyal dog, went missing on the New South Wales frontier. His employer, John Jamieson, suspected he may have been killed by local Aborigines. Jamieson armed himself and set out with two men towards a local Aboriginal camp. There he 'arrested' ten Aborigines, including five children, and accused them of being responsible for the disappearance of Preston. After intense questioning and threats, the Aboriginal children eventually revealed that an Aboriginal man called 'Hole-in-the-book' had murdered Preston. The savage brute had even slayed his dog![20]

Most disturbing of all was the fact that the Aborigines also confessed – in response to Jamieson's unrelenting interrogation – that Hole-in-the-book had actually dismembered, roasted and cannibalised Preston. Upon request, and under duress, bones and innards from the cannibalised victim were produced. Jamieson and his posse rode on. After eventually tracking down and capturing Hole-in-the-book, preparations were made for an immediate hanging. Seeing the rope, Hole-in-the-book broke free and made a run for it. He was gunned down by Jamieson and killed.[21]

The matter appeared settled. Except that on 3 January 1827, eleven days after his disappearance, Henry Preston walked out of the bush alive. He had been lost and had walked around eighty kilometres trying to find his way home. No one must have been more shocked than John Jamieson. Preston's reappearance changed everything and Jamieson was now arrested and charged with the manslaughter of Hole-in-the-book. However, at Jamieson's trial:

Two surgeons testified that, in their opinion, the bones discovered were human bones. Those witnesses who had contact with the local Aboriginal group testified that the Aborigines had identified Hole-in-the-Book as Preston's murderer. One doctor testified that the Aborigines claimed that a black woman had eaten the murdered man's arm and that, even after Preston was found alive, they maintained that a 'flour-headed' man had been killed and eaten.[22]

The court found Jamieson innocent on the grounds that his assumption that Hole-in-the-book had cannibalised Preston constituted 'justifiable homicide'.[23] Or in other words, the fact that Preston hadn't actually been killed or eaten didn't matter. What mattered was that Jamieson believed that he had. In this case, coerced 'confessions' and colonial anxiety of being cannibalised by 'black savages' provided legal justification for murder.

::

Perth's newspapers carried the macabre and gory details of the Francis Dunne case to a curious West Australian public. After they were charged with the murder of little Francis Dunne, Mullagelly and Yaradee appeared in the Supreme Court on 3 October 1873 in front of Acting Chief Justice Hocking. It was argued that on 5 October 1865 the two men had 'feloniously, wilfully and with malice' kidnapped, killed and eaten young Francis Edward William Dunne, 'the son of a farmer residing at Champion Bay' (Geraldton). As *The Inquirer* reported:

> The particulars of the case are sad and revolting in the extreme. The Crown Solicitor in addressing the jury said it had fallen to his lot, for the first time in the history of the colony, to detail in a court of justice the details of a murder accompanied by cannibalism.[24]

Young Francis Dunne was described by the Crown prosecutor as 'a fair-headed, plump, fresh-complexioned boy' – the perfect target for hungry black cannibals. According to the prosecutor, on the day of the murder in 1865 four Aborigines had been walking from the Geraldine Mines when they discovered the young white boy 'picking gum'. As *The Inquirer*, paraphrasing one of the accused cannibals, recounted:

> Being sulky and hungry, one of the natives went up to the child and throttled him, and subsequently killed him by hitting him on the nape of the neck with a

dowark. They carried the body a distance of about two miles, and, having made a fire, roasted it and then eat it. Billoo eat two fingers, Mullagelly partook of the buttocks, Yarradee eat part of the legs, Nungdamara (the missing native) eat the child's heart and also portions of his legs. [25]

Indeed, they ate 'the whole child between them, (except the feet, head and arms) as they were very hungry'. [26]

Afterwards the Aborigines allegedly wrapped the boy's head, hands and feet up in his clothes and threw them down Megrew's Well where they were to be accidentally discovered, nine months later, by a horrified Frank Parker. Their appetite satiated, they then returned to their own country in the Murchison River district. Concluding its coverage of the trial, *The Inquirer* recorded that:

> Such, briefly told, are the revolting details of this horrible murder…The prisoners, in fact, acknowledged the truthfulness of the statement volunteered by the native Billoo, who had turned Queen's evidence. The jury, after a few minutes deliberation, found the prisoners guilty, and sentence of death was recorded. This concluded the business of the sessions, and the Court rose at a quarter past six o'clock. [27]

In his official confession taken in Geraldton and later submitted to the Supreme Court in Perth, Mullagelly had freely admitted to having 'roasted' and eaten young Francis Dunne. He also confessed to throwing the boy's clothes in the well. Mullagelly made an 'X' for his signature, and the statement was also signed by Toby, the Aboriginal translator. [28] Intriguingly, however, the most damning evidence against the two 'native cannibals', Mullagelly and Yaradee, actually came from another Aborigine, Billoo, who had been involved in the murder but saved himself from the hangman's rope by testifying for the prosecution. Or as the *Perth Gazette* reported:

> There was another native, named Billoo, in custody on the same charge, but, being a mere lad when the murder was committed, he was admitted Queen's evidence. [29]

Billoo was about fourteen years old at the time of the court case and according to the Police, he had 'lived with whites since he was a child'. When news of the gruesome discovery at Megrew Well had spread, it was Billoo who had actually attended the crime scene in the company of Police Corporal Sullivan. Seven years later Billoo was arrested and charged as an accomplice in the murder of little Francis Dunne on the basis of Mullagelly's confession.[30]

It was Billoo whose evidence had been transcribed and published in the local newspapers, including his confession that the Aborigines had killed Dunne after coming across him in the bush, because they were hungry and 'sulky'. According to Billoo it was Yaradee's idea to murder the little boy, and it had been Yaradee who had attacked and killed young Dunne with his dowark. Mullagelly had carried the dead boy on his back a distance of about two miles before they built a fire to cook him over, like he was a felled kangaroo. Billoo confessed to eating at least two fingers of the child, while the others ate the rest of the corpse.[31] Billoo, who was about six years old when these horrible events had taken place, said that he was only a 'little fellow' at the time, not much taller or older than the Dunne boy whom he helped cannibalise.[32]

Billoo is a fascinating character. Although he participated in the cannibalisation of young Francis Dunne in 1865, he later played the key role in sending his two Aboriginal friends to the gallows. He was no more than a child himself when Dunne was murdered, a highly vulnerable fourteen-year-old witness when the case went to trial in 1873. Besides saving himself from the hangman's rope, it is intriguing to ponder what he must have made of the proceedings that seemed to depend so much upon his words and memory.

At their Supreme Court trial, Mullagelly and Yaradee were apparently given the chance to cross-examine Billoo, although, according to the court translator, they said only that, 'the evidence given by Billoo was the truth'.[33] The Jury retired, the verdict was delivered, and the two Aboriginal men were sentenced to death. Mullagelly and Yaradee were hanged at Perth Gaol on 16 October 1873.[34] They were the first, and last, West Australians to hang for murder accompanied by cannibalism. The Dunne family continued to mourn the loss of their child, and most white colonists, who passionately supported the execution of the two Aborigines, went to bed thinking that at last the savage and cannibalistic tendencies of 'the natives' had been revealed for the whole world to see.

::

In the remote northern and interior regions of Western Australia, Christianity and pastoral invasion were virtually synchronic. Violence between pastoralists (often backed by police) and Aborigines defending their lands was frequent. Everywhere the defeated Aboriginal survivors – ravaged by introduced diseases and affected by the loss of traditional hunting grounds as much as by the superiority of European bullets – often coagulated around Christian missions. While the missionaries denounced violence by settlers against Aboriginal people and sometimes offered the only effective sanctuary from further bloodshed, the Christian missions consciously presented themselves to the Colonial government as the only institutions present, willing and capable of 'saving' Aboriginal people from the 'backwardness' of their own uncivilised ways. The government, in turn, saw the Christian missions as playing an essential role when it began removing de-tribalised Aboriginal 'fringe dwellers' from the outskirts of remote towns.

While denouncing the behaviour of those who abused Aborigines, Christian missionaries were caught in a contradictory position. Protestant and Catholic missions were built upon Aboriginal land and in many ways their success depended upon the ongoing dispossession and social dislocation of the Aborigines they had ambitions to 'save'. In general, Aborigines entered the Missions in large numbers only when their traditional societies were substantially weakened by the corrosive activities of white expansion (pastoralism, mining, etc.). The Missions provided sanctuary for defeated peoples. Moreover, although Christians taught that all men were brothers in Christ, many of the Missions forbade marriages between whites and blacks (as was the Law) and where possible, even prevented marriages between Aboriginal 'full bloods' and 'half castes'. Christian missionaries were not immune from the racial prejudice of the age. [35]

Increasingly, missionary attentions fell upon Aboriginal children, whom they considered to be ripe for salvation. It was here that they felt they had the best chance of saving souls and rebuilding Aboriginal society in their own spiritual image. It was an orientation that was to eventually produce the 'stolen generations' and all its tragedies.

Besides Christian missionaries, by the 1870s another group of people to display a distinct interest in Aboriginal society and their children were anthropologists. Among the most famous of these was Daisy Bates, who for thirty-five years of her life lived alongside outback Aborigines. While dutifully maintaining her lady-like demeanour (she always dressed in a long heavy skirt, hat and gloves, despite the heat), Daisy is credited with being a founder of the anthropological study of Australia's Indigenous people. Her book, *The*

Passing of the Aborigines, also served to reassure white Australians that kind, enlightened people like herself were doing all they could, as the phrase went, to 'smoothe the pillow' of a dying race.[36]

On the inside cover of the 1966 edition of *The Passing of the Aborigines*, Daisy is photographed sitting on the porch behind a row of flowers. Umbrella in hand and with a face of grim benevolence, she appears like an anthropological Mary Poppins – the woman who gave up everything to live among Aboriginal Australians. The introduction to the volume, penned by Arthur Mee, is heliographic.

> The race on the fringe of the continent has been there about a hundred years, and stands for Civilization; the race in the interior has been there no man knows how long, and stands for Barbarism. Between them a woman has lived in a little white tent for more than twenty years, watching over these people for the sake of the Flag, a woman alone, the solitary spectator of a vanishing race. She is Daisy Bates...[37]

Daisy shared the pessimism of some within the white establishment regarding the futility of missionary work among Aborigines. In a section of *The Passing of the Aborigines* detailing how Catholic Bishop Salvado of New Norcia sent five Aboriginal boys to Rome to study for the priesthood, Daisy retells how they 'died in Europe, with the exception of one, who returned to New Norcia, promptly flung away his habit, made for the bush and died there'. Her conclusions were profoundly dismal:

> It was the same story everywhere, a kindness that killed as surely and as swiftly as cruelty would have done. The Australian native can withstand all the reverses of nature, fiendish droughts and sweeping floods, horrors of thirst and enforced starvation – but he cannot withstand civilization... There is no hope of protecting the Stone Age from the twentieth century![38]

Daisy's essential thesis was that if Australia was to be brought into the fold of British civilisation (and she clearly believed it should) then the entire indigenous population of Australia should be left to die in peace as the scientific laws of nature and human progress ordained. In her words, 'To save and civilize the race we are supplanting is an impossibility, for they are physically uncivilizable, and are inevitably doomed to perish.'[39]

If nothing else Daisy was certainly an extraordinary woman. After arriving in Australia in 1883, she eventually took up a position in the Kimberley region of Western Australia. It was there, a solitary white woman living among Aborigines, that she found her life's calling. Still, while Daisy was embraced by many Aborigines, who apparently gave her the name of 'Kabbarli' (grandmother spirit), she often betrayed that trust. Her role, for example, in the enforced exile of Aborigines suffering from venereal disease to islands off the coast of Western Australia, and in assisting in the abduction of 'half-caste' children, was one she neither regretted nor repudiated.[40]

In *The Passing of the Aborigines* Daisy regales readers with numerous horrifying stories of Aboriginal cannibalism. For example, in the middle of the book we meet 'Dowie, the Insatiable Cannibal', who ate 'four baby sisters' and grew big and strong. The story of Dowie is a bizarre moral fairy-tale of Aboriginal depravity – Dowie, who wanted to eat his own mother; Dowie, who drank blood regularly and 'greedily'; Dowie, whose 'huge mouth twisted and moved with every ugly emotion of his mind'; Dowie, who ate his first wife. And so on, until Dowie finally goes mad from his murderous dietary desires. The story ends with Dowie, 'blind and demented', being discovered 'naked and exhausted' by Daisy Bates. We are then asked to believe that Bates, in white gloves and long skirt, single-handedly lifts Dowie on to her back and carries him more than a dozen miles back to camp. 'A few days later,' she writes, 'Dowie died.' She then digs his grave with her bare hands, a final merciful act for a depraved baby-eating savage.[41]

Elsewhere in *The Passing of the Aborigines* Daisy writes about cannibalism among the Aborigines near the border between South and Western Australia:

> I use the word cannibal advisedly. Every one of these central natives was a cannibal…Human meat had always been their favourite food…Everyone of the natives whom I encountered on the east-west line had partaken of human meat…[42]

These were no harmless imaginings. Bates's fantasies about regular contact with ravenous cannibals, which elevated her status in the eyes of her peers, touched the core fears of white settlers. What is debatable is whether Daisy's cannibalism 'observations' were simply sensationalised misunderstanding, or deliberately deceitful. For example, after some concerns were raised about her work, Bates provided scientific evidence of Aboriginal cannibalism when she sent bones recovered from one alleged incident to the South Australian Museum. The bones turned out to be those of a feral cat.[43]

Daisy's cannibalism obsession was not only disparaging and inaccurate, the entire premise of her book was false. The Aboriginal people of Australia did not die out or 'pass'. Daisy, undeterred, continued to intervene in the public debate regarding what to do about Australia's Indigenous people. In a 1921 article in Perth's *Sunday Times* newspaper, for example, she wrote that, 'As to the half-caste, however early they are taken or trained, with very few exceptions, the only good half-caste is a dead one.' She claimed that she was still acquainted with 'a few old and young cannibals' from among the 'northern natives' and asserted that, 'Western Australia, in proportion to population, has done more for the Aborigines since her inception as a colony than any other State in the Commonwealth.'[44]

Following the release of her book *The Passing of the Aborigines*, Daisy Bates was praised in England as a 'saint' and the 'greatest woman in the Empire'. She died in 1951, aged ninety-one. She was a patriotic Britisher, a 'humane' imperialist and a woman who denied her own Irish Catholic roots in order to climb the colonial social ladder. The churches may have provided the moral reasoning and physical institutions essential for the destruction of Aboriginal family life, but anthropologists like Daisy Bates provided the crucial scientific justification for the systematic abduction and removal of Aboriginal children.

::

Despite the fact that Australia's impressive and unique Aboriginal cultural heritage is a source of pride for a growing number of non-Indigenous Australians, the widespread misunderstanding of Aboriginal cultural practices continues. For example, the idea that many Aboriginal people were cannibals still maintains some currency in Australian society. Adherents of this view include the former far-right politician, Pauline Hanson, who claimed in her 1997 ghost-written book, *The Truth*, that white Australians need not apologise for the 'stolen generations' until Aborigines apologised to the Chinese they had cannibalised in Queensland during the nineteenth century.[45]

Hanson and other far-right cranks could certainly draw on a battalion of respectable dead anthropologists to support their contention that cannibalism was widely practised in traditional Aboriginal society. Behind it all, however, was a concerted political attack on the idea that Aboriginal claims for land rights and social justice were historically justified. David Ettridge, then President of the One Nation Party, was quoted as saying that Hanson's book 'was put forward to correct misconceptions about Aboriginal history and was relevant to the debate on Aboriginal welfare spending'. Ettridge argued that white concern for modern-day Aborigines should be 'balanced a little bit by the alternative view of whether you feel sympathy for people who eat their babies'.[46]

As Colin Tatz of Macquarie University argues, much of the evidence to support claims of Aboriginal cannibalism was based upon the findings of Daisy Bates and other nineteenth-century social Darwinists.

> In my view, the evidence – and I've read most of it – is fragmentary and inconclusive. The fact is that we don't have a single eyewitness account of aboriginal cannibalism. Everyone heard it from someone else. And what they heard, as Maddock rightly says, is that in some, not all, mourning and mortuary rituals, portions of a deceased relative's body were seen to be carried about. In some clans, when a prominent person died in the prime of life, there was consumption of parts of the body as a way of perpetuating the existence of the dead one. Daisy Bates was, and remains, notoriously unreliable and sensationalist – on practically every subject from aboriginal cannibalism to aboriginal cricket.[47]

Tatz was joined by other academics, such as anthropologist Michael Pickering, who claimed to have investigated 440 claims of Aboriginal cannibalism that allegedly took place between the 1700s and 1940s. Pickering claimed that he could find no proof in any of the 440 claims of Aboriginal cannibalism that any such acts ever took place. He was reported in the press as saying that, 'Many people who made the claims were known to have killed Aborigines', while 'others had relied on second and third-hand accounts and some misinterpreted rituals'. He was similarly prepared to state, however, that some groups of Aborigines 'practised ritual consumption in rare circumstances where eating a part of the body was seen as perpetuating the dead person's existence'.[48]

Under the headline 'WA claims back Hanson', the 24 April 1997 edition of *The West Australian* argued that there were accusations of Aboriginal cannibalism in colonial Western Australia, but offered no real evidence to support the allegations. The 1873 case of the two convicted West Australian Aboriginal cannibals, Mullagelly and Yaradee, therefore stands as a unique historical and legal moment. The essential point, however, is to understand that their behaviour was disturbingly exceptional.

Caught between their collapsing traditional culture and the expanding European colony, Francis Dunne's Aboriginal killers lived (literally) on the margins of two contending cultural worlds in deep conflict with one another. What is disappointing are the questions that were not asked in court, or the answers that were not recorded, about the circumstances that had led the Aboriginal men to kill the innocent white child in the first place. The court, and the press, appeared content with the assumption that native bloodlust was at play. Billoo's comment, however, that the Aborigines were 'sulky' prior to the murder, seemed to hint at a pre-existing sense of chagrin and hostility. Who or what were the men 'sulky' about? To what extent did Francis Dunne appear before them as prey, or to what extent was he simply the personification of a society that had destroyed their ancient way of life, including the prevalence of traditional bush foods? Or in other words, was this simply savagery, or was it the misplaced rage (and hunger) of the dispossessed? We can only speculate.

At the time Mullagelly and Yaradee were hanged, ideas about the innate inferiority and savagery of Aborigines were still ascendant. A decade later in 1883 an American 'showman', R. A. Cunningham, took nine Aborigines from Queensland for 'display' as part of Barnum and Bailey's Circus. Promoted as 'savage cannibals' they travelled the world as a sideshow curiosity. They all died before returning to Australia. In 1892 the same showman took another eight Aborigines overseas for exhibition. Only two made it home six years later. At least one of those who died overseas, Tambo, was embalmed and displayed at a 'dime museum' in Cleveland, Ohio.[49]

As Roslyn Poignant has argued in her book *Professional Savages*, in travelling circuses exotic indigenous people were exhibited alongside 'the congenitally impaired', and presented as freaks of nature. Darwinist pseudo-science was employed to lend legitimacy and wonder to the spectacle. Barnum & Bailey's 1883 travelling exhibition, for example, was billed as the 'Ethnological Congress of Strange and Savage Tribes'. The show included Zulus, Sioux Indians and the aforementioned eight Aborigines from Queensland.[50]

The Australian Aborigines caused particular excitement in the United States, as reported in the *Baltimore Morning Herald* during May 1883:

The Australian Cannibals
To-day their first appearance in Public in a Civilised Country

This strange group arrived in Baltimore yesterday in the charge of one of Mr Barnum's agents direct from Northern Australia. They were captured in the wilds of that desolate region and while on route from San Francisco, have attracted more attention than any human beings every before seen in civilization.[51]

The Aborigines led the circus parade along with Jumbo the Elephant and were allegedly viewed by an estimated 30,000 people.[52] The circus enthusiastically promoted the alleged savagery of the Aborigines. Or as one newspaper advertisement proclaimed:

A tribe of Male and Female
AUSTRALIAN CANNIBALS
Also kown as Bushmen, Black Trackers and Boomerang Throwers. These are the only one of their monstrous, self-disfigured and hopelessly embruited race, ever lured from the remote, unexplored and dreadful interior wilds, where they wage an endless war of extermination, that they may gratify their hellish appetite and
GORGE THEMSELVES UPON EACH OTHER'S FLESH[53]

The advertisement went on to describe the Aboriginal cannibals as having, 'bestiality, ferocity and treachery stamped upon their faces; their cruel eyes reflecting but a glimmering of reason; having no gift of speech beyond an ape-like gibberish, utterly unintelligible to any one else; they are but one step removed from brutes in human form.'[54] In fact they spoke English, much to the dismay of some circus viewers.

The Aborigines toured the United States before being exhibited in London, Dublin, Glasgow, Copenhagen and Moscow. As their numbers were thinned by alcoholism, tuberculosis and the misery of their lives far from their ancestral homes, it became harder for promoters to present them as a dangerous threat to civilisation. Nevertheless, an English-language poster produced in Berlin in 1884 still announced the presence of the 'Australian Cannibal Boomerang Throwers' in the city.[55]

By the end of the nineteenth century even white Australians were becoming interested in exhibiting 'exotic' Aborigines. In 1888, for example, a group of Aboriginal people were 'displayed' at the Melbourne Zoo as part of the Centennial Exhibition. An Aboriginal family from Coranderk

Station – Tommy and Rosy Avoca and their two children – were brought into town, dressed in possum and kangaroo skins, told to sit under a bark shelter surrounded by spears and boomerangs, and urged to look as 'native' as possible.[56]

By the time of the centenary of Australia's colonisation in 1888 the pseudo-science of racial progress was thoroughly entrenched, with *The Age* in Melbourne proclaiming that 'a natural law' was pushing aside the Aborigines and 'providing for the survival of the fittest'. However much this 'may clash with human benevolence', the overall benefits 'to mankind at large' were self-evident. Moreover, in case some people's consciences were troubled, 'Human progress has all been achieved by the spread of the progressive races and the squeezing out of the inferior ones'. As such, the Aborigine was a lost cause, 'and we need not therefore lament his disappearance'.[57] After all, cannibals are undeserving of sympathy.

8

'Wicked Orientals' and the New Fremantle Gallows, 1889

Science attempts to overcome the cruelties of hanging. Opposition to Chinese immigration leads to the gradual development of the White Australia Policy. A Malay worker is condemned to death for murdering his master.

In 1883 the middle of nowhere was about thirty miles from Roebourne. The nights were empty and quiet on the Cheritah sheep station, with only the sounds of the bush and the crackling murmur of working men talking around the campfire to keep you awake. Which is why it was unusual that at around midnight on 2 July 1882 Wallace McLeod was not awakened from his sleep when one of his Chinese workers was being hacked to death. McLeod slept through the bloodcurdling screams and instead he was awoken by a frightened Chinese employee who had come running to the house. The Chinaman told him that an awful attack had been committed by Ah Kett against Foo An Moy. McLeod roused his overseer, Guy Thompson, and promptly made his way to the 'Chinamen's Hut'.

The sky was dark but McLeod could make out the shadow of Ah Kett standing in the doorway of the Chinamen's Hut. He shouted for Ah Kett and all the other Chinamen to come outside. Ah Kett was reluctant until McLeod, using Thompson's pistol, threatened to shoot him if he did not step outside immediately. Slowly all the Chinese filed out of the hut, including Ah Kett and two other Chinamen from his fencing crew – all of whom were supposed to be camping near the station's fence line, nine miles away in the bush.

Thompson and McLeod ventured cautiously into the hut. It was too dark to see anything so McLeod struck a match and lit one of the lamps. As the darkness retreated he could see that on a narrow bed lay Foo Ah Moy with awful gaping wounds to the right side of his head. He was covered in blood. Before he died in this strange land so far from his ancestral home, Foo Ah Moy whispered to McLeod that Ah Kett had chopped him up with a tomahawk. Meanwhile the other Chinese workers stood outside in the dark saying nothing. A small sharp tomahawk, covered in blood, was later discovered in the dirt nearby.[1]

Almost ten years earlier in October 1873 the editor of *The Perth Gazette* had railed against a seemingly insane proposal advanced in a rival newspaper:

> An absurd project, a project which but for its very absurdity would be iniquitous, has been mooted in a leading article in the *Inquirer* newspaper. The writer proposes that Chinese immigration into this colony should be fostered and encouraged. Chinese forsooth![2]

While forgiving the writer from *The Inquirer* his sin of ignorance, the editor of the *Perth Gazette* proclaimed that:

> In Melbourne the Chinese are hissed and hooted. Some people even propose to banish them altogether from Victoria. The plea that is addressed against them is that of their gambling proclivities. Gambling is the least and best of their vices; and it is charged against them because people of any modesty dare not, at least in public, mention their actual crimes. We should be sorry to make such groundless charges. We should be the first to advocate the cause of the friendless and those who are causelessly, cruelly oppressed. 'All men are equal,' but only so long as they maintain their title to humanity. When men are beasts, they are simply 'not wanted' in a Christian community.[3]

Given such public hostility it is remarkable that the Chinese ever made it to Western Australia at all. However, convict transportation to Western Australia ceased in 1868. Self-government, under the British Crown, had been granted two years later and Western Australia's first elected government (by male suffrage only) was largely composed of men who were sympathetic to those business interests who complained most loudly about the shortage of cheap workers.[4] By the late 1870s the Legislative Council was under increasing pressure to assuage this labour shortage, particularly in the remote north of the colony. There was a formal proposal to subsidise the importation of cheap Chinese labour. Men like Ah Kett and Foo Ah Moy were the indispensable vanguard of that Chinese migration, but many more were to join them. With the support of the Western Australian parliament, between 1884 and the end of the century more than two thousand Chinese ventured to the colony as indentured labourers. These Chinese workers were all male and almost all were recruited from Singapore.[5]

Although initially concentrated in remote farming or mining areas, by the late 1880s the Chinese were becoming a visible minority group within the growing urban areas of the colony. Chinese businesses – most famously, laundries – started to contribute to a growing perception that little 'Chinatowns' were sprouting up everywhere. The popular mood, which had never been especially favourable towards the Chinese, now turned decidedly poisonous.

Formal legislation to restrict Chinese migration to Australia was introduced in New South Wales, Queensland, South Australia and Victoria between July and December of 1888.[6] In Western Australia, where the dependence upon cheap Asian labour in the north of the colony was particularly noticeable, parliament passed anti-Chinese immigration restrictions while it continued to subsidise the importation of Chinese indentured labourers![7] In 1892, even as the Fremantle Lumpers' Union was organising a 'Monster Meeting' of seven hundred dock workers to protest against Chinese immigration, prominent businessmen were writing to the newspapers arguing the economic rationale for the importation of Chinese labour. As late as 1893 the *West Australian* was still advertising, on its front page no less, the services of McAlister & Co. who provided 'Native Servants, Coolies, Cooks, Boys' from Singapore to local employers.[8]

However, it was the premier of the colony, Sir John Forrest, the legendary West Australian explorer and politician, whose interventions into the political debate best reflected the polite conventions of late nineteenth-century parliamentary prejudice. During the November 1897 introduction of Western Australia's immigration restriction bill, Forrest had explained to the parliament that 'grave anxiety' had been caused among the God fearing white people of Western Australia by the 'influx of coloured people'. He urged members to take legislative action to protect the cultural, moral and racial integrity of the colony.[9] A year later John Forrest took his views into the national arena. At the Federation Convention of 1898 Forrest told delegates that, 'It is no use, to shut our eyes to the fact that there is a great feeling all over Australia against the introduction of coloured persons.' 'It goes without saying,' he continued, 'that we do not like to talk about it, but it is so.'[10]

::

Australia has always been a diverse and multicultural country. Besides the hundreds of unique languages and cultural groups that made up pre-1788 Aboriginal society, the British colony established in Sydney Cove was never homogenous. There was a language, ethnic and cultural gap between the mainly Gaelic Irish and the English. There were visible populations of Pacific Islanders, Indians and even Africans present in The Rocks in Sydney and throughout colonial Australia. Keith Windshuttle claims that at 'least 1000 of the convicts sent to Australia before 1850 were not white'.[11]

Nevertheless, as the Australian colonies established themselves during the nineteenth century ideas of race, blood and Empire grew in importance to white Australians. Aborigines and Asians, in particular, were viewed as undesirable and potentially threatening. The hostility was greatest where these minorities were most visible and present – Aborigines in remote farming areas, Asians on the goldfields and in frontier towns like Broome. The growing attempt to cohere six remote colonies into an Australian nation intensified attempts to define and exclude those who lay outside the imagined national 'family'.

The Federal Immigration Restriction Act of 1901 became the legislative cornerstone of the much reviled – but occasionally still lamented – 'White Australia Policy'. The Act itself has dated badly, its legislative prose heavy with the sort of *fin de siecle* casual prejudices no contemporary parliamentarian would dare utter outside the privacy of the members' toilets. The section on 'prohibited immigrants', for example, not only forbade entry to any person incapable of writing out a dictated passage of fifty words in a European language, but also excluded 'any idiot or insane person'; and any person suffering from a 'contagious disease of a loathsome or dangerous character'.[12] Exemptions, however, could be made for any person who was a member of 'the King's regular land or sea forces'. Therefore, in theory at least, a British lunatic with syphilis might have been able to visit Australia as long as he was serving in the Army. A wealthy and healthy Chinese doctor who could only speak Mandarin could not.

The common-sense historical view of the growth of hostility towards the Chinese in Australia during the nineteenth century is that it was the regrettable byproduct of extensive Chinese migration to the goldfields of Victoria in the 1850s and New South Wales a decade later. For example, the doyen of Australian history, Manning Clark, described the violent anti-Chinese riots at Lambing Flat in NSW during 1861 as stemming from 'madness in the blood of the diggers' who were 'disgusted' or 'resentful' of the Chinese miners. When the European miners vented their rage on the Chinese camp 'civilized men were converted into brutes'. In Clark's analysis, racial attacks on Chinese at Lambing Flat and elsewhere ensured that 'radicalism and colonial nationalism were indelibly stained by racial intolerance and ruffianism'.[13]

In keeping with such arguments, the creation of 'White Australia' policies by various colonial parliaments at the end of the century, and the Federal Immigration Restriction Act of 1901, are often seen as a response by otherwise dignified Australian gentlemen to the hysterical racism of their electors. What this commonsense view of anti-Chinese racism neglects is that even as compared to the distant and generally unresponsive parliaments of today, parliamentarians of the nineteenth century were comparatively free to shape legislation in their collective interests as men of property. So why did the colonial parliaments pass anti-Chinese immigration legislation during the late nineteenth century against the wishes of some major business interests (especially in Queensland and Western Australia) who desired cheap Asian labour? The answer rests in the fact that concepts of European superiority were central to the ideological fabric of Australia decades before a single Chinese miner set sail for the Victorian goldrush, or a single stone was thrown at Lambing Flat. Or in other words, these gentlemen passed anti-Chinese legislation because it corresponded with their own beliefs regarding the undesirability of widespread Asian migration to Australia.

Which is not to say that there weren't individuals who spoke out against explicitly anti-Asian immigration restrictions. They did so, not least of all, because open racism cut against the ideals of the British Empire. The Empire prided itself on the image of a harmonious multi-ethnic family of colonies under the British monarchy and spanning the globe. Explicit legislative racism was viewed as impolite, un-gentlemanly and altogether un-British. In 1888, for example, the British Secretary of State, Lord Knutsford, had written to the Australian colonial premiers (who were meeting in conference) to inform them that 'placing Chinese emigrants on different footing to subjects of any other power' would be neither advisable nor acceptable to the Crown.[14] Such opposition was one of the reasons why the eventual Acts restricting Chinese and other Asians tended to focus on language and health, rather than upon race, as a basis for exclusion.

Ironically it had been Western Australia, where the importation of cheap Asian labour ended much later than in the other colonies, that had pioneered the use of a language test as a means of exclusion. Borrowing from the experience of the Natal colony in South Africa, the genius of the language dictation test was that although the intent was to block entry to unwanted 'coloured people', there was nothing in the Act that specifically mentioned race at all. Nevertheless, John Forrest, when introducing the 1897 bill to the Western Australian Legislative Assembly, claimed that the language test:

> ...will not be asked in the case of one of our own race, nor do I suppose that the test will be applied to any but the persons whom we all have on our minds.[15]

Just who was 'on our minds' was clear enough. Three Chinese workers had boarded a ship in Hong Kong that was heading for Western Australia a week before the new language-based restrictions became law. When they arrived at the port of Albany in January 1898 they were immediately subjected to a language dictation test and denied entry.[16]

With time the language test became the basis of the Federal Immigration Restriction Act. Again the intent was racial even if the legislation politely avoided any mention of a White Australia. During the first year of the Act a total of 459 Chinese failed the dictation test and were denied entry. Of the 1,300 migrants who were subjected to a dictation test by the new Commonwealth authorities during the first seven years of the Act, only fifty-two passed. After 1909 and until the White Australia Policy was abolished in the late 1950s, not a single person passed the dictation test.[17]

Behind all of this was a desire in the minds of Australia's 'Founding Fathers' to avoid the racial problems of other white settler states. In particular, they were determined to avoid the mistake of the United States of America where African slavery had created a racially divided labour market. In the northern states of America the economy relied upon free labour and modern industry. In the south prior to 1865 plantation slavery and economic backwardness predominated. The net result of this state of affairs – Australian parliamentarians were aware – had been immense profits followed by a bloody civil war that nearly tore the country to pieces. In their more sombre moments, Australian parliamentarians and capitalists could imagine a similar north-south economic divide developing in Australia with cheap Chinese indentured labourers dominating a plantation-style economy in the north (especially in Queensland) and a modern free market economy in the south-eastern states. Therefore, as Australia edged towards Federation its parliamentary gentlemen generally desired evolution towards a single free labour market based upon an exclusively European settler population.

When the Immigration Restriction Bill was introduced to the new Federal Parliament in 1901, speakers rose to confirm these prejudices. Edmund Barton, the prime minister, spoke of the need to 'secure the future' of Australia 'against the tide of inferior and unequal Asians arriving from the north'. Alexander Paterson, from Queensland, attacked the 'uncivilised habits' of the Chinese. George Reid, Leader of the Opposition, supported the bill and noted the 'problem caused by coloured people in the United States'. Opposition was muted. John Watson's principal comment, as leader of the Labor Party in the new parliament, was that the legislation did not 'go far enough'.[18] Anti-Chinese feeling, therefore, was neither exclusive to the working class 'deranged mobs' of Lambing Flat, nor confined to the parliamentary debating chamber. In Australia – six isolated colonies on the remote edge of the British Empire – anti-Chinese immigration restrictions appealed to the core beliefs of a diverse range of European settlers.

The pervasiveness of anti-Chinese prejudice was felt within the recesses of nineteenth-century popular culture. Asian invasion fantasies found a receptive audience. The Chinese were represented within these stories as sinister and sneaky infidels.[19] The Chinese also provided plenty of material for editorialists and cartoonists. In the words of constitutional historian Helen Irving:

> Cartoons, caricatures and purple prose images of Asians were drawn so crudely and repulsively, that they represent now a barrier to understanding the imagination of the nineteenth century on this issue. The issue of 'colour' was unequivocally a racist issue, but it was much more than this. As much as anything, it was a type of cultural strategy in the process of nation building.[20]

Most white Australians remained ignorant of Chinese culture and language, relying instead upon stereotypes of the Chinese as devious opium-smoking exotics. The fear of Chinese raping or seducing European women was particularly strong. In the 1881 census the number of Chinese in Australia amounted to 38,532 people. Of these, however, only 259 were women.[21] Without Chinese wives to comfort them, and satiate their alleged oriental lusts, it was feared that imported Chinese labourers would prey upon white women. Yet, despite the social obstacles placed in their way, there were numerous genuine 'mixed-race' relationships. For example, there were approximately 470 marriages between European women and Chinese men in colonial Victoria. Even between 1855 and 1860, when anti-Chinese racism was on the rise in Victoria, there were fifty-nine cases of European women (almost half were Irish) marrying Chinese men.[22] At a time when European women were viewed as a precious economic, emotional and sexual resource, such relationships were disturbing to many white Australians.

The social pressure on individuals within these 'mixed marriages' must have been tremendous. Every public moment of their lives was scrutinised or became a matter for ridicule. For example, in early 1859 an Irish-born woman called Mary Ah Ping appeared in Castlemaine Magistrates Court charged with threatening to murder her Chinese husband, William. The *Mount Alexander Mail* delighted in detailing the court proceedings:

> Mary Ann Ping, who appeared at the bar with the embellishment of a black eye, was charged with threatening the life of her husband, Chinaman named Ah Ping. It appeared that the Celestial being desirous of taking unto himself a European wife, selected the prisoner, but the union would not appear to have been a felicitous one, for the lady got drunk and threatened the life of her Mongolian lord.[23]

Repression followed ridicule. In 1910 twenty-two European women who 'consorted' with Chinese were arrested for vagrancy by the Western Australian police. As historian Jan Ryan explains:

> The courts did not distinguish between prostitutes and those living in long term relationships with Chinese. When convicted, they received three to six months hard labour, as did the Chinese – for 'harbouring' a vagrant. Clearly, Chinese men were not seen as home providers or supporters if 'white' women were involved. Churches, the press and the law intervened to deter women from choosing a Chinese partner.[24]

The Chinese who, like other migrants, had come to Western Australia to make their fortunes and start a new life, found themselves increasingly vilified and ostracised. They also found their ability to enter the colony, or to work in particular areas or occupations, severely restricted by a series of prohibitive laws – The *Sharks Bay Pearl Shell Fishery Act (1886)*; The *Goldfields Act (1886)*; *Act to Regulate and Restrict Chinese Immigration (1886)* among others.[25]

Despite these pieces of discriminatory legislation, however, the Chinese population in the colony continued to rise during the 1880s and 1890s. Gold, immigrant ambition and the desire of some sections of capital to exploit cheap indentured Asian labour meant that loopholes in the restrictions were continually discovered and exploited. It was not until 1901, and the birth of the Australian nation, that the Western Australian door was finally and decisively slammed shut on the Chinese.

::

The *West Australian*'s report on the Supreme Court trial of Foo Ah Moy's killer started with the headline, 'Murder of a Chinaman':

> Ah Kett, a Chinaman, was charged with having at Roebourne, on the 2nd July last, wilfully murdered a fellow countryman named Ah Moy; and Soon Kee and Ah Tong, two other Chinamen, were charged with having aided and abetted Ah Kett in the commission of the crime.[26]

The trial commenced just after eleven o'clock on the morning of Friday 5 January 1883. Mr S. H. Parker opened the prosecution's case, alleging that a 'diabolical murder had been committed'. According to Mr Parker, Foo An Moy worked around the 'homestead' on Wallace McLeod's station and slept in a nearby hut with some other Chinese workers. Ah Kett and his two co-accused worked about nine miles away doing fencing and usually camped there. It was through Foo An Moy that Mr McLeod discovered that another Chinaman, Ah Hook, who was also working in the fencing crew, had been stealing sheep from the station. Ah Hook was arrested and taken to gaol. The prosecution's case hinged upon the fact that the three remaining Chinamen of the fencing crew, friends of the thieving Ah Hook, knew that Foo An Moy was McCleod's informant and that he was to give evidence in court. Ah Hook was due to stand trial for sheep stealing in Roebourne only days after the murder of Foo An Moy.[27]

On the night of the crime the three accused rode nine miles from their bush camp to the McLeod homestead. At about eleven o'clock, while everyone was asleep, they crept into the hut that Foo An Moy shared with three other Chinese workers. It was dark and quiet. Minutes later one of the Chinese who shared the hut was awakened by terrible screams coming from the bed of Foo An Moy. Jumping to his aid the witness saw the shadow of Ah Kett above the bed hitting Foo An Moy with a tomahawk. The witness, with the help of another Chinese worker, eventually restrained Ah Kett but the damage had been done. According to the Crown prosecutor, the tomahawk 'had been sharpened to the sharpness of a razor' and Foo An Moy had been 'mercilessly hacked' by Ah Kett, 'his head being almost severed from his body'. Besides the wounds to his face and skull, Foo An Moy's chest was also opened, with some of his entrails showing. Remarkably, he was still alive.[28]

While Ah Kett sat on a nearby bed resting, one of the Chinese set off to the main house to awaken the boss, Wallace McLeod. When McLeod arrived soon afterwards with his overseer, he immediately ordered all the Chinese out of the hut. Although the hut was small (sixteen feet by eleven feet) the night was dark – making it difficult to see who was inside. As the Chinese workers shuffled out from the hut it was discovered that not only was Ah Kett inside, but also two other men from the fencing crew, Soon Kee and Ah Tong. Somehow, despite having his head almost severed from his body, Foo An Moy survived more than an hour after the attack – long enough to speak to McLeod and to ask for a drink of water. Before he died he told McLoed that it had been Ah Kett who attacked him.[29]

Wallace McLeod, with his overseer's pistol in his hand, separated Ah Kett and the two other Chinese fencers from the other Chinese, and marched the three men over to the homestead. McLeod and Thompson, the overseer, chained the three Chinese up before turning them over to the police the following day.[30] The accused were then transported to Perth to stand trial for the murder of Foo An Moy.

The prosecutor ended his opening statement by declaring that Ah Kett was an unrepentant murderer:

> When charged with the crime he offered no denial, but, on the contrary, seemed to glory in it; and no doubt the object in view in committing the offence was to prevent the deceased from giving evidence against the other man who had been committed to trial for sheep-stealing. Apart from this, it appeared from Ah Kett's own confession that a rooted ill feeling existed between him and the deceased; so that, so far as this prisoner was concerned, the jury would have little or no difficulty in finding him guilty; and, as he had already said, the only question for their consideration was whether the evidence satisfied them that the other two prisoners were present aiding and abetting.[31]

The case was not without its moments of cross-cultural difficulty. For example, according to one report:

> A Chinaman, Ah King, was affirmed to speak the truth as an interpreter, when it was discovered that he could understand the language of only one of the prisoners. After some delay the services of another Chinaman, Cooh, a prisoner of the Crown, were secured, who could speak to Ah Kett fluently, and to the two others but indifferently. Upon the charge being translated to Ah Kett, he replied he did not remember the day, and the other two denied it.[32]

Two Chinese witnesses appeared to testify against Ah Kett, as did Wallace McLeod, his former employer, and Guy Thompson, the station overseer. While giving evidence McLeod broke down after describing the horrible injuries and slow death of Foo An Moy in the 'Chinamen's Hut' on his station. Court was temporarily adjourned so that McLeod could compose himself. When the trial resumed McLeod was allowed to sit in a chair for the remainder of his evidence, rather than stand in the witness box.[33]

The next witness was Guy Thompson, the overseer. Thompson testified that the morning after the murder he had spoken to the chained Ah Kett. Affecting his best (worst) Chinese-English accent, Thompson testified that he had asked Ah Kett, 'Why for you kill "Hoppy?"' (Foo An Moy's nickname). To which Ah Kett allegedly replied, 'Me no likee Hoppy, and Hoppy no likee me.' In his final summation the Chief Justice returned to these comments, insisting that they were full of meaning. The Chief Justice also instructed the jury with regard to the legal interpretation of aiding and abetting murder, the crime Ah Kett's co-accused were charged with. While he seemed to lead the jury towards dismissal of the aiding and abetting charges, he reminded them that Ah Kett had confessed to the crime and should expect little mercy. The Chief Justice gratuitously added that he was 'glad in this instance it was not a white man who had been murdered, but that it was a case of Chinaman against Chinamen.'[34]

It took the jury just ten minutes to find Ah Kett guilty of murder. Soon Kee and Ah Tong were acquitted of aiding and abetting. Ah Kett was sentenced to death by the Chief Justice of the Supreme Court and taken away. Before he was led from the court, Ah Kett yelled out that he had, indeed, murdered Foo An Moy. He remained unrepentant, much to the condescending dismay of the Chief Justice.[35]

Ah Kett was hanged at Perth Gaol on a Saturday morning, 27 January 1883. Another condemned murderer named Collins was hanged at the same time. The *Daily News* reported the last moments of the two men's lives. Although Collins slept soundly the night before his execution:

> …it was very different with the doomed Celestial. He became very nervous yesterday, and as the night drew on his agitation increased to such a degree that he did not go to bed until about one o'clock this morning, and afterwards he was very restless in his sleep. Each of the men eat a good breakfast this morning, and about seven o'clock the irons, with which they had been manacled since receiving their dread sentence, were struck off their limbs. As soon as this was done Collins shook his legs, and said with firmness, 'Free at last!', while the Chinaman phlegmatically enjoyed a smoke.[36]

Any sense of freedom was momentary. Soon afterwards the death bell started tolling in the prison. The two men were pinioned and led from their cells. One reporter wrote that as the two condemned prisoners walked, 'the foreigner turned ghastly pale and trembled excessively'. It was just after eight o'clock. Ah Kett and Collins were marched to the execution yard, accompanied by warders and the hangman. Collins maintained his bravado while Ah Kett appeared deeply troubled. According to the *West Australian*:

> When the procession reached the yard where the gallows was erected, the unhappy man, upon viewing the ghastly instrument of death, changed colour, and a shudder seemed to pass over his frame; but recovering himself almost immediately, he walked, unassisted, to the steps of the scaffold.[37]

The sun crept over the wall of the prison and broke upon the gallows as the two hooded men stood beside each other awaiting execution. The hangman pulled the lever. Collins dropped and died instantly while Ah Kett struggled for a few moments after going through the trap door. The reason was that Ah Kett had anticipated the drop and attempted to 'spring', causing the hangman's knot under his chin to move. The witnesses watched him convulse at the end of the noose before death eventually overtook him.[38]

Although appearing to be a simple case of malicious assault and murder, there was no doubt in the mind of the editor of the *West Australian* newspaper regarding the true importance of the Ah Kett case, along with other recent Supreme Court cases involving Aborigines and former convicts.

> Regarding the most prominent local events in the immediate past there is nothing very pleasant to say. Partly owing to the now, happily, fast disappearing remnant of a class of men bred up in vicious ways; partly owing to the number of the aboriginal population; partly owing to the mixture of different races brought in contact together – crimes of violence are of most unfortunate frequency amongst our community.[39]

Or in other words, convictism, Asian immigration and race mixing led to murder.

::

There were Asians present at the Swan River Colony from the earliest days. Indeed, the first Chinese arrived in 1829, only a few months after the arrival of Captain Stirling himself. The Chinese man in question was a carpenter named Moon Chow, who eventually made his home in Fremantle. After almost two decades in the colony Moon Chow married a European woman and started a family. The children of Moon Chow were the first Chinese-Australians born at Swan River. Moon Chow is generally considered by historians to have been the only Chinese in the colony until indentured servants were recruited from Singapore in 1847.[40]

However, perhaps Moon Chow was not alone. In a December 1832 letter to England, for example, James Purkis complained that the 'English servants we brought here are not worth much; we find that the Lascars, Javanese, and Chinese, who have emigrated here, are much better labourers'. Purkis himself had a native Hawaiian working for him.[41] We also know that in October 1847 and May 1848 the Swan River government paid for the recruitment of fifty-one Chinese men from Singapore to try and ease the labour shortage in the colony.[42] The census of that year listed ninety 'Mahomedans and Pagans' living in the Colony – the 'pagans' included Chinese Taoists and Buddhists.[43] Such people, however, were exotic minorities rather than members of a cohesive Chinese immigrant community. Many of the Chinese, it is assumed, moved to Victoria after the beginning of the 1850s gold rush there. Some remained, however, including Ah Chong – murdered by Edward Bishop in 1854.[44]

The next Chinese to be specifically recruited from Singapore for service in the Swan River Colony arrived during the 1870s when the colony was in the midst of a post-convict labour shortage. The decision of the Western Australian government to sponsor this scheme caused consternation among the other Australian colonial governments who lodged a specific complaint with the British government following the 'Intercolonial Conference' of January 1881.[45] The greatest number of Chinese, however, were recruited between 1884 and 1898. Although they were all lumped together as 'Chinamen' in the public mind, they were a remarkably ethnically and culturally diverse group. For example:

> Just one page of the register listing Chinese coming to Western Australia in April 1889 records 33 emigrants from 13 different districts and five major linguistic groups: Cantonese, Hokkien, Halham, Teochiu and Huichiu.[46]

Initially at least, the Chinese had been afforded some cultural concessions when they arrived in Western Australia. For example, Chinese were exempted from swearing on the Bible in a courtroom. By the 1890s, however, the conservative press delighted in ridiculing the cultural practices and language difficulties of Chinese witnesses appearing in courts of justice.[47]

Western Australia's white population had grown slowly since 1829. In the sixty years since Captain Fremantle first stepped ashore the European population had only increased to 45,660.[48] By the time the Federal Immigration Restriction Act was passed in 1901 Western Australia had become home for 1,526 Chinese men and forty-three Chinese women. Only a tiny number of Chinese men (3 per cent) had Chinese wives and families living with them. About 100 of the Chinese were children of 'mixed race' relationships. Almost half the Chinese population lived in Perth/Fremantle, with the rest (54 per cent) being scattered throughout the remote coastal towns and the dry vastness of the rural interior. Those who lived and worked in Perth or Fremantle tended to coagulate in particular areas. Murray Street in Perth was known for its Chinese shops while South Terrace and Bannister Streets in Fremantle were notorious for their Chinese laundries and other establishments (including dubious 'gambling dens' and alleged brothels). There were even suburban Chinese shops in Leederville and Beaconsfield.[49]

Notwithstanding the pervasiveness of gambling and the consumption of alcohol among the European population,[50] newspapers continued to focus upon Chinese 'Opium Dens' and 'Fan-tan Houses' as an exotic and decadent threat to colonial society. For example, there was a vocal anti-Chinese rally in Fremantle during January 1892 after the Lumpers' Union called upon dock workers to 'Roll up, Working Men of W.A., and give your Vote against being dragged down to the level of a Chinaman!'[51] During March a petition opposing Chinese immigration was forwarded to the West Australian parliament. The petition blamed illegal gambling on the Chinese, and coincidentally (or perhaps not) a new Police Act focusing upon illegal gambling came into effect less than a month later. Raids on Chinese gambling 'dens' took place in York, Albany and Fremantle. Most of the raids netted no more than a half-dozen Chinese who were discovered playing cards together. The attention of the police and press seemed to be out of all proportion to the crime.[52]

By 1901 the Chinese community of Western Australia was in decline. For those small numbers of Chinese still living in remote outposts of the colony, this meant isolation. For those living in Chinese communities in Perth or Fremantle, however, there was some attempt to petition and protest against the hostility and discrimination. For example, representatives of the Perth Chinese community wrote to the Australian prime minister and the Empress Dowager to complain against the unjust imposition of the Immigration Restriction Act.[53] Regrettably, they were spectacularly unsuccessful in their attempt to have the legislation amended or repealed.

::

Ah Kett was the first Chinese to be legally hanged in Western Australia, and among the last dozen human beings to be subjected to the old method of execution in Perth Gaol. The 'ghastly instrument of death' that hanged him had changed little over the previous centuries, and the newspapers reported that he had convulsed for a while after the fatal drop.[54] Although hanging remained an awkward, cruel and 'unscientific' enterprise, the late nineteenth century was a bold progressive age. Rationalism and science were on the rise. Reformists hoped that not even the primitive act of hanging could withstand their modernising gaze.

When public execution was formally abolished in Western Australia (except for cases involving Aborigines) during the 1870s, Perth Gaol became the official, private, site of state executions. In small regional towns, however, there continued to be some local hangings. Following the completion of a new 'modern' gallows at Fremantle Prison in 1888, it became Western Australia's official hanging prison. People were brought from all over the colony to die upon its scaffold. Over the following ninety years, forty-three men and one woman would be hanged there.

Not far from the condemned cells at Fremantle Prison is the Anglican chapel, which looks out over the central prison courtyard and catches the yellowing afternoon light as the sun sinks over the Indian Ocean. Painted on the wall of the Anglican Chapel, the only room in the prison without bars on the windows, are The Ten Commandments. Painted by a convict during the 1870s, the Sixth Commandment, 'Thou shalt do no murder', seems strangely out of place in a hanging prison. Western Australians of the late nineteenth century struggled to see the irony in the fact that a colony founded by self-proclaimed followers of the world's most famous victim of capital punishment – Jesus Christ – permitted judicial killing.

At Fremantle Prison most hangings took place in the early morning. The prisoner was woken at 5:30 am and given breakfast. The condemned was then offered the comfort of a religious advisor, and a cup of tea or whiskey, before being led to the gallows with their arms pinioned. The actual hanging usually took place just after at 8:00 am. The time it took to walk from the condemned cell to the awaiting noose was about one minute. Inside the gallows room were usually a doctor, a religious representative, the hangman, along with a small number of prison officials and reporters from the local newspapers. The condemned's head was discretely covered with a hood. After falling through the trapdoor the body was left to hang for at least thirty minutes before being officially declared dead by the attending doctor.[55]

Although the new, private, Fremantle gallows was completed in 1888, the first hanging did not take place there until March 1889. The impending execution of Jimmy Long, aka Long Jimmy, gave the public and press pause to contemplate the appropriateness of capital punishment in Western Australia. In a long article originally published in The Daily News (4 March), and republished in The Inquirer (6 March), the editor expressed his doubts:

> Perhaps one of the most remarkable social features of the present age, owing in all probability to the greater extension of education, is the general disgust with which capital punishment is now regarded by the vast majority of all respectable members of every civilized community.[56]

Remarkably, given the public belief in the innate superiority of British culture typical of the age, the newspaper denounced the English criminal code as being, historically speaking, 'of the most barbarous blood-thirsty nature'. Even at a date 'within the memory of our fathers', stealing was 'punishable with the most disgraceful death in the Mother Country'. Although the writer praised recent reforms to the British legal code that had reduced the number of capital offences to two – murder and high treason – he commented that, 'law reform in the British Empire has not kept pace with the march of humanitarianism'. Nevertheless, 'there is but little doubt that even in England the abolition of capital punishment for murder is a question of only a little more time'.[57]

The writer then went on to debate the theological arguments surrounding capital punishment throughout the British Empire.

> In the Mother Country the advocates of the infliction of the death penalty for murder base their arguments upon the authority of Holy Writ, and triumphantly quote the text – "Whoso shedeth man's blood, by man shall his blood be shed".[58]

However, a 'little reflection' was required:

> In the first place: the command in question was binding only upon the ancient Jews; whose criminal punishments were based upon the *lex talionis* – or law of retribution. The principle was inflicting on the culprit exactly the same injury he inflicted on his victim – thus under the old Jewish dispensation the law was – "An eye for an eye, a tooth for a tooth;"... [59]

The writer went on to argue that to 'contend that such laws are binding upon mankind after the advent of the Christian dispensation is simple absurdity'. If such was to be the case, then supporters of the death penalty in Western Australia 'are surely under the logical obligation to demand that also adultery should be punished with death, yet we are convinced that no sane person would venture to seriously propose such a thing these days'.[60]

Moreover, while the legal code relating to capital punishment in England was 'bad enough', it was 'in a still worse state in the Australian colonies' where the fear of the convictism had ensured that rape and unlawful wounding remained capital offences in some colonies. There was 'no reason', according to the author, 'why such sanguinary laws should be allowed to any longer disgrace our statute books'.[61] While the writer accepted that the popular and legislative mood was still against an outright abolition of the death penalty (the writer was correct, this would not occur in Western Australia until almost a century later!), he felt that urgent reform was required in the methodology of execution. What was needed were laws that guaranteed a 'speedy death' for the condemned, rather than a situation where a person was 'tortured out of existence'.[62]

> In England such precautions are taken, for there before the execution the hangman is supplied with the doomed criminal's height, weight and previous occupation. Furnished with such particulars the executioner is able to so calculate the length of the 'drop' he will give the prisoner so as to insure instantaneous death.[63]

The author was making reference to the 'Long Drop' method of hanging which had been devised in Britain in 1872 by William Marwood, the Crown's official hangman. Marwood developed a method of execution where the intent was to quickly break the neck of the condemned, rather than strangle him or her. Marwood, who had watched several executions before becoming a hangman himself, had observed that while too little drop resulted in strangulation, too much could easily result in decapitation. His solution was a scientific table of weights and measures where the preferred fatal drop could be precisely calculated. By making the condemned fall rapidly for a predetermined distance, the hangman could ensure that the resulting jerk upwards of the noose (which was placed under the left jaw), would throw the head backwards, severing the spinal cord and breaking the neck. Death would come promptly and without any macabre drama. Or so it was believed.

According to the writer in *The Inquirer* the development of the Long Drop resulted in a more modern and compassionate form of hanging. However, in 'this Colony such humane precautions are not taken'. The executioner had no prior opportunity to see, or measure, the condemned until virtually the moment of execution:

> The fatal rope is adjusted beforehand, and it is simply a matter of pure accident whether the 'drop' be of the right length so as to insure speedy death. Had the English plan been adopted here, several extremely painful scenes which have occurred in the execution yard of the Perth prison during the last six years would have been obviated.[64]

The author was referring to previous hangings where men's necks did not break properly (including Ah Kett) and instead the condemned prisoner slowly suffocated to death at the end of the rope. In some cases men convulsed and could be heard gurgling under the execution hood. Supporters of a more modern and scientific form of hanging hoped that the opening of the new gallows in Fremantle Prison would ensure that such gruesome events could now be avoided. The *West Australian*, by contrast, placed its article about the opening of the new gallows in a 'commodious room' in Fremantle Prison, next to an article asking 'is the world growing wickeder'.[65] It would not be easily swayed from its belief in the ongoing necessity of the public hangman.

The notion of a humane hanging was an illusion anyway. As V. A. C. Gatrell has argued in his mammoth study of hanging in England:

> Even after the introduction of the long drop in the 1880s, designed to dislocate the cervical vertebrae and rupture the spinal cord, consciousness was thought sometimes to be lost only after two minutes 'or thereabouts'; the heart could beat for several minutes longer, while muscular convulsions could set in after a few minutes' pause. If the long drop was misjudged, decapitation might ensure as well.[66]

Still, it was no accident that the editor's argument against capital punishment was published in *The Inquirer* on 6 March 1889, alongside the official report of the first hanging inside Fremantle prison. Jimmy Long was a Malay labourer who had murdered his 'master' aboard a pearling boat at Cossack. He died by the Long Drop method of hanging at the freshly painted Fremantle gallows on the morning of 2 March 1889.

::

In 1889 Cossack was in the middle of an economic boom, being the major northern port and a centre for the pearling industry before Broome displaced it from this position. In many ways Cossack represented the contradictions inherent in the immigration debate that had been percolating in Western Australia since the decision was first made to import substantial numbers of Chinese labourers during the 1880s. By 1895 the town had about 400 residents, more than half of whom were Asian. Chinatown in Cossack had its own Chinese and Japanese shops, along with its own brothel and other community 'services'.

Without cheap Asian labour it was believed that the northern pearling industry, and the town, could not survive. The presence of so many strange non-British people, however, seemed to bode ill for the future of a pure white Western Australia. To many Europeans it also seemed as though the Asians in the town were forgetting their rightful place in society.

For example, when the *West Australian* published 'Nor'-West News' in February 1892, the column was full of reports of recent crimes perpetrated by non-Europeans in Cossack and Roebourne. These included the violent robbery of 'a Chinaman at Japan Town'; a 'Manilaman' and some Chinese servants charged with refusing to return to their masters; fresh reports of thieving 'natives'; the case of an Arab who assaulted police; and the impending trial of a Chinese charged with murdering a white man. The correspondent also reported an 'army of Chinese loafers' who lived outside of town and were spoiling the region's reputation.[67] The overall impression was of a wild frontier settlement overrun with malingering, duplicitous and dangerous Asians and 'coloureds'. The Jimmy Long case provoked similar fears.

Although tried and sentenced at Roebourne, Jimmy Long had been transferred to Fremantle Prison in order to become the new gallows first victim. When a Catholic priest working in the prison tried to make contact, Jimmy declared he was a Muslim and kept the counsel of a fellow Malay prisoner as his religious advisor instead. The two men prayed together and prepared for Jimmy Long's fateful appointment.[68] According to *The Inquirer*, Jimmy Long was 'a tall man, of upright and even somewhat dignified carriage and demeanour'. He was around fifty and his hair and beard were greying. Jimmy claimed that he had only stabbed his master after being left aboard the boat he was working on for a week without food, and after drinking alcohol heavily. When his master returned an argument broke out and Jimmy stabbed Mr Claude Kerr to death with his 'krase – or native dagger'. *The Morning Herald* claimed Jimmy Long was 'usually inoffensive' but had been 'maddened with drink' on the night of the murder. The court found the attack was unprovoked.[69]

In *The Inquirer's* account of Jimmy Long's hanging, extensive details were given of the dimensions, outlook and construction of the 'New Execution Room' at Fremantle, even pointing out that 'the whitewashed walls of the chamber reflect the light which is freely admitted by the large skylights in the roof'. Care was taken to emphasise that the latest hanging methods were used, including the careful positioning of the rope so as to ensure the breaking of the neck. As such, 'the fatal noose' was adjusted so that 'the knot was just under the left side of the chin'. A moment later, 'the soul of the murderer was launched into eternity'.[70]

> He fell without a movement, nor was even a muscular quiver of limbs perceptible. Dr. White, who was present, declared that death must have been instantaneous, as the neck was dislocated. The length of the drop given was just about 6ft., and as the rope (a piece of ordinary Manilla, an inch in circumfurence) stretched at least 30 inches, the drop in reality was about 8ft. 6 in.; and as Long weighed about 10st. 8lbs., sudden death was then assured.[71]

The Morning Herald offered a similarly approving account of proceedings. Its reporter had also been permitted to join the officials and journalists witnessing the hanging, a dozen people in total, and commented that Jimmy Long's 'anxiety was extreme' as he approached the gallows. The reporter remarked that after entering the 'execution chamber' it took less than two minutes to place Jimmy Long in an appropriate position for death, 'the man standing perfectly quiet meanwhile, once looking up at the rope'. Jimmy Long died quickly and with dignity, the 'entire arrangements were as good and decorous as they could well be, and a great improvement on those which formerly obtained at the Perth Prison'. Indeed, one attending reporter went so far as to claim that it 'was the most humane and orderly execution he had ever witnessed'.[72]

Or in other words, it was generally agreed that this was a thoroughly British, Christian, modern and scientific hanging. Fremantle Prison had triumphed over the cruelty of the suffocating rope. Faith had been restored in the science of execution. Only a few months later the *West Australian* would go so far as to denounce the 'contemptible and maudlin sentimentality' of those who now continued to oppose hanging.[73]

However, while science could improve the conditions under which the condemned died, it could not change the social processes and prejudices that led certain people to the gallows in the first place. There were seventeen men hanged upon the new gallows at Fremantle Prison between 1889 and 1904. All of them were 'foreigners' – two Afghans, six Chinese, one Malay, two Indians, one Greek, one Frenchman and four 'Manilamen'. Not one was a 'Britisher'. Justice in *fin de siecle* Western Australia was many things, but like the colony's immigration policy, it certainly wasn't colour blind.

9

Murder in a Coolgardie Mosque, 1896

Gold transforms Western Australia. Two Afghan cameleers argue and a man is shot dead in a place of worship. A Muslim is hanged under Christian law.

While eating breakfast at a café in the Eastern Goldfields town of Kalgoorlie, I was reminded of the curious relationship between Islam and the Western world. Coffee was, of course, introduced to Westerners by the Turks, whose Muslim empire had once extended deep into Europe. Islam forbids the drinking of alcohol by its adherents and dark aromatic coffee filled the social void. The Turks shared their love of the beverage with visiting traders, scholars and diplomats who, in turn, carried the practice of coffee drinking back to France, England and elsewhere.

Staring at my plate, I was confronted with another reminder of this history of contending civilisations. Legend has it that the innocuous fluffy croissant is so-named and so-shaped because of the Turkish siege of Vienna in 1683. The siege was a defining moment in European history, representing the high-tide of armed Muslim expansion under the Ottoman Empire. As the story goes, during the siege a Viennese baker going about his business early one morning heard Turkish soldiers attempting to tunnel into the city beneath his bakery. Reporting the tunnel to the Viennese defenders, the Turks were routed as was, eventually, the entire Muslim siege of the city. The entrepreneurial baker, seizing his moment in history, produced a special commemorative pastry treat shaped like the Muslim crescent (as represented on the modern Turkish flag). Thus the croissant (meaning crescent in French). From that day to this, supposedly, millions of Westerners around the world – including those breakfasting in Kalgoorlie – unconsciously commemorate the Muslim expulsion from Europe.

I was not in Kalgoorlie to ruminate over the decline of Islam's European empire, but in order to assist a friend and colleague with a research project on prostitution. Rae Frances had requested I visit a famous Kalgoorlie brothel, Langtree's 181, and take one of its history tours. The theme-oriented rooms of the brothel had become a major tourist attraction in Kalgoorlie and were now, allegedly, more profitable than the money generated from the oldest profession in the world within the confines of those same rooms. Despite my fascination, I found some of the information cruelly inaccurate. For example, while encouraged to empathise with the attractive 'French girls' who were brought to Western Australia and tricked into prostitution, or the English prostitutes who worked the tent brothels of the Coolgardie goldfields and drank themselves to death, little sympathy was exhibited towards the male Afghan camel drivers who brought water to Kalgoorlie before the laying of the 'golden pipeline'. In the Afghan Room named after them, our brothel tour guide explained that:

> The Afghans provided the first major means of transport in Kalgoorlie with the camel trains. These guys were actually despised by the Australians. Big time. Because of the way they treated them. Their main job was bottling water. They'd go down the local dams, have a drink themselves, have a bit of a wash in it. Wash their camels, and then bottle the water for the Aussies. We were dropping like flies. We didn't know why…That's because we were being poisoned by the camels and the different diseases in their fur and their skin. These guys didn't get along very well with the Aussies at all. But we did need them because they were the first major means of transport.[1]

The curiously misplaced décor of the Afghan Room, with its attempted 'Arabian Nights' eroticism, remains a fitting memorial to the much-maligned Afghans whose camels helped keep Kalgoorlie alive in an era before trains and running water, in a place where their religion, culture and ethnicity marked them out for dark rumours and misunderstanding.[2]

::

On the morning of 10 January 1896 Tagh Mahomet rose at dawn and went to the Mosque – which adjoined his house – to pray. He was thousands of miles from home in a strange and alien land. Afghanistan is notoriously mountainous. Coolgardie, his adopted home, would have appeared monotonously flat by comparison. Both places shared searing heat and aridity. Tagh Mahomet was a tremendously successful businessman and devout Muslim. At well over six feet tall and of 'stout build', he was known, according to *The Kalgoorlie Miner,* 'to pretty well everyone at Coolgardie'. He must have cut a stunning figure. The newspaper described his typical dress as being an 'ample white turban, embroidered jacket, baggy white pants, and long chain'. He had been in Australia for eighteen years, and in Coolgardie since the gold rush first began.[3]

Tagh and his brother Faiz had established a wealthy camel train company that at its peak employed almost 100 (mainly Afghan) workers. Based in Coolgardie, Faiz and Tagh's camels brought precious supplies, including water, across the desert to the thriving town. By 1896 Coolgardie and nearby Kalgoorlie were possibly the two fastest growing towns in Australia – every day brought new people seeking their fortunes, new investment money, new businesses.

As Tagh prayed at the Coolgardie mosque – his head dutifully facing west as the morning sun rose behind him – his brother Faiz Mahomet was in far off Geraldton on business. After saying his dawn prayers Tagh returned to his lodgings only to be summoned again by the Muslim prayer leader. It was still not yet five o'clock in the morning. Tagh walked the ten paces from his house back to the mosque with his brother-in-law, Kheir. Outside the mosque he ran into Goulam Mahomet, a fellow Afghan cameleer, who was in the company of Surwah, another Afghan. After exchanging a few words Tagh and Kheir entered the Mosque. Inside Tagh prayed again – facing towards Mecca. He was interrupted from his prayers by Surwah, who asked Tagh why he was angry at Goulam. Tagh replied that the whole thing was a misunderstanding. Tagh remained kneeling with his back to the main door of the Mosque.[4]

Growing increasingly agitated, Goulam Mahomet then entered the mosque. Much to the consternation of the Muslim prayer leader, Goulam did not remove his shoes. Goulam quickly walked to where Tagh was praying on his knees. Reaching into his long coat, Goulam pulled out a gun and shot Tagh in the back. Tagh collapsed and never said another word, dying beside his prayer mat. Afghans, rushing to the mosque after hearing the gun shot, carried Tagh to a nearby tent where they respectfully covered his face with a white cloth.[5]

Goulam meantime walked quietly from the mosque and made no attempt to escape. After telling a friend what he had done, he was escorted to a building near the police station and told to wait while his friend went and discussed the matter with the constabulary. Goulam stood quietly as the dawn light of the desert broke upon the street. Constable Brown was amazed to still find him waiting there when he came out of the station a few minutes later. Goulam handed over his pistol and was then arrested and charged with murder.[6]

::

Gold transformed Western Australia. When convict transportation ceased in 1868 the non-Aboriginal population of the colony was around 22,000 people. Almost half of these were former convicts who had been dragged to Swan River against their will. With the Coolgardie gold rush, however, for the first time tens of thousands of people voluntarily made their way to Western Australia to settle, mine, and hopefully prosper. Between 1892 and 1901 the settler population of Western Australia grew from just 58,569 people to 193,601. Almost 36,000 people arrived in 1896 alone.[7] The entire colony was affected. In January 1896, for example, it was reported that prospectors heading to Coolgardie from the eastern colonies were arriving in Albany in such great numbers that dozens were sleeping in the streets. Plans were afoot for a major hotel and other substantial infrastructure investments.[8]

Gold was first discovered in remote Coolgardie in September 1892, and in nearby Kalgoorlie the following year. Within weeks of the first major strike at Coolgardie there were several hundred men camped in the area prospecting – enough people to justify a police constable and his 'Aboriginal assistant' being sent to Coolgardie with a tent, two revolvers, handcuffs and a bundle of office forms, and told to maintain law and order.[9] Life was tough. Over the first year the severe lack of water periodically drove miners from Coolgardie, or killed them. And still, at Coolgardie and in numerous surrounding claims, the gold piled up. Inconceivable amounts of it.

Vera Whittington captures the contagious urgency of the initial Coolgardie gold rush during 1892–1893:

> Swirls of red dust rose as wagons, drays, coaches, carts, traps, camel trains, horsemen leading pack-horses, arrived and departed, loaded and unloaded. Neighing snorting horses, groaning snarling camels, banging hammers, busy saws, shouting men, ringing anvils…vied with smells of food being cooked, of

chaff, of piles of animal manure, of decaying garbage. Dirt, noise, smells and heat filled the days...At night, lights gleamed through thin walls; hotel bars buzzed with excited talk and boasting of new finds, banter and laughter... Round hundreds of camp-fires diggers and teamsters smoked clay pipes as they swapped yarns and cemented mateship...[10]

Tents were pitched alongside houses made from gum trees, iron sheeting, packing cases and hessian sacks. Pragmatism ruled over aesthetics. The hard dusty main street of Coolgardie was made wide enough to turn a camel train around in. Riders and pedestrians entering town for the first time had to watch out for the towering gum trees unevenly dispersed along the middle of Bayley Street – they provided what little shade was available and had been kept by the town's planners.

Along with the pick-and-shovel prospectors, Coolgardie attracted large numbers of mining engineers, financial speculators and businessmen seeking opportunities. Even the young American geologist Herbert Hoover, destined to become one of the most unpopular presidents in United States' history, made a career for himself on the goldfields.[11] By 1896 there were 690 mining companies tied to the Western Australian goldfields listed on the London Stock Exchange. By 1898 Coolgardie had a population of around 20,000 people, with an estimated 10,000 more based on surrounding goldfields. Coolgardie was also home to six banks, twenty-six hotels, two theatres, several breweries, two stock exchanges, several schools and a half dozen competing newspapers. The value of gold exports from Western Australia rose from £1,148 in 1886 to £6,007,000 by 1900. By then gold made up 88 per cent of the colony's export income.[12]

At least forty Western Australian goldfields towns spectacularly rose and fell during the last decade of the nineteenth century and the first decade of the twentieth century on the strength of elusive yellow dust. Some contemporary sleepy towns of dwindling population and diminishing fortune – Kanowna, Broad Arrow, Kookynie, Menzies among others – were once at the centre of Western Australia's social, political and economic development. Therefore it was not without justification that newspapers sometimes referred to Coolgardie or Kalgoorlie (depending on the period and where your sympathies lay) as 'the Westralian Johannesburg'. Although the goldfields were overwhelmingly male dominated (with the notable exception of the aforementioned prostitutes), supporters held out great hopes that, 'in a few months there will be a great increase in the proportion of lady residents'. It was therefore necessary to make 'the social life of the people as attractive as possible'.[13]

Yet, despite the hopes of politicians, social planners and newspaper editors, Coolgardie and Kalgoorlie remained predominately male towns. They were tough places to work and live. The population was generally transient and despite grand public works, the towns declined as soon as the gold ran out. Nothing appeared permanent.

There was also a strong sense of danger on the goldfields. Men stole from one another and 'claim jumped'. Men died of thirst, or were crushed to death inside improperly dug mines. The miners drank too much (the absence of water was a good excuse to imbibe other fluids), and suffered in the heat and dust. The flies and filth of the mining camps were atrocious. And so the Gold Rush dragged in its wake the corpses of men who were greedy, or stupid, men who sought redemption for past sins, who were desperate for fortune, or just wanted to experience the adventure of the ravenous search for the golden rock. For many, Coolgardie or Kalgoorlie became a final resting place.

The rudimentary nature of Coolgardie, a town that had risen out of a mining camp in the middle of a desert, had all kinds of civic consequences. For example, in December 1894 the Reverend Thomas Trestrail wrote to the newspapers:

> ...complaining about the barbarous state of things existing at the Coolgardie cemetery. He asserts that bodies are thrown into shallow graves anyhow, and no record is kept of the burials. Foul odours are he says, commencing to arise from the cemetery, and the present state of affairs is a terrible disgrace to civilization.[14]

Lacking a clean water supply, outbreaks of typhoid tore through mining camps and killed dozens at a time. Between 1894 and 1900 about 2,400 cases of typhoid (with 208 deaths) passed through the Coolgardie government hospital alone. These figures do not take into account those who died without receiving medical treatment in outlying mining camps. Across the goldfields at least 151 men also died in mining accidents between 1896 and the end of the century.[15]

Coolgardie itself was a rough, dangerous and unhealthy place to live. In 1894 the first white baby born in Coolgardie, a little boy, died within a day. In the first twenty days of 1895 an outbreak of fever killed forty-nine people. It was symptomatic of the craziness of the gold rush that the identities of twenty-eight of the deceased were unknown. Men rushed to Coolgardie and died often without leaving any record of who they were or where they came from. The local newspapers started publishing 'Missing Friends' columns where relatives, often mothers or wives, would plead for information concerning a young man last seen heading to Coolgardie to make his fortune. The unidentified dead, meanwhile, were hastily buried in Coolgardie cemetery, twigs stuck in a mound of parched dirt sometimes being all that was used to mark a final resting place.[16]

::

Among the tens of thousands who were rushing to Coolgardie and Kalgoorlie to make their fortunes were not only white 'British' Australians, but foreigners of all varieties and faiths. In this context, the term 'Afghan' was widely deployed by Europeans to describe any Muslim from what is now Afghanistan or the bordering regions of India and Pakistan. Afghans predominated in the provision of camels necessary for the delivery of goods (and people) in the remote and dry Eastern Goldfields where there was no railway and no regular supply of water. It was camels and the Afghan cameleers that provided Kalgoorlie and Coolgardie with a supply lifeline to the world. By the late 1890s there were more than two thousand Afghans working in outback Australia. In these remote corners of the continent, the visible presence of so many strange 'Mahomedans' (as Muslims were called) was an exotic challenge to the sensibilities of colonial Australia.[17]

The Afghan cameleers worked at tremendous risk to their own lives. They operated in the most inhospitable parts of the colony and often travelled long distances where they had to negotiate the unfamiliar bush, as well as relations with Aborigines. Sometimes even their own camels could turn on them. For example, in December 1894 *The Inquirer* reported a case where:

> An Afghan has been found at a spot forty miles from Anna Creek station, seriously injured. He was attacked by camels, and lay 3 days and nights exposed without food and water. He was ultimately found by a boundary rider, and taken to a neighbouring station. Shortly afterwards, whilst lying helpless in bed, a snake crept over him, the reptile being killed by the station cook.[18]

Although a sizeable Afghan community had been present in South Australia since 1866, by the 1890s Coolgardie was the centre of Afghan Australia.

In 1898 there were fifty-four camel companies in the town, with the majority of these being run by Muslims (mostly Afghans). The cameleers had built a Mosque and a community – referred to as 'Ghantown' or 'the Afghan Camp' by Europeans – on the fringes of white society. (Ghantown was located at the eastern end of Bayley Street.) Around 300 Muslims lived around Coolgardie with about eighty regularly attending Friday prayers at the Mosque. The community was serviced by a *Mullah* (prayer leader) and three community preachers. All the community lacked were women, although in 1907 one wealthy Afghan married a French prostitute from Kalgoorlie who converted to Islam and moved to Coolgardie with him.[19]

At the centre of the Muslim-Afghan community were Tagh and Faiz Mahomet. They were undeniably the richest and most successful Afghans in Coolgardie, and quite possibly the whole of Australia, at the time. Faiz had arrived in South Australia around 1876, while he was still in his early twenties, and had moved to Coolgardie with his brother Tagh in October 1892, one month after the discovery of gold there. Together they established the most successful camel transport business in Australia and accumulated a fortune. Faiz and Tagh were also generous benefactors of local charities and public services – financially contributing to the Coolgardie hospital and fire service, among others.[20]

By 1898 Tagh and Faiz Mahomet's company owned 444 of the 1649 camels operating in Coolgardie. Their largest competitor owned only 142 camels, and most of their rivals owned less than twenty-five.[21] The two brothers employed nearly 100 Afghans and Tagh and Faiz Mahomet's business regularly advertised on the front page of the *Coolgardie Miner*, the only Afghan business to be able to afford to do so. The Mahomet brothers established camel stations across Western Australia (Coolgardie, Geraldton, Cue, Mullewa), sunk their own wells and developed essential supply routes that were widely utilised by white miners and the colonial authorities.[22]

The Mahomet brothers were originally from Kandahar in Afghanistan – a place better known these days as the last known address of Osama bin Laden and his Taliban hosts. Although Faiz and Tagh became rich servicing the Coolgardie goldfields, as Afghans they struggled for acceptance. For example, in December 1894 James Cardew wrote to the *Coolgardie Miner* about 'The Afghan Question'. Principle among his complaints was that Afghans were getting rich while white miners struggled to prosper:

We have allowed them [Afghans] to buy land, to sink wells, and to take possession of a portion of the Cattle Swamp. Faiz Mahomet holds a Miner's Right – What business has he with such?[23]

Describing Faiz as 'the pernicious Afghan', Mr Cardew called upon white miners to 'hunt them gently before they become a greater nuisance than they already are'.[24] The following edition of the *Coolgardie Miner* carried, as usual, a front page advertisement for Faiz and Tagh Mahomet, 'Camel Proprietors'. Inside, the editor, the famous demagogue Frederick Vosper, attacked the presence of Afghans on the goldfields – 'Like the fever and the drought, and just as paralysing, they have come to stay.'[25]

Nevertheless, Faiz and Tagh took their opportunities to prove themselves to the Coolgardie establishment. Just the rumour of a new discovery of gold could cause hysterical flight into the wilderness. During October 1893 dozens of men raced seventy miles to the north of Coolgardie to 'Siberia', a previously unknown patch of bush where forty ounces of gold had been discovered by prospectors. Without water to sustain them or their horses, men became dehydrated, disoriented and died without ever reaching Siberia. In an attempt to deal with the disaster that was unfolding, Coolgardie's authorities sent teams out with water to rescue the prospectors. The supporters of this operation included Tagh and Faiz Mahomet, whose camels were deployed at their company's own expense. When the town of Coolgardie offered to refund the brothers, Faiz refused, explaining that 'these men are the sons of God, and therefore I have saved them'.[26] Although they were neither white nor Christian, Faiz and Tagh's wealth and philanthropy made them honorary members of Coolgardie's business elite.

The murder in the mosque of Tagh Mahomet therefore convulsed Coolgardie's Muslim community. Faiz was notified by telegraph in Geraldton and he headed back to Coolgardie immediately. Although the railway to Coolgardie would not be completed until March, Faiz hired a 'saloon carriage' to be attached to the first available goods train making its way to Southern Cross, before taking other transport to Coolgardie. Because of Muslim rules regarding the speedy burial of the dead, *The Kalgoorlie Miner* initially reported that Faiz would not be able to be present when his brother was buried in the restless hot sand of Western Australia.[27]

Perhaps because of Tagh Mahomet's wealth and standing, the cultural issues surrounding his Muslim burial were handled with considerable sensitivity by the civil authorities and the press. For example, as *The Kalgoorlie Miner* reported:

> On Friday afternoon a telegram was received from the Government giving permission for the burial of the body of Tagh Mahomet. This authority did away with the necessity of a post-mortem examination, but before the interment Dr Ellis was permitted to satisfy himself as to the cause of death without, of course, in any way touching the body with an instrument or otherwise, as for an unbeliever to do so would be against the principles of the Koran.[28]

Immediately after receipt of the government telegram Coolgardie's Muslim community prepared to bury Tagh Mahomet. To the consternation of some European onlookers, there was no coffin. Instead Tagh was carried in a funeral shroud upon the shoulders of his fellow Afghans and placed in a grave. Fruit and coins were passed around to the hundreds of mourners and spectators.[29] Then, just as Tagh's corpse was about to be covered with dirt, an urgent telegram arrived from Faiz Mahomet requesting that his brother's funeral be delayed and that his corpse be placed in a lead coffin.[30] It was a departure from Islamic funeral rites, but Tagh's body was taken back from the gravesite. Faiz Mahomet would not be denied his right to bury his brother.

::

Only fifteen months before Tagh Mahomet's murder, on 13 October 1894 several white men (and their sixteen-horse wagon team) were camped in the area of Point Malcolm when some Afghan cameleers (and 200 camels) arrived. According to the white men one of the Afghans, Noor Mahomet, was seen washing his feet at the water hole – the only source of drinking water (he was probably performing his ablutions prior to evening prayers, as is required of Muslims). Thomas Knowles confronted the Afghan and after an argument he pushed the cameleer into the water. As Noor Mahomet yelled for help about a dozen Afghans arrived on the scene. According to the evidence offered by white witnesses at a later inquest, the Afghans were 'armed with sticks, stones, rifles and revolvers'. Knowles was attacked and hit in the face with a stone. In response Knowles pulled a revolver and fired a shot that seriously wounded Noor Mahomet. A struggle ensued for control of the revolver. During the fight Knowles fired a second shot that killed another of the Afghans.[31]

Thomas Knowles was eventually subdued by the remaining Afghans and tied to a nearby tree. The whites, outnumbered by the Afghans, claimed that Knowles was 'shamefully treated, being kicked and beaten with sticks and stones'. Two of Knowles' white workmates, John Hatfield and Ernest Langheim, were also tied up for a period of about eighteen hours before the Afghans handed them all over to a local station owner. Knowles was initially charged with manslaughter for the killing of John (although his name was actually 'Jehan') Mahomet, and with the 'unlawful wounding' of Noor Mahomet. When Noor later died of his wounds, the second charge was also upgraded to manslaughter.[32]

Before an inquest could begin the court had to send to Perth for a copy of the Qur'an for the Afghan witnesses to swear upon. Shan Awio, speaking through an interpreter, gave very different evidence to that of the white witnesses. According to Shan, he and Noor Mahomet were at the water hole when confronted by Knowles and another white man. After an argument, Knowles kicked Noor into the water. All hell broke loose. Then, during the resulting struggle Knowles 'aimed at John Mahomet, and shot him in the stomach', killing him. The Afghans overwhelmed Knowles and his two companions while one of the whites was loading ammunition into a rifle.[33]

The white men's story was of Afghan cameleers flagrantly disregarding the cultural etiquette of a communal water hole by using it to wash their feet. In this version, an argument ensued and Knowles only pulled his revolver and accidentally discharged it after being set upon by an Afghan mob. In the Afghan version of the story, however, a man was attacked without reason and then two Afghans were shot dead for defending their countryman. To the white witnesses it was a case of justified manslaughter. To the Afghans it was murder.

There was no doubt where the sympathies of Coolgardie's white miners lay. The *Coolgardie Miner*, under the editorship of Frederick Vosper, had already been agitating against the Afghan presence, with Vosper arguing that 'opulent Asiatics' were taking over the goldfields. Among their other imagined crimes was the fact that:

> ...to our sorrow we have seen the slaves of these semi-barbarous foreigners working at footpath making in the streets of Coolgardie, while men of our own kith and kin – our own blood – hungry with longing for remunerative employment to tide over exemption – have had to stand and look on impotently, with the rage of despair in their hearts.[34]

Alarmist in the extreme, Vosper's *Coolgardie Miner* claimed that not even the town's prostitutes were safe from the Asiatic menace – 'The flesh-pots are smoking, and the Afghan is sniffing them with ravenous expectation.' Even the fact that many Muslim Afghans did not drink alcohol was threatening. The 'dusky exiles' may indeed have been 'abstemious', but this just meant they had more money to save and buy Australian land with. Calling on all white miners to 'unite in defence of our rights against these invaders', the newspaper claimed that to do otherwise would lead to 'the subjugation of the white race in Western Australia'.[35]

The Knowles case gave focus to the discontent. In late December 1894 a large 'Anti-Afghan Agitation' was held in Coolgardie. Vosper was centrally involved and the meeting was advertised in the *Coolgardie Miner* under the banner:

> Hooshstah!
> Miners! Miners! Miners!
> Storekeepers!
> Business men!
> White men! Workmen!
> The
> Black and Tan Torture
> Is Here!
> The
> Yellow Agony is Coming!
> Roll up! Roll up!
> One and All!!!
> To A
> Mass Meeting
> To be Held
> This Evening (Saturday)
> At 8 P.M.[36]

The meeting was convened outside the offices of the *Coolgardie Miner* on Bayley Street, not far from the office of Faiz and Tagh Mahomet. Almost three thousand Europeans turned up to hear the speeches. Or as *The Inquirer* later reported:

> A big meeting was held in Bayley street last week to consider the Afghan question. About three thousand people were present, Councillor McKenzie

presiding. He said the matter was so serious that white men must take action. The Afghans were increasing so much that they were becoming aggressive and insolent, when Europeans protested against them polluting water.[37]

According to the Councillor, Thomas Knowles was 'a quiet and inoffensive man, who resented the Afghans washing in common drinking water, and only used the revolver when set upon by a mob of Afghans'.[38]

The following speaker at the Coolgardie rally was none other than Frederick Vosper who moved a motion that 'this meeting views with alarm and indignation the encroachments of Afghans, Coolies and Asiatics upon this field'. Vosper voiced his passionately held belief that 'the introduction of inferior races degraded the whole community', and that Western Australia should 'prohibit the landing of all Afghans, Chinese, Japanese, Indians, Coolies or any other coloured race'. The motion was carried unanimously. The meeting then adopted a resolution to form an 'Anti-Afghan League' and to send correspondence to the premier informing him of the meeting's resolve. The meeting ended with Councillor McKenzie informing the crowd that a petition in support of Thomas Knowles would be circulated and sent to the Supreme Court. He also expressed his personal hope that the jury would acquit Knowles of all charges.[39]

Soon afterwards the 'Anti-Asiatic League' of Coolgardie (presumably 'Anti-Afghan' hadn't cast a wide enough net) convened an organising meeting to set out its aims and objectives. The League's committee immediately sent a telegram to Knowles in Albany Gaol, the text of which read:

> Public meeting held here, sympathise strongly your misfortune. Anti-Asiatic League formed, willing to raise funds your defence, if needed.[40]

Knowles' reply arrived in Coolgardie shortly afterwards by telegram: 'Re: your wire. Many thanks. Will accept your proposition.'[41]

The Anti-Asiatic League obviously struck a chord with white miners in Coolgardie. Only a week later newspapers reported that attendance at several subsequent Anti-Asiatic League meetings had been very good (about 600 to 800 people), with several 'strong speeches' being given. One miner, returning from an outlying goldfield, told a meeting that:

> He had found water one night and the next morning eight Afghans appeared, and refused to let him have any. They took possession of the soak, and pelted

him off with stones. He then sent his black boy to the camp for his revolver, when the Afghans changed their tone, and wanted to be friendly. He further stated that if he had his revolver when stoned, he would have shot some of his assailants.[42]

The implication was obvious. The Afghans were out of order and Knowles had only done what any reasonable 'Britisher' would do when faced with such Asiatic insolence. One newspaper report ended by noting that, 'A subscription has been taken up for the defence of Knowles, and already £30 has been collected.'[43]

It is unclear what Faiz and Tagh Mahomet thought of all of this. One can assume, however, that they would have been troubled. Both men lived within earshot of the rowdy Bayley Street rally that formed the 'Anti-Afghan League' in December 1894. The words of Vosper and others were particularly directed at them. To the gentlemen of the League the Mahomet brothers were a prime example of imported Asiatics rising above their station. While the Mahomet brothers remained publicly silent, Vosper's *Coolgardie Miner* (which continued to take the Mahomet's advertising money) published a letter from Perth by Mr Jim Mohand of the 'Afghan Committee':

> The people at Coolgardie must remember more than half of the population of the world is coloured, and we lose no time in making it known if justice is denied us. I don't think the people of Australia generally have forgotten that we have been the means of saving hundreds of lives on the goldfields with camels. The Afghans have been about 30 or 40 years in Australia, and nothing has ever been said of them, although they have been very badly treated at times. However, this case will put things on a different footing.[44]

Mr Mohand had a point. For example, when 120 Afghans and 354 camels had unexpectedly arrived in Fremantle aboard the *Abergeldie* in September 1887, they had been treated with peculiar interest rather than hostility. A journalist from *The Weekly Times* went aboard and interviewed some of the Afghans, noting (without rancour) in his report that a few were wearing parts of army uniforms, 'and these were evidently "loot" from British soldiers during campaigns in Afghanistan'. The Afghans and their camels even camped for a while at South Beach in Fremantle, providing a fascinating spectacle for locals.[45]

On the morning of 5 January 1895 the trial of Thomas Knowles commenced in Albany, with a newspaper correspondent reporting that the 'case is exciting great interest amongst miners in the town, the court being crowded'. Knowles pleaded not guilty. The trial proceeded rapidly and at the end of the day the jury, 'after short retirement', found Knowles not guilty. According to the report, the 'verdict was received with loud cheers in the Court'. Thomas Knowles walked free.[46]

The news was greeted with celebration in Coolgardie. In the *Coolgardie Miner* Vosper proclaimed that:

> It is a matter for congratulation for every white man on this field that [Thomas] Knowles has been acquitted of the two charges of manslaughter preferred against him. Had he been hanged or imprisoned the insolence of the Asiatic population, already unbearable, would have known no bounds, and the gross offences which led to the unfortunate shooting match would have been multiplied on every side.[47]

Indeed Vosper believed an important message had been sent to the Afghan population on the Goldfields with regard to their use of precious water.

> The verdict given will show the Afghans that they cannot in future destroy or pollute the means of livelihood of the whites...We trust that no jury may be found to disgrace itself by a verdict of 'guilty' in any case where a charge of manslaughter is made, in the face of the provocation that Knowles and others have received.[48]

Apparently, sometimes murder wasn't murder at all. Indeed, where water and the polluting influence of Afghans was concerned, it wasn't even manslaughter.

::

Tagh Mahomet's death was the lead news story in *The Kalgoorlie Miner* on 11 January 1896. In an article dated the day before, the newspaper reported that:

> At daylight this morning Goulam Mahomet shot Tagh Mahomet dead while at prayers at the Afghan camp. Tagh Mahomet was a member of the well-known firm of Faiz and Tagh Mahomet, the pioneer camel men of West Australia, and was very popular on the fields.[49]

Thirty-seven year old Tagh's charitable contributions to the local hospital were noted, as was the fact that the crime 'is supposed to be the outcome of some old grudge'. It was remarked that, 'No post-mortem examination was held, as it is against the Mahomedan religion for a Christian to handle the body of a Mahometan after death'. Then in bold type, *The Kalgoorlie Miner* offered readers a 'Graphic Description of the Dastardly Deed' as well as information on the 'Cool Behaviour of the Murderer'.[50]

Illuminatingly, *The Kalgoorlie Miner* reported that, 'As far as Coolgardie is concerned, the terrible crime of murder had not so far sullied the police records, but I regret to say we can make this boast no longer' And yet, 'General satisfaction lies in the fact that the tragedy was not committed by a white man, but by an alien'. While remarking that Tagh Mahomet was, along with his brother, among the best known and most respected residents of Coolgardie, the murder was described as 'of a most cowardly and cold-blooded nature'.[51] It was revealed that Goulam had lived in Perth for several years. He had come to Coolgardie with Mildool Khan, who was allegedly the first Afghan to settle permanently in West Australia.[52]

On 17 January the inquest into the death of Tagh Mahomet was held at the Police Court in Coolgardie. The hearing was open to the public and 'was filled to overflowing with onlookers'. A copy of the Qur'an was produced for the Afghan witnesses to swear upon, and no less than two translators were present in the court. A mullah from the Coolgardie mosque, described incorrectly as a 'Mahomedan priest' in the *Kalgoorlie Miner*, gave evidence along with a number of other Afghans. When questioned about why the murder of Tagh in the Mosque on a Friday was considered particularly heinous to Afghans, one of the witnesses explained that 'Friday is the same with us as Sunday is to you'.[53]

Arrested and deposed in Coolgardie, on 8 April 1896 Goulam Mahomet was tried for murder in front of Justice Stone in Perth. Two Afghan cameleers and two Muslim mullahs from Coolgardie appeared as witnesses.[54] In his defence, the twenty-seven year old insisted that he and Tagh Mahomet had argued in the street in Coolgardie on one occasion and that Goulam had grabbed Tagh by the beard and punched the rich Afghan businessman. Both men came from an Afghan tribal culture where insults to personal dignity were often resolved with bloodshed. According to *The Inquirer*:

Ever after, Goulam dreaded that Tagh was seeking to have him assassinated in revenge, and the life the man led was one of hunted fear. It was declared at the trial that large bribes had been offered by Tagh to some Afghans to kill his insulter, and, acting under such an impression, Goulam took the life of his supposed enemy.[55]

Goulam claimed that on the morning of the murder when he had run into Tagh Mahomet outside the Mosque, the rich cameleer had 'deliberately insulted him by neglecting to give him the usual Moslem salute as they met'.[56] Besides reiterating the allegations that Tagh had offered to pay people to kill Goulam, the defence also suggested that Goulam was high on hashish ('hemp-root' or 'heras' in the newspapers) and not in full control of himself when he killed Tagh.[57] The jury did not accept Goulam's defence and after a fifteen-minute deliberation, he was found guilty of murder.

::

On 23 March 1896, only two months after his brother's murder, Faiz Mahomet must have cast a worrying eye over the dramatic arrival of the railway in Coolgardie. Ten thousand people turned out to welcome the first train. There was a massive celebratory parade with the fire brigade and contingents from all the local civic associations. The Afghans put on a special display. Dressed in 'full Oriental costume', Afghan cameleers rode thirty-one camels in the parade and later presented special gifts to the attending dignitaries.[58] It was a last hurrah. The railway meant that Coolgardie was no longer cut off from the rest of 'civilisation' (in this case, civilisation meant the railway station at Southern Cross). The following month the *Coolgardie Miner* proposed moving the entire Afghan camp no less than two miles outside the town limits.[59] The age of the camel was drawing to a close.

A month later Goulam Mahomet was tried for Tagh Mahomet's murder. After the court passed a death sentence upon him, Goulam was taken to Fremantle Prison to await his execution. In his cell he continued to pray to Allah, the same God worshipped by his Christian jailers, as he prepared for death. During 1896 Mullah Mirza Khan petitioned the government for a change in the food regulations governing Muslim prisoners at Fremantle Prison. Islam, like Judaism and Christianity in its early years, maintains strict dietary rules. Among other things, the faithful must not eat pork, the flesh of birds of prey, meat that has been killed improperly (including by violent blows) and are expected to fast during Ramadan. The response of the Premier's Department to the 'Mahomedan' was that, 'here the Mahomedan is in the Britisher's country and if he does not like his treatment he can clear out'. The Premier himself, John Forrest, advised his under-secretary to write back to the petitioner – 'Reply that the best way to avoid the treatment he objects to is for Mahomedans to avoid gaols.'[60]

Therefore Goulam Mahomet, a man who was supposed to be spiritually preparing himself for death, was unable to eat halal meat while in Fremantle Prison. Instead, according to the newspapers, Goulam 'drinks large quantities of milk, and eats much fish and bread, while he frequently takes baths'.[61] Goulam also continued to receive visits from Muslim friends, and from Mullah Mirza Khan, who prayed with him and prepared him for the hangman's rope.

On the morning of 2 May 1896 Goulam Mahomet was led from his cell to the gallows inside Fremantle Prison. According to *The Inquirer*:

> He behaved well up to the last moment. Like a true Mussulman [Muslim], he displayed very little concern at his approaching death, saying that what was to be would be, and that, although he had killed Tagh Mahomet, he was no murderer, the deed being an act of self defence.[62]

Goulam had slept and prayed upon his prayer mat during 'his last night on earth'. He awoke at dawn on Saturday morning and was joined soon after by Mirza Khan who led him in prayers from the Qur'an. Although Goulam declined breakfast, he did request a final cup of tea before his execution.[63] Goulam Mahomet walked barefoot from his cell to the gallows and wore Afghan clothing rather than prison uniform ('spotless white pantaloons and smock' in the words of *The Inquirer*). Goulam approached the noose proclaiming his faith in a language his executioners couldn't understand. One of the reporters later asked the attending mullah and was told that Goulam had been chanting that, 'there is no God but the one God, and Mahomet is his Prophet'.[64]

It was eight o'clock in the morning. Outside the sun was shining brightly. Inside the execution chamber the atmosphere was sombre. Present were the various officials responsible for dispensing with human life, and five reporters who had been allowed in as witnesses. With keen scientific observation *The Inquirer* reported that the hangman's rope was 'a piece of new Manilla seven-eighths of an inch in thickness, and noosed with a ring or thimble instead of a knot'.[65] The hangman, 'a little old man named Burrell', a former transported convict, placed the noose around Goulam's neck. The condemned man kept swaying back and forth and uttering his prayers.[66]

Before he was hooded, Goulam was asked if he had any last words. He said farewell to a few Muslim friends who had been allowed in to witness his execution and then spoke to his executioners and the attending reporters in English:

> I am in the last moments of my life. In true faith of a Mussulman and knowing that I shall soon be with Allah, I will tell the truth. I am an innocent man. Tagh Mahomet was a rich man, but I not kill him for money. Tagh Mahomet gave people money to kill me. I shot him because he wanted to kill me; but it was not murder. I had no murder in my heart. I went away three times because he was going to kill me. He had anger towards me. He was a rich man, and I am not. He sure to kill me some of these days. Tagh Mahomet insulted me in the mosque at the last moment, and in a moment I shoot him.[67]

Then came a remarkable speech from a man about to die.

> I gave myself up. I believed there was justice in Englishmen; but now I not believe there is justice. I give my life into their hands, and they not do justice to me. I am innocent! I am innocent! I am innocent! Why then, hang me? If I English, I not be hung. An Englishmen shoot two Afghans, and he was let go. Thanks to God, I am not guilty before that one Judge, before whom I shall be soon.[68]

Goulam was referring to the Knowles case of 1894 – a case that was notorious among the Afghan cameleers for its injustice. Goulam then made reference to Britain's unsuccessful attempt to militarily subjugate Afghanistan. The disastrous British defeat in the First Afghan War of 1838–42, involving the massacre of retreating troops along Afghanistan's narrow mountain passes in the middle of winter, represented one of the most humiliating defeats in British military history. Of the approximately four thousand British soldiers of the Kabul garrison, only a handful made it out alive.

> English not friends to the Afghans. They will not forget; they can't forget. I am a Musselman [Muslim]. I'll soon be in joy this time. I die innocent.[69]

With his final testament finished, the mullah passed a copy of the Qur'an to Goulam who 'kissed it fervently'.[70] The execution hood was placed over his head and Goulam resumed his prayers. At eighteen minutes past eight in the morning Goulam plunged through the trap door. *The Inquirer* meticulously recorded the grisly details:

> The fall was 8ft., and as Goulam weighed 10st. 4 lb., the force was quite sufficient to break the neck. The victim drew his legs up convulsively two or three times, and then became still. The death work had been well carried out.[71]

The newspaper had noted that, 'Death was almost instantaneous and certainly was inflicted without pain.'[72] It was important to maintain the illusion that British Christian justice abhorred the infliction of suffering and was precise, clean and effective.

Unlike the Muslim murderer Jimmy Long, the first person to be hanged at Fremantle Prison, Goulam Mahomet died as a member of the local Muslim community and his treatment after his execution reflected this. Goulam Mahomet had lived in Perth for several years before he moved to Coolgardie and remained in contact with local Muslims during his incarceration. In a census held two years later it was revealed that there were twenty-three Muslims in Fremantle and eighty in Perth. All were male. In the absence of a Mosque Fremantle's Muslim community utilised two other buildings for religious observance, with at least half the community regularly turning out for Friday prayers. There were four Muslim prayer leaders servicing adherents in Perth and Fremantle.[73]

With the 'death work' completed, Goulam's body was taken down from the gallows and handed over to his Muslim friends. His corpse was taken to the prison morgue where it was washed, wrapped in white linen and placed in a prison coffin with flowers on top. Goulam Mahomet was taken from Fremantle Prison by a procession of about twenty 'Afghans, Bengali and Punjabis' who 'carried his coffin in turns' and chanted Muslim prayers. Arriving at the nearby old Fremantle cemetery, 'the coffin was placed on the ground so that the dead man faced the sun, and, kneeling in a row, the Mohammedans indulged in their service for the dead, accompanying it with many gestures and mute supplications.'[74]

The murder of Tagh Mahomet and the execution of Goulam Mahomet were big news in Western Australia. Even as Goulam's coffin was carried from prison, newspaper reporters dutifully traipsed behind it and were obviously intrigued by the spectacle of mourning Muslims on the streets of Fremantle.

One noted that there was no gateway to the segregated Muslim section of the graveyard and that Goulam Mahomet's coffin had to be 'hoisted over the wall' by his friends, before being placed in a waiting grave. Each of the Muslims attending the funeral threw a handful of dirt into the grave before it was properly filled in. In a remarkable gesture, the Muslims made sure Fremantle's gawking European residents were not excluded. After Goulam was buried, repeating a scene that had occurred at Tagh Mahomet's burial three months earlier, 'plentiful supplies of dates, almonds, and oranges were distributed among the crowd of curious spectators' by the Muslim mourners.[75]

::

In 1897 Frederick Vosper, the political voice of the *Coolgardie Miner* and the Anti-Afghan League, was elected to the West Australian Legislative Assembly for the seat of North-East Coolgardie. Thomas Knowles and his anti-Afghan animus had obviously served Vosper well. Three years later the Australian colonies federated. With the subsequent passing of the Immigration Restriction Act and the improvement of railway and water supplies to the Eastern Goldfields, the Afghan Muslim population withered. Their indispensable role in the expansion of Western Australia complete, the Afghan cameleers were now unwelcome 'aliens' in a land that no longer needed them.

Nevertheless, on 28 June 1901 Hugh Mahon, the federal Member for Coolgardie, stood on the floor of the new national parliament, and repeated the libel that the dwindling Afghan population were taking 'forcible possession' of waterholes across the Goldfields and excluding 'white men'. Mahon requested the prime minister of Australia consider deporting the entire Afghan population and enforce the 'absolute exclusion' of Afghans from future migration to Australia. When the prime minister wrote to the West Australian authorities requesting confirmation of the veracity of Mahon's allegations, he received a stark reply from the police commissioner, who declared that:

> Reports and rumours of Afghans polluting the water and taking forcible possession of dams have been received by the police on various occasions, but, on enquiry, no evidence was available to substantiate the same.[76]

Although Afghans had constituted a sizeable and visible minority within West Australia in 1896, by 1911 they were a measly 0.05 per cent of the state's population. Although during the 1890s there were more than a thousand Afghans in West Australia, by 1933 there were only 153 Afghans in the entire country.[77] Tagh, Faiz and Goulam's people were largely gone from Australia.

These days when most Australians think of Islam or Afghanistan they think of the Taliban, Osama bin Laden, and terrorism. It has been forgotten that many of the Afghan 'asylum seekers' who wash up on our shore in refugee boats share much history in common with us. Woomera detention centre, for example, is situated in a remote region of South Australia that was regularly traversed by nineteenth-century Afghan cameleers as they carried supplies across the outback. The Ghan, the celebrated rail service between Darwin and Adelaide, is named after these Afghan cameleers. We could do much better in Western Australia to celebrate the Muslim contribution to our own history.

::

On one visit to Kalgoorlie I had the opportunity to travel deep into the outback north-east of the town with an academic friend of mine, and an Aboriginal *Wongatha* elder, Geoffrey. After driving in the heat and dust for an hour or so, we pulled to the side of the road and followed Geoffrey on foot into the scrub. Less than a hundred metres from the road was a well-disguised and substantial enclosed well – more than enough to water an entire camel train. Geoffrey explained to us that there was a natural source of water below ground and that Afghan cameleers had built this well, and kept its location secret, as they traversed the Eastern Goldfields. He had no idea when it was built, except that it was 'gold rush times'. He learnt of its existence from Aboriginal elders who were the custodians of this land, and its precious supply of water, long before the Afghans or Europeans came.

Standing in the bush admiring the cunning of the Afghan cameleers I wondered if the well had been built by Faiz and Tagh Mahomet's company? I thought of Faiz, the suave businessman, who built a business empire on the backs of camels, and who was probably the best known and most respected Afghan in Western Australia. Still, in August 1896, seven months after his brother's murder, when Faiz applied for naturalisation as a British subject – pointing out that he had lived in Australia for twenty-two years – his application was denied. Or as a letter to him from the Colonial Under-Secretary explained:

I am directed to inform you that it is fully admitted that you have proved yourself a good citizen of the Colony and the decision arrived at in refusing you a Certificate of Naturalisation has no personal reference, but is part of the Policy of the Government.[78]

In 1897, the year after Tagh's death, the *Amir* of Afghanistan awarded Faiz Mahomet a special gold medal honouring his charitable service to his homeland as well as to the country he had made his adopted home – Australia.[79] But what became of Faiz? We know his business fell upon hard times, that he lived in Perth for a period between 1900 and 1905 (where he contributed to the building of the Perth mosque), and there was a brief mention in the *Kalgoorlie Miner* during 1907 that Faiz Mahomet had returned to Afghanistan 'last year'. He died soon after.[80]

Although Faiz and the other Afghan cameleers were eventually driven from Australia – unwanted and unneeded anymore – they left behind traces of their presence. These tokens included not only secret bush wells, but the more easily observable wild camels that now roam the West Australian desert. The expansive canyon-like streets of Kalgoorlie and Coolgardie, built wide enough so that you could turn a camel train around, are another reminder of the time when Afghan camels were the Eastern Goldfields' lifeline to the world.

The Afghans also left their graves. These final resting places of our Muslim pioneers are mostly forgotten and untended these days. For example, in the sandy and sparse Coolgardie Cemetery are the graves of sixteen Afghans, including Tagh Mahomet. The text of Tagh's elaborate gravestone is in Arabic and English. The headstone is decorated with an engraved vine of hearts and flowers. The English reads:

Sacred to the memory
Of
Tagh Mahomed
Who Died By The Hand Of An Assassin At Coolgardie Jan – 10th 1896
Aged 37 Years.
His End Was Peace.[81]

The Arabic text beneath carries the words of the *Shahadah* (holy affirmation) from the Qur'an. 'There is no God but God,' it reads, 'and Muhammad is his

Prophet.' Tagh's lonely grave is a reminder of the time when he and his brother Faiz were the undisputed camel kings of Coolgardie, before the railway, the Immigration Restriction Act and the murderous rage of Goulam Mahomet took everything away.

10

The Market Gardener, White Westralia and the Empire of the Rising Sun, 1908

An unstable Japanese man commits a crime of passion. Race, mental illness and murder create legal intrigue in post-Federation Western Australia.

When the Japanese Zero fighter planes flew over Broome on the morning of 3 March 1942 the pilots could hardly believe their luck. Tipping their silver wings and staring down at the remote pearling town scrunched between the turquoise blue of the ocean and the blood red dirt, they could see that Broome was crowded with Allied aircraft. Not only was the airstrip undefended, but there were a dozen sea planes parked in Roebuck Bay with the morning sun shimmering on the water at low tide.[1]

The Japanese pilots took turns diving from the hot blue sky and strafing their targets. The Allied planes burst into flames on the airstrip, or were shot to pieces and sank in the ocean. It was a good day for the Empire of the Rising Sun.

Many of the seaplanes in Roebuck Bay were full of refugees – men, women and children who had fled the seemingly unstoppable advance of the Japanese Army across Southeast Asia. A total of twenty-eight American, Dutch, Australian and British planes were destroyed that morning. It is conservatively estimated that at least fifty Dutch civilians died on the Dornier seaplanes, or drowned as they sank. More than thirty wounded US Servicemen died on a Liberator bomber shot down off Cable Beach. In total about 100 people, military and civilian, were killed. There was only one Japanese casualty. The Zero of Warrant Officer Osamu Kudo was hit by ground fire, crashed into the sea, and he was killed.

After the Japanese attack the general consensus among the remaining Broome residents was that the 3 March raid was probably the precursor to a full-scale Japanese invasion of Australia. A long rusty convoy of civilian vehicles attempted to evacuate Broome. They believed that the greatest fear of White Australia was finally becoming a reality – the yellow hordes were on their way.

::

Thirty-four years earlier the United States' Pacific Fleet – consisting of sixteen impressive cruisers, battleships and destroyers – visited Australia. Commonly referred to as 'the Great White Fleet', their visit during August 1908 resulted in some of the biggest public gatherings in the history of Sydney or Melbourne. Tens of thousands came to get a look at the impressive might of the US Navy.

The fleet had been invited to Australia by Prime Minister Alfred Deakin, who was secretly supplementing his governmental stipend with journalistic work for the London newspapers. Despite an obvious conflict of interest, Deakin reported anonymously on how the Australian government (which he led) had won popular support by inviting the Great White Fleet to Australia. Deakin argued that:

> Nowhere in the Empire, and perhaps nowhere outside of the Southern States of the Union [meaning the USA], is the import of the colour question more keenly realised than in the Commonwealth. The ties of kinship are potent too, and when these happen to be invoked in connection with a visit of the imposing American fleet to an ocean in which the Union Jack has foregone its old supremacy the significance of the invitation given by our Government assumes its true proportions.[2]

The West Australian, summarising the response of the American press to the visit of the US Pacific Fleet to Australia, noted that an improved American–Australian relationship would be 'a barrier against the extension of Japanese rule in the Pacific'. In anticipation of the fleet's expected arrival in Albany, a West Australian Reception Committee was formed to prepare extravagant festivities, and special trains were organised from Perth. Even in dusty land-locked Kalgoorlie the Western Argus carried six full pages of enthusiastic text and accompanying photographs (still a developing journalistic art) of the US Fleet's earlier visit to Sydney.[3]

On 11 September 1908 the Great White Fleet arrived in Albany. The following day the West Australian waxed lyrical about the 'mammoth warriors of the deep that slid swiftly and symmetrically into the Sound yesterday'. It was an impressive spectacle of 'power and beauty' that thrilled the people of Western Australia who came in droves to see it. The town of Albany had apparently never experienced anything quite like the visit 'in her wildest dreams of gorgeous glamour and bustling activity'. Across the state various newspapers reported on the excitement the visit of the US Navy had provoked.[4]

It was another sensation that had prompted the invitation to the Great White Fleet in the first place – fear of Japan. Uniquely, Japan had been able to avoid colonisation by any European power by modernising, industrialising and expanding through war. The Meiji Restoration of 1868 had succeeded in turning Japan into arguably the most powerful nation in Asia. Between 1894 and 1910 Japan waged three major successful military campaigns – one in China that humbled the Asian giant, one against Russia that represented the first humiliating defeat for a modern European nation in Asia, followed by the colonial annexation of Korea. Although Britain signed a friendship treaty in 1894, Australians remained distinctly uncomfortable with Japan's rise.

The very same year that the Great White Fleet visited Australia, 1908, a man was murdered outside Pinjarra, in the southwest of the state, in a crime of madness and passion. The killer was Japanese. The victim was a 'Britisher'. It was a powerful elixir for public interest.

::

In late 1906 a man called James Shaw[5] moved to a small farm south of Perth in the West Murray. On the farm, about nine miles from Pinjarra, he worked producing a market garden and lived with his wife and five children. Around November 1907 Shaw entered a business partnership with Oki Iwakichi, a local Japanese fisherman who had been in Western Australia for about twelve years. The first Japanese residents of the Murray region had arrived during the 1890s, and although the community was small there were a number of Japanese fishermen and market gardeners in the area.[6] A verbal agreement was entered into by which Oki and Shaw decided to share the costs of a market garden, fishing and poultry business. Shaw leased a farm for four years (with the help of Oki's money) and the two men agreed to split all costs and profits arising from the joint venture. According to *The Evening Mail*:

For a while matters progressed smoothly, then Shaw, finding that things were dull in the West Murray district, journeyed to the metropolitan district, where he remained for a considerable period, paying occasional visits to the farm.[7]

Shaw's fifteen-year-old son, Carol, assisted with the fishing and worked the farm with Oki. Although Oki was now living on the farm, the business floundered. After a delay of some months, Shaw eventually returned to the West Murray farm in early August 1908 and promptly suggested the business be sold and that his family move on. Oki was distinctly unhappy and had the temerity to insist that if that was to be the case, then half of everything on the farm was his. After some argumentation, and a further short-term absence of Shaw, the two men agreed to shut down the business and split the goods between them. But as the *Evening Mail* later reported:

> For the next three weeks relations prevailing the two men appear to have been strained. Oki became very unsettled and peculiar in his manner. He complained of 'a big lump' which came up in his throat, and refused to join the family for meals.[8]

As the day of the Shaw family's evacuation from the West Murray farm approached, Oki became visibly depressed and irrational. He kept begging Shaw to reconsider and at one point lay in bed with a rifle at his side, claiming that 'he would hurt no one but himself'. The following day, Sunday 23 August 1908, Oki refused to get out of bed and stayed in his 'singlet and pyjamas' all day. He refused to join the Shaw family for lunch, claiming that he might be poisoned. That evening he again missed the meal and after the family retired to bed the distressed Oki kept pacing the house, bothering the sleep of Mr Shaw. Eventually, harsh words were spoken between Shaw and Oki with Shaw remarking that they would have to 'settle things' or else Oki would have to move out so the family could get some sleep.[9]

Oki was clearly mentally disturbed by this point and Mary, James Shaw's wife, quietly suggested to her husband that she go get some rope in order to tie Oki up. Carol sat in the 'sitting room' while his mother took a hurricane lamp outside to find some rope. Mr Shaw got up and came into the sitting room to speak to his son. Oki could be heard bumbling around in the nearby kitchen. And then, to Carol's amazement, Oki suddenly burst into the room brandishing a shotgun which, without warning, he promptly fired into James

Shaw's chest. With Shaw bleeding to death on the floor, and his son screaming for help, Mary Shaw came running back to the house. Oki escaped into the night. With his wife at his side, Shaw proclaimed 'Mary, old girl, I'm shot,' before lapsing into unconsciousness.[10]

Running from the house where his father still lay dying, Carol Shaw had to swim the Murray River to raise the alarm. A rider was sent into town for a doctor and the police, while the neighbours came to the Shaw homestead to search for Oki. According to the *Evening Mail*, under the heading 'King Death':

> The lamp of life burnt feebly for a little over an hour, and then James Henry Shaw – enemy of no man, departed for 'The bourne from whence no traveller returns'.[11]

All that night and throughout the next day the police and 'black trackers scoured the neighbouring country for the fugitive murderer'. It was not until Tuesday night, two days after the murder, that Oki was captured after he turned up at a neighbour's house suffering from exposure.[12] He was arrested for murder.

::

Officially the Australian nation was not born until the first morning of 1901. On that day the old British colonies ceased to exist, supplanted by the new federal Commonwealth of Australia. The new nation, made up of six states and governing an entire continent, had a total population of less than four million people. Despite the popularity of a literary culture based around farming life and the outback, most Australians lived in cities. One-quarter of the nation lived in Melbourne and Sydney alone. The rest remained mainly clustered in coastal outposts of the British Empire – Perth, Hobart, Brisbane – or coagulated in dry outback centres like Coolgardie or Broken Hill.

At the official ceremony held in Sydney's Centennial Park on 1 January 1901, proceedings took place under the folds of the British Union Jack, 'God Save the Queen' was sung by those assembled to give birth to the new nation, and toasts of honour were drunk to the British monarchy. It could not have been otherwise. There was no Australian national anthem to sing and no Australian flag to fly. There wasn't even an agreed permanent national capital. Although a design for an Australian flag was officially selected later in 1901, it was not until the Flag Act of 1953 that it displaced the British flag at the ceremonial centre of Australian life. Similarly, 'Advance Australia Fair' did not become the national anthem (winning out over the unofficial anthem, 'Waltzing Matilda') until 1984.[13] Even more remarkably, it was not until the Nationality and Citizenship Act of 1948 that the government started to legally define Australian citizenship as being uniquely separate from being a subject of the British Empire.[14]

Of the 3,773,801 people who made up the Commonwealth of Australia in 1901, almost a quarter had been born in Great Britain. Of the remainder of the white Australians, most had a parent or grandparents who had been born in the British Isles. Australia did, however, still have significant non-European populations – including 29,907 Chinese, 3,602 Japanese and 10,428 Pacific Islanders. Still, such inchoate 'multiculturalism' needs to be kept in perspective. Only 40,000 people, or 1 per cent of the nation, were Asian – significantly less than the estimated 94,000 Aborigines who were marginalised within the new Federal Commonwealth.[15]

The founders of Australian Federation were, essentially, dreamers and idealists. Although Federation is sometimes presented by historians as a mercenary business deal (customs union), or a racist pact (White Australia Policy), at its core was a common agreement to construct a nation from a disparate and isolated set of colonies at the ends of the earth. The new Federal Commonwealth would be proudly British in its culture, composition and political orientation. One example of this commitment was represented in the fact that on the day the nation was born it was already at war, with Australian colonial troops fighting for the British Empire against the Boxers in China and the Boers in South Africa.

Western Australia had been a reluctant participant in the coming together of the Australian colonies under a single federal government – only signing up at the last moment. However, as with all matters in Western Australia during the 1890s, the Goldfields proved hugely influential. The presence of large numbers of 'tothersiders', miners originally from the Eastern colonies, in towns like Kalgoorlie and Coolgardie swung the political balance against remaining outside the federal pact. In December 1899 the Eastern Goldfields had assembled delegates in Coolgardie who resolved to secede from Western Australia if it failed to join the new nation and threatened to federate with the rest of Australia as an independent state. Around 28,000 locals signed a petition in favour of 'Separation for Federation'.

A successful referendum on Federation was eventually held in Western Australia on 31 July 1900, twenty-two days after Queen Victoria had already signed the Constitution bill in London. Even John Forrest's belated attempt to offset the overwhelmingly male pro-Federation votes of the Goldfields by granting women the vote was not sufficient to keep Western Australia out of the Commonwealth. The Goldfields voted overwhelmingly in favour of federation – 26,330 votes for and only 1,813 against. The 'Yes' votes of the Goldfields, in turn, made up almost 60 per cent of the state total and effectively secured Western Australia's place in the new Commonwealth.[16]

Western Australia, which became the last state to join the Commonwealth of Australia, made up almost a third of the total landmass of the continent. Without Kalgoorlie and Coolgardie, Australia might never have been, as Edmund Barton famously put it, 'a continent for a nation and a nation for a continent'. And in the same way that it seemed natural and inevitable that Australia should one day become a single country (rather than six self-governing colonies under the Crown), it was similarly logical and self-evident to Barton and all the 'Founding Fathers' that this new nation should unashamedly proclaim itself to be a 'white man's country'. To many Australians the Japanese remained a barely tolerated alien minority within the new Commonwealth. Or as the large 'triumphant arch' constructed upon The Esplanade in Perth proclaimed in bold, visionary and exclusive terms – 'One People, One Destiny'.[17]

::

At Oki Iwakichi's murder trial, held in what one newspaper rather grandiosely described as a 'sombre palace of justice' only one month after the American 'Great White Fleet' had left Australia, it took two full days to hear the evidence.[18] A translator was required for Oki so that he could understand what was going on. Oki sat motionless in the courtroom – 'He might have been a statue cast in bronze, but for the careless flicker of his eyelids.' Although his appearance had apparently improved since the coronial inquest, he still appeared dishevelled and strange to the reporters covering the case. Moreover, at each adjournment of the court, 'the officials were forced to rouse him from his apathetic lethargy'. The trial ended as everyone expected, with Oki Iwakichi being found guilty of murder and sentenced to death. He was taken to Fremantle Prison to await the gallows.[19]

The 18 October edition of *The Sunday Times*, reporting on 'The West Murray Tragedy', revealed that a petition that included the signatures of five of the jurors who had found Oki guilty of murder had been sent to the Executive Council requesting that the death sentence be commuted to life in prison. The petition was turned down and a date was set for the execution – Tuesday, 27 October at eight in the morning.[20] As the 'end of his earthy existence' approached, in the words of *The Evening Mail*, Oki Iwakichi was 'in a placid and undemonstrative mood' according to the newspaper's sources inside Fremantle prison. With only days left to live, Oki 'expressed regret' regarding the murder of James Shaw. Although he was a Buddhist, Oki was visited regularly by a Catholic priest, Father Wheeler, who succeeded in baptising Oki into the faith on the very morning of his hanging. On the way to his execution Oki apparently 'shuffled' passively off to his death 'with closed eyes and downcast head'.[21]

Inside the gallows room the grim execution ritual began. The *Evening Mail* described Oki's executioner as wearing a 'sinister black mask over his face'.[22] Oki stood silent as the white hood was placed over his head and the noose adjusted around his neck. When the priest finished his prayers and asked if Oki had any final words, Oki said nothing. The priest asked again. Again nothing. The priest stepped forward and whispered in Oki's ear – 'Jesus, lover of my soul' – words that Oki quietly repeated. The ritual complete except for one final gruesome act, the priest stepped back and the bolt was pulled on the drop. Oki fell five feet into the darkness until the rope yanked the life out of him.[23]

A reporter from *The Evening Mail* explained the importance of the execution to the newspaper's readers:

> Happily, in Australia murder is a crime that is comparatively rare, and it is not often that the hangman is called upon to perform his grisly duties. The West Murray murder was one of somewhat remarkable features, showing as it did some sidelights of a sordid and repulsive nature. The law is the law, and that the murderer in this case was an alien weighed not one iota in the trial and subsequent deliberations of the jury. Putting aside the the question of capital punishment altogether it has to be admitted that this morning Oki Iwakichi deservedly suffered for his dastardly and brutal crime.[24]

Twenty-one people, including six journalists, had witnessed Oki's hanging in the execution room of Fremantle Prison. Most were prison warders. None mourned his passing.

::

In 1901 when the Federal Commonwealth came into existence an estimated 3,602 Japanese existed within an Australian nation of 3,773,801 people. As such, the Japanese made up only a minuscule .0009 per cent of the population of the country. In Western Australia there were 658 Japanese men and 209 women. Of the 867 Japanese in the state, 366 of them (almost half the total) resided in Broome.[25] In earlier times many white Australians had displayed a curious and active interest in exotic Japan. There was much about the culture – including its focus on order, personal strength and cleanliness – that appealed to the nineteenth-century European mind and contrasted sharply with stereotypes about degraded and dirty 'Chinese coolies'.

Possibly the first Japanese to visit Western Australia were the Kioto Troupe – a travelling band of acrobats who, in November and December of 1873, performed in front of the governor and for packed audiences in the Perth Town Hall. The troupe appeared in Fremantle, Perth and several other towns in the south-west of the colony. An advertisement in the *Western Australian Times* informed interested readers that the troupe consisted of 'Japanese Jugglers, Foot Balancers, Top Spinners, Rope Walkers, Acrobats, Shoulder Balancers, etc, etc, etc, in their wonderful and pleasing Entertainments that created such a wonderful sensation in every part of the world that they have visited'.[26] It was pointed out that previous audiences had included 'H.M The Queen', as well as 'The Crowned Heads of Europe'. Western Australian audiences were apparently entranced by the antics of the performers, who seemed to confirm the view that the Japanese, although Asian, were somehow 'different', disciplined, and more deserving of respect.[27]

Similarly, in December 1894 Miss Georgia Cayvan, who had visited Japan, provided a public lecture that was later reproduced in *The Inquirer*. In the lecture Japanese women were described as 'dainty little ladies' and unfamiliar Japanese culture was explained in favourable terms. Interestingly, the speaker was particularly concerned by recent attempts by wealthy Japanese to forego traditional dress in favour of European attire.

> It is enough to make the angels weep to see them change this dress, which suits them so beautifully, for the European attire, in which they lose every vestige of the piqant, dainty grace. They wear our things as badly as we wear theirs, which is saying a great deal. The shoes seem most disastrous in effect, for a Japanese lady walks in them as if she had had a glass to[o] much.[28]

The first Japanese migrant workers started arriving in Western Australia during the 1880s. They played a crucial role in the establishment of several remote towns including Cossack (in the Pilbara) where in 1893 there were only 141 Europeans resident, as compared to 225 Asians.[29] With the gold rush of the 1890s Japanese joined the Chinese, Afghans and other non-European minorities trying to eke out a position for themselves in the frontier towns of Kalgoorlie, Coolgardie and elsewhere. Although Japanese businessmen like Muramatsu Jiro attempted to 'assimilate' and were able to build up substantial financial interests in the colony, it did not protect him from later being stripped of the right to residency – an injustice Jiro unsuccessfully appealed all the way to the High Court.[30]

By the 1890s it was not just Japanese men who were taking the boat to Western Australia. Japanese prostitutes and brothel madams worked on the Kalgoorlie and Coolgardie goldfields, as well as establishing a highly visible presence in Broome and other remote towns. The 1901 census recorded 209 Japanese-born women as being resident in Western Australia.[31] When Albert Calvert travelled through Western Australia in 1896 he was highly conscious of the presence of these Japanese women. In remote Roebourne he observed:

> Near the river there is a Japanese village. In nearly all the towns of the North-West dwell frail sisters of the East. Carnarvon alone refuses to countenance this form of social evil. The other centres are content to ban the aliens from the European quarter. The Japanese courtesan is always young, sometimes comely, and invariably partial to plenty of soap and water.[32]

In other words, 'laundries' and 'bath houses' were well-known fronts for Japanese brothels. Similarly, Japanese prostitutes, referred to as 'dressmakers' and given exemptions under the Immigration Restriction Act, catered to the Japanese men who worked in the pearling industry in Broome. There were apparently twenty-one Japanese dressmakers in Broome between 1916 and 1941, despite the fact that, as Emma Hopkins argues, it was 'highly unlikely that there would have been enough work to sustain these businesses' given the tiny female population of the town. Moreover, 'not a single advertisement' for dress-making services 'appears in the town newspaper'. Shiba Lane in Broome was well known as the centre of the Japanese gambling and red light district.[33]

Although the Immigration Restriction Act of 1901 represented a definite hardening of attitudes towards Asian migration, the Japanese were able to maintain their positions in niche occupations – particularly as pearl divers, laundry workers, rural cooks or market gardeners. The fact that these occupations were so closely associated with Asian labour partially protected them being taken over by Europeans. What many white Australians were not prepared to countenance was the idea that some Japanese might be rising above their 'natural station'. For example, when in 1909 the Australian government approved a Japanese doctor to come and practise in Broome the local white community were incensed. The *Broome Chronicle* published letters and commentary in opposition to the proposal on the grounds that it would set a 'grave precedent because the Chinese and Afghan populations of the North might make similar demands, and the next request might be for Asiatic lawyers and others'.[34]

When the Immigration Restriction Act was debated in September 1901, Alfred Deakin, Attorney-General of the new Federal Commonwealth, spoke not only for his parliamentary colleagues but for the majority of white Australians when he said that:

> ...no motive operated more powerfully in dissolving the technical and arbitrary political divisions which previously separated us than the desire that we should be one people and remain one people without the admixture of other races. It is not necessary to reflect upon them even by implication. It is only necessary to say that they do not and cannot blend with us; that we do not, cannot, and ought not to blend with them.[35]

In the same parliamentary debate John Watson, leader of the Labor Party, similarly opposed the 'racial contamination' threatened by 'these coloured people' coming to Australia.[36] In June 1901 *The Bulletin* published an article entitled 'The Jap on the Horizon', where it was argued that the Australian population objected to Japanese immigration:

> ...because they introduce a lower civilization. It objects because they intermarry with white women, and thereby lower the white type, and because they have already created the beginnings of a mongrel race...[37]

Japanese prostitution was one thing, but it was miscegenation that really struck terror into the hearts of white Australians.

::

At Oki Iwakichi's trial Mrs Mary Shaw, James' widow, had given evidence.[38] She was, according to the *West Australian*, calm and collected.[39] She said that she had been married to her husband James for seventeen years and that she had known Oki for about two years in total. After her husband and Oki had entered into business together Oki had moved into 'a room adjoining the stables'. He had stayed in the 'out house' until about three months prior to the murder, when he moved into the sitting room in the main house where Carol Shaw, her oldest son, also slept at night. In her version of Oki's breakdown there were multiple threats by Oki to shoot himself. Oki mentioned that 'everything was dark' for him following the failure of his business partnership with Shaw. Mary's husband forcibly removed the gun from Oki and told him that, 'Mrs is afraid of it.' At this point Oki was crying because he would never see his mother or brothers again. Although Shaw had initially humoured him in his attempt to get the rifle off him, he now gave the rifle to his wife for safe-keeping and went to bed.[40]

The next day Oki stayed in bed and complained about a lump in his throat. According to Mary, however, he also begged her husband to shoot him – an enticement he declined. That night Oki was very distraught, disturbing the sleep of the family while rummaging around the house. Mary spelt out 'r-o-p-e' to her husband (Oki, presumably, could not spell in English) and then went out looking for something to tie Oki up with. Shortly afterwards she heard the fatal gunshot and her son cry out, 'You dog!' When she rushed into the sitting room her husband was bleeding on the floor. Carol was pummelling Oki with his fists in the corner of the room. Oki, however, was able to escape from the house and was chased by Carol, who ended up throwing the hurricane lamp at him in frustration. Oki got away. The next time Mary Shaw saw Oki was in court.[41]

There was, however, one interesting comment right at the end of Mary Shaw's testimony. Asked if she thought Oki had reason to kill her husband, she replied:

> I know no particular reason for this man Oki to have shot my husband, except that of breaking up the home.[42]

Such comments led some to believe that there was more to the relationship between Oki and Mary Shaw than met the eye. After all, they had lived on the farm together when her husband was away. Was Oki in love with her?

Some evidence pointed to as much. For example, Oki had been captured in the house of Forrest Charles Carruthers. In his evidence before the court Mr Curruthers mentioned that before being arrested by the police, Oki had told him:

> ...me very sorry, twice, Mrs Shaw all spoil me. You think me happy, I said I don't know Oki, I don't think so. He said which way Mrs Shaw. I said gone Pinjarrah funeral. He caught hold of my hand which was on the door and said me go out and die.[43]

Curruthers had his wife make Oki some tea while he waited for the police to arrive – 'All the time he was having his meal, he kept repeating Mrs Shaw all spoil me, before me good man.' Curruthers also mentioned that Oki did not mention the man that he had killed, James Shaw, once during the whole time he was at Curruthers' house, just his widow. Similarly, in evidence before the court Gitaro Kariya, Oki's cousin, claimed that once when he turned up at the Shaw's house, James Shaw had pointed at Mary, asking, 'Is she my wife or Oki's wife?' Kariya asserted that, indeed, Mrs Shaw was 'your wife'.[44]

Was James Shaw suspicious of something, or did he just think Oki was developing dangerous notions about his beloved? The most telling evidence, however, came from the pen of Oki himself. The Crown Prosecutor read several translated letters that Oki had written to his cousin prior to the murder. The first letter read:

> Me and the Missus about one and a half years ago been like man and wife. If me not here all the children will starve and now they want me to go and separate us. That make me very cross and something come up in my throat. Me have been supporting all Mrs Shaw's family. Old man never look after the house and family. Mrs Shaw all cause of trouble. If you think statement not true you can ask everybody...[45]

A second letter by Oki, read in translation to the court, alleged:

> Me, Missus and old man quarrel. Me penniless and cannot do anything. I think go to other side of the world altogether...Missus said old man know nothing and she hint at separation and want me to live with her.[46]

The letter ended with a threat to suicide – 'Good-bye to everybody' – and a suggestion that his cousin sell up his estate after his death. Remember, Oki wrote, 'Mrs Shaw owe me £63'.

Was Oki delusional? Was the lonely Japanese man simply lovestruck, imagining a relationship with Mary Shaw which did not really exist? Or was Mrs Shaw a romantic manipulator, encouraging Oki's notions and using him to keep her family fed during tough times? Was there some credibility to his charge that they had previously had a sexual relationship? At the trial Mary Shaw was asked uncomfortable questions by the Prosecutor regarding the allegations in Oki's letters. First the translation of the letters was read to her:

Witness: Is that Oki's writing?

Mr Barker [Prosecutor]: It is a translation of Oki's writing.

Witness: There is no truth in it.

Mr Barker: Oki goes on to say that he supported the family.

Witness: It was my son who did the supporting when my husband was unable to send enough money for us.

Mr Barker: He says you wanted a separation so that you and he might live together.

Witness (indignantly): There was nothing of the kind. There is not truth in it.[47]

The defence cross-examined Mary Shaw, alleging that Oki had bought clothing for her children and paid the maternity expenses when her twins had been born. Furthermore, according to the defence, when Mr Curruthers had challenged Mary Shaw regarding her relationship with Oki, she had allegedly told him that 'I had to do this because Harry would not help me'. Mary Shaw denied this, adding that, 'we all hate Mr Curruthers'.[48]

Remarkably, on the final day of the trial the judge decided that the letters that Oki had written and in which he had made allegations about a sexual relationship with Mrs Shaw were so badly written that their true meaning was not clear and that they could not therefore be considered reliable. They were discounted as evidence.[49]

::

Why had the court simply dismissed Oki Iwikachi's letters? Were they really that poorly written, or maybe the prosecution simply decided that Oki would hang anyway (no one was disputing he shot Shaw), so why ruin a grieving widow's reputation over it? Especially a widow with five white children to look after. Regardless, Oki Iwikachi was hanged soon after in Fremantle, thousands of miles from his ancestral home in Japan. In Fremantle he was isolated. In the north of the state, however, remained Australia's most prominent and thriving Japanese community.

Broome was established in 1883 to act as base of operations for the then immensely profitable business of harvesting mother-of-pearl shell. Before plastic took over our world, pearl shell was widely used for buttons and many other essential domestic items. By the 1920s Broome's 400 pearl luggers were responsible for harvesting about 80 per cent of the mother-of-pearl shell on the world market.[50]

Broome, more than any other Australian town, had a long relationship with Japan. There were already 322 Japanese living in tiny isolated Broome in 1891, and the population continued to grow after that time.[51] So much so that by the late 1890s Broome, in the words of historian David Day, had taken on 'the appearance of being an Asian township'.[52] Unlike the situation in the rest of the colony, in Broome the Japanese were at the centre of economic and cultural life, dominating the local pearling industry and establishing their own vibrant neighbourhood and social hierarchy. The Japanese had their own hospital in Broome, complete with their own specially imported Japanese doctor. They also had their own brothels and gambling houses in Shiba Lane. In 1916 Australia's first soya sauce factory was even opened. Until 1941, despite the White Australian Policy, the Japanese remained a prominent ethnic group in town.[53]

The Japanese of Broome had done everything they could to emphasise their patriotic attachment to their new country. Outside the Japanese Club was an archway with 'God Save the King', meaning the British one, emblazoned upon it in both English and Japanese.[54] British and Japanese flags were prominently displayed at all community functions. The Japanese community even collected money for the families of local Anzacs killed during World War One.[55] Broome's European population, including those who wrote for the local newspaper, were particularly impressed by Japanese ceremonies honouring their community's own dead.

Western Civilization could learn quite a little from the Orient in the way of caring for the last resting place of their relatives and friends. On outgoing tides this week one could see miniature luggers, laden with food, etc., sailing out to solace the departed spirits of those Japanese who have found watery graves while searching for the elusive pearl.[56]

A senior Japanese businessman in Broome, Umeda Nobutaro, was apparently fond of promoting the friendship between Australia and Japan by reference to a parable regarding a hard-boiled egg. The egg was 'white and yellow in the same shell together forming a harmonious whole, yet each separate, distinct and unmixed'.[57] Such perspectives were reassuring to the European community and Broome remained a racially segregated town. Even the famous Sun Picture Theatre, now a tourist attraction, had separate fees, entry doors, and seating for white, Asian and Aboriginal patrons.[58]

At times the segregation, sexual and class tensions could explode into violence. In December 1920 serious rioting broke out in Broome between the Japanese and Koepangers (Timorese). The rioting developed after a Koepanger allegedly stabbed a Japanese pearl diver at around nine o'clock one night. According to the *West Australian*, the 'Japanese turned out in force, armed with mangrove clubs, pieces of bar iron, and iron piping'. Isolated Koepangers were attacked and beaten. By eleven o'clock the police had sworn in twenty 'special constables' in an attempt to stop the violence. When that failed all returned World War One soldiers were summoned, with eighty volunteering to form patrols and restore the peace. The rioting subsided after midnight, but resumed the next morning. It was then that:

> ...all the whites were called out and mustered at the police station. Armed patrols were formed, and the Riot Act was read to the Japanese by the Resident Magistrate. All the hotels were closed. The Koepangers were mustered under the protection of armed white guards. As the result of the disturbances two Japanese were killed and four others are in hospital, while four Koepangers are also in hospital badly hurt.[59]

At its peak the riots had involved up to about 400 Koepangers and possibly as many as 800 Japanese.[60]

In 1939 when World War Two broke out, albeit without Japanese involvement, the population of Broome was around 1,500 people. There were only 150 white men and 400 white women and children in Broome, as compared to 269 Japanese, 75 Malays, 188 Koepangers, 107 Chinese, and 21 Manilamen (Filipinos). As such, the minority white population numbered about 550 as compared to an Asian population of 660, and about 400 Aborigines.[61] During June of 1941, six months before Japan bombed Pearl Harbor, West Australian police were issued with arrest warrants for Japanese living in their area.[62] Then in December 1941, immediately following Japan's devastating attack on Pearl Harbor, 212 Japanese residents of Broome who had been identified as 'enemy aliens' were rounded up and deported to an internment camp.

Included in the Broome arrests were twenty women and nine children under the age of thirteen (the youngest was four months old). Of the women, fourteen were over the age of sixty and had entered Australia more than forty years earlier – before the Immigration Restriction Act of 1901. All of the children had been born in Western Australia.[63] Although only about 30 per cent of the German and Italian population of Australia were interned, 97 per cent of Japanese resident in Australia at the time of the outbreak of war soon found themselves behind barbed wire.[64] Occasionally, however, some Japanese-Australians were able to avoid arrest, exposing the remarkable contradictions of the internment policy. For example, William Kobe Michimoto served in the Australian armed forces while his Japanese father was arrested in Geraldton and taken away to an internment camp.[65]

With Australia at war, anti-Japanese propaganda was broadcast on ABC Radio and published in the newspapers. Following the devastating raid on Broome, one government advertisement from 25 March 1942 commented that, 'The maps he made on our luggers, bring Japanese bombers to Broome.' The advertisement ended with the revealing slogan, 'We've always despised them – NOW WE MUST SMASH THEM!'[66]

Today the Japanese cemetery in Broome is a tourist attraction. There are 707 unique Japanese-style graves, representing the lives of 919 Japanese who died in or around Broome.[67] The tall sandstone graves are intricately carved with neat rows of Japanese characters. They tell the stories of the mainly young Japanese men who died diving for precious pearl shell or were lost at sea. Like the engine of one of the Allied planes destroyed by the Japanese during the 1942 raid and now mounted outside the Qantas departure gate at Broome airport, the Japanese graveyard speaks of another time and place in our history.

There is no memorial for Oki Iwikachi. After Oki was hanged in Fremantle the Sheriff's Deputy sent copies of the documents relating to his execution to the Consulate General of His Imperial Japanese Majesty in Martin Place, Sydney. The Consul General wrote back a polite reply on 3 December 1908 thanking them for the correspondence.[68] Oki Iwakachi had been legally disposed of. A marginalised migrant in a country that barely tolerated his presence, he was easily forgotten.

II

Martha Rendell and the Manufacture
of a Suburban Monster, 1909

The police and press discover a monster lurking in suburban Perth. Children die mysterious deaths and a woman is accused of murder.

Indulging my illicit passion for cheap literature I came across an interesting find in a second hand bookstore a few years ago. The *Australian Murder Almanac* not only offered me '150 Years of Chilling Crime' but also promised '28 Gripping Yarns'. Although published in 1993 the book definitely had a 1940s *noir* look and feel to it, not least of all in its seamless blending of journalism, crime and sensationalism. The fifth story (one is hesitant to call it a chapter) particularly stood out – 'Perth Woman Made History On Gallows'. The introductory paragraph was magnificently lacking in subtlety:

> Martha Rendall was a murderous sadist who took sexual pleasure from the agony of children. Still considered the nation's most vicious female killer, she entered the history books on October 6, 1909, when she became the last woman to be hanged in Western Australia.[1]

Intrigued, I read on:

> Every night in the winter months of 1907, a terrible drama was enacted in the bedroom of a drab weatherboard cottage in the suburb of East Perth. In a bed lay a wasted little girl, continually racked with coughing while a short but shapely brunette of about thirty-five watched. As the woman swayed back and forth in her chair, she would break into laughter as each tormented moan from the small figure on the bed filled the room.[2]

According to the *Murder Almanac* the woman was none other than Martha Rendell, 'one of Australia's most monstrous murderers, who killed three of her step-children with apparently no other motive than pure sadism'.[3] Frightening stuff.

Some years later, waiting at Sydney airport for a flight to Perth, I noticed a glossy 'true crime' publication of considerable thickness entitled *Australia's Serial Killers*. Promising to be the 'Definitive History of Serial Multicide' in our country, chapter six featured none other than 'The Murderous Mistress', Martha Rendell. Apparently Rendell had graduated from being simply one of Australia's most vicious and diabolical killers, to being 'among the most sadistic serial child killers the world has ever known'.[4]

Martha Rendell had also been physically transformed during the ten years between the two publications. Now described as tall and 'voluptuous', Martha Rendell the 'disruptive mistress' was accused of first destroying the 'Morris family's blissful existence' by moving in to their home, and of then poisoning three of her lover's children to death. Finally uncovered by a young Police Inspector with 'Sherlock Holmes tendencies', Rendell was charged with murder and eventually hanged in Fremantle Prison. If nothing else, the aforementioned Police Inspector, Harry Mann, obviously possessed superhuman insight – he was quoted in the *Murder Almanac* as saying that Martha Rendell 'delighted in seeing her victims writhe in agony and from it derived sexual satisfaction'.[5]

Afterwards I kept wondering who Martha Rendell really was. Could there have been another explanation for the Morris children's deaths? For example, the urban environment of Perth at the turn of the century was notoriously dangerous. During the 1890s even Perth's drains were lethal. Or as Tom Stannage has written with regard to the suburb where the Morris children died:

> In East Perth alone the drain received refuse from a tannery, soap factory, brickworks, factories, stables, laundries, four saw mills, foundries, and so on. By the turn of the century the drain was regarded as 'a disgrace to the Council', and local children were warned not to go near it. One of the open drains, in Coolgardie Street, was known as the 'fever drain'.[6]

The open drain in Coolgardie Street was only a short walk from the Morris family's home. East Perth was not alone in posing a significant health hazard to the young. As one researcher has detailed:

Perth, because of its climate and its flies, and because it was still in many ways a frontier town, retained the doubtful privilege of having the worst IMR [Infant Mortality Rate] in the Commonwealth, although positive action by health authorities and an increasing knowledge of health care practices amongst mothers by 1914 greatly reduced the threat of infant death from weanling diarrhoea.[7]

Weanling diarrhoea is an illness where pathogenic micro-organisms cause 'progressive weakening as diarrhoea and poor nutrition react together in a vicious spiral which is accelerated by poor environmental sanitation, inadequate hygiene within the home and parental ignorance.'[8] During the late nineteenth and early twentieth centuries weanling diarrhoea killed many small children in Perth.

The government was aware of the health threat posed by Perth's urban environment. As Martha Rendell sat in the dock of the Supreme Court charged with murder, the West Australian parliament debated bills on public sewerage, water supply, public education, liquor licensing and vaccination.[9] These were all contentious issues of social reform, with one Perth resident writing to the *West Australian* voicing their opposition to mandatory childhood vaccination:

> In many other localities people are, prompted by conscientious reasons, put to the expense of moving, and even leaving the State for various periods, in order to dodge the compulsory officer, for whom there is a dislike verging on hate. One man told me that he had two of his children, each the picture of health, vaccinated, and that both of these died in very great pain within two months.[10]

The same edition of the newspaper also carried numerous medical advertisements in the form of supposed letters from happy customers about how to cure the urban ailments of consumption, 'hacking coughs,' 'liver trouble,' as well as 'nervousness and heart palpitation.' Women were the target of special advertisements offering them soaps and other domestic consumables that promised 'perfect complexions and soft, glossy hair' among other benefits. Preying on insecurities (some things never change), one advertisement offered the 'perfect bust' and asked 'Are you thin and scraggy, flat-chested, spare bosomed, and a walking skeleton?'[11]

Overall, Perth in 1909 was, like many other urban industrial centres, a city obsessed with its health, appearance and welfare. It was also a city that was dangerous for children, with many still dying from simple diseases or from unknown causes. Other dangers lurked within the home.

::

It took five days for all the sordid details in the Martha Rendell murder trial to unfold. Under the headline 'A City Sensation', the *West Australian* gave the opening of the case in the Supreme Court on the morning of 7 September 1909 extensive coverage. Although she was blamed for the deaths of three of the Morris children between July 1907 and October 1908, Martha Rendell was only charged with the murder of thirteen-year-old Arthur J. Morris. Rendell, who was about forty, and her fifty-year-old de facto Thomas Morris (charged as an accessory) were led up the steps from the Supreme Court basement straight into the dock to face Justice McMillan. Both pleaded not guilty. The Crown Solicitor, Mr A. E. Barker, opened the prosecution's case.[12]

In his opening statement Mr Barker pointed out to the jury that a coronial inquiry held in August had already found Martha Rendell responsible for the death of Arthur Morris, but that 'did not bind the present jury in any way'.[13] He contended that Martha had deliberately poisoned Arthur in the family's home in Robertson Street, East Perth. Mr Barker conceded that while his only evidence was 'circumstantial', it was nevertheless overwhelming. Accordingly, Martha Rendell had killed Arthur and two other Morris children with an 'irritant poison' commonly known as 'spirits of salts' (hydrochloric acid). In concluding his opening statement, Mr Barker said:

> ...he wished to refer to the peculiar conduct of Mrs Rendall since the matter had got into the ears and mouths of the public. The medical evidence went very far to prove that she had endeavoured to create on her own throat an appearance to give the impression that she was suffering from the same complaint as that from which the children had suffered.[14]

Having reminded the jury that a coronial jury had already determined Martha was responsible for the death of Arthur Morris, and planted the idea that Martha had attempted to cover up the murder by faking a medical complaint, the first witness was then called. It was none other than Sarah Morris, wife of Martha Rendell's co-accused and mother of the murdered children.

Sarah and Thomas Morris, a carpenter, had been married in Melbourne around 1887. The couple moved to Adelaide where they lived for some time, before moving to Perth. Sarah testified that her marriage to Thomas had been troubled, however, with the principal cause of the 'unhappy relations' between her and her husband being 'a third party coming on the scene in the person of Martha Rendall'. Rendell was presented by Sarah Morris as a manipulative and murderous whore – a woman who broke up an otherwise happy family and then killed her children.[15]

Mrs Morris's cross-examination by the defence focused upon her own role in the family's destruction. Accordingly, Thomas Morris had brought his wife and five children to Western Australia for a new start around 1904. About a year later Thomas ejected Sarah from the family home in East Perth. The *West Australian* recorded the following exchange between Sarah Morris and Martha Rendell's lawyer:

> Did your husband not ask you to turn over a new leaf shortly after he came over here? – No, he had the other woman to live with.
> Did you not continue your drinking habit? – That did not drive him away.
>
> Re-examined by Mr Barkley, witness said that when she was living with her husband he used to turn her out at night. He often struck her. Since her husband had left her she had earned a livelihood by washing, cleaning and sewing.[16]

Hardly an ennobling picture of domestic bliss on behalf of any of the parties concerned. The defence continued to focus upon the bereaved mother of the dead children as an incompetent who was unable to adequately provide for her hungry children because of her alcoholism.

Most interesting of all, however, was the evidence of a surviving teenage son, seventeen-year-old William 'Willie' Morris. Called as the next witness, he had no recollection of any beatings or other mistreatment at the hands of Mrs Rendell or his father. He did recall that his sister Annie (who was seven) had been sick with diphtheria and typhoid before she fell into her mysterious terminal illness. He also recalled Martha Rendell 'taking to her bed' with sickness at some point.[17]

At the conclusion of the first day's evidence the overall impression was not of Martha Rendell being a sadistic sexual monster who murdered children, but of a working class family struggling with poverty, alcoholism and a failed relationship. A marriage had broken up. The father had asked another woman to move into the family home in East Perth and look after his children. Three children had died mysterious deaths, but apart from the strenuous assertions of the prosecution, there was no compelling evidence that Martha Rendell was in any way responsible.

::

Western Australia was one of only two Australian colonies to grant women the vote prior to Federation in 1901. Which is not to say that the colony was a bastion of feminist sentiment. In 1830 the ladylike Eliza Shaw had written about her female indentured servant, describing her as 'the idlest, dirty, sauciest slut that ever got into any persons family'.[18] Such views of working class women were common. By contrast, middle-class life was supposed to be one of dignified ladylike restraint and blissful matrimony. During the 1850s the *Perth Gazette* regularly printed articles that instructed young ladies on how to live a respectable life. Articles like 'A Little Lesson for Well-disposed Wives' venerated personal hygiene, marriage and motherhood while providing examples for the younger generation to emulate.[19] Even in 1901 there were many men (and not a few women) who still regarded 'modern women' – that is to say, those who aspired to be educated, to vote and possibly to have a job outside the home – to be morally degenerate.

At the same time there were women who were campaigning for an extension of their rights. For example, during September 1909, while Martha Rendell was on trial for her life, Miss Jessie Ackermann gave a lecture in St. Andrew's Hall in Perth on women's work around the world. Miss Ackermann paid particular attention to 'sweating' (sweat-shop labour) and to the gains made by women workers in Australia. Although she feared that the 'evils of the old world threatened the new world' and 'that sweating might become an element' in Perth, she called upon women to continue in the vanguard of the struggle:

> The whole world was going to follow the example set by this new country. It was not only moral suasion they must use, but legal suasion as well. They must make it impossible for conditions which destroyed humanity to exist.[20]

Not everyone was as worried as Miss Ackermann and her supporters about the scourge of 'sweating'. The political establishment in Western Australia remained much more concerned about social propriety. Those who scorned the institution of marriage, or pushed the boundaries of socially acceptable behaviour, risked sanction. In 1909 the state only had an official population of 285,193 people. Still, during the legal calendar year of 1 July 1908 until 30 June 1909 criminals charged with no less than 12,685 offences appeared in court. A remarkable 43.91 per cent of committed offences that went to trial were 'attributable to drink'. Many other 'Offences against good order' were also committed, however, with fifteen cases of 'evil fame', 680 charges of threatening or indecent language, and even twenty-four offences relating to 'Bathing without a costume'. There were also five murders.[21] The murders occurred at a time when fresh scientific ideas about criminality and breeding were taking hold. In the words of Janet Browne:

> Psychiatrists identified degenerative 'types' among their inmates using the new medium of photography, and criminologists such as the Italian writer Cesare Lombroso proposed that there were physical stigmata to be seen in social deviants. These were sometimes linked explicitly with apish features.[22]

Popular culture, science and politics intersected. In 1886 Robert Louis Stevenson had published *The Strange Case of Dr Jekyll and Mr Hyde*, where Dr Jekyll's evil other self embarks upon a reign of terror. People believed that there were real life Dr Jekylls and Mr Hydes living among them – monsters in suburbia. In 1909 the case of the Martha Rendell the child murderer spectacularly combined these elements in the minds of many Western Australians.

::

The second day of Martha Rendell's murder trial was more dramatic than the first. The public gallery was crowded with spectators as the Crown Prosecutor resumed his case, calling to the stand fourteen-year-old Edward George Morris, the other surviving Morris son. Edward testified that he had purchased 'spirits of salts' for Martha Rendell, whom his father made him call 'mother'. He recalled that his sister Olive (who was five) and brother Arthur, had complained about sore throats prior to their deaths and that Martha had 'painted' their throats with something. He was asked specifically if he had ever seen Martha use 'spirits of salts' on his dead siblings. He had not. The damning part of his testimony, however, came when he recalled that Arthur had been sick for about two months before his death.

Arthur was always crying, particularly when his throat was being painted…This year witness ran away from home. He had a sore throat at the time. Willie [his brother] advised him to run away. Witness did not know what to attribute his sore throat to, but his tea was bitter in taste. He remembered his father on one occasion saying to Mrs. Rendall, 'I have only got two left now', and Mrs. Rendall replying, 'Anyone would think I was the cause of it.' His father thereupon said, 'So you are.'[23]

At an earlier coronial inquiry both Thomas Morris and Martha Rendell had denied this conversation ever took place, while Willie Morris had actually testified that before he died Arthur had told him that he suspected Martha Rendell was poisoning him with spirits of salts.[24] At the Supreme Court trial Edward testified that Martha used 'to give Olive a beating for the least little thing'. He claimed that he had been threatened by Martha, who told him in April 1909, after the deaths of three of his siblings, that 'he had better take plenty of Epsom salts or he would be the next to go.'[25] It was through the testimony of young Edward Morris that the noose started to tighten around Martha Rendell's neck.[26]

It grew tighter still after the evidence of a neighbour, Mrs Carr. She testified that it was the weeks of pained cries by Arthur Morris that had led her to suspect Martha Rendell of slowly killing the children. She had told the woman on numerous occasions to take the sick boy to the hospital. She claimed that on one occasion she had even heard the dying boy cry out, 'Murder! Police! Save me, Mrs. Carr.' She also said that peering through the window of the Morris's house, she had seen Arthur vomiting, for which he was beaten by Martha Rendell and then thrown back into bed. Another time, after being shown the medicine Martha was giving Arthur, she allegedly told Rendell, 'Surely to God you are not using that! Why, it would kill a horse.' When asked by the defence why she had not contacted the police, Mrs Carr testified that she had not done so because she believed, falsely, that Martha Rendell was the mother of the children. Then, recalling the treatment of poor Arthur Morris at the hands of Rendell, Mrs Carr broke down in court.[27]

This was the sort of sensational testimony that the newspapers and public desired. The image of Martha Rendell as an uncaring monster grew further with the evidence of David Lewis, a baker, who testified that on one occasion he had seen Arthur Morris struggling to get out of his sick bed, to which

Martha Rendell simply laughed. Some time later Martha told the baker that young Arthur had died:

> Witness thereupon said he had been wondering what had become of the boy, and had not seen his death announced in the papers. Mrs. Rendall said, in reply, that she could put half-a-crown to better advantage than in advertising.[28]

However, just as the circumstantial evidence was building, Mary Burgess was called to the witness box – a friend of Martha Rendell and Thomas Morris for the previous two years. She testified that she too had told Martha to take poor Arthur to the hospital. However, she also confirmed that Martha had a sore throat of her own that 'was assuming the same appearance as Olive's throat'. She had suggested the sick children be removed to the hospital not because she feared for Martha's care of them, but because 'she thought that by that means Mrs Rendall would be relieved of some of her work, as she always appeared to be on her feet'. According to Mary Burgess, Martha laboured tirelessly while caring for her five stepchildren.[29]

In the newspaper reports of the second day of her Supreme Court trial, Martha Rendell started to emerge as the female monster the media were craving. To newspaper readers and court spectators she seemed to be the very inversion of everything a woman was supposed to be – peaceful, motherly, emotional. Instead, Martha was portrayed as an uncaring cold-hearted wretch who was determined to kill off five burdensome children belonging to another woman's husband.

::

Nineteenth- and early twentieth-century women were supposed to be gentle peacemakers, not fearsome murderers. Indeed, to the extent that woman appeared in accounts of criminal trials it was usually as reluctant witnesses or defenceless victims. In January 1865, for example, the newspapers reported the case of James Fox, charged with assaulting his wife Mary. In the words of a witness in the case:

> I saw Fox, on 30 November, kick his wife and she fell down with her child in her arms, and on her rising to get up I saw him kick her twice afterwards, from the distance I was at he appeared to kick her with all his force, and left

her lying there; in 10 minutes afterwards he passed through my gate and I then saw he had heavy boots on.[30]

In his defence James Fox attributed 'all his woes to his wife's objection to his having been a convict'.[31] Similarly, in Fremantle during October 1882 a man named John Heap was charged with stabbing his wife while in a drunken rage. Although he was found guilty of the charge, the jury issued a 'strong recommendation to mercy on account of the bad character of his wife'. Throughout the trial, Heap had continually alleged that his wife was a drunkard.[32] *The Weekly Times* reported another case in September 1887 where a man appeared in court for assaulting his wife:

> The complainant said that the defendant jumped on her, danced over her body, and she was one mass of bruises through his treatment, simply because she would not give him money for drink. The defendant made a long rambling statement to the bench, to the effect that the story told by his wife was a pure fabrication. This was the defendant's 73rd appearance and he was committed to prison for two months with hard labour.[33]

Although the courts sometimes provided justice, women were often blamed for their own misery. In November 1884 *The Inquirer* reported that:

> A very painful scene occurred in the City Police Court on Friday morning. A woman, whom her husband refused to support, had previously made several applications to Mr Leake, and a short time ago he granted her a summons against her unnatural husband who had added to his cruelty by beating the unfortunate woman.[34]

However, by the time the case came to court the woman had returned to her husband and dropped the charges. He deserted her soon afterwards, leaving her to throw herself, once again, upon public charity and the mercy of the court. She was taken before the Police Magistrate to see 'what could be done' to help her:

> Mr. Leake refused to issue another summons against the inhuman husband, on the ground that if he did so she would no doubt again refuse to prosecute him, and said the best thing she could do was to return to her husband and claim

support from him for herself and her children. Thereupon the woman became almost mad with anger and disappointment, and shrieked a torrent of words in a manner which was perfectly sickening to hear. Ultimately she had to be gently removed from the Court by two constables.[35]

The Inquirer found the temptation to editorialise irresistible. Referring to 'vagabond husbands' who deserted their 'wretched wives' and 'miserable children', the newspaper was disgusted by the alcoholic proclivities of these men. The same edition of the newspaper published a reader's condemnatory letter regarding 'Larrikinism at Fremantle', and the general impression was of a society faced with the potential moral collapse of the working classes. There was a fear in late nineteenth-century Western Australia that rapid expansion in population had also brought about a corresponding expansion of crime, alcoholism and harlotry that was corroding society's moral fibre.

The newspaper's coverage of the aforementioned case revealed the social complexities, and domestic injustices, of its age perfectly. The husband was referred to as 'unnatural' and 'inhuman' because his behaviour was at odds with contemporary notions of the family. A husband provided for his family. He was supposed to be hardworking and strong. Children were to be seen and not heard. And the role of the wife was to raise the children, support her husband, and be the temperate moral core of the family. When men publicly violated those norms they called into question the sanctity of the Christian family and the moral fabric of society. However, when an abandoned woman, bereft of financial support and caught in an emotional sinkhole, lost her composure in a courtroom it was a 'sickening' and un-ladylike spectacle. Indeed, her very sanity was called into question.

Part of the problem was that insanity was actually barely understood in the nineteenth and early twentieth century. How to 'treat' mental illness was a question that vexed authorities. In Western Australia where the immensity of isolation, the infernal heat and the comparative absence of 'civilising influences' were generally considered to be contributing factors in the mental fragility of Perth's citizens, mental health was a serious concern. The arrival of 10,000 male convicts to Western Australia between 1850 and 1868 contributed to the pressures on the colony's mental health.

In 1855 Governor Fitzgerald was already writing, despairingly, that 'the proportion of lunatics among the prisoners is numerically greater than among freeman'. In 1860 Dr Attfield, colonial surgeon at the Convict Establishment, reported on the large number of convict 'lunatics' who had previously been committed or treated in England for insanity. In this context, it is worth noting that insanity was entangled with nineteenth-century notions of propriety. So, as Norman Megahey has written, although 'many convict "lunatics" were said to be suffering from delusions or to be incoherent, it was not the presence of these symptoms alone which resulted in committal...Descriptions of the behaviour of Imperial male "lunatics" frequently included reference to violence, incorrigibility, insubordination and refusal to work'.[36]

The social conditions of the most desperate cases among the working poor – the pitiful houses they lived in, their struggle to eke out an existence – were generally considered to be a symptom, rather than a cause, of emotional or mental breakdown. Of the men committed between 1857 and 1865, one-quarter died within two years of arriving at the Fremantle Lunatic Asylum. Interestingly, alcohol abuse was often given as the cause of death. The Annual Report of the Fremantle Lunatic Asylum for 1860 also commented that most male inmates were 'exceedingly ignorant and uneducated men'.[37]

What all of this hints at was the overwhelming pressure of social class and the prejudices of the doctors and administrators who oversaw mental health in Western Australia. Poverty and vagrancy remained serious problems in Perth and Fremantle during the late nineteenth century. Between 1887 and 1893 more than 90 per cent of the men committed to the Fremantle Lunatic Asylum were paupers. A woman, 'Nora F.' ended up in the Poor House with five of her children when her husband developed cancer. After six months she developed mental problems and was eventually committed to the asylum.[38]

Mentally disturbed individuals who did appear before the courts often became a source of public ridicule. For example, in December 1894 *The Inquirer* recorded the case of a middle-aged man named Walter Mockett, who was charged with being of 'unsound mind'. Mockett was brought before Magistrate Cowan:

'I am an angel of the Lord,' he said in answer to the charge. 'How long have you been so,' asked Mr. Cowan. 'Oh for about 6 months,' said the celestial one. 'And does it agree with you' said the Court. 'Yes sir.' Mockett was remanded for medical examination.[39]

The failure of the government to cope with mental illness was compounded by its inability to understand the special strains and pressures – social, economic, and emotional – on women. For example, in March 1864 the neighbours of 'Anne T.' wrote to the governor of the colony highlighting her mental breakdown and respectfully requesting she be committed to the lunatic asylum. Nothing was done. A month later Anne abandoned her baby and husband and walked into the bush where she was discovered several days later in a desperate physical and mental state. She was arrested and then charged with desertion of her family and with indecently exposing herself. She was sentenced to one month's hard labour before she was certified insane and sent to the lunatic asylum.[40]

The lunatic asylum was the final destination for women who had somehow 'failed' as mothers or wives, who had transgressed against the social mores of the age, or for whom life had simply become too much to bear. 'Mary K.' of York was a case in point. She was committed in 1894 with her one-month-old baby, who was taken from her shortly afterwards. She was so depressed after the removal of her child that she required spoon-feeding and attempted suicide. Despite being condemned as a 'homicidal maniac', her asylum record revealed that she was not to be released without informing the police first as her husband intended to murder her! Perhaps the real source of Mary's mental debility lay within the violence of her marriage? Regardless, Mary remained as a confined 'lunatic' for the rest of her life, eventually dying at the Claremont Hospital for the Insane in 1934.[41]

During September 1887 the 'Ladies Column' in *The Weekly Times* published advice on 'How to deal with hysteria' among women, recommending that the best 'remedy is just enough cold water to make the patient thoroughly uncomfortable'.[42] While the newspaper claimed that 'true womanliness dreads to make a scene', it was society's inability to understand mental and emotional disturbance, or to cope with the social dysfunction that seemed to plague all too many working class families, that led so many of these people into asylums, prison or to their deaths.

::

The third day of Martha Rendell's trial was most notable for the medical evidence of Dr Cleland. Forensic science was still in its infant stage in 1909 and the murder charge against Martha Rendell seemed to hinge upon proving that someone had poisoned the three Morris children. Dr Cleland had previously worked for the West Australian government and at the time of the Rendell trial was employed by the government of New South Wales. He had travelled all the way from Sydney (a considerable undertaking in 1909) in order to give evidence. According to Dr Cleland he had become involved in the case of the Morris children while Arthur, the last to die, was still alive. Dr Cuthbert, who had attended the children, had originally prescribed a medicine for Martha Rendell to swab the children's sore throats with. It was alleged by the prosecution, however, that Martha had caused the sore throats in the first place by mixing the children's tea with diluted Spirits of Salts. After the sore throats developed she allegedly substituted the prescribed medicinal throat swab for Spirits of Salts and exacerbated the condition – slowly poisoning the children to death.

Dr Cuthbert originally passed on to Dr Cleland two pieces of affected membrane from the throat of Arthur Morris. After examining the membrane, Dr Cleland was perplexed enough by the results (he had never seen anything like it) to personally visit Arthur Morris in the company of Dr Cuthbert. According to one court reporter's account of Dr Cleland's testimony:

> The boy looked to be very ill. He was small in size, and witness was surprised to learn at the time that he was considerably older than eight or nine years. When he saw the boy Mrs. Rendall was present. The membranous condition of the boy's throat was not marked on the two occasions on which he saw him, although he was informed by Dr Cuthbert that it was not then so bad as it had been.[43]

Dr Cleland was so perplexed by the boy's condition that he read a paper in front of the Western Australian branch of the British Medical Association in order to solicit advice from his fellow medical practitioners as to a probable cause of the illness. No diagnosis was forthcoming. It was then put to Dr Cleland that the perplexing state of the membrane from Arthur's throat may have been caused by exposure to dangerous chemicals.

> Are spirits of salts an ordinary commercial form of hydrochoric acid? – Yes, an irritant poison.
> Is it known to have caused death? – Yes, in many cases.
> Were the conditions you saw consistent with death resulting from hydrochloric acid administered by swabbing the throat? – Yes.[44]

Next Dr Cleland gave an account of the post-mortem examination of Arthur Morris that Martha Rendell had insisted she be allowed to attend. Remarkably, Martha forbid Dr Cleland to remove biological matter from the dead boy's throat or stomach for examination. This was of considerable importance to the prosecution's case.

Did she display any emotion? – No; her apparent callousness was a subject which was remarked upon afterwards.[45]

Indeed, while Arthur Morris's death was not consistent with any disease known to Dr Cleland or any other doctor at the autopsy, they all agreed that, 'there was something queer about the case'. Indeed, Dr Cleland's professional conclusion was that Arthur Morris's passing had been caused by 'death from an irritant poison'.[46]

Under cross-examination the defence tried to get Dr Cleland to admit that during his two trips to the Morris's house to visit the dying boy Martha Rendell appeared to not be completely devoid of womanly feeling. He would not even concede this small point, choosing instead to answer that, 'Well, there seemed to be an extraordinary desire on her part to be present' at the autopsy.[47] The implication – of a conspiracy to cover up her evil deeds – was obvious to everyone in the court. After some additional medical evidence the case was adjourned until the following morning. Martha Rendell must have gone to sleep that evening certain that the trial was going against her, but still quietly confident that she could escape the gallows. After all, no one wanted to hang a woman.

::

Much of the circumstantial evidence against Martha Rendell focused upon her 'unwomanly' conduct. She was the de facto stepmother of five children. A woman in her early forties, she also had children of her own in South Australia whom she had abandoned in order to live with Thomas Morris – a fact that would have perturbed most of the jury. The *Sunday Times* claimed that Martha, who was illiterate, had been 'led astray' while young. She had two children but had never been married. The overall impression was of a lowly, conniving woman of loose moral virtue.[48]

Although the times were slowly changing, in 1909 women were still expected to be bounteous, maternal and matrimonial. Men were supposed to be honourable and husbandly. Bad marriages were to be endured. Indeed, it is worth noting that the day after Martha Rendell's trial ended the Legislative Assembly in Perth was debating, in the words of the *Daily News*, 'Protecting Women' and 'The Illegitimate Child Problem'. Not by accident, the newspaper's coverage of the parliamentary debate was published on the same page as its coverage of Martha Rendell's trial.[49]

During the nineteenth century it was quite normal for young women to enter a seemingly endless cycle of pregnancy and child-rearing from the time of their marriage until the onset of menopause. The case of Elizabeth Eddison, a sixteen-year-old girl who married a twenty-six-year-old farm worker named Charles Holly in Toodyay during 1852 was by no means abnormal. Elizabeth had her first child nine months after her wedding. By October 1862, when Elizabeth was still only twenty-seven, she had given birth to eight children in ten years. More pregnancies followed, although the pace slackened. By October 1879 Elizabeth had begat fourteen children, three of whom, tragically, died before reaching four years of age. Elizabeth only lived twelve years after her last pregnancy, dying in 1891 at the age of fifty-six.[50]

For those who wanted to avoid, or simply could not afford nor countenance, an unwanted pregnancy, there were few options. Most birth control was neither safe nor effective. For those who fell pregnant there was, however, the possibility of abortion. Remarkably, abortifacients were relatively easy to acquire during the nineteenth century. Besides herbal remedies passed down among women from one generation to the next, the *Perth Gazette*, the colony's premier newspaper, carried regular advertisements for Holloway's Pills which diplomatically promised to cure 'disorders peculiar to women'. Indeed, among the many medicinal properties offered by Holloway's Pills were the fact that it 'corrects and regulates the monthly courses' of women. While it is unclear how many women purchased the pills, there was clearly a big enough market to make newspaper advertising worthwhile.[51]

However, if the pregnancy could not be aborted, more desperate measures were sometimes engaged. In his *Treatise on the Police of the Metropolis*, P. Colquhoun listed some of the 160 crimes that could result in the punishment of death in Britain during the 1760s. Treason and Petty Treason (or 'petit treason', meaning murder of your husband or master) topped the list, followed by Murder, Arson and Rape, as well as the then widely feared crimes of Sodomy, Piracy, Destroying Ships, and Highway Robbery. Still further down the list of capital offences were the unremarkable crimes of

Sacrilege, Sending Threatening Letters, and Robbery of the Mail. One crime, however, now stands out simply because of the remarkable language deployed – 'Concealing the death of a Bastard Child'. Infanticide was a hanging offence in Britain. Indeed, between 1703 and 1772 approximately 12 per cent of the women hanged at London's Tyburn gallows were executed for infanticide.[52]

Infanticide was also a serious problem in the Swan River Colony. During the nineteenth century the absence of effective contraception resulted in both unwanted pregnancies and many unexpected children. Sometimes these babies were the result of surreptitious dalliances between master and servant. Being the mother of an 'illegitimate' child was a fearful stigma for a white woman to bear. Poverty was another complicating factor. Where the father refused to acknowledge the child as being his shared responsibility, the economic, emotional and social pressures on young mothers were tremendous. Unable to cope, some, in a fit of desperation, chose infanticide instead.

The legal system struggled to deal with what was a largely unacknowledged, but relatively widespread, social problem. While some mothers were charged with murder for killing their babies, others were dealt with under lesser charges. In 1830 a female 'servant maid', Elizabeth Gamble, was accused of burning her hut down in order to dispose of an unwanted baby. Evidence provided by her mistress, Sarah Drummond, included the fact that when 'upbraiding her with her want of affection and attention' to the child, Elizabeth Gamble replied, 'Maam, if I had a pair of shoes or even slippers, I would no longer be bothered with the child, but to take it down to Fremantle, and throw it on the deck of the ship to the Father of it.' Despite the suspicious circumstances, Elizabeth Gamble was cleared of deliberately killing her baby because of, 'the absence of the usual motives to infanticide, viz. the dread of losing a situation and of being unable to provide for the child as Mrs. Drummond had never threatened to dismiss the Woman, and had repeatedly assured her that the child should be taken care of'.[53]

Another tragic and pathetic case was that of Catherine Kelly, an 'unemployed serving girl', accused of murdering her baby son during 1862. In court Catherine was accused of having secretly given birth in the Perth Servants Home's toilet and that she afterwards disposed of the baby by dropping it into the sewerage pit where it drowned in human waste. Catherine's defence was that the baby had accidentally fallen into the cesspit. Witnesses testified to the fact that Catherine wept afterwards and that she, 'appeared to be almost out of her mind to me...I was terribly frightened and told her to go see the Matron'. Catherine was found not guilty.[54]

In another tragic case in April 1887, an eighteen-year-old domestic servant called Theresa Arnold was accused of 'concealment of birth'. After secretly giving birth, her dead child had been placed in a box and hidden from her 'master'. She pleaded guilty and was given one week in prison, the attorney-general commenting that:

> ...the Crown had no wish to press at all hardly in this case. Of course they could not help feeling that there was a far more guilty one than the prisoner, who had left her to face her sorrow and her shame; and the Court had no desire to see the girl further punished, with any great severity.[55]

It is difficult not to mourn these lost babies. But it is also hard not to feel for the mothers; usually young themselves, mostly poor, often devoid of anyone they could turn to for medical or emotional advice. Most of them had left their own family back in Europe. At Swan River they had no strong familial networks to support and sustain them. In desperation they committed one of the cruellest crimes imaginable, infanticide. And quite remarkably, given the times, the legal system often treated them with leniency.

::

Martha Rendell could expect no such compassion. As her trial entered its fourth day the case against her was building. Dr Cumpston, who conducted the post-mortem of Arthur Morris with Dr Cleland, testified to Martha's bizarre behaviour. She appeared unfazed by the gruesome nature of the post-mortem examination but refused permission for necessary tissues to be taken from the boy's throat or stomach. It was also noted that the doctor had examined Mrs Rendell's throat and found that it was mildly affected 'by the application of a caustic'. The implication was that Martha swabbed her own throat with diluted Spirits of Salts in order to cover up her role in poisoning Arthur.[56]

Sitting in the dock Martha Rendell must have also worried over the evidence of the next witness, Dr Macauley, who testified that he was a nose and throat specialist and that he had been visited by Martha. He examined her and found 'white membrane' on her throat. Martha told him she was concerned it might be diphtheria, 'as members of the family who had died had suffered from that complaint, and that they had had a condition of throat precisely the same as her own.' The doctor, who was visited by Martha six or seven times, determined she did not have diphtheria. However, he also concluded that her troubles were caused by something being applied to the back of her throat. When he asked Martha if she was swabbing her throat with anything, 'she replied in the negative'. In the doctor's opinion Martha was 'humbugging' and her behaviour was suspicious.[57]

The court resumed the following morning for the final day of evidence in Martha Rendell and Thomas Morris's trial. The star witness that day, Saturday 11 September 1909, was Detective-Sergeant Harry Mann. It had been Mann who initially responded on 9 April to a report from Thomas Morris that his son Edward was missing. Edward was later discovered at his mother's house in the nearby suburb of Subiaco. Following the boy's interview with Detective-Sergeant Mann the first allegations were made about poisoning at the hands of Martha Rendell, and the murder investigation began. It was this same Detective-Sergeant Mann who had also attended the exhumation of the three Morris children and who had arrested Thomas Morris and Martha for murder.[58]

The Detective-Sergeant testified that he had visited the Morris house in East Perth and spoken to female neighbours. According to the women, some of whom were called as witnesses, Martha Rendell was a cruel monster. Under cross-examination Detective-Sergeant Mann was asked whether the 'ladies' were 'a little bit annoyed' over the fact that 'the two accused were not married?' Mann conceded that the women may have been bothered by Thomas Morris and Martha Rendell's improper relationship, but the Detective-Sergeant did not see this as in any way impinging upon their judgement of the conduct of the accused.[59]

Later that day the prosecution's case closed.[60] Remarkably, no witnesses were called for the defence. Unlike the earlier coronial investigation, Martha Rendell did not take the stand to argue that she was a misunderstood woman, pilloried for allegedly killing the children she fed and cared for.[61] What the jury made of her decision to maintain her silence in the Supreme Court was probably reflected in their final judgement. Before they could reach a verdict however, the jury had to sit through a four-hour closing argument by Mr Barker, the Crown Solicitor. The two defence lawyers also spoke 'at considerable length'. The public gallery of the court was at full capacity as the lawyers prowled the room.[62]

In his two hour summing up of the evidence, Justice McMillan commented upon the fact that the case had engaged the public mind. He urged the jurors not to be influenced by newspaper reports pertaining to the case. He also encouraged the jurors to only consider the charge of murder against Martha Rendell and Thomas Morris and not to dwell upon the fact that at the time of the crime 'they were living a life of immorality'.[63] With that in mind the jury retired for four hours before returning a verdict of guilty against Martha Rendell. Thomas Morris, meanwhile, was found not guilty of abetting the murder of his three children. Apparently Morris 'looked like a physical wreck and it was with difficulty that he walked out of the dock'.[64]

Martha Rendell now sat alone, her seven-day trial over. According to the *West Australian*:

> Martha Rendall, who betrayed little emotion on hearing the verdict, protested her innocence when asked if she had anything to say. She said she was not guilty of the crime.[65]

The *Sunday Times* reported that, 'The unhappy creature looked dazed, haggard, uncertain, abandoned, and helpless.'[66] The judge then spoke directly to her:

> Martha Rendall, the jury have come to the conclusion that you are guilty, and they have come to that conclusion after a long and patient inquiry, and after giving careful attention to the evidence. They have found you guilty of one of the most horrible crimes of which I have ever heard. You are a woman who is apparently responsible for her actions. No one has suggested that you are mad. If you are in your senses, you must be a moral deformity. Throughout the whole of the case I have been astonished at your demeanour...The jury has done its duty and now I must do mine.[67]

With that the judge passed sentence of death upon Martha Rendell, condemning her to be hanged by the neck until dead. Rendell, according the *West Australian*'s reporter, 'seemed greatly agitated, and looked anxiously about the court, but displayed little emotion'.[68] Martha would face death alone.

::

The otherwise uneventful year of 1686 proved to be a turning point in the history of women and the British legal system. In that year Alice Molland became the last woman to be hanged in Britain for being a witch. While those female 'offenders' who came after her would never have to endure the vicious religious zealotry of her persecutors, the British legal system remained notoriously unforgiving of female criminals. For example, while the punishment for 'coining silver' was hanging, where the offender was female it was accompanied by the special post-mortem punishment of burning at the stake. An estimated 20,000 spectators watched Phoebe Harris die at the stake in June 1786 before her corpse was set alight and incinerated. She was not the last woman to expire this way, but times were slowly changing. After a similar execution in 1788, the year Australia was first colonised, one English newspaper denounced the legal system for allowing such cruelties to take place – 'Shame on it, thus to attack the female sex, who by being the weaker body, are more liable to error, and less entitled to severity.' The last legal burning of a woman at the stake took place in March 1789 and the practice was abolished in Britain the following year.[69]

After Margaret Sullivan was hanged and burnt at the stake in 1788 the crowd 'amused themselves with kicking about her ashes.'[70] Occasionally, however, the spectacle of an otherwise 'respectable' woman facing capital punishment would elicit compassion or admiration from the assembled crowd. For example, before she was hanged on 6 April 1752 for the crime of poisoning her father, Mary Blandy had begged her executioners, 'for the sake of decency, gentlemen, don't hang me high'. Mary, a middle-class murderess, had attempted to secure a £10,000 dowry promised by her father. Found guilty of his murder and sentenced to death, Mary was allowed to have her hands tied in front of her with black ribbons so she could hold her bible up until the very last moment of her life. Her mild-mannered fear that the assembled crowd might be able to look up her skirt after she was dead impressed those concerned with female modesty. Although her hanging was a public spectacle, in death Mary Blandy became a strange symbol of female propriety upon the gallows.[71]

Although Western Australia was extremely reluctant to hang female offenders, the circumstances of the Martha Rendell case seemed to excite people's minds for revenge. Not even Thomas Morris, who had been acquitted, could escape the judicious gaze of the press. The *Sunday Times*, reflecting upon the fact that Thomas and Martha were not married, commented that, 'If the man had not violated the moral and sociological laws, Martha Rendall would not be in the condemned cell today awaiting the terrible summons of the hangman.'[72]

Before Martha Rendell could be taken to the gallows, however, a petition was delivered to the premier of the state pleading with him to commute her death sentence on grounds of doubt regarding the evidence against her and the fact that she was a woman. The premier declined to intervene. That same weekend, the last before Martha's scheduled execution, a public meeting was convened in Perth to discuss her case. It was resolved to form 'a society for the abolition of capital punishment' in Western Australia. Meanwhile, numerous letters appeared in the West Australian opposing Martha Rendell's impending execution. One reader argued that in addition to the dubious scientific evidence used to condemn her (in that no one really knew what killed the children), there was also the fact that 'the supposed improper relations existing between the two accused had tremendous influence with the jury and public'. As such, 'on the evidence produced I would not hang a dog'.[73]

Not everyone was feeling merciful. Mary-Ann Martin wrote to the West Australian to declare that:

> Hanging seems too good for such as Martha Rendall. She should be given spirits of salts in the same way as she administered it to the poor children. There are still a few right feeling mothers left in Western Australia.[74]

Every detail of the case was analysed and discussed in print. When the Legislative Assembly was disrupted as one of its members rose to plead for the premier to commute Martha Rendell's death sentence, his long speech beseeching the premier to show mercy, along with the responses of the attorney general and the premier, were subsequently published in the West Australian. The Daily News even ran two columns detailing Morris and Rendell's 'Last Kiss' at the Leederville police station.[75] It was the obsessive interest of the public and press that compelled the sheriff to eventually declare that henceforth no journalists would be allowed to witness hangings at Fremantle Prison, a significant break with tradition. Martha Rendell would be the first person to hang without reporters attending to record the event.[76]

Martha, meanwhile, languished in her death cell. On the evening of Tuesday 5 October she met with the superintendent of the prison and told him:

> I am to meet God tomorrow morning. I am not afraid. It's a terrible thing. I will be brave. I will be brave because I am innocent.[77]

Martha was even prepared to declare her innocence before God and in print in the *West Australian* and *Daily News*. Despite 'all that was said and done and in spite of the mental anguish which I have suffered', Martha declared that she was 'innocent before God and man of having done anything that injured the children in any degree'. She claimed she had never applied Spirits of Salts to the children and ended with the words:

> I believe it would be contrary to my most solemn convictions to profess to man to be innocent when before God I should be found guilty, which would be to me dying with a lie on my lips and a crime on my soul unconfessed – unforgiven. I pray to God to give me grace to forgive those who have sworn falsely my life away.[78]

In case any additional drama was needed, Rendell was visited shortly after making her statement by Thomas Morris, her de facto and the father of the children she had been found guilty of murdering. According to the newspapers, Thomas Morris came to farewell his beloved and obviously still believed her to be innocent of the crime she was about to pay for with her life. Prison officials later claimed that the scene was a highly emotional one with 'both Morris and the unfortunate woman being utterly broken up'. Thomas Morris had earlier written to the *West Australian* proclaiming Rendell's innocence in a letter that was reproduced in full in several other newspapers.[79]

It was all to no avail. Martha Rendell was hanged in Fremantle Prison on the morning of 6 October 1909. In the words of the *West Australian*, 'As she had lived, so she died – stoic and emotionless to the end, and even when the great Inquisitor Death faced her on the scaffold her lips did not utter one word which would confirm or otherwise the doubting and misgivings entertained regarding her guilt.'[80] If Martha Rendell had secrets, she was not confessing them to the hangman.

::

In the aftermath of the hanging of Martha Rendell the newspapers, and the public, had opportunity to ponder the ongoing controversy surrounding the crime. The *Daily News* attempted to cater for the public's seeming insatiable appetite by offering no less than eight columns of coverage of Martha's execution.[81] Of particular interest to all the newspapers seemed to be the alleged 'physical and mental abnormality' of Martha Rendell herself. What particularly bothered people was that, as the *West Australian* explained:

> Through all the sordid details of a gruesome and nerve-racking trial the woman never quailed, but sat stolid and brazen, whilst her partner in the dock, man though he was, was prostrated by the strain of the terrible ordeal.[82]

Similarly, the *Daily News* was disturbed by the fact that 'the death sentence had not produced insomnia or loss of appetite' in Martha Rendell while she awaited execution in Fremantle Prison. In short, Martha Rendell was a female 'enigma'.[83] She was supposed to break down. She was supposed to weep and plead for mercy. Perhaps if she had done so her life might have been spared. But it was contrary to her character to do so and so she was hanged.

Martha Rendell was also the first alleged female murderess to be photographed for the newspapers. At her trial she endured the 1909 equivalent of a media gauntlet. On 12 September the *Sunday Times* – which somewhat ostentatiously presented itself as 'the Biggest Sunday paper in the British Empire' – published a large, if somewhat blurry, action photograph of Rendell, accompanied by Thomas Morris and police officers, entering the court. In the picture Rendell is wearing a heavy dark dress and a large hat with a veil as she turns towards the camera. Similarly, in a scene which was still unusual in 1909, but would soon become commonplace, Morris was photographed shielding his face with his hand as the police hurried him and Martha towards the courthouse steps.[84]

The following edition of the *Sunday Times*, published after Rendell had been found guilty, offered the only two surviving portrait photographs of Martha for readers to contemplate. The photographs had obviously been taken at a local studio before her imprisonment. One accompanying action photograph showed a large crowd awaiting the verdict outside the Supreme Court. Another showed people crowding around the 'Black Maria' as Martha was being led away after being condemned to death. Overall, there was something distinctly modern and vulgar in the morbid sense of celebrity built around Martha Rendell's trial.[85]

The press had not been permitted to attend Martha's hanging and they recited their displeasure on the pages of their newspapers. Standing outside the gates of Fremantle Prison the waiting reporters were made aware of Martha Rendell's execution by two female warders whose 'half-suppressed weeping' revealed that the hanging had been completed. The press was, however, able to interview some of the witnesses afterwards. According to the *West Australian*, 'Never was an execution better performed, or less likely to satisfy appetites for the sensational.' The *Daily News* quoted a warder as saying that Rendell was composed to the very end – 'she was the gamest condemned prisoner I have yet seen.'[86]

During her final hours on earth Martha had declared her undying love for Thomas Morris. Her hair was plaited to facilitate her execution. While on the gallows with the noose around her neck, the hangman 'wound a strap' around her 'light print skirt' in order to avoid any improper displays as she fell through the trapdoor. Martha stood silent listening to the final prayers of her religious advisor. A pariah in life, she was the model of female propriety upon the gallows, causing one newspaper to comment that 'whether innocent or guilty', Martha was 'truly a most remarkable woman.'[87]

Martha Rendell was only the third woman to be hanged in Western Australia and was almost the last woman to be hanged in Australia.[88] In the public mind Martha Rendell had become the personification of suburban evil. However, in the portrait photograph originally published in the *Sunday Times* Martha looks distinctly...normal. Taken in happier times, she was photographed wearing her dark wavy hair up in a bun, in what was the fashion for ladies of her age. She does not have the appearance of a sultry mistress, nor of a deranged child killer. She appears like any other working class woman approaching middle age – some wrinkles, the flesh under her chin starting to sag, but her eyes still sparkling and bright. After her hanging Martha was buried in Fremantle Cemetery by Thomas Morris. Only a married couple, friends of Morris and Rendell, and two female warders from the prison attended. The press and curious onlookers maintained a respectful distance.[89] The woman was dead, the monster lived on.

12

The Unforgiving Rope

When the founding of the Australian Federal Commonwealth was officially celebrated in Perth during January 1901, the mayor of the city, the Honourable W. G. Brookman, told those assembled on that auspicious occasion that he would lead them, if not to the promised land, then certainly to some land nearby. Brookman summoned up the majesty of previous civilisations – 'Citizens of Perth, follow me and I will make this city a fairer Athens and a freer Rome.'[1]

At the time of Federation Western Australia had an official population of 184,124 people. Of these, however, only 52,663 had been born in the state, while around 70,000 had been born elsewhere in Australia. Approximately 50,000 residents of Western Australia had been born overseas – with 25,376 coming from England and 9,862 from Ireland. As such, English (14 per cent) and Irish-born (5 per cent) migrants together constituted nearly a fifth of the state's total population. About 36 per cent of West Australians lived in the Perth–Fremantle area. Only a tiny 3 per cent lived in the remote north, while a remarkable (and never again achieved) 32 per cent of the population lived inland on the Eastern Goldfields.[2]

While there may have been some cause for optimism in hoping that the Coolgardie–Kalgoorlie nexus would create Australia's first genuinely thriving major urban area in the arid centre of the continent, it was not to be. As soon as the gold rush weakened, inland towns like Broad Arrow, Kanowna and Menzies withered. During the first half of the twentieth century, Perth remained the focus of growth and development in the state, and the Kimberley remained splendidly remote. Indeed, by comparison to today's interconnected 'global village', in 1901 even Perth was remarkably isolated. In an age before air travel, Perth was connected to the rest of Australia and the world mainly through telegraph and commercial shipping. The journey to Adelaide, the nearest major city, took three days by sea. Overland travel was difficult, dangerous and took considerably longer.

Although the Federal Commonwealth of Australia became a legal reality on 1 January 1901 many historians claim that a true sense of Australian nationhood was not born until World War One and the crucible of Gallipoli. Although this is an increasingly contentious proposition, there is no doubt that Gallipoli was a turning point in Australian history. After World War One this 'race of athletes', as the Australians were described by English war correspondent Ashmead-Bartlett, were increasingly conscious of the isolated uniqueness of their continental experiment. They may not have still been rushing around, as Ashmead-Bartlett described them at Gallipoli, 'searching for fresh enemies to bayonet', but nor were they entirely at ease with their society and the legacy of their history.[3]

In the north of Western Australia, for example, relations between whites, Aborigines and Asians remained tense. During June 1919 the premier of Western Australia wrote to the prime minister suggesting that, 'a timely visit by a gunboat would probably have a good effect towards dispelling racial feeling at Broome'. He also complained of 'renegade Whites' who were working alongside Asian fishermen.[4] The fiction of a secure 'White Australia' was always desperately hard to maintain in the remote north-west.

In February 1879 when a touring English cricketer wanted to insult the local spectators who invaded the pitch at the Sydney Cricket Ground, he reached back into Australia's past to find a suitable colonial epithet – 'You sons of convicts', he said in disgust.[5] Although no convicts arrived in Western Australia after 1868, the influence of the penal period was felt well into the twentieth century. Or as Tom Stannage wrote in 1979, in a comment that reflects his own times as much as the period he was writing about:

> When transportation ceased in 1868 the spiritual and social effects of convictism lingered and even today few people of convict descent would openly acknowledge their family's past.[6]

While locals are not nearly so reluctant to divulge a convict antecedent these days, there is no doubt that the issue of convicts and crime distorted West Australian society.

The issue of Aboriginal crime also continued to plague the establishment. In 1911 the Chief Protector of Aborigines reported on a number of inter-tribal killings outside Laverton, in the Eastern Goldfields. While he asserted, as one would expect a representative of the state government to do, that within 'the four corners of settlement, our own laws must, of course, supersede' Aboriginal tribal custom, he remained somewhat uneasy. 'It is questionable,' he wrote, 'if any good result is obtained by interfering with tribal customs in the unoccupied portions of the state where the Aborigines are living in their natural way and amenable to their own laws.'[7]

That same year, 1911, there was a clash between cattle drovers and Aborigines along the remote Canning Stock Route. The battle, almost certainly over access to water, resulted in the deaths of two whites and one of their Aboriginal assistants. In response a mounted police patrol was sent out to find and punish the perpetrators. The difficulties of policing in such an environment were revealed by the fact that it took the police ninety-two days to complete their patrol, during which they travelled 1,162 miles. Along the way they had numerous violent encounters with 'hostile Aborigines' in which a number were shot dead. Nevertheless, the police returned to Halls Creek content that they had imposed justice upon 'the natives.'[8]

Meanwhile, those Aborigines who lived under Western Australia's (British-derived) laws continued to be treated harshly. In 1895 the noted explorer and politician Alexander Forrest had argued that:

> Natives who were taken to Rottnest were pampered too much, and, when liberated, were as bad as when they were first imprisoned; but when they had to do a hard day's work, chained to a wheelbarrow, and occasionally flogged for bad conduct, they generally recognised that it was not desirable to spear cattle or break the law in any way.[9]

Aborigines continued to be marked out for 'special treatment'. It has been calculated that 66 per cent of the death sentences handed down in Western Australia were to Aborigines. Aborigines were also 39 per cent of the 154 people hanged between 1840 and 1964. In all, sixty-one Aborigines faced the hangman's noose. As such, despite forming a dwindling minority of the state's growing population, they formed a disproportionately large portion of its prison population. While the number of death sentences declined with the closing of the West Australian frontier, the last Aborigines to be executed were Nooluillinah (or Woormillanah) and Mullabudden, hanged at Derby Gaol on 12 May 1900.[10]

Despite the scientific pretence of hanging being a quick and painless form of capital punishment, the very words of the traditional death sentence – 'hanged by the neck until dead' – revealed that twentieth century hanging continued to be an imprecise art. For example, when Charles Henry Odgers was hanged in Fremantle on 14 January 1914 for the murder of a married woman whom he had been romantically involved with, not everything went according to plan. The *West Australian* later reported that Odgers had accidentally been decapitated during the hanging.[11]

Even professional hangmen struggled with their involvement in executions. In January 1904, following the hanging of Chinese murderer Ah Hook in Fremantle Prison, a rare glimpse into the mind of the executioner was provided when it was reported that:

> The hangman Burrowes, who officiated at the last five executions, died about two months ago, and his place was taken by a much younger man, who carried out his duties with precision, but who was considerably affected by the task, and vowed that he would not do similar work again.[12]

Eighteen people were hanged in Western Australia between 1900–1909, the largest number hanged in any state in Australia. New South Wales, with a population many times larger, only hanged twelve people during the same period. Queensland formally abolished capital punishment in 1922, with New South Wales following in 1955 and Tasmania in 1968. Victoria, the Northern Territory, Australian Capital Territory and South Australia all abolished capital punishment between 1973 and 1976.[13] Western Australia, however, was the last state in Australia to turn its back upon gallows justice. Although the last hanging took place in 1964, the law that permitted execution was not expunged from the law books until 1984.

It took 155 years for capital punishment to be abolished in Western Australia, and only sixteen years for people to start agitating for its reintroduction. In March 2000 a minor controversy erupted in the West Australian parliament after a petition was handed in calling for a referendum on the issue of the death penalty. Premier Richard Court, told the *West Australian* that he was personally in favour of the death penalty. Dr Geoff Gallop, Labor Leader of the Opposition, accused the Liberal government of 'reaching for the noose' in order to distract the public from the financial scandals that were starting to weigh heavily upon the government.[14]

The *West Australian* covered the death penalty controversy in some depth, publishing the views of various religious spokespeople, the WA Law Society, the Human Rights and Equal Opportunity Commission, and even the federal attorney general, all of whom were opposed to the reintroduction of the death penalty. Such a view was also articulated by Tony Cooke, the son of Eric Edgar Cooke – the last man to be hanged in Western Australia. Mr Cooke accused Premier Court of using a 'pseudo debate' about capital punishment as a 'political stunt'.[15]

The petition to the parliament calling for a reintroduction of the death penalty was signed by 2,743 West Australians and had been organised by a retired eighty-year-old farmer from Greenough named Ruth Gould. Mrs Gould said that, 'they took the death penalty away and society has deteriorated'. She felt 'we have become a sick society – there is no respect, no honour', and even offered to 'pull the trigger' on convicted murderers herself.[16] The *West Australian* published interesting figures from a national survey of 2,000 voters conducted between November and December of 1999. The survey revealed that while about 46 per cent of voters across Australia strongly supported the reintroduction of the death penalty, the figure for Western Australia was 54 per cent. Put bluntly, more than half of surveyed West Australians wanted to bring back the public executioner. Only 29 per cent said 'the death penalty was not acceptable'.[17]

These West Australians were not alone in their longing for a return of the gallows. In another national survey conducted by Newspoll in August 2003, people were asked whether they were personally 'in favour or against' the introduction of capital punishment in Australia for people found guilty of terrorism. According to Newspoll 56 per cent of respondents answered that they would be in favour of the death penalty for convicted terrorists like the Bali bombers.[18]

However, given that no state-sanctioned hangings have actually taken place in Australia since the 1960s, hanging has moved into the private sphere where it continues to be a popular means of committing suicide. Tragically, this is particularly the case with Aboriginal Australians who had no tradition of hanging prior to the arrival of Europeans. Given that Indigenous Australians have a suicide rate about 40 per cent higher than the national average, the predominance of hanging as a method of death is especially symbolic. Suicide by hanging is intentionally confronting, hurtful and disturbing. There is perhaps no greater and more tragic irony in the social history of hanging in Australia, that this most potent weapon of terror deployed against Aborigines during colonial times is now the preferred method of Aboriginal self-harm.[19]

Overall, when one looks back over the history of capital punishment in Western Australia, one sees that despite lofty rhetoric around Christian justice or the humane science of execution, hanging was never applied fairly nor impartially upon West Australians. Nor was it ever clean or precise. On the western frontier the distortions and prejudices of the British colonial legal system were magnified. The noose was dangled in front of the poor, the desperate and the deranged as a warning. The gallows were a potent symbol of an unforgiving social order that was determined to stamp its moral authority over one-third of the Australian continent.

As the western frontier closed at the start of the twentieth century, as the descendants of the Swan River colonists felt less threatened and isolated, so too did the 'need' for the public hangman dissipate. By the middle of the century hanging had become an embarrassing anachronism. For those who enforced the laws of the land, capital punishment came to be seen as a cruel and undesirable course of action to be deployed only against especially heinous criminals (such as the infamous Edgar Cooke), who could be speedily dispatched when media outcry and public fear demanded such a course of action. The belated decision in 1984 to remove capital punishment from the law books once and for all was part of a broader campaign to 'modernise' Western Australia.

These days the gallows at the defunct Fremantle Prison are a ghoulish attraction. Tourists are led into the dim chamber with its whitewashed walls to contemplate life and death in this place of perdition. Few take photographs. Visitors are cautioned to keep back from the gaping dark hole where forty-four people took their final fatal drop out of this world. The sensitive or faint of heart grimace in distaste at this unsightly reminder of our brutal past and politely make their way to the exit at the end of the execution chamber. And a quiet few just stand and stare at the unforgiving rope that still hangs above the trapdoor. The rope does not move with the breeze nor change with the seasons. The noose's brass eyelet neither rusts nor shines. Once the ultimate manifestation of state retribution, the hangman's rope now appears as little more than a grim historical curio summoned from the dark recesses of our social and legal history. May it ever remain so.

Notes

Author's Note

1   C. T. Stannage, *The People of Perth: A Social History of Western Australia's Capital City*, Perth City Council, East Perth, 1979, p. 332; B. Purdue, *Legal Executions in Western Australia*, Foundation Press, Victoria Park, 1993.

Introduction: Young John Gavin and the Spectacle of Death

1   P. Hetherington, *Settlers, Servants & Slaves: Aboriginal and European Children in Nineteenth-century Western Australia*, UWA Press, Nedlands, 2002, pp. 16–17, 38–40.

2   ibid., pp. 38–40.

3   *The Perth Gazette and Western Australian Journal*, 6 April 1844; B. Purdue, *Legal Executions in Western Australia*, Foundation Press, Victoria Park, 1993. See also, P. Casellas, 'Did young John deserve to hang?', *The West Australian*, 22 September 2007.

4   *The Perth Gazette and Western Australian Journal*, 6 April 1844. For more on the trial, see *Case 304: Regina Vs John Gavin, April 1844*, State Records Office, Perth.

5   *The Perth Gazette and Western Australian Journal*, 6 April 1844.

6   ibid.

7   ibid.

8   V. A. C. Gatrell, *The Hanging Tree: Execution and the English People, 1770-1868*, Oxford University Press, Oxford, 1994, p. 87.

9   T. Castle, 'Constructing Death: Newspaper reports of executions in colonial New South Wales, 1826-1837', *Journal of Australian Colonial History*, Vol. 9, 2007, p. 67.

10   Arago quoted in J. Bailey, *The White Divers of Broome: The True Story of a Fatal Experiment*, Macmillan, Sydney, 2001, p. 16.

11   F. K. Crowley, *Australia's Western Third*, Macmillan & Co., London, 1960, p. 5. Of course there had been an earlier small military outpost established at King George's Sound (Albany) in 1826.

12   ibid., p. 1.

13   G. Orwell, *The Collected Essays, Journalism and Letters of George Orwell*, Vol. 3, Penguin, 1978, pp. 109–11.

14   J. S. Battye, *Western Australia: A History from its Discovery to the Inauguration of the Commonwealth*, UWA Press, Nedlands, 1978, pp. 120–1.

1. The Basest Treachery and Blackest Ingratitude: Barrabong and Doodjeep Versus the British Empire, 1840

1   M. Dash, *Batavia's Graveyard: The True Story of the Mad Heretic Who Led History's Bloodiest Mutiny*, Phoenix, London, 2002, pp. 242, 307. The exact numbers killed are difficult to ascertain – obviously the mutineers kept no precise records. The most accurate report, written afterwards, suggested that a total of ninety-six 'men and boys', twelve women and seven children were murdered.

2   ibid., pp. 242–3, 248–54.

3   ibid., pp. 259–61, 263–6.

4   ibid, pp. 258–9, 290.

5   S. Leys, *The Wreck of the Batavia & Prosper*, Black Inc, Melbourne, 2005, p. 7.

6   D. & M. Preston, *A Pirate of Exquisite Mind. The Life of William Dampier: Explorer, Naturalist and Buccaneer*, Corgi Books, Sydney, 2005, p. 17.

7   ibid., pp. 21, 23–4. In Swift's parody of British imperialism, *Gulliver's Travels*, imaginary Lilliput is located off the coast of New Holland.

8   ibid., pp. 34–6, 245–6. I have worked with Bardi-Djawi people for many years and have had the opportunity to listen to some of these stories myself.

9   ibid., pp. 247–8.

10   ibid., p. 374.

11   Quoted in E. Jaggard, 'Why W.A. Settled?', in *On This Side: Themes and Issues in Western Australian History*, Bookland, East Perth, 1985, p. 129.

12   Statham-Drew, P., *James Stirling: Admiral and Founding Governor of Western Australia*, UWA Press, Crawley, 2003, pp. 29, 36. Stirling's military career had been quite remarkable – he fought the Americans in the war of 1812 and had met the exiled South American revolutionary, Simon Bolivar, in Jamaica. Stirling's first ship, the *Brazen*, was allegedly used for an important secret meeting between Bolivar's top advisors and a British envoy off the Venezuelan coast in 1817.

13   On Stirling's exploration of the Swan River in 1827, see ibid., pp. 69–87.

14   ibid., pp. 78–9.

15   C. Duff, *A Handbook on Hanging: Being A Short Introduction to the Fine Art of Execution*, Nonsuch, Stroud, 2006 (1928), p. 149. See also Capital Punishment UK, *The history of judicial hanging in Britain*, <www.capitalpunishmentuk.org/hanging1.html>.

16   Capital Punishment U.K., *The History of Judicial Hanging in Britain*; A. Brooke & D. Brandon, *Tyburn: London's Fatal Tree*, Sutton Publishing, Thrupp, 2004, p. 181.

17   V. A. C. Gatrell, *The Hanging Tree: Execution and the English People, 1770-1868*, p. 57.

18   A. Brooke & D. Brandon, *Tyburn: London's Fatal Tree*, p. vi.

19   V. A. C. Gatrell, *The Hanging Tree: Execution and the English People, 1770-1868*, pp. 7–8, 616–18. See also, A. Brooke & D. Brandon, *Tyburn: London's Fatal Tree*, p. viii.

20   V. A. C. Gatrell, *The Hanging Tree: Execution and the English People, 1770-1868*, p. 18; A. Brooke & D. Brandon, *Tyburn: London's Fatal Tree*, pp. 69, 74.

21   M. Clark, *History of Australia abridged by Maichael Cathcart*, Penguin, Ringwood, 1995, p. 3.

22   V. A. C. Gatrell, *The Hanging Tree: Execution and the English People, 1770-1868*, pp. 9, 267–8.

23   A. Brooke & D. Brandon, *Tyburn: London's Fatal Tree*, p. 74.

24   Capital Punishment U.K., *The History of Judicial Hanging in Britain*.

25   V. A. C. Gatrell, *The Hanging Tree: Execution and the English People, 1770-1868*, pp. 11, 571, 579–83, 618–19; A. Brooke & D. Brandon, *Tyburn: London's Fatal Tree*, pp. 61, 69.

26   W. Tench (Flannery, T. (ed.), *1788*, Text Publishing Company, Melbourne, 1996, p. 50.

27   R. Hughes *The Fatal Shore*, Vintage, New York, 1986, p. 91.

28   As reproduced in W. Tench, *1788*, p. 69.

29   ibid., p. 102.

30 ibid., p. 152.

31 Account of David Collins, as reproduced in T. Flannery (ed.), *The Birth of Sydney*, Text Publishing Company, Melbourne, 1999, pp. 147–8.

32 See *Sydney Gazette* of 2 October 1803, as reproduced in ibid., pp. 184–7.

33 R. Drewe, *The Shark Net*, Penguin, Victoria, 2000, p. 7. For more on the early Swan River legal system, see E. Russell, *A History of the Law in Western Australia and its Development from 1829 to 1979*, UWA Press, Nedlands, 1980, pp. 8–20.

34 See, for example, Stirling's Despatch to Lord Glenelg of 3 December 1837. Letter reproduced as 'Document 55: Social Conditions in Western Australia. 1837' in C. M. H Clark, *Select Documents in Australian History, 1788-1850*, Angus & Robertson, Sydney, 1950, p. 88.

35 E. Russell, *A History of the Law in Western Australia and its Development from 1829 to 1979*, p. 134.

36 P. Statham-Drew, *James Stirling: Admiral and Founding Governor of Western Australia*, pp. 355–6; B. Purdue, *Legal Executions in Western Australia*, Foundation Press, Victoria Park, 1993, pp. v–vi. Helia later drowned attempting to escape from Rottnest Island. The Executive Council was made up of leading colonial officers and was formed in 1832 to advise the Governor. In 1839 and 1867 the Executive and Legislative Councils were expanded to incorporate nominated colonists and became, in essence, a mini-parliament. In 1870 the Legislative Council became an elected body. Full democratic self-government was not achieved until 1890.

37 *The Perth Gazette and Western Australian Journal*, 25 May 1839. See also B. Purdue, *Legal Executions in Western Australia*, p. 1. All the reports from the *Perth Gazette* relevant to the Cook case are also reproduced in G. Blackburn, *Conquest and Settlement: The 21st Regiment (Royal North British Fusiliers) in Western Australia 1833-1840*, Hesperian Press, Victoria Park, 1999, pp. 80–5.

38 *The Perth Gazette and Western Australian Journal*, 25 May 1839.

39 *The Perth Gazette and Western Australian Journal*, 25 May 1839; 6 June 1840; 11 July 1840. R. H. Bland was Resident Magistrate of the York District at this time. He published an account of his involvement in the case as R. H. Bland, 'A Few Particulars Concerning the Aborigines of Western Australia in the Early History of that Colony', *The Journal of the Anthropological Institute of Great Britain and Ireland*, Vol. 16 (1887), pp. 340–3. An electronic version of this document is now available on the JSTOR database, <www.jstor.org>.

40 *The Perth Gazette and Western Australian Journal*, 4 July 1840.

41 ibid.

42 ibid., 18 July 1840.

43 G. Blackburn, *Conquest and Settlement: The 21st Regiment (Royal North British Fusiliers) in Western Australia 1833-1840*, p. 85.

44 Emphasis in original. *The Inquirer: A Western Australian Journal of Politics and Literature*, 23 September 1840.

45 *The Inquirer: A Western Australian Journal*, 20 October 1841; 12 January 1842. See also, G. Blackburn, *Conquest and Settlement: The 21st Regiment (Royal North British Fusiliers) in Western Australia 1833-1840*, pp. 64–7.

46 *The Perth Gazette and Western Australian Journal*, 25 May 1833.

47 N. Green, *Broken Spears: Aboriginals and Europeans in the Southwest of Australia*, Focus Education Services, Perth, 1984, p. 219, n. 27.

48 *The Perth Gazette and Western Australian Journal*, 2 March 1833.

49 ibid., 16 March 1833.

50 ibid., 6 April 1833.

51 Interestingly, John Velvick had earlier been involved in a violent dispute with black Muslim 'Lascars' who were living in Perth. He was sentenced to three months prison for assault. See

C. T. Stannage, *The People of Perth: A Social History of Western Australia's Capital City*, p. 69.

52   *The Perth Gazette and Western Australian Journal*, 4 May 1833.

53   ibid., 18 May 1833.

54   G. F. Moore, *Diary of Ten Years Eventful Life of an Early Settler in Western Australia*, UWA Press, Nedlands, 1978, p. 188.

55   *The Perth Gazette and Western Australian Journal*, 25 May 1833; I. Edwards, *Headlines of History: A Chronicle of Western Australian History*, Flying Fish Ventures, Perth, 2002, p. 38.

56   *The Perth Gazette and Western Australian Journal*, 25 May 1833.

57   ibid.

58   ibid. Also, 'Document 2.24. Perth Gazette: The Execution of an Aborigine, May 1833', in M. Aveling (ed.), *Westralian Voices*, UWA Press, Nedlands, 1979, p. 99.

59   Irwin's report as quoted in P. Statham-Drew, *James Stirling: Admiral and Founding Governor of Western Australia*, p. 247.

60   ibid., p. 247.

61   For a full report, see *The Perth Gazette and Western Australian Journal*, 13 July 1833.

62   ibid. Interestingly, the *Perth Gazette* criticised the Keats boys for deploying deceit in order to kill Yagan. *The Perth Gazette and Western Australian Journal*, 20 July 1833.

63   *Morning Herald*, 13 December 1834; *The Perth Gazette and Western Australian Journal*, 13 July 1833.

64   ibid., 25 May 1839; 6 June 1840; 11 July 1840.

65   ibid., 4 July 1840.

2. Edward Bishop and the Convict Stain, 1854

1   The above details, and quotes, were principally drawn from court testimony and witness depositions collected in *Case #616: Regina -V- Edward Bishop, Quarter Sessions – 4th October 1854*, State Record Office, Perth.

2   J. S. Battye, *Western Australia: A History from its Discovery to the Inauguration of the Commonwealth*, UWA Press, Nedlands, 1978, p. 257.

3   C. T. Stannage, *The People of Perth: A Social History of Western Australia's Capital City*, p. 14.

4   On the debate over why convicts were introduced to Western Australia see, for example, P. Statham, 'Why Convicts II: The Decision to Introduce Convicts to Swan River', *Studies in Western Australian History*, No. 4, December 1981, pp. 11–17.

5   G. F. Moore, *Diary of Ten Years Eventful Life of an Early Settler in Western Australia*, p. 185.

6   I. Berryman (ed.), *Swan River Letters: Vol. 1*, Swan River Press, Glengarry, 2002, p. 259. On the Lascars, see C. T. Stannage, *The People of Perth: A Social History of Western Australia's Capital City*, p. 69.

7   P. Statham (ed.), *The Tanner Letters: A Pioneer Saga of Swan River and Tasmania, 1831-1845*, UWA Press, Nedlands, 1981, p. 54. Ironically, Tanner left Western Australia in 1853 in protest against the importation of convicts.

8   P. Cowan (ed.), *A Faithful Picture: The Letters of Eliza and Thomas Brown at York in the Swan River Colony*, Fremantle Arts Centre Press, Fremantle, 1991, p. 50.

9   See, Fremantle Prison Website, *Who Came From Where*, <www.fremantleprison.com.au/history/history8.cfm >. Also, T. Stannage & L. Stevenson, 'Why Convicts?', in *On This Side: Themes and Issues in Western Australian History*, Bookland, East Perth, 1985, pp. 148–151; S. Taylor, 'Who Were the Convicts: A Statistical Analysis of the Convicts Arriving in Western Australia in 1850/51, 1861/62, and 1866/68', *Studies in Western Australian History*, No. 4, December 1981, pp. 29, 34–6, 39–40.

10   'Document 3.17: The Colonial Chaplain: Report on the Library, 1855', in M. Aveling (ed.), *Westralian Voices*, UWA Press, Nedlands, 1979, p. 151.

11   M. Clark, *History of Australia*, p. 338.

12   G. C. Bolton, 'Western Australia Reflects on its Past' in C. T. Stannage (ed.), *A New History of Western Australia*, UWA Press, Nedlands, 1981, p. 677.

13   M. Clark, *History of Australia*, pp. 180–1. P. Statham-Drew, *James Stirling: Admiral and Founding Governor of Western Australia*, pp. 29, 36.

14   R. T. Appleyard & T. Manford, *The Beginning: European Discovery and Early Settlement of Swan River Western Australia*, UWA Press, Nedlands, 1979, p. 112.

15   Cottesloe (ed.), *Diary And Letters of Admiral Sir C.H. Fremantle*, Fremantle Arts Centre Press, Fremantle, 1979, pp. 67–8.

16   ibid. p. 62.

17   E. Jaggard, 'Why W.A. Settled?', in *On This Side: Themes and Issues in Western Australian History*, Bookland, East Perth, 1985, pp. 138–139. On bad publicity, see I. Berryman (ed.), *Swan River Letters: Vol. 1*, pp. 17, 20.

18   Stirling's 1829 report published in England and reproduced in I. Berryman (ed.), *Swan River Letters: Vol. 1*, pp. 53–6.

19   I. Berryman (ed.), *Swan River Letters: Vol. 1*, Swan River Press, Glengarry, 2002, p. 10.

20   ibid., p. 23.

21   ibid., p. 174.

22   Moore quoted in J. K. Ewers, *The Western Gateway: A History of Fremantle*, UWA Press, Nedlands, 1971, p. 11.

23   I. Berryman (ed.), *Swan River Letters: Vol. 1*, p. 178; M. Clark, *History of Australia*, p. 187. Also, P. Statham-Drew, *James Stirling: Admiral and Founding Governor of Western Australia*, pp. 180–1, 456.

24   By 1850, twenty-one years after settlement had commenced, the population of the Swan River Colony consisted of only 5,254 Europeans. By comparison, in 1850, after only fourteen years of settlement, South Australia had a population ten times that size – 52,904 settlers. P. Statham-Drew, *James Stirling: Admiral and Founding Governor of Western Australia,*, pp. 456, 457–8; A. Hasluck, *Unwilling Emigrants: A Study of the Convict Period in Western Australia*, Oxford University Press, Melbourne, 1978, p. 29.

25   P. Statham-Drew, *James Stirling: Admiral and Founding Governor of Western Australia*, pp. 457–8. Interestingly, Captain Fremantle had recorded in his diary in September 1832, during his second visit to Swan River, that he thought the Colony's only salvation lay in becoming a penal settlement. See, Cottesloe (ed.), *Diary And Letters of Admiral Sir C.H. Fremantle*, p. 90.

26   T. Stannage & L. Stevenson, 'Why Convicts?', p. 153.

27   *Case #616: Regina -V- Edward Bishop, Quarter Sessions – 4th October 1854.*

28   E. Russell, *A History of the Law in Western Australia and its Development from 1829 to 1979*, pp. 138–9.

29   Eight jurors were listed in the court records. *Case #616: Regina -V- Edward Bishop, Quarter Sessions – 4th October 1854,*

30   *Case #616: Regina -V- Edward Bishop, Quarter Sessions – 4th October 1854.*

31   ibid.

32   ibid.

33   ibid

34   ibid. On Aboriginal evidence, see E. Russell, *A History of the Law in Western Australia and its Development from 1829 to 1979*, pp. 317, 319.

35   *Case #616: Regina -V- Edward Bishop, Quarter Sessions – 4th October 1854.*

36   P. Cowan (ed.), *A Faithful Picture: The Letters of Eliza and Thomas Brown at York in the Swan River Colony*, p. 57.

37   ibid., pp. 57–8.

38 ibid., p. 136.
39 N. Ogle, *The Colony of Western Australia: A Manual for Emigrants, 1839*, John Ferguson, St Ives, 1977, pp. v, 43, 84–5.
40 ibid., pp. 83, 119.
41 ibid., pp. 161–2.
42 *Case #616: Regina -V- Edward Bishop, Quarter Sessions – 4th October 1854*.
43 ibid.
44 *The Inquirer*, 11 October 1854.
45 ibid.
46 ibid.
47 ibid. See also, *Perth Gazette*, 13 October 1854.
48 *The Inquirer*, 18 October 1854.
49 ibid. See also, *Perth Gazette*, 13 October 1854.
50 *The Inquirer*, 18 October 1854.
51 ibid.
52 *The Inquirer and Commercial News*, 2 November 1859.
53 ibid.
54 *The Inquirer and Commercial News*, 8 January 1862.
55 ibid.
56 ibid.
57 ibid.
58 ibid.
59 ibid.

3. Richard Bibby and the Law of the Frontier, 1859

1   P. Statham-Drew, *James Stirling: Admiral and Founding Governor of Western Australia*, p. 136. Stirling's proclamation was officially dated 18 June 1829. However, it was first publicly read a day earlier in Fremantle by Captain Irwin.
2   *Secret Instructions to Lieutenant Cook 30 July 1768*, 30 June 1768. Full document available online at internet at Documenting a Democracy, <http://www.foundingdocs.gov.au>.
3   ibid.
4   A good abridged version of Cook's journal from his 1770 exploration of the east coast of Australia is reproduced in J. Hirst (ed.), *The Australians: Insiders & Outsiders on the National Character since 1770*, Black Inc., Melbourne, 2007, pp. 5–7.
5   A similar point is made in D. Day, *Claiming a Continent: A New History of Australia*, Angus & Robertson, Sydney, 1997, p. 26.
6   R. Hughes, *The Fatal Shore: The Epic of Australia's Founding*, p. 1.
7   W. Tench *1788*, p. 40.
8   ibid.
9   ibid., p. 58.
10 D. Day, *Claiming a Continent: A New History of Australia*, Angus & Robertson, Sydney, 1997, p. 3. More recently, there has been growing historical debate about the legal implications of the British seizure and the relevance and applicability of the concept of *terra nullius*, which played such an important role in the historic Mabo decision in the High Court. For an overview of this issue, see A. Fitzmaurice, 'The Genealogy of *Terra Nullius*', *Australian Historical Studies*, Vol. 38, No. 129, April 2007, pp. 1–15.
11 For more on the points developed here, see H. Reynolds, *Aboriginal Sovereignty*, Allen & Unwin, Sydney, 1996, pp. 16–38.
12 P. Statham-Drew, *James Stirling: Admiral and Founding Governor of Western Australia*, p. 214.
13 Quoted in H. Reynolds, *Aboriginal Sovereignty*, p. 26.

14   G. F. Moore, *Diary of Ten Years Eventful Life of an Early Settler in Western Australia*, p. 146.
15   For Batman and his treaty, see T. Flannery (ed.), *The Explorers*, Text Publishing, Melbourne, 1998, pp. 163–70.
16   Quoted in E. Russell, *A History of the Law in Western Australia and its Development from 1829 to 1979*, p. 29.
17   Quoted in P. Statham-Drew, pp. 305–6.
18   Quoted in ibid., p. 211.
19   Document 2.27: 'E.W. Landor: "How the Laws of England Affect the Natives"', in M. Aveling (ed.), *Westralian Voices: Documents in Western Australian Social History*, UWA Press, Nedlands, 1979, pp. 101–103; D. Day, *Claiming a Continent: A New History of Australia*, p. 109.
20   Quoted in P. Statham-Drew, *James Stirling: Admiral and Founding Governor of Western Australia*, pp. 355–6.
21   *The Perth Gazette and West Australian Journal*, 13 July 1839.
22   P. Statham-Drew, *James Stirling: Admiral and Founding Governor of Western Australia*, p. 212.
23   *Case 802: Regina -V- Richard Bibby, Quarter Sessions, 5th October 1859*. For the newspaper's account of the court case, see *The Inquirer and Commercial News*, 12 October 1859, or *Perth Gazette*, 7 October 1859.
24   *Case 802: Regina -V- Richard Bibby, Quarter Sessions, 5th October 1859*, State Record Office, Perth.
25   ibid.
26   M. Grellier, 'The Family: Some Aspects of its Demography and Ideology in Mid-nineteenth Century Western Australia', in C. T. Stannage (ed.), *A New History of Western Australia*, p. 475.
27   B. Bennett, *Australian Short Fiction: A History*, University of Queensland Press, St Lucia, 2002, pp. 92–4.
28   G. F. Moore, *Diary of Ten Years Eventful Life of an Early Settler in Western Australia*, p. 337.
29   *The Perth Gazette and West Australian Journal*, 8 March 1845.
30   Interestingly, John Drummond had played a crucial role in the capture of Barrabong – one of the first two people to be legally hanged in Western Australia. In court Barrabong confessed to the murder of Sarah Cook and her baby daughter south of York during May 1839. For Drummond's own account of the capture of Barrabong, see *The Perth Gazette and Western Australian Journal*, 11 July 1840. On Drummond and Kabinger, see N. Green, *Broken Spears: Aboriginals and Europeans in the Southwest of Australia*, Focus Education Services, Perth, 1984, p. 224, n. 157; G. Blackburn, *Conquest and Settlement: The 21st Regiment (Royal North British Fusiliers) in Western Australia 1833-1840*, p. 86, n. 27; *Episodes in Western Australia's Policing History*, Western Australia Police – Media and Public Affairs, Perth, 2006, p. 3.
31   *Case 802: Regina -V- Richard Bibby, Quarter Sessions, 5th October 1859*. See also, *The Inquirer*, 12 October 1859; *Perth Gazette*, 7 October 1859.
32   Evidence collected for *Case 802: Regina -V- Richard Bibby, Quarter Sessions, 5th October 1859*. See also, *The Inquirer*, 12 October 1859; *Perth Gazette*, 7 October 1859.
33   ibid.
34   P. Statham-Drew, *James Stirling: Admiral and Founding Governor of Western Australia*, p. 75.
35   Cottesloe (ed.), *Diary And Letters of Admiral Sir C.H. Fremantle*, pp. 37–9.
36   ibid., p. 55.
37   ibid., p. 34.
38   ibid., p. 43.
39   ibid., pp. 87–8, 90, 91.

40 ibid., pp. 91–2.

41 ibid., p. 92.

42 C. T. Stannage, *The People of Perth: A Social History of Western Australia's Capital City*, p. 43.

43 *Case 802: Regina -V- Richard Bibby, Quarter Sessions, 5th October 1859.*

44 ibid.

45 Details from *Register of Heritage Places – Assessment Documentation, Butterabby Graves*, 31/03/2006, pp. 4–5. Available at <http://register.heritage.wa.gov.au/PDF_Files/B%20-%20 A-D/05109%20Butteraby%20Graves%20(P-AD).PDF>

46 *Case 802: Regina -V- Richard Bibby, Quarter Sessions, 5th October 1859.*

47 ibid.

48 Interestingly, the *Perth Gazette* later claimed that Bibby had played a role in a near-fatal attack on a prison warder by a convict during 1855 for which the prisoner, George Williams, was hanged. Bibby, it was alleged, had handed Williams the shovel with which he had violently attacked the warder and encouraged the assault. Bibby was never charged. *Perth Gazette*, 21 October 1859.

49 *The Inquirer and Commercial News*, 12 October 1859.

50 *Perth Gazette*, 21 October 1859.

51 G. F. Moore, *Diary of Ten Years Eventful Life of an Early Settler in Western Australia*, 1978, p. X.

52 ibid., p. 120.

53 ibid., pp. 122–3.

54 ibid., p. 184.

55 On Pinjarra, see ibid pp. 240–3. Also, P. Statham, 'James Stirling and Pinjarra: A battle in more ways than one', *Studies in Western Australian History*, No. 23, 2003, pp. 167–94.

56 Quoted in G. F. Moore, *Diary of Ten Years Eventful Life of an Early Settler in Western Australia*, p. 191. Moore's version of Yagan's speech was based on his knowledge of *Nyoongar* and conjecture derived from 'the tone and manner'.

57 ibid., pp. 191–2.

58 ibid., pp. 199–200.

59 ibid., p. 206.

60 ibid., p. 267. See also, *Perth Gazette and Western Australian Journal*, 30 May 1835; *Perth Gazette and Western Australian Journal*, 6 June 1835.

61 G. F. Moore, *Diary of Ten Years Eventful Life of an Early Settler in Western Australia*, p. 271.

62 *The Inquirer and Commercial News*, 19 October 1859.

63 ibid.

64 ibid., 26 October 1859.

65 ibid.

66 ibid.

4. 'Great Is Our Sin': Rape, Sodomy and the Hanging of Joseph McDonald, 1861

1 See the convict database at the Fremantle Prison website: <http://www.fremantleprison. com>. For information on WA Convict ships see <http://members.iinet.net. au/~perthdps/convicts/con-wa10.html>.

2 The court sat for the first time in July 1861. E. Russell, *A History of the Law in Western Australia and its Development from 1829 to 1979*, pp. 136–7, 153.

3 B. Purdue, *Legal Executions in Western Australia*.

4 *The Inquirer and Commercial News*, 9 January 1861.

5 *Perth Gazette*, 11 January 1861.

6 ibid., 18 January 1861.

7   F. K. Crowley, *Australia's Western Third*, Macmillan & Co., London, 1960, p. 34.

8   See the convict database at the Fremantle Prison website: <http://www.fremantleprison. com>. For information on WA Convict ships see <http://members.iinet.net. au/~perthdps/convicts/con-wa10.html>.

9   J. Gascoigne, *The Enlightenment and the Origins of European Australia*, Cambridge University Press, Port Melbourne, 2002, p. 1.

10   See, The National Archives of Ireland, on the internet at <www.nationalarchives.ie/topics/ transportation/transportation.html>.

11   P. O'Farrell, *The Irish In Australia*, UNSW, Sydney, 1993, p. 22.

12   W. Tench, *1788*, p. 209.

13   P. O'Farrell, *The Irish In Australia*, p. 22.

14   Account of David Collins, as reproduced in T. Flannery (ed.), *The Birth of Sydney*, p. 162.

15   P. O'Farrell, *The Irish In Australia*, p. 23.

16   ibid.

17   ibid., p. 39.

18   ibid.

19   G. F. Moore, *Diary of Ten Years Eventful Life of an Early Settler in Western Australia*, p. 214. 'Keening', or *Caoineadh* in Gaelic, is a traditional Irish lament for the dead.

20   B. Reece, 'The Irish and the Aborigines', in T. Foley & F. Bateman (eds), *Irish Australian Studies: Papers Delivered at the Ninth Irish-Australian Conference, Galway, April 1997*, Crossing Press, Sydney, 2000, pp. 194–5.

21   ibid., p. 199.

22   C. T. Stannage, *The People of Perth: A Social History of Western Australia's Capital City*, pp. 36–7.

23   *Perth Gazette and Independent Journal of Politics and News*, 13 January 1854. Fr Thomas O'Neil was from Clonmel in Ireland. He had come to Western Australia with Bishop Salvado in August 1853. He died in Western Australia during April 1854, only a few months after the incident at the prison. See, *Perth Gazette and Independent Journal of Politics and News*, 28 April 1854.

24   *Case 852: Regina Versus Joseph McDonald, 4 January 1861*, State Records Office, Perth.

25   *Perth Gazette*, 2 September 1853.

26   ibid.

27   *The Inquirer*, 7 September 1853.

28   *The Inquirer and Commercial News*, 1 February 1865.

29   T. Stannage & L. Stevenson, 'Why Convicts?', p. 157.

30   *The Inquirer and Commercial News*, 1 February 1865.

31   *The Inquirer*, 12 July 1853.

32   R. T. Appleyard, 'Western Australia: Economic and Demographic Growth, 1850-1914', in C. T. Stannage (ed.), *A New History of Western Australia*, pp. 213, 214.

33   See, for example, M. Grellier, 'The Family: Some Aspects of its Demography and Ideology in Mid-nineteenth Century Western Australia', in C. T. Stannage (ed.), *A New History of Western Australia*, pp. 497–8.

34   *The Inquirer*, 31 May 1854. Quoted in C. Kazakoff, *Irish Assisted Single Female Migration to Western Australia 1850-1870*, Honours Dissertation, University of Notre Dame Australia, 2003, pp. 55–6.

35   Quoted in ibid., p. 59.

36   *The Inquirer*, 11 May 1853.

37   ibid., 25 May 1853. The reference to Smithfield, which means next to nothing to most readers today, would have been a widely understood historical allusion at the time. John Frith was a Protestant martyr who was burned at the stake at Smithfield on 4 July 1533 on

the orders of King Henry VIII of England. Ironically, Henry VIII was excommunicated from the Catholic Church a week later. Many nineteenth-century writers, including Charles Dickens, made reference to Frith and Smithfield.

38 *The Inquirer*, 11 May 1853; *The Inquirer*, 25 May 1853. The potential divisiveness of the issue of religion was again exhibited in April 1854 when rumours circulated that the newly appointed governor (Arthur Kennedy) was both Irish and Catholic. One letter writer to *The Inquirer* argued that the appointment was 'objectionable to the large majority of the community, and so pregnant with danger to their peace and religious freedom'. *The Inquirer*, 5 April 1854.

39 C. Kazakoff, 'Irish Assisted Single Female Migration to Western Australia 1850-1870', p. 77.

40 During 1854 the Legislative Council voted six to four in favour of the importation of female convicts. The plan was never acted upon.

41 P. Eddin, 'In Changing the Law of the Land, Six Justices Turned to Its History', *New York Times*, 20 July 2003.

42 C. T. Stannage, *The People of Perth: A Social History of Western Australia's Capital City*, p. 98.

43 *The West Australian*, 5 April 1887; *The West Australian*, 6 April 1887. See also, J. Bavin-Mizzi, 'An Unnatural Offence: Sodomy in Western Australia from 1880 to 1900', p. 114.

44 *The West Australian*, 5 April 1887; *The West Australian*, 6 April 1887.

45 ibid., 6 April 1887.

46 ibid.

47 ibid.

48 R. Hughes, *The Fatal Shore: The Epic of Australia's Founding*, p. 264.

49 ibid., pp. 264–72. Such judicial violence was not limited to Australia. In England the government hanged fifty 'sodomites' between 1805 and 1832 alone. V. A. C. Gatrell, *The Hanging Tree: Execution and the English People, 1770-1868*, pp. 100–1.

50 M. Clark, *History of Australia*, p. 19; R. Hughes, *The Fatal Shore: The Epic of Australia's Founding*, p. 264.

51 R. Hughes, *The Fatal Shore: The Epic of Australia's Founding*, pp. 529–30.

52 ibid., p. 530.

53 ibid., pp. 271, 538.

54 ibid., p. 271.

55 M. Foucault, *The History of Sexuality: Volume 1, An Introduction*, Pantheon Books, New York, 1978, p. 43.

56 See, *Convict Ships to the Swan River Colony at Fremantle, Western Australia*, <http://gsaglobal.net/theoutlife/history/australianconvictships.html>.

57 J. Bavin-Mizzi, 'An Unnatural Offence: Sodomy in Western Australia from 1880 to 1900', p. 111.

58 *Case 602: Regina Versus Edwin Gatehouse, Quarter Sessions, 5 July 1854*, State Records Office, Perth.

59 *The Inquirer*, 12 July 1854.

60 *Executive Council Minutes, 10 July 1854*. Available in microfilm under Australian Joint Copying Program, CO20, Reel 1121, Battye Library, Perth.

61 J. Bavin-Mizzi, 'An Unnatural Offence': Sodomy in Western Australia from 1880 to 1900', p. 116.

62 ibid.

63 *The Inquirer and Commercial News*, 14 December 1894.

64 J. Bavin-Mizzi, 'An Unnatural Offence': Sodomy in Western Australia from 1880 to 1900', p. 118.

65 ibid., pp. 102–103, 113.

66   M. Clark, *History of Australia*, p. 86.

67   B. Purdue, *Legal Executions in Western Australia*, p. 9.

68   J. Bavin-Mizzi, 'An Unnatural Offence': Sodomy in Western Australia from 1880 to 1900', p. 107.

69   ibid., p. 117.

70   *The West Australian*, 5 January 1883.

71   J. Bavin-Mizzi, 'An Unnatural Offence: Sodomy in Western Australia from 1880 to 1900', p. 105.

72   In the Western Australian context, see for example the case of John Horgan in C. T. Stannage, *The People of Perth: A Social History of Western Australia's Capital City*, pp. 196–205.

73   C. Kazakoff, 'Irish Assisted Single Female Migration to Western Australia 1850-1870', pp. 69, 75, 84, 88. Also, T. McClaughlin, '"I was nowhere else": casualties of colonisation in eastern Australia in the second half of the nineteenth century', in T. McClaughlin (ed.), *Irish Women in Colonial Australia*, Allen & Unwin, St Leonards, 1998, pp. 142–62.

74   C. Darwin, *The Voyage of the Beagle*, Anchor Books, New York, 1962, p. 497.

5. Vengeance Is Mine Saith the Lord, the Law and the 'Treacherous Natives', 1865

1   The gravesite is roughly sixteen kilometres south of the town of Mullewa. *Register of Heritage Places – Assessment Documentation, Butterabby Graves*, 31/03/2006. Available at <http://register.heritage.wa.gov.au/PDF_Files/B%20-%20A-D/05109%20Butteraby%20Graves%20(P-AD).PDF>.

2   *Supreme Court Case 152: Regina vs. Garder and 4 other Ab. Natives*, State Record Office, Perth. The men's names (in the same order) are also sometimes spelt as Garolee, Wangatyackoo, Yermakarra, Charlacarra and Williakarra.

3   *Register of Heritage Places – Assessment Documentation, Butterabby Graves*, 31/03/2006, pp. 4–6. Davis's Tibradden station was also the scene of Richard Bibby's murder of Billimarra in 1859. The constable involved in that case, Joseph Watson, was also involved at Butterabby. For more see Chapter 3.

4   *Perth Gazette & W.A. Times*, 6 January 1865. Also, *The Inquirer and Commercial News*, 11 January 1865.

5   ibid. Also, *The Inquirer and Commercial News*, 11 January 1865. Bott's statement was reproduced in full in *The Inquirer*.

6   There seems to be some debate over the movements of Tunstill and her daughter during this time. Some accounts say they joined Rudd on the initial ride into Champion Bay to report the attack on Bott, but most claim she stayed behind with the wounded man until Rudd returned from Champion Bay with the police.

7   *Perth Gazette & W.A. Times*, 6 January 1865; *The Inquirer and Commercial News*, 11 January 1865.

8   I. Berryman (ed.), *Swan River Letters: Vol. 1*, pp. 77–8.

9   *The Fremantle Observer*, 15 April 1831.

10   I. Berryman (ed.), *Swan River Letters: Vol. 1*, p. 110.

11   P. Statham-Drew, *James Stirling: Admiral and Founding Governor of Western Australia*, p. 327.

12   See Warburton's account in T. Flannery (ed.), *The Explorers*, Text Publishing, Melbourne, 1998, pp. 290–301.

13   P. Jones, *Ochre and Rust: Artefacts and Encounters on Australian Frontiers*, Wakefield Press, Kent Town, 2007, pp. 93–4.

14   P. Crawford & I. Crawford, *Contested Country: A history of the Northcliffe area, Western Australia*, UWA Press, Nedlands, 2003, p. 35.

15   *The Perth Gazette and West Australian Journal*, 23 February 1833.

16 A similar point is made in D. Day, *Claiming a Continent: A New History of Australia*, p. 51.

17 J. S. Battye, *Western Australia: A History from its Discovery to the Inauguration of the Commonwealth*, pp. 304–5.

18 *The Perth Gazette and West Australian Journal*, 20 April 1833.

19 ibid., 30 March 1833.

20 ibid., 13 April 1833.

21 An Aboriginal man, Mumbleby, was found guilty of the manslaughter of Rudd and sentenced to life in prison. He had also been arrested by Constable Joseph Watson. See, *The Inquirer and Commercial News*, 11 January 1865. The *Perth Gazette* was appalled by the court's verdict, clearly believing it to be a case of murder, and editorialised against the jury's decision. See, *Perth Gazette & W.A. Times*, 13 January 1865.

22 *Perth Gazette & W.A. Times*, 6 January 1865.

23 *The Inquirer and Commercial News*, 11 January 1865.

24 ibid. Two of the accused Aborigines, Garder and Wangayakoo, were Elieu's uncles.

25 ibid., 15 February 1865.

26 ibid.

27 ibid.

28 ibid.

29 ibid., 22 February 1865.

30 The 'noble savage' idea is usually credited to the French philosopher Rousseau. It was a concept that had broad influence over late eighteenth-century thought. See, P. Watson, *Ideas: A History from Fire to Freud*, Phoenix Books, London, 2005, pp. 737–8.

31 Some of Dampier's account of his exploration is reproduced in T. Flannery (ed.), *The Explorers*, pp. 26–8.

32 The full titles of the books were: *On the Origin of Species by Means of Natural Selection, or the Preservation of Favoured Races in the Struggle for Life*, and *Descent of Man, and Selection in Relation to Sex*. Ironically, Darwin actually said very little about the evolution of humanity in *Origin of Species*, although the implications of his theory were clear. He did address the question of human evolution more directly in *Descent of Man*.

33 Darwin didn't actually use the term 'survival of the fittest' to encapsulate his theory until the fifth edition (1869) of *On the Origin of Species*. J. Browne, *Darwin's Origin of Species*, Allen & Unwin, Crow's Nest, 2006, p. x, 72, 110.

34 P. Statham-Drew, *James Stirling: Admiral and Founding Governor of Western Australia*, pp. 305–306.

35 Quoted in G. Blackburn, *Conquest and Settlement: The 21st Regiment (Royal North British Fusilers) in Western Australia, 1833-1840*, Hesperian Press, Victoria Park, 1999, p. 44.

36 Quoted in ibid.

37 *The Perth Gazette and West Australian Journal*, 1 November 1834; *The Perth Gazette and West Australian Journal*, 15 November 1834; G. F. Moore, *Diary of Ten Years Eventful Life of an Early Settler in Western Australia*, pp. 240–3. See also, P. Statham, 'James Stirling and Pinjarra: A battle in more ways than one', *Studies in Western Australian History*, No. 23, 2003, pp. 167–94.

38 G. F. Moore, *Diary of Ten Years Eventful Life of an Early Settler in Western Australia*, p. 243.

39 B. Kercher, *An Unruly Child: A History of Law in Australia*, Allen & Unwin, St Leonards, 1995, p. 6.

40 P. Statham-Drew, *James Stirling: Admiral and Founding Governor of Western Australia*, p. 305.

41 Quoted in ibid., p. 343.

42 Quoted in G. Blackburn, *Conquest and Settlement: The 21st Regiment (Royal North British

Fusilers) in Western Australia, 1833-1840, pp. 18–19.
43 ibid., pp. 27–8.
44 P. Cowan (ed.), *A Faithful Picture: The Letters of Eliza and Thomas Brown at York in the Swan River Colony 1841-1852, 1831-1845*, Fremantle Arts Centre Press, Fremantle, 1991, p. 131.
45 *Perth Gazette & W.A. Times*, 19 May 1865; *Perth Gazette & W.A. Times*, 26 May 1865. Although young, Brown was appointed a Justice of the Peace as a reward for his service in finding the dead explorers.
46 *Episodes in Western Australia's Policing History*, Western Australia Police – Media and Public Affairs, Perth, 2006, pp. 4–5.
47 Information and quotes regarding the Explorers' Monument taken from B. Scates, 'A Monument to Murder: Celebrating the Conquest of Aboriginal Australia', *Studies in Western Australian History*, Vol. 10, April 1989, pp. 21–31.
48 Interestingly, in 1876 Maitland's brother Kenneth was tried three times (!) for the murder of his wife Mary Anne. He was eventually found guilty and hanged on 10 June 1876. See B. Purdue, *Legal Executions in Western Australia*, pp. 26–7.
49 B. Scates, 'A Monument to Murder: Celebrating the Conquest of Aboriginal Australia', p. 27.
50 *The Inquirer and Commercial News*, 8 February 1865.
51 Quoted in P. Cowan, *Maitland Brown: A View of Nineteenth Century Western Australia*, Fremantle Arts Centre Press, Fremantle, 1988, pp. 79–80.
52 B. Scates, 'A Monument to Murder: Celebrating the Conquest of Aboriginal Australia', pp. 28–9.
53 P. Cowan, *Maitland Brown: A View of Nineteenth Century Western Australia*, p. 87.
54 *The Inquirer and Commercial News*, 12 July 1865.
55 ibid.
56 ibid.
57 ibid.
58 *Perth Gazette & W.A. Times*, 21 July 1865.
59 ibid.
60 ibid.
61 ibid.
62 *The Inquirer and Commercial News*, 19 July 1865.
63 V. A. C. Gatrell, *The Hanging Tree: Execution and the English People, 1770-1868*, pp. 59–60.
64 ibid. p. 61.
65 *The Inquirer: A Western Australian Journal of Politics and Literature*, 23 September 1840.
66 J. McGuire, 'Judicial Violence and the "Civilizing Process": Race and the Transition from Public to Private Executions in Colonial Australia', *Australian Historical Studies*, No. 111, October 1998, p. 192.
67 *The Inquirer and Commercial News*, 17 October 1855.
68 J. McGuire, 'Judicial Violence and the "Civilizing Process": Race and the Transition from Public to Private Executions in Colonial Australia', p. 192.
69 ibid., p. 195.
70 ibid., p. 201.
71 *Perth Gazette & W.A. Times*, 6 January 1865. David Reader was found guilty of manslaughter and sentenced to three years' prison.
72 J. McGuire, 'Judicial Violence and the "Civilizing Process": Race and the Transition from Public to Private Executions in Colonial Australia', p. 202; B. Purdue, *Legal Executions in Western Australia*, pp. 36–9.
73 Quoted in J. McGuire, 'Judicial Violence and the "Civilizing Process": Race and the

Transition from Public to Private Executions in Colonial Australia', p. 202. See also, N. Green, *The Forrest River Massacres*, Fremantle Arts Centre Press, Fremantle, 1997, pp. 59–60.

74   M. Aveling (ed.), *Westralian Voices: Documents in Western Australian Social History*, pp. 100–1.

75   B. Purdue, *Legal Executions in Western Australia*, pp. 61, 79.

76   J. McGuire, 'Judicial Violence and the "Civilizing Process": Race and the Transition from Public to Private Executions in Colonial Australia', p. 202.

77   The memorial stone was erected in 1975 by the Keeffe family who have owned the property that includes the Butterabby gravesite since 1912. The Keeffe family's dedication to preserving the unique heritage of the Butterabby site is to be commended. *Register of Heritage Places – Assessment Documentation, Butterabby Graves*, 31/03/2006.

6. Bernard Wootton and the Fenian Disease, 1867

1   F. Wheen, *Marx's Das Kapital: A Biography*, Allen & Unwin, Crow's Nest, 2006, pp. 68–9.

2   K. Marx, *Capital: A Critique of Political Economy*, Vol. 1, Progress Publishers, Moscow, 1986, pp. 717–19.

3   F. Wheen, *Marx's Das Kapital: A Biography*.

4   *Perth Gazette and W.A. Times*, 11 October 1867.

5   *Perth Gazette and W.A. Times*, 11 October 1867; *The Inquirer and Commercial News*, 9 October 1867.

6   ibid.

7   ibid.

8   ibid.

9   ibid.

10   ibid.

11   J. M. Dixon, 'Melbourne 1865: Gorillas at the Museum', in C. Rasmussen (ed.), *A Museum for the People: A History of Museum Victoria and its Predecessor Institutions, 1854-2000*, Scribe Publications, Carlton North, 2001. Article is also available on the internet at <*www.museum. vic.gov.au/history/gorrilas.html*>.

12   *Perth Gazette and W.A. Times*, 11 October 1867; *The Inquirer and Commercial News*, 9 October 1867.

13   P. Watson, *Ideas: A History from Fire to Freud*, p. 914.

14   C. Darwin, *The Voyage of the Beagle*, pp. 431, 443.

15   J. Browne, *Darwin's Origin of Species*, pp. 66–7.

16   ibid., p. 67.

17   R. McGregor, *Imagined Destinies: Aboriginal Australians and the Doomed Race Theory, 1880–1939*, Melbourne University Press, Carlton, 1997, p. 23; J. Browne, *Darwin's Origin of Species*, pp. 1, 42.

18   J. Browne, *Darwin's Origin of Species*, pp. 1, 42.

19   J. Browne, 'Darwin in Caricature: A Study in the Popularisation and Dissemination of Evolution', *Proceedings of the American Philosophical Society*, Vol. 145, No. 4, December 2001, pp. 496–509.

20   See, for example, J. Mandelstam, 'Du Chaillu's Stuffed Gorillas and the Savants from the British Museum', *Notes and Records of the Royal Society of London*, Vol. 48, No. 2, July 1994, pp. 227–45; J. Browne, *Darwin's Origin of Species*, pp. 93–9.

21   Owen was an opponent of Charles Darwin and did not believe that apes and humans were related. J. Mandelstam, 'Du Chaillu's Stuffed Gorillas and the Savants from the British Museum', pp. 231, 233. See also, J. Browne, *Darwin's Origin of Species*, pp. 98–9.

22   The seminal work of L. Perry Curtis Jr has placed these developments in historical context.

L. P. Curtis Jr, *Apes and Angels: The Irishman in Victorian Caricature*, New York, 1971.

23   ibid., pp. 13, 17, 100.

24   C. Treadgold, 'Bushrangers in Western Australia: Incidents of '67', 1939, pp. 49–53.

25   *Perth Gazette and W.A. Times*, 11 October 1867; *The Inquirer and Commercial News*, 9 October 1867.

26   ibid.

27   ibid.

28   ibid.

29   *Perth Gazette*, 23 September 1853.

30   See the convict database at the Fremantle Prison website. <http://www.fremantleprison. com>. For information on WA Convict ships: <http://members.iinet.net.au/~perthdps/ convicts/con-wa10.html>.

31   R. Erickson, 'Friends and Neighbours: The Irish of Toodyay' in B. Reece (ed.), *The Irish in Western Australia: Studies in West Australian History*, No. 20, 2000, pp. 49–50.

32   T. Stannage & L. Stevenson, 'Why Convicts?', p. 154.

33   Quoted in H. Zinn, *A People's History of the United States*, HarperCollins, New York, 1999, pp. 176–7.

34   Rossa's Hotel was at Chatham Square in what is now Chinatown. T. Anbinder, *Five Points: The Nineteenth Century New York City Neighbourhood That Invented Tap Dance, Stole Elections, and Became the World's Most Notorious Slum*, Plume, New York, 2002, p. 329.

35   K. Amos, *The Fenians in Australia, 1865-1880*, UNSW Press, Sydney, 1988, p. 22.

36   *The Inquirer and Commercial News*, 20 November 1867.

37   V. A. C. Gatrell, *The Hanging Tree: Execution and the English People, 1770-1868*, pp. 48, 50.

38   *The Inquirer and Commercial News*, 18 December 1867.

39   V. A. C. Gatrell, *The Hanging Tree: Execution and the English People, 1770-1868*, p. 46. Also, C. Duff, *A Handbook on Hanging: Being A Short Introduction to the Fine Art of Execution*, Nonsuch, Stroud, 2006 (originally published 1928), pp. 201–5; A. Brooke & D. Brandon, *Tyburn: London's Fatal Tree*, p. 200.

40   K. Amos, *The Fenians in Australia, 1865-1880*, p. 85. Interestingly Flood was given a pardon in May 1869 and left Western Australia.

41   *The Inquirer and Commercial News*, 15 January 1868.

42   Quoted in K. Amos, *The Fenians in Australia, 1865-1880*, pp. 111–13. Kelly was given a pardon in 1871. He then relocated to Sydney where he was active in local Fenian politics before moving back to America in 1875.

43   Quoted in P. O'Farrell, *The Irish in Australia*, p. 51.

44   *The Inquirer and Commercial News*, 22 January 1868.

45   After a period of neglect, historians and fiction writers have turned their attentions to the Fenians and the *Catalpa* rescue once again. See, for example, T. Keneally, *The Great Shame: The Story of the Irish in the Old World and the New*, Random House, Sydney, 1998.

46   *New York Times*, 20 August 1876.

47   ibid.

48   R. Douglas, L. Harte & J. O'Hara, *Drawing Conclusions: A Cartoon History of Anglo-Irish Relations 1798-1998*, The Blackstaff Press, Belfast, 1998, pp. 67–8.

49   *The Inquirer and Commercial News*, 2 October 1867.

50   *Perth Gazette and W.A. Times*, 11 October 1867.

51   For more see M. Brown, 'Probationary Prisoner 5270: Thomas Bushell', *Studies in Western Australian History*, No. 4, December 1981, pp. 51–5.

52   ibid., p. 51.

53   ibid., p. 52.

54   *The Inquirer and Commercial News*, 13 September 1865. Also, M. Brown, 'Probationary

Prisoner 5270: Thomas Bushell', p. 53.

55 *The Perth Gazette & W.A. Times*, 8 September 1865. Also, M. Brown, 'Probationary Prisoner 5270: Thomas Bushell', p. 54.

56 Quoted in G. Bolton, 'The Fenians Are Coming, The Fenians Are Coming', *Studies In Western Australian History*, No. IV, December 1981, p. 64.

57 Quoted in ibid., p. 65.

58 *Perth Gazette and W.A. Times*, 17 April 1868.

59 ibid., 1 May 1868.

60 *Perth Gazette and W.A. Times*, 1 May 1868; *The Inquirer and Commercial News*, 29 April 1868.

61 ibid.

62 *The Herald (Fremantle)*, 25 April 1868. Griver, a Spanish Benedictine, had arrived in Perth in 1849. He became Bishop of Perth in 1871 and died in 1886.

63 *Perth Gazette*, 24 July 1868.

64 A. Gill, '"To the Glorious, Pious and Immortal Memory of the Great and Good King William": The 12th of July in Western Australia, 1887-1930', *Studies in Western Australian History*, No. 10, April 1989, pp. 75–83.

65 M. Mortimer, '"An ordinary commonplace outbreak of everyday dirty bigotry": Walter Dwyer and the St Patrick's Day Procession in Perth, 1919', *Australian Journal of Irish Studies*, Vol. 5, 2005, p. 85.

66 ibid., p. 86.

7. Cannibalism and Stolen Children: The Strange Case of Mullagelly, 1873

1 P. Statham, 'James Stirling and Pinjarra: A battle in more ways than one', p. 171; P. Statham-Drew, *James Stirling: Admiral and Founding Governor of Western Australia*, p. 174.

2 For an overview of the case, see B. Purdue, *Legal Executions in Western Australia*, pp. 23–4; *The Inquirer and Commercial News*, 8 October 1873; *Perth Gazette & W.A. Times*, 10 October 1873.

3 *Perth Gazette & W.A. Times*, 10 October 1873.

4 *The Inquirer and Commercial News*, 8 October 1873.

5 *The Inquirer and Commercial News*, 8 October 1873. Also, *Perth Gazette & W.A. Times*, 10 October 1873.

6 *The Inquirer and Commercial News*, 8 October 1873; *Perth Gazette & W.A. Times*, 10 October 1873.

7 ibid.

8 B. K. De Garis, 'Political Tutelage 1829-1870', in C. T. Stannage (ed.), *A New History of Western Australia*, p. 299.

9 *The Inquirer and Commercial News*, 8 October 1873.

10 ibid.

11 ibid.

12 ibid.

13 ibid.

14 For example, in 1861 a settler with the macabre, but fitting, name of Mr Death was accused of poisoning Aborigines. Mr Death, of Wanneroo, had placed poisoned flour near some tobacco in a locked storage room inside his house. Some Aborigines stole the flour and an Aboriginal child died of strychnine poisoning. Aborigines had broken into his house previously and the police suspected that Mr Death had placed the poisoned flour near the tobacco on purpose. In court a white witness offered evidence that, 'Death complained of the natives and said he had laid a trap for them'. The judge summed up the case for the jury by reminding them that with regard to poisoning, 'it would be

equally murder with respect to a native or a white man'. Despite the judge's instructions, the jury found Mr Death not guilty. See, *The Inquirer and Commercial News*, 9 January 1861.

15   *The Inquirer and Commercial News*, 1 October 1873.

16   ibid.

17   T. Flannery (ed.), *Watkin Tench 1788*, Text Publishing, Melbourne, 1996, pp. 53–4.

18   N. Ogle, *The Colony of Western Australia: A Manuel for Emigrants, 1839*, pp. 48–9.

19   K. Biber, 'Cannibalism and Colonialism', *Sydney Law Review*, Vol. 27, No. 4, December 2005, p. 626.

20   ibid., pp. 623–4.

21   ibid.

22   ibid., p. 637.

23   ibid., pp. 623–4.

24   *The Inquirer and Commercial News*, 8 October 1873.

25   ibid. Also, *Perth Gazette & W.A. Times*, 10 October 1873.

26   *Perth Gazette & W.A. Times*, 10 October 1873.

27   *The Inquirer and Commercial News*, 8 October 1873.

28   *Supreme Court Case 595: Regina vs Yaradee and Mullagelly*, 1 October 1873, State Record Office, Perth. (Documents include witness depositions.)

29   *Perth Gazette & W.A. Times*, 10 October 1873.

30   ibid.

31   *The Inquirer and Commercial News*, 8 October 1873; *Perth Gazette & W.A. Times*, 10 October 1873.

32   *Perth Gazette & W.A. Times*, 10 October 1873.

33   ibid.

34   *The Inquirer and Commercial News*, 5 November 1873; *The Herald*, 18 October 1873.

35   On some of these issues, see, M. Zucker, *From Patrons to Partners: A History of the Catholic Church in the Kimberley* (Second Edition), Notre Dame Press, 2005, pp. 38, 49.

36   Some historians claim that Bates is often incorrectly credited with coining this phrase. See, B. Reece, 'The Irish and the Aborigines', in T. Foley & F. Bateman (eds), *Irish Australian Studies: Papers Delivered at the Ninth Irish-Australian Conference, Galway, April 1997*, Crossing Press, Sydney, 2000, f. 13. Bates' book was not published until 1938, after she left the outback.

37   D. Bates, *The Passing of the Aborigines*, Heinemann, Melbourne, 1966 (1938), pp. xi, xiv.

38   ibid, pp. 67–8.

39   D. Bates from a 1907 lecture delivered in the presence of the Governor-General, quoted in R. McGregor, *Imagined Destinies: Aboriginal Australians and the Doomed Race Theory, 1880–1939*, Melbourne University Press, Carlton, 1997, pp. 55–6.

40   On this point, see also R. Hall, *Black Armband Days: Truth from the Darkside of Australia's Past*, Vintage, Sydney, 1998, pp. 147–70.

41   D. Bates, *The Passing of the Aborigines*, pp. 144–52.

42   ibid., p. 195.

43   This is a main point of Richard Hall's chapter on Daisy Bates. See, R. Hall, *Black Armband Days: Truth from the Darkside of Australia's Past*, pp. 147–70. See also, P. Jones, *Ochre and Rust: Artefacts and Encounters on Australian Frontiers*, pp. 291–2.

44   *The Sunday Times*, 2 October 1921.

45   See, (Anon), *P. Hanson: The Truth*, St Georges Publishing, Parkholme, 1997. Also, *The West Australian*, 23 April 1997; K. Biber, 'Cannibalism and Colonialism', p. 626.

46   *The West Australian*, 23 April 1997.

47   C. Tatz, 'Pauline Hanson's Aboriginal "blood libel"', *Australian Jewish News*, 2 May 1997, published online at <www.ajn.com.au/pages/archives/one-nation/one-nation-19.html>.

48 *The West Australian*, 23 April 1997. See also, *The West Australian*, 24 April 1997.
49 Information from *Captive Lives: Looking for Tambo and His Companions*. Printed material accompanying the Australian Museum's presentation, August 1999.
50 R. Poignant, *Professional Savages: Captive Lives and Western Spectacle*, UNSW Press, Sydney, 2004, pp. 11, 84, 87.
51 From *Baltimore Morning Herald* of 7 May 1883, quoted in R. Poignant, *Professional Savages: Captive Lives and Western Spectacle*, UNSW Press, Sydney, 2004, p. 89.
52 R. Poignant, *Professional Savages: Captive Lives and Western Spectacle*, UNSW Press, Sydney, 2004, p. 90.
53 Quoted in ibid., p. 91.
54 Quoted in ibid.
55 Poster reproduced in ibid., p. 173.
56 P. Edmonds, 'The Le Souef Box: Reflections on Imperial Nostalgia, Material Culture and Exhibitionary Practice in Colonial Victoria', *Australian Historical Studies*, No. 127, April 2006, pp. 133–5.
57 *The Age* article is reproduced in R. Evans *et al.* (eds), *1901: Our Future's Past*, Pan Macmillan Australia, Sydney, 1997, p. 47.

8. 'Wicked Orientals' and the New Fremantle Gallows, 1889

1 From evidence presented in the Supreme Court trial. See *The West Australian*, 9 January 1883; *The Inquirer and Commercial News*, 10 January 1883.
2 *Perth Gazette & W.A. Times*, 3 October 1873.
3 ibid.
4 Self-government came slowly, and incrementally, to Western Australia. Between 1829 and 1832 all power rested with the governor. In 1832 the Executive Council was formed (consisting of four leading colonial officers) to advise the governor. In 1839 and 1867 the Executive and Legislative Councils were expanded to incorporate nominated colonists and became, in essence, a mini-parliament. In 1870 the Legislative Council became an elected body. It was elected by male suffrage with a property qualification. Full self-government was not achieved until 1890, although women were still excluded from voting.
5 J. Ryan, 'The Business of Chinese Coolie Immigration', in F. Broeze (ed), *Private Enterprise, Government and Society: Studies in Western Australian History*, No. 13, 1992, p. 24.
6 H. Irving, *To Constitute a Nation: A Cultural History of Australia's Constitution*, Cambridge University Press, Melbourne, 1999, p. 101.
7 See A. Atkinson, 'Placing Restrictions Upon Them: Controlling "Free" Chinese Immigrants and Capital in Western Australia', *Studies in Western Australian History*, No. 16, 1995.
8 See, *The West Australian*, 16 January 1892; 11 October 1893.
9 J. Martens, 'When WA led the way to a whiter Australia', *The West Australian*, 10 June 2006.
10 H. Irving, *To Constitute a Nation: A Cultural History of Australia's Constitution*, p. 100.
11 K. Windschuttle, 'Was Twentieth-Century Australian Racism A Myth', *The Australian*, 12 June, 2004.
12 *Immigration Restriction Act 1901*.
13 M. Clark, *History of Australia*, pp. 308–12.
14 H. Irving, *To Constitute a Nation: A Cultural History of Australia's Constitution*, pp. 101–2.
15 J. Martens, 'When WA led the way to a whiter Australia'.
16 ibid.
17 ibid. Also, G. Blainey, *A Shorter History of Australia*, Mandarin, Port Melbourne, 1995, p. 135.
18 Immigration Restriction Bill 1901, *Parliamentary Education Office*. See also, R. Hall, *Black Armband Days: Truth From the Dark Side of Australia's Past*, pp. 132–46.
19 For more, see J. Webb and A. Enstice, *Aliens and Savages: Fiction, politics and prejudice in*

Australia, HarperCollins, Sydney, 1998; R. Evans *et al.* (eds), *1901: Our Future's Past*, Pan Macmillan Australia, Sydney, 1997, pp. 197–9; B. Bennett, *Australian Short Fiction: A History*, University of Queensland Press, St Lucia, 2002, pp. 43–4.

20   H. Irving, *To Constitute a Nation: A Cultural History of Australia's Constitution*, p. 100.

21   J. Ryan, *Chinese Women and The Global Village*, University of Queensland Press in association with the API Network and Curtin University of Technology, St Lucia, 2003, p. 26.

22   P. Rule, 'Challenging Conventions: Irish-Chinese Marriages in Colonial Victoria', in T. Foley & F. Bateman (eds), *Irish Australian Studies: Papers Delivered at the Ninth Irish-Australian Conference, Galway, April 1997*, Crossing Press, Sydney, 2000, p. 206.

23   Quoted in P. Rule, 'Challenging Conventions: Irish-Chinese Marriages in Colonial Victoria', in T. Foley & F. Bateman (eds), *Irish Australian Studies: Papers Delivered at the Ninth Irish-Australian Conference, Galway, April 1997*, p. 209.

24   J. Ryan, *Chinese Women and The Global Village*, p. 37.

25   A. Atkinson, 'Placing Restrictions Upon Them: Controlling "Free" Chinese Immigrants and Capital in Western Australia', *Studies in Western Australian History*, No. 16, 1995; J. Gentilli, 'Western Australia's Chinese Immigration Policy', *Early Days: Journal of the Royal Western Australian Historical Society*, Vol. 9, Part. 2, 1984, p. 78.

26   *The West Australian*, 9 January 1883.

27   *The West Australian*, 9 January 1883; *The Inquirer and Commercial News*, 10 January 1883.

28   ibid.

29   ibid.

30   ibid.

31   *The West Australian*, 9 January 1883.

32   *The Inquirer and Commercial News*, 10 January 1883.

33   *The West Australian*, 9 January 1883; *The Inquirer and Commercial News*, 10 January 1883.

34   ibid.

35   ibid.

36   *The Daily News*, 27 January 1883.

37   *The West Australian*, 30 January 1883.

38   *The Daily News*, 27 January 1883.

39   *The West Australian*, 19 January 1883.

40   P. Mallabone, 'Towards a Multi-Cultural Society', in *On This Side: Themes and Issues in Western Australian History*, Bookland, East Perth, 1985, p. 44; J. Gentilli, 'Western Australia's Chinese Immigration Policy', p. 77; A. Atkinson, 'Early Chinese in Western Australia', *Chung Wah Association 85th Anniversary Magazine*, Perth, 1995. Also available at <www.nw.com.au/~ysyow/chungwah/85/early.html>.

41   I. Berryman (ed.), *Swan River Letters: Vol. 1*, p. 259.

42   A. Atkinson, 'Early Chinese in Western Australia'.

43   J. Gentilli, 'Western Australia's Chinese Immigration Policy', p. 78.

44   See Chapter 2 of this book.

45   J. Gentilli, 'Western Australia's Chinese Immigration Policy', p. 82.

46   A. Atkinson, 'Early Chinese in Western Australia'.

47   J. Ryan, 'Humour and Exclusion: Chinese Minorities and the Conservative Press in late Nineteenth Century Western Australia', in B. Shoesmith (ed.), *Studies in Western Australian History*, No. 15, 1994, pp. 26–7.

48   R. T. Appleyard, 'Western Australia: Economic and Demographic Growth, 1850-1914', p. 216.

49   J. Gentilli, 'Western Australia's Chinese Immigration Policy', p. 78; P. Mallabone, 'Towards a Multi-Cultural Society', in *On This Side: Themes and Issues in Western Australian History*, Bookland, East Perth, 1985, p. 45; A. Atkinson, 'Early Chinese in Western Australia'.

50   *The West Australian*, 27 December 1881.

51   ibid., 12 January 1892.

52   J. Ryan, 'Humour and Exclusion: Chinese Minorities and the Conservative Press in late Nineteenth Century Western Australia'. See also, *The West Australian*, 3 May 1892; *The West Australian*, 27 June 1892.

53   A. Atkinson, 'Early Chinese in Western Australia'.

54   *The West Australian*, 30 January 1883.

55   Details on hanging at Fremantle from the *Fremantle Prison History Page*. Available at <www.fremantleprison.com.au>.

56   *The Inquirer and Commercial News*, 6 March 1889.

57   ibid.

58   ibid.

59   ibid.

60   ibid.

61   ibid.

62   ibid.

63   ibid.

64   ibid.

65   *The West Australian*, 25 February 1889.

66   V. A. C. Gatrell, *The Hanging Tree: Execution and the English People, 1770-1868*, p. 46.

67   *The West Australian*, 23 February 1892.

68   *The Inquirer and Commercial News*, 6 March 1889.

69   *The Inquirer and Commercial News*, 6 March 1889; *The Morning Herald*, 4 March 1889; *The West Australian*, 4 March 1889.

70   *The Inquirer and Commercial News*, 6 March 1889.

71   ibid.

72   *The Morning Herald*, 4 March 1889. For another account of the hanging, see *The West Australian*, 4 March 1889.

73   *The West Australian*, 19 October 1889.

9. Murder in a Coolgardie Mosque, 1896

1   From transcript of Langtrees 181 Brothel Tour, 3 October 2002.

2   S. Adams and R. Frances, 'Lifting the Veil: The sex industry, museums and galleries', *Labour History*, No. 85, Winter 2003, pp. 47–64. (This article is also available online at <www.historycooperative.org/journals/lab/85/adams.html>).

3   *The Kalgoorlie Miner*, 11 January 1896.

4   Details from trial of Goulam Mahomet from *Supreme Court Case 2595: Regina Vs Goulam Mahomet, 8 April 1896*, State Record Office, Perth. Also, as reported in *The Inquirer and Commercial News*, 8 May 1896; *The Inquirer and Commercial News*, 17 January 1896; *The Kalgoorlie Miner*, 18 January 1896; *Coolgardie Miner*, 18 January 1896.

5   *Supreme Court Case 2595: Regina Vs Goulam Mahomet, 8 April 1896*. Also, as reported in *The Inquirer and Commercial News*, 8 May 1896; *The Inquirer and Commercial News*, 17 January 1896; *The Kalgoorlie Miner*, 18 January 1896; *Coolgardie Miner*, 18 January 1896.

6   All the above general details collated from *Supreme Court Case 2595: Regina Vs Goulam Mahomet, 8 April 1896*; *The Inquirer and Commercial News*, 8 May 1896; *The Inquirer and Commercial News*, 17 January 1896; *The Kalgoorlie Miner*, 11 January 1896; *The Kalgoorlie Miner*, 18 January 1896; *Coolgardie Miner*, 18 January 1896.

7   D. Gava, 'Gold: Did it Transform Society?', in *On This Side: Themes and Issues in Western Australian History*, Bookland, East Perth, 1985, p. 168; V. Whittington, *Gold and Typhoid:*

Two Fevers, UWA Press, Nedlands, 1988, p. 4; R. T. Appleyard, 'Western Australia: Economic and Demographic Growth, 1850-1914', p. 220.

8   *The Inquirer and Commercial News*, 17 January 1896.

9   V. Whittington, *Gold and Typhoid: Two Fevers*, p. 31.

10   ibid., p. 36.

11   Hoover arrived in Coolgardie in 1897 and later became manager of the Sons of Gwalia mine. While in Western Australia he wrote awful love poetry to a barmaid, was photographed riding an Afghan camel (which he despised) and got rich. W. J. Coughlin, 'Into the Outback', *Stanford Magazine*, March/April 2000. Hoover was a graduate of Stanford University.

12   R. T. Appleyard, 'Western Australia: Economic and Demographic Growth, 1850-1914', p. 226; D. Gava, 'Gold: Did it Transform Society?', in *On This Side: Themes and Issues in Western Australian History*, Bookland, East Perth, 1985, p. 161; V. Whittington, *Gold and Typhoid: Two Fevers*, UWA Press, Nedlands, 1988, p. 88.

13   *The Inquirer and Commercial News*, 1 May 1896.

14   ibid., 14 December 1894.

15   V. Whittington, *Gold and Typhoid: Two Fevers*, p. 187.

16   ibid., pp. 51, 71, 82, 187.

17   B. Cleland, *The Muslims in Australia: A Brief History*, Islamic Council of Victoria, 2002 (2000), pp. 13, 18. It is worth noting that the Afghans were so successful in dominating the camel industry that even when the cameleers were Turkish or Arab, they were still commonly referred to as Afghans.

18   *The Inquirer and Commercial News*, 7 December 1894.

19   B. Willis, 'From Indispensability to Redundancy: The Afghans in Western Australia, 1887-1911', *Papers in Labour History*, No. 9, June 1992, pp. 42, 53–54; B. Cleland, *The Muslims in Australia: A Brief History*, pp. 13, 18. On the marriage of 'Madam Violette' and Gool Mahomet, see E. McKewon, *The Scarlet Mile: A Social History of Prostitution in Kalgoorlie, 1894–2004*, UWA Press, Crawley, 2005, p. 27.

20   *The Kalgoorlie Miner*, 11 January 1896; B. Willis, 'From Indispensability to Redundancy: The Afghans in Western Australia, 1887-1911', pp. 42–3.

21   B. Cleland, *The Muslims in Australia: A Brief History*, p. 13.

22   *Coolgardie Miner*, 1 December 1894. B. Willis, 'From Indispensability to Redundancy: The Afghans in Western Australia, 1887-1911', pp. 43, 45.

23   *Coolgardie Miner*, 15 December 1894.

24   ibid.

25   ibid., 18 December 1894. Vosper became the editor of the *Coolgardie Miner* earlier in 1894.

26   B. Willis, 'From Indispensability to Redundancy: The Afghans in Western Australia, 1887-1911', p. 50; V. Whittington, *Gold and Typhoid: Two Fevers*, pp. 38–9. Also, *The Inquirer and Commercial News*, 18 December 1896.

27   *The Kalgoorlie Miner*, 11 January 1896.

28   ibid., 13 January 1896.

29   ibid.

30   Tagh apparently had a wife and four children in Afghanistan and originally Faiz planned to send his body back to Afghanistan. This, however, was simply not possible. Tagh was buried in Coolgardie instead. *The Kalgoorlie Miner*, 13 January 1896; *Coolgardie Miner*, 13 January 1896.

31   Coverage of the inquest as reported in *The Inquirer and Commercial News*, 14 December 1894.

32   *The Inquirer and Commercial News*, 14 December 1894; *The Inquirer and Commercial News*, 21 December 1894. Also, B. Willis, 'From Indispensability to Redundancy: The Afghans in

Western Australia, 1887-1911', p. 51.

33   Coverage of the trial as reported in *The Inquirer and Commercial News*, 14 December 1894.

34   *Coolgardie Miner*, 18 December 1894.

35   ibid.

36   ibid., 22 December 1894.

37   *The Inquirer and Commercial News*, 28 December 1894. Also, *Coolgardie Miner*, 25 December 1894.

38   ibid.

39   ibid.

40   ibid.

41   *The Inquirer and Commercial News*, 28 December 1894.

42   *The Inquirer and Commercial News*, 4 January 1895. Also, *Coolgardie Miner*, 29 December 1894; *Coolgardie Miner*, 5 January 1895.

43   *The Inquirer and Commercial News*, 4 January 1895. Also, *Coolgardie Miner*, 5 January 1895.

44   *Coolgardie Miner*, 12 January 1895.

45   *The Weekly Times*, 1 October 1887.

46   *The Inquirer and Commercial News*, 11 January 1895. Also, B. Willis, 'From Indispensability to Redundancy: The Afghans in Western Australia, 1887-1911', pp. 51–52.

47   *Coolgardie Miner*, 12 January 1895.

48   ibid.

49   *The Kalgoorlie Miner*, 11 January 1896.

50   ibid.

51   ibid.

52   ibid.

53   *The Kalgoorlie Miner*, 18 January 1896; *Coolgardie Miner*, 18 January 1896; *The Coolgardie Pioneer*, 22 January 1896.

54   *Supreme Court Case 2595: Regina Vs Goulam Mahomet, 8 April 1896.*

55   *The Inquirer and Commercial News*, 8 May 1896. Also, *The West Australian*, 9 April 1896.

56   *The Inquirer and Commercial News*, 8 May 1896; *The West Australian*, 9 April 1896. The newspapers were referring to the fact that Tagh apparently neglected to say 'As-salamu 'alaykum' (Peace be upon you) or the response, 'Wa-'alaykum as-salam' (And upon you, too, be peace) to Goulam, as is customary in most Muslim parts of the world.

57   *The West Australian*, 9 April 1896; *Western Mail*, 10 April 1896.

58   *Coolgardie Miner*, 24 March 1896; V. Whittington, *Gold and Typhoid: Two Fevers*, pp. 127–8.

59   *Coolgardie Miner*, 11 April 1896.

60   'Document 2.13: Premier's Department: A Muhammedan Prisoner, 1896', in M. Aveling (ed.), *Westralian Voices* pp. 83–4. This is the same imam, or mullah, who attended to Goulam Mahomet's spiritual needs while in prison. It was common in the nineteenth century for Islamic names to be translated several different ways – thus, *Mirza* in some accounts and *Miza* in others. The same is true of the different spellings (sometimes in the same document) of the name of the prophet – *Mahomet, Mahomed, Muhammed, Mohammed* or *Mohammad*. Where possible I have tried to standardise the spelling of names of the main personalities so as to avoid unnecessary confusion.

61   *The Inquirer and Commercial News*, 1 May 1896; *The Inquirer and Commercial News*, 8 May 1896. Also, *Daily News*, 2 May 1896.

62   *The Inquirer and Commercial News*, 8 May 1896. Also, *Daily News*, 2 May 1896; *The West Australian*, 4 May 1896.

63   *The Inquirer and Commercial News*, 8 May 1896.

64   *The Inquirer and Commercial News*, 8 May 1896; *Daily News*, 2 May 1896; *The West Australian*, 4 May 1896.

65   *The Inquirer and Commercial News*, 8 May 1896.
66   *The Inquirer and Commercial News*, 8 May 1896; *Daily News*, 2 May 1896; *The West Australian*, 4 May 1896.
67   *The Inquirer and Commercial News*, 8 May 1896; *The West Australian*, 4 May 1896.
68   *The Inquirer and Commercial News*, 8 May 1896. A slightly different version was published in *Daily News*, 2 May 1896.
69   *The Inquirer and Commercial News*, 8 May 1896; *The West Australian*, 4 May 1896; *The Western Mail*, 8 May 1896.
70   *The Inquirer and Commercial News*, 8 May 1896.
71   *The Inquirer and Commercial News*, 8 May 1896. Also, *The West Australian*, 4 May 1896.
72   *The Inquirer and Commercial News*, 8 May 1896.
73   B. Cleland, *The Muslims in Australia: A Brief History*, p. 12.
74   *The Inquirer and Commercial News*, 8 May 1896; *The West Australian*, 4 May 1896.
75   ibid. By 1897, only a year after Goulam Mahomet's burial, the old Fremantle cemetery was already overcrowded. It was also too close to the centre of Fremantle, which was rapidly expanding due to the gold rush. When a new Fremantle Cemetery was opened in 1898 further from town, some bodies from the old cemetery were disinterred and relocated to the new graveyard. Goulam Mahomet was not among them. The old cemetery was covered over and eventually became part of the grounds of a local public school. Goulam Mahomet, the murderer of Tagh the Coolgardie cameleer, remains buried there.
76   *Report by Fred Hare, Commissioner of Police, 1 August 1901*, NAA: A6, 1901/1910, p. 10. Available from the National Archives of Australia online exhibition, *Uncommon Lives*, at <http://uncommonlives.naa.gov.au/detail.asp?iID=787&lID=9&cID=103>. See also, *Question by Hugh Mahon, Member for Coolgardie, to the Prime Minister, Edmund Barton, 28 June 1901*, NAA: A6, 1901/1910, p. 6. Also available from the *Uncommon Lives* exhibition.
77   B. Willis, 'From Indispensability to Redundancy: The Afghans in Western Australia, 1887-1911'; B. Cleland, *The Muslims in Australia: A Brief History*, p. 25.
78   Quoted in B. Willis, 'From Indispensability to Redundancy: The Afghans in Western Australia, 1887-1911', p. 53.
79   *Morning Post*, 29 April 1896; V. Whittington, *Gold and Typhoid: Two Fevers*, p. 161.
80   *Kalgoorlie Miner*, 4 May 1907; 'Mahomet, Faiz', *Australian Dictionary of Biography – Online Edition*, <http://www.adb.online.anu.edu.au/biogs/A100371b.htm>. In December 1896 Faiz Mahomet wrote to *The Inquirer* offering condolences on behalf of the entire Afghan community for the axe murder of a European in Fremantle at the hands of an insane Afghan, Jumna Khan, who had worked for Faiz. Jumna Khan was hanged the following March. Interestingly, Faiz offered financial for the family of the murder victim. *The Inquirer and Commercial News*, 18 December 1896. See also, C. Fox, 'Jumna Khan', *Studies in Western Australian History*, No. 16, 1995. Both Tagh's daughters came to Western Australia in 1907 to contest his will. Tagh's not inconsiderable wealth had been in guardianship since his murder in 1896. The case involved complicated family disputes. See, *Western Mail*, 15 June 1907.
81   On the gravestone Tagh's last name is spelt as 'Mahomed' rather than 'Mahomet'. His age was listed as 37, although the newspapers usually gave his age as being 45.

10. The Market Gardener, White Westralia and the Empire of the Rising Sun, 1908

1   Details regarding the Japanese raid on Broome are mainly from M. W. Prime, *Broome's One Day War: The Story of the Japanese Raid on Broome 3rd March 1942*, Broome Historical Society, 2004.

2   Deakin in the London *Morning Post*, 2 March 1908. Reproduced in R. Evans *et al.* (eds), *1901: Our Future's Past*, Pan Macmillan Australia, Sydney, 1997, p. 238.

3   *The West Australian*, 3 September 1908; *The Western Argus*, 8 September 1908.

4   *The West Australian*, 12 September 1908. See also, for example, *The Western Argus*, 15 September 1908.

5   Sometimes incorrectly referred to as 'William Shaw' in the press.

6   N. Jones, *Number 2 Home: A Story of Japanese Pioneers in Australia*, Fremantle Arts Centre Press, Fremantle, 2002, p. 34.

7   *The Evening Mail*, 27 October 1908.

8   ibid.

9   ibid.

10   ibid.

11   ibid.

12   ibid.

13   R. Evans *et al* (eds), *1901: Our Future's Past*, pp. 12–13.

14   ibid., H. Irving, *To Constitute a Nation: A Cultural History of Australia's Constitution*, pp. 157–8.

15   R. Evans *et al.* (eds), *1901: Our Future's Past*, p. 187.

16   D. Gava, 'Gold: Did it Transform Society?', p. 172.

17   *The West Australian*, 2 January 1901.

18   For accounts of the trial, see *The Evening Mail*, 27 October 1908; *The West Australian*, 8 October 1908.

19   ibid.

20   *The Sunday Times*, 18 October 1908.

21   *The Evening Mail*, 24 October 1908; *The Evening Mail*, 27 October 1908.

22   *The Evening Mail*, 27 October 1908.

23   ibid.

24   ibid.

25   R. Evans *et al.* (eds), *1901: Our Future's Past*, p. 187; J. Easton, 'Japanese War Brides in Western Australia: Immigration and Assimilation in the Nineteen Fifties', *Studies in Western Australian History*, No. 16, 1995.

26   *The Western Australian Times*, 1 December 1874.

27   N. Jones, *Number 2 Home: A Story of Japanese Pioneers in Australia*, p. 24.

28   *The Inquirer and Commercial News*, 14 December 1894.

29   N. Jones, *Number 2 Home: A Story of Japanese Pioneers in Australia*, p. 27.

30   ibid., p. 30.

31   ibid., p. 48.

32   Quoted in ibid., p. 60.

33   E. Hopkins, 'The Colour Confusion: A Study of the Japanese Community in Broome During the White Australia Policy, 1901-1941', Unpublished Honours Thesis, University of New South Wales, 2000, p. 79. The name 'Shiba Lane' was eventually corrupted as 'Sheba Lane'. The Lane was originally named after Mr K. Shiba, owner of a restaurant in the area.

34   N. Jones, *Number 2 Home: A Story of Japanese Pioneers in Australia*, p. 76.

35   R. Evans *et al.* (eds), *1901: Our Future's Past*, p. 209.

36   ibid., p. 210.

37   ibid. p. 211.

38   *Supreme Court Case 4074: Rex Vs Oki Iwakichi 6 October 1908*, State Records Office, Perth.

39   *West Australian*, 8 October 1908.

40   *Supreme Court Case 4074: Rex Vs Oki Iwakichi.*

41 ibid.
42 ibid.
43 ibid.
44 ibid.
45 *The West Australian*, 8 October 1908.
46 ibid.
47 ibid.
48 ibid.
49 ibid.
50 M. Schaper, 'The Broome Race Riots of 1920', *Studies in Western Australian History*, No. 16, 1995.
51 E. Hopkins, 'The Colour Confusion: A Study of the Japanese Community in Broome During the White Australia Policy, 1901-1941', p. 9.
52 D. Day, *Claiming a Continent: A New History of Australia*, p. 188.
53 N. Jones, *Number 2 Home: A Story of Japanese Pioneers in Australia*, p. 143.
54 ibid., p. 95.
55 E. Hopkins, 'The Colour Confusion: A Study of the Japanese Community in Broome During the White Australia Policy, 1901-1941', p. 55.
56 *Nor West Echo* of 1 September 1923, quoted in N. Jones, *Number 2 Home: A Story of Japanese Pioneers in Australia*, p. 100.
57 Quote from undercover intelligence officer in 1939, reporting to Perth on Japanese community of Broome. See N. Jones, *Number 2 Home: A Story of Japanese Pioneers in Australia*, p. 153.
58 E. Hopkins, 'The Colour Confusion: A Study of the Japanese Community in Broome During the White Australia Policy, 1901-1941', p. 71.
59 Details and quotes from *The West Australian*, 22 December 1920; *The West Australian*, 23 December 1920.
60 For more, see M. Schaper, 'The Broome Race Riots of 1920'.
61 C. Choo, 'The Impact of War on the Aborigines of the Kimberley', in J. Gregory (ed.), *On the Homefront: Western Australia and World War II*, UWA Press, Nedlands, 1996, p. 135.
62 N. Jones, *Number 2 Home: A Story of Japanese Pioneers in Australia*, p. 175.
63 ibid., pp. 176–7.
64 E. Hopkins, 'The Colour Confusion: A Study of the Japanese Community in Broome During the White Australia Policy, 1901-1941', pp. 87–8.
65 William was saved from a similar fate, perhaps, because his Irish mother had separated from his father and William had been living under his mother's maiden name, Murphy. See N. Jones, *Number 2 Home: A Story of Japanese Pioneers in Australia*, p. 187.
66 *Daily News*, 25 March 1942. Also reproduced ibid., p. 136.
67 E. Hopkins, 'The Colour Confusion: A Study of the Japanese Community in Broome During the White Australia Policy, 1901-1941', p. 25.
68 Copies of correspondence available in file for *Supreme Court Case 4074: Rex Vs Oki Iwakichi*.

11. Martha Rendell and the Manufacture of a Suburban Monster, 1909

1 P. Dasey, *An Australian Murder Almanac: 150 Years of Chilling Crime*, Griffin Paperbacks, Adelaide, 1993, p. 17.
2 ibid., p. 17.
3 ibid., p. 17.
4 P. B. Kidd, *Australia's Serial Killers: The Definitive History of Serial Multicide in Australia*, Macmillan, Sydney, 2006, pp. 58–65.

5   P. Dasey, *An Australian Murder Almanac: 150 Years of Chilling Crime*, Griffin Paperbacks, Adelaide, 1993, p. 17; P. B. Kidd, *Australia's Serial Killers: The Definitive History of Serial Multicide in Australia*, Macmillan, Sydney, 2006, pp. 58–65.

6   C. T. Stannage, *The People of Perth: A Social History of Western Australia's Capital City*, p. 253. Coolgardie Street in East Perth is now Coolgardie Terrace.

7   M. Durey, 'Infant Mortality in Perth, Western Australia, 1870-1914: a Preliminary Analysis', in L. Layman (ed.), *Bosses, Workers and Unemployed: Studies in Western Australian History*, No. 5, December 1982, p. 65.

8   ibid.

9   *The West Australian*, 10 September 1909; *The West Australian*, 11 September 1909.

10   *The West Australian*, 11 September 1909.

11   *The West Australian*, 11 September 1909; *Sunday Times*, 19 September 1909.

12   *The West Australian*, 8 September 1909. For full coverage of the case, see also, *Sunday Times*, 12 September 1909.

13   For newspaper coverage of the Coronial investigation, see *The Sunday Times*, 15 August 1909; *The West Australian*, 11 August 1909; *The West Australian*, 12 August 1909; *The West Australian*, 13 August 1909; *The West Australian*, 17 August 1909.

14   *The West Australian*, 8 September 1909.

15   ibid.

16   *The West Australian*, 8 September 1909. Also, *Sunday Times*, 12 September 1909.

17   *The West Australian*, 8 September 1909.

18   Quoted in T. W. Mazzarol, 'Tradition, Environment and the Indentured Labourer in Early Western Australia', *Studies in Western Australian History*, No. 3, 1978, p. 30.

19   See, for example, C. T. Stannage, *The People of Perth: A Social History of Western Australia's Capital City*, pp. 101–2.

20   *The West Australian*, 7 September 1909.

21   J. E. Thomas, 'Crime and Society', in C. T. Stannage (ed.), *A New History of Western Australia*, , p. 637.

22   J. Browne, *Darwin's Origin of Species*, pp. 124–5.

23   *The West Australian*, 9 September 1909. Also, *Sunday Times*, 12 September 1909.

24   *The Sunday Times*, 15 August 1909.

25   *The West Australian*, 9 September 1909.

26   ibid.

27   *The West Australian*, 9 September 1909; *Sunday Times*, 12 September 1909.

28   *The West Australian*, 9 September 1909.

29   ibid.

30   *Perth Gazette & W.A. Times*, 6 January 1865. See also, *The Inquirer and Commercial News*, 11 January 1865.

31   ibid.

32   *The Inquirer and Commercial News*, 10 January 1883.

33   *The Weekly Times*, 3 September 1887.

34   *The Inquirer and Commercial News*, 5 November 1884. Also, *The Daily News*, 1 November 1884.

35   *The Inquirer and Commercial News*, 5 November 1884.

36   N. Megahey, 'More Than A Minor Nuisance: Insanity in Colonial Western Australia', in C. Fox (ed.), *Historical Refractions: Studies in Western Australian History*, No. XIV, 1993, pp. 47–8.

37   ibid., pp. 50–1.

38   ibid., pp. 52, 56.

39   *The Inquirer and Commercial News*, 7 December 1894.

40   ibid., p. 42.

41   ibid., pp. 55–6.

42   *The Weekly Times*, 24 September 1887.

43   *The West Australian*, 10 September 1909.

44   ibid.

45   ibid.

46   ibid.

47   ibid.

48   *Sunday Times*, 19 September 1909.

49   *The Daily News*, 16 September 1909.

50   M. Grellier, 'The Family: Some Aspects of its Demography and Ideology in Mid-Nineteenth Century Western Australia', p. 473.

51   ibid., pp. 488, 508.

52   'Document 9: Crimes Punishable by Death. 1765-9', in C.M.H Clark, *Select Documents in Australian History, 1788-1850*, Angus & Robertson, Sydney, 1950, pp. 13–14. Also, A. Brooke & D. Brandon, *Tyburn: London's Fatal Tree*, p. 92. Infanticide was outlawed under the 1624 'Act to Prevent the Murdering of Bastard Children'.

53   'Document 2.8: Magistrate's Report: The Death of a Baby, Feb. 1830', in M. Aveling (ed.), *Westralian Voices*, pp. 75–8.

54   'Document 2.9: Extracts from Supreme Court Depositions, Jan. 1863', in M. Aveling (ed.), *Westralian Voices*, pp. 78–9. Also, C. T. Stannage, *The People of Perth: A Social History of Western Australia's Capital City*, p. 114.

55   *The West Australian*, 5 April 1887.

56   *The West Australian*, 11 September 1909.

57   ibid.

58   *The West Australian*, 13 September 1909.

59   ibid.

60   ibid.

61   Thomas Morris had also testified at the earlier coronial investigation. *The West Australian*, 13 August 1909.

62   *The West Australian*, 14 September 1909.

63   *The West Australian*, 15 September 1909.

64   ibid.

65   ibid.

66   *Sunday Times*, 19 September 1909.

67   *Sunday Times*, 19 September 1909; *The West Australian*, 15 September 1909.

68   *The West Australian*, 15 September 1909; *Sunday Times*, 19 September 1909.

69   V. A. C. Gatrell, *The Hanging Tree: Execution and the English People, 1770-1868*, pp. 337–8. Also, A. Brooke & D. Brandon, *Tyburn: London's Fatal Tree*, p. 62.

70   V. A. C. Gatrell, *The Hanging Tree: Execution and the English People, 1770-1868*, p. 337.

71   See, V. A. C. Gatrell, *The Hanging Tree: Execution and the English People, 1770-1868*, Oxford University Press, p. 51; Capital Punishment U.K., *Mary Blandy – Patricide*, <http://www.capitalpunishmentuk.org/blandy.html>.

72   *Sunday Times*, 19 September 1909.

73   *The West Australian*, 5 October 1909; *The West Australian*, 6 October 1909; *The Daily News*, 6 October 1909.

74   *The West Australian*, 5 October 1909.

75   *The Daily News*, 15 September 1909.

76   *The West Australian*, 6 October 1909; *The Daily News*, 5 October 1909.

77   *The West Australian*, 6 October 1909.

78   *The West Australian*, 6 October 1909; *The Daily News*, 5 October 1909.
79   *The West Australian*, 6 October 1909; *The Western Argus*, 5 October 1909.
80   *The West Australian*, 7 October 1909.
81   *The Daily News*, 6 October 1909.
82   *The West Australian*, 7 October 1909.
83   *The Daily News*, 15 September 1909; *The West Australian*, 7 October 1909.
84   *Sunday Times*, 12 September 1909.
85   *Sunday Times*, 19 September 1909.
86   *The West Australian*, 7 October 1909; *The Daily News*, 6 October 1909.
87   ibid.
88   The last woman executed in Australia was Jean Lee, who was hanged in Melbourne
      on 19 February 1951 for murder. She was 31 years old and had been used as 'bait' by
      her two male accomplices in an attempt to lure and rob a 73-year-old SP bookmaker
      in Carlton. See, J. Main, *Hanged: Executions in Australia*, Bas Publishing, Seaford,
      2007, pp. 254–61.
89   *The West Australian*, 7 October 1909; *Sunday Times*, 19 September 1909.

12. The Unforgiving Rope

1   Quoted in C. T. Stannage, *The People of Perth: A Social History of Western Australia's
      Capital City*, 1979, p. 214.
2   R. T. Appleyard, 'Western Australia: Economic and Demographic Growth, 1850-1914'
      pp. 221–2, 225.
3   An abridged version of Ashmead-Bartlett's Gallipoli report is reproduced in J. Hirst (ed.),
      The Australians: Insiders & Outsiders on the National Character since 1770, Black Inc.,
      Melbourne, 2007, pp. 46–8.
4   *Letter from the Premier of Western Australia to the Acting Prime Minister, 23 June 1919*,
      Ref: NAA: A1, 1920/2207, p. 23. Available from the National Archives of Australia
      online exhibition, *Uncommon Lives*, at <http://uncommonlives.naa.gov.au/detail.
      asp?ilD=655&IID=9&cID=89>.
5   *Sydney Morning Herald* of 10 February 1879 quoted in J. Hirst (ed.), *The Australians:
      Insiders & Outsiders on the National Character since 1770*, p. 100.
6   C. T. Stannage, *The People of Perth: A Social History of Western Australia's Capital City*, p. 1.
7   Quoted in J. E. Thomas, 'Crime and Society', p. 645.
8   *Episodes in Western Australia's Policing History*, p. 9.
9   Quoted in J. E. Thomas, 'Crime and Society', p. 648–9.
10   B. Purdue, *Legal Executions in Western Australia*, pp. 42, 57–79.
11   *The West Australian*, 15 January 1914.
12   *The West Australian*, 12 January 1904.
13   Victoria holds the ignoble record of being the last state in Australia to legally execute a
      criminal. Ronald Ryan was hanged in 1967. I. Postas & J. Walker, 'Capital Punishment',
      Trends & Issues in Crime and Criminal Justice, Australian Institute of Criminology,
      Canberra, February 1987, p. 2.
14   *The West Australian*, 17 March 2000. Labor, under Gallop, won the state election a year
      later.
15   ibid.
16   ibid.
17   ibid.
18   Survey details available at <Newspoll.com.au>.
19   T. Elliott-Farrelly, 'Australian Aboriginal Suicide: The need for an Aboriginal suicidology?',
      Australian e-Journal for the Advancement of Mental Health, Volume 3, Issue 3, 2004; C. Tatz,

'Aboriginal suicide is different: Aboriginal youth suicide in New South Wales, the Australian Capital Territory and New Zealand: towards a model of explanation and alleviation', *Criminology Research Council Report*, CRC-Funded Report available at <http://www.aic. gov.au/crc/reports/tatz/>.

Select Bibliography

Books

Amos, K., *The Fenians in Australia, 1865-1880*, UNSW Press, Sydney, 1988.

Appleyard, R. T. & Manford, T., *The Beginning: European Discovery and Early Settlement of Swan River Western Australia*, UWA Press, Nedlands, 1979.

Aveling, M. (ed.), *Westralian Voices: Documents in Western Australian Social History*, UWA Press, Nedlands, 1979.

Bates, D., *The Passing of the Aborigines*, Heinemann, Melbourne, 1966.

Battye, J. S., *Western Australia: A History from its Discovery to the Inauguration of the Commonwealth*, UWA Press, Nedlands, 1978.

Bennett, B., *Australian Short Fiction: A History*, UQP, St Lucia, 2002.

Beresford, Q. & Omaji, P., *Our State Of Mind: Racial Planning and the Stolen Generations*, Fremantle Arts Centre Press, Fremantle, 2000.

Berryman, I. (ed.), *Swan River Letters: Vol. 1*, Swan River Press, Glengarry, 2002.

Blackburn, G., *Conquest and Settlement: The 21st Regiment (Royal North British Fusiliers) in Western Australia 1833–1840*, Hesperian Press, Victoria Park, 1999.

Briscoe, G., *Counting, Health and Identity: A history of Aboriginal health and demography in Western Australia and Queensland, 1900-1940*, Aboriginal Studies Press, Canberra, 2003.

Brooke, A. & Brandon, D., *Tyburn: London's Fatal Tree*, Sutton Publishing, Thrupp, 2004.

Browne, J., *Darwin's Origin of Species*, Allen & Unwin, Crow's Nest, 2006.

Choo, C., *Mission Girls: Aboriginal Women on Catholic Missions in the Kimberley, Western Australia 1900-1950*, UWA Press, Crawley, 2001.

Clark, M., *History of Australia abridged by Michael Cathcart*, Penguin, Ringwood, 1995.

——, *Select Documents in Australian History, 1788-1850*, Angus & Robertson, Sydney, 1950.

Cottesloe (ed.), *Diary And Letters of Admiral Sir C.H. Fremantle*, Fremantle Arts Centre Press, Fremantle, 1979.

Cowan, P. (ed.), *A Faithful Picture: The Letters of Eliza and Thomas Brown at York in the Swan River Colony*, Fremantle Arts Centre Press, Fremantle, 1991.

——, *Maitland Brown: A View of Nineteenth Century Western Australia*, Fremantle Arts Centre Press, Fremantle, 1988.

Crawford, P. & Crawford, I., *Contested Country: A history of the Northcliffe area, Western Australia*, UWA Press, Nedlands, 2003.

Crowley, F. K., *Australia's Western Third*, Macmillan & Co., London, 1960.

Darwin, C., *The Voyage of the Beagle*, Anchor Books, New York, 1962.

Dasey, P., *An Australian Murder Almanac: 150 Years of Chilling Crime*, Griffin Paperbacks, Adelaide, 1993.

Dash, M., *Batavia's Graveyard: The True Story of the Mad Heretic Who Led History's Bloodiest Mutiny*, Phoenix, London, 2002.

Day, D., *Claiming a Continent: A New History of Australia*, Angus & Robertson, Sydney, 1997.

Douglas, R., Harte, L. & O'Hara, J., *Drawing Conclusions: A Cartoon History of Anglo-Irish Relations 1798-1998*, The Blackstaff Press, Belfast, 1998.

Drewe, R., *The Shark Net*, Penguin, Victoria, 2000.

Duff, C., *A Handbook on Hanging: Being A Short Introduction to the Fine Art of Execution*, Nonsuch, Stroud, 2006.

Edwards, I., *Headlines of History: A Chronicle of Western Australian History*, Flying Fish Ventures, Perth, 2002.

Evans, R. et al. (eds), *1901: Our Future's Past*, Pan Macmillan Australia, Sydney, 1997.

Ewers, J. K., *The Western Gateway: A History of Fremantle*, UWA Press, Nedlands, 1971.

Flannery, T. (ed.), *The Birth of Sydney*, Text Publishing, Melbourne, 1999.

—— (ed.), *The Explorers*, Text Publishing, Melbourne, 1998.

Foley, T. & Bateman, F. (eds), *Irish Australian Studies: Papers Delivered at the Ninth Irish-Australian Conference, Galway, April 1997*, Crossing Press, Sydney, 2000.

Gascoigne, J., *The Enlightenment and the Origins of European Australia*, Cambridge University Press, Port Melbourne, 2002.

Gatrell, V. A. C., *The Hanging Tree: Execution and the English People, 1770-1868*, Oxford University Press, Oxford, 1994.

Green, N., *Broken Spears: Aboriginals and Europeans in the Southwest of Australia*, Focus Education Services, Perth, 1984.

——, *The Forrest River Massacres*, Fremantle Arts Centre Press, Fremantle, 1997.

Gregory, J. (ed.), *On the Homefront: Western Australia and World War II*, UWA Press, Nedlands, 1996.

Haebich, A., *Broken Circles: Fragmenting Indigenous Families 1800-2000*, Fremantle Arts Centre Press, Fremantle, 2000.

Hall, R., *Black Armband Days: Truth from the Darkside of Australia's Past*, Vintage, Sydney, 1998.

Hasluck, A., *Unwilling Emigrants: A Study of the Convict Period in Western Australia*, Oxford University Press, Melbourne, 1978.

Hetherington, P., *Settlers, Servants & Slaves: Aboriginal and European Children in Nineteenth-century Western Australia*, UWA Press, Nedlands, 2002.

Hirst, J. (ed.), *The Australians: Insiders & Outsiders on the National Character since 1770*, Black Inc., Melbourne, 2007.

Hughes, R., *The Fatal Shore: The Epic of Australia's Founding*, Vintage Books, New York, 1998.

Irving, H., *To Constitute a Nation: A Cultural History of Australia's Constitution*, Cambridge University Press, Melbourne, 1999.

Jones, N., *Number 2 Home: A Story of Japanese Pioneers in Australia*, Fremantle Arts Centre Press, Fremantle, 2002.

Jones, P., *Ochre and Rust: Artefacts and Encounters on Australian Frontiers*, Wakefield Press, Kent Town, 2007.

Kercher, B., *An Unruly Child: A History of Law in Australia*, Allen & Unwin, St Leonards, 1995.

Kidd, P. B., *Australia's Serial Killers: The Definitive History of Serial Multicide in Australia*, Macmillan, Sydney, 2006.

Leys, S., *The Wreck of the Batavia & Prosper*, Black Inc., Melbourne, 2005.

Main, J., *Hanged: Executions in Australia*, Bas Publishing, Seaford, 2007.

Marx, K., *Capital: A Critique of Political Economy*, Vol. 1, Progress Publishers, Moscow, 1986.

McClaughlin, T. (ed.), *Irish Women in Colonial Australia*, Allen & Unwin, St Leonards, 1998.

McDonald, H., *Blood, Bones and Spirit: Aboriginal Christianity in an East Kimberley Town*, Melbourne University Press, Carlton South, 2001.

McGregor, R., *Imagined Destinies: Aboriginal Australians and the Doomed Race Theory, 1880-1939*, Melbourne University Press, Carlton, 1997.

McKewon, E., *The Scarlet Mile: A Social History of Prostitution in Kalgoorlie, 1894-2004*, UWA Press, Crawley, 2005.

Moore, G. F., *Diary of Ten Years Eventful Life of an Early Settler in Western Australia*, UWA Press, Nedlands, 1978.

O'Farrell, P., *The Irish In Australia*, UNSW, Sydney, 1993.

Ogle, N., *The Colony of Western Australia: A Manual for Emigrants, 1839*, John Ferguson, St Ives, 1977.

Orwell, G., *The Collected Essays, Journalism and Letters of George Orwell*, Vol. 3, Penguin, 1978.

Poignant, R., *Professional Savages: Captive Lives and Western Spectacle*, UNSW Press, Sydney, 2004.

Preston, D. & M., *A Pirate of Exquisite Mind. The Life of William Dampier: Explorer, Naturalist and Buccaneer*, Corgi Books, Sydney, 2005.

Purdue, B., *Legal Executions in Western Australia*, Foundation Press, Victoria Park, 1993.

Reynolds, H., *Aboriginal Sovereignty*, Allen & Unwin, Sydney, 1996.

Russell, E., *A History of the Law in Western Australia and its Development from 1829 to 1979*, UWA Press, Nedlands, 1980.

Ryan, J., *Chinese Women and The Global Village*, University of Queensland Press in association with the API Network and Curtin University of Technology, St Lucia, 2003.

Stannage, C. T. (ed.), *A New History of Western Australia*, UWA Press, Nedlands, 1981.

——, *The People of Perth: A Social History of Western Australia's Capital City*, Perth City Council, East Perth, 1979.

Statham, P. (ed.), *The Tanner Letters: A Pioneer Saga of Swan River and Tasmania, 1831-1845*, UWA Press, Nedlands, 1981.

Statham-Drew, P., *James Stirling: Admiral and Founding Governor of Western Australia*, UWA Press, Crawley, 2003.

Tench, W. (Flannery, T. ed.), *1788*, Text Publishing Company, Melbourne, 1996.

Watson, P., *Ideas: A History from Fire to Freud*, Phoenix Books, London, 2005.

Webb, J. & Enstice, A., *Aliens and Savages: Fiction, politics and prejudice in Australia*,

Harper Collins, Sydney, 1998.

Westralian History Group (eds), *On This Side: Themes and Issues in Western Australian History*, Bookland, East Perth, 1985.

Wheen, F., *Marx's Das Kapital: A Biography*, Allen & Unwin, Crow's Nest, 2006.

Whittington, V., *Gold and Typhoid: Two Fevers*, UWA Press, Nedlands, 1988.

Zucker, M., *From Patrons to Partners: A History of the Catholic Church in the Kimberley* (Second Edition), Notre Dame Press, 2005.

Journal Articles

Adams, S. & Frances, R., 'Lifting the Veil: The sex industry, museums and galleries', *Labour History*, No. 85, Winter 2003.

Atkinson, A., 'Placing Restrictions Upon Them: Controlling "Free" Chinese Immigrants and Capital in Western Australia', *Studies in Western Australian History*, No. 16, 1995.

Bavin-Mizzi, J., '"An Unnatural Offence": Sodomy in Western Australia from 1880 to 1900', *Studies in Western Australian History*, No. 14, 1993.

Biber, K., 'Cannibalism and Colonialism', *Sydney Law Review*, Vol. 27, No. 4, December 2005.

Bland, R. H., 'A Few Particulars Concerning the Aborigines of Western Australia in the Early History of that Colony', *The Journal of the Anthropological Institute of Great Britain and Ireland*, Vol. 16 (1887).

Bolton, G., 'The Fenians Are Coming, The Fenians Are Coming', *Studies In Western Australian History*, No. 4, December 1981.

Brown, M., 'Probationary Prisoner 5270: Thomas Bushell', *Studies in Western Australian History*, No. 4, December 1981.

Browne, J., 'Darwin in Caricature: A Study in the Popularisation and Dissemination of Evolution', *Proceedings of the American Philosophical Society*, Vol. 145, No. 4, December 2001.

Castle, T., 'Constructing Death: Newspaper reports of executions in colonial New South Wales, 1826-1837', *Journal of Australian Colonial History*, Vol. 9, 2007.

Durey, M., 'Infant Mortality in Perth, Western Australia, 1870-1914: A Preliminary Analysis', *Studies in Western Australian History*, No. 5, December 1982.

Easton, J., 'Japanese War Brides in Western Australia: Immigration and Assimilation in the Nineteen Fifties', *Studies in Western Australian History*, No. 16, 1995.

Edmonds, P., 'The Le Souef Box: Reflections on Imperial Nostalgia, Material Culture and Exhibitionary Practice in Colonial Victoria', *Australian Historical Studies*, No. 127, April 2006.

Erickson, R., 'Friends and Neighbours: The Irish of Toodyay', *Studies in West Australian History*, No. 20, 2000.

Fitzmaurice, A., 'The Genealogy of Terra Nullius', *Australian Historical Studies*, Vol. 38, No. 129, April 2007.

Fox, C., 'Jumna Khan', *Studies in Western Australian History*, No. 16, 1995.

Gentilli, J., 'Western Australia's Chinese Immigration Policy', *Early Days: Journal of the Royal Western Australian Historical Society*, Vol. 9, Part. 2, 1984.

Gill, A., 'To the Glorious, Pious and Immortal Memory of the Great and Good King William': The 12th of July in Western Australia, 1887-1930', *Studies in Western Australian History*, No. 10, April 1989.

Mandelstam, J., 'Du Chaillu's Stuffed Gorillas and the Savants from the British Museum', *Notes and Records of the Royal Society of London*, Vol. 48, No. 2, July

1994.

Mazzarol, T. W., 'Tradition, Environment and the Indentured Labourer in Early Western Australia', *Studies in Western Australian History*, No. 3, 1978.

McGuire, J., 'Judicial Violence and the 'Civilizing Process': Race and the Transition from Public to Private Executions in Colonial Australia', *Australian Historical Studies*, No. III, October 1998.

Megahey, N., 'More Than A Minor Nuisance: Insanity in Colonial Western Australia', *Studies in Western Australian History*, No. 14, 1993.

Mortimer, M., '"An ordinary commonplace outbreak of everyday dirty bigotry": Walter Dwyer and the St Patrick's Day Procession in Perth, 1919', *Australian Journal of Irish Studies*, Vol. 5, 2005.

Ryan, J., 'Humour and Exclusion: Chinese Minorities and the Conservative Press in late Nineteenth Century Western Australia', *Studies in Western Australian History*, No. 15, 1994.

——, 'The Business of Chinese Coolie Immigration', *Studies in Western Australian History*, No. 13, 1992.

Scates, B., 'A Monument to Murder: Celebrating the Conquest of Aboriginal Australia', *Studies in Western Australian History*, Vol. 10, April 1989.

Schaper, M., 'The Broome Race Riots of 1920', *Studies in Western Australian History*, No. 16, 1995.

Statham, P., 'James Stirling and Pinjarra: A battle in more ways than one', *Studies in Western Australian History*, No. 23, 2003.

——, 'Why Convicts II: The Decision to Introduce Convicts to Swan River', *Studies in Western Australian History*, No. 4, December 1981.

Taylor, S., 'Who Were the Convicts: A Statistical Analysis of the Convicts Arriving in Western Australia in 1850/51, 1861/62, and 1866/68', *Studies in Western Australian History*, No. 4, December 1981.

Treadgold, C., 'Bushrangers in Western Australia: Incidents of "67"', *Early Days: Journal and Proceedings of the Western Australian Historical Society*, Vol. 3, Part 2, 1939.

Willis, B., 'From Indispensability to Redundancy: The Afghans in Western Australia, 1887-1911', *Papers in Labour History*, No. 9, June 1992.

Newspapers Consulted
Coolgardie Miner.
Morning Herald.
Perth Gazette.
Perth Gazette and Independent Journal of Politics and News.
Perth Gazette & W.A. Times.
Sunday Times.
The Daily News.
The Evening Mail.
The Fremantle Observer.
The Herald (Fremantle).
The Inquirer.
The Inquirer: A Western Australian Journal.
The Inquirer: A Western Australian Journal of Politics and Literature.
The Inquirer and Commercial News.
The Kalgoorlie Miner.

The Perth Gazette and Western Australian Journal.
The Weekly Times.
The West Australian.
The Western Australian Times.

Court Files

Case 304: *Regina Vs John Gavin, April 1844*, State Records Office, Perth.
Case 602: *Regina Vs Edwin Gatehouse, Quarter Sessions, 5 July 1854*, State Records Office, Perth.
Case 616: *Regina Vs Edward Bishop, Quarter Sessions, 4 October 1854*, State Records Office, Perth.
Case 802: *Regina Vs Richard Bibby, Quarter Sessions, 5 October 1859*, State Records Office, Perth.
Case 852: *Regina Vs Joseph McDonald, 4 January 1861*, State Records Office, Perth.
Supreme Court Case 152: Regina Vs Garder and 4 other Ab. Natives, State Records Office, Perth.
Supreme Court Case 595: Regina Vs Yaradee and Mullagelly, 1 October 1873, State Records Office, Perth.
Supreme Court Case 2595: Regina Vs Goulam Mahomet, 8 April 1896, State Records Office, Perth.
Supreme Court Case 4074: Rex Vs Oki Iwakichi, 6 October 1908, State Records Office, Perth.

Websites

Fremantle Prison Official Website, <www.fremantleprison.com.au>.
Cartlann Náisiúnta na hÉireann (National Archives of Ireland), <www.nationalarchives.ie/topics/trasportation/transportation.html>.
Register of Heritage Places, <http://register.heritage.wa.gov.au>.
National Archives of Australia – Documenting a Democracy Project, <http://www.foundingdocs.gov.au>.
Tatz, C., 'Aboriginal suicide is different: Aboriginal youth suicide in New South Wales, the Australian Capital Territory and New Zealand: towards a model of explanation and alleviation', *Criminology Research Council Report*, <http://www.aic.gov.au/crc/reports/tatz/>.
Tatz, C., 'Pauline Hanson's Aboriginal "blood libel"', *Australian Jewish News*, 2 May 1997 published online at, <www.ajn.com.au/pages/archives/one-nation/one-nation-19.html>.
WA Convict Ships, <http://members.iinet.net.au/~perthdps/convicts/con-wa10.html>

Unpublished Theses

Hopkins, E., 'The Colour Confusion: A Study of the Japanese Community in Broome Du White Australia Policy, 1901-1941', Honours Dissertation, University of New South 2000.
Kazakoff, C., 'Irish Assisted Single Female Migration to Western Australia 1850-1870', Hon Dissertation, University of Notre Dame Australia, 2003.

Index

About the Author

Simon Adams has chosen to work in places most 'normal' people avoid –
Cuba, South Africa, Northern Ireland, East Timor. Along the way he was
a witness to the Eastern European anti-Communist revolutions of 1989,
nearly died of dengue fever in Vietnam, and worked with former political
prisoners in South Africa. He continues to be actively involved in global
issues of social justice.

The author of four history books, Simon is a Professor of History at
Monash University and is currently serving as Deputy Pro-Vice Chancellor
(International) of Monash's South African campus. Although he now lives
in Johannesburg, his heart is in Fremantle, Western Australia. He has three
children and still secretly dreams of being a pirate.